PART 2

GREGG SHORTHAND FOR THE ELECTRONIC OFFICE

PART 2

GREGG SHORTHAND FOR THE ELECTRONIC OFFICE

SHORT COURSE

SERIES 90

LOUIS A. LESLIE
CHARLES E. ZOUBEK
GREGG A. CONDON

Shorthand written by **Jerome P. Edelman**

Gregg Division
McGraw-Hill Book Company

New York Atlanta Dallas St. Louis San Francisco Auckland
Bogotá Guatemala Hamburg Johannesburg Lisbon London
Madrid Mexico Montreal New Delhi Panama Paris San Juan
São Paulo Singapore Sydney Tokyo Toronto

Sponsoring Editor: Barbara Oakley
Shorthand Production Manager: Jerome P. Edelman
Shorthand Production Supervisor: Mary C. Buchanan
Shorthand Production Assistant: Louise Intorrella
Art & Design Supervisor/Interior Design: Karen Tureck
Photo Editor: Mary Ann Drury
Production Supervisor: Frank Bellantoni

Cover Design: Renee Kilbride and Karen Tureck
Cover Photographer: Karen Leeds
Cover Office Equipment:
Olivetti ET231 • Courtesy Docutel/Olivetti Corp.
Xerox Telecopier 455 • Courtesy Xerox Corp.
Saturn PABX • Courtesy Siemens Communication Systems, Inc.
Wang 01S115 • Courtesy Wang Laboratories Inc.

Section Photography:
Section 1: © Michal Heron 1983
Section 2: © Michal Heron 1983
Section 3: Karen Leeds
Appendix Photography: Courtesy Haworth, Inc.
Interior Photography: © Michal Heron 1983

Interior Office Equipment:
Red Book Courtesy American Hotel Association Directory Corporation,
Magna III Word Processor Courtesy A.B. Dick Company

Library of Congress Cataloging in Publication Data

Leslie, Louis A., date–
Gregg shorthand for the electronic office, short course, part 2.

1. Shorthand—Gregg. I. Zoubek, Charles E., date II. Condon, Gregg A., date III. Title.
Z56.2.G7L49 1983 653'.4270424 83-13584
ISBN 0-07-037917-3

Gregg Shorthand for the Electronic Office, Short Course, Part 2, Series 90

1 2 3 4 5 6 7 8 9 0 DOCDOC 8 9 0 9 8 7 6 5 4 3

To The Student

In Part 1, you learned the alphabet of Gregg Shorthand as well as brief forms, word beginnings, word endings, and phrases.

You now have at your command the tools for writing *any* word in shorthand. Welcome to the world of Gregg writers!

Part 1 was devoted to the basics of shorthand and of English, because those basics are extremely important. Part 2 will continue to stress the basics, but it will also include some other things that will enhance your study of shorthand. You will learn about a variety of ways that shorthand can be used personally and professionally. Some of the exercises you write in shorthand will illustrate those uses. You will also learn a little about word processing and the electronic office. (There's a word processing glossary at the back of this book.) You will learn about three commonly used letter styles, and you will prepare your typewritten transcripts following these styles.

As a shorthand writer, you are already aware of the importance of listening—if you don't listen, you will miss out on the dictation. But listening is an important part of communication even when you are not taking dictation. Part 2 will describe ways in which you can become a better listener—and a better communicator.

Part 2 will not only be devoted to increasing your dictation speed; it will also help you develop good transcription skills and increase your transcription speed. Just as you take timings in your typing class, you will take timings in your shorthand class—the only difference is that the words are written in shorthand. What a challenge! As you progress through the program, you will discover that it becomes easier and easier to do the transcription exercises, and you will see your speed increase.

Features Of Gregg Shorthand For The Electronic Office, Part 2

The appearance of this part of the program continues that of Part 1—all shorthand is written on lines, special words and marks of punctuation are highlighted in color, and, most importantly, the book is bound at the top for ease in transcribing from the text material. The special features of Part 2 are as follows:

Building Professional Skills

The opening segment of each lesson covers a variety of topics—the professional and personal uses of shorthand, techniques for improving listening skills, formatting directions for three common letter styles, and punctuation checkups. Another professional skill is covered in each lesson in a Communication Checkup that reviews similar words or spelling-family exercises.

Building Transcription Skill

The second segment of each lesson contains three exercises that will help you build your transcription skill. The first is a Transcription Warmup in which you will practice transcribing four lines of shorthand words. The second is a Transcription Speed Building exercise. Both the warmup and the speed builder are word counted in standard typewriting words so that you can take timings on the material. You will compete against yourself in an attempt to boost your transcription speed. The third exercise is a Transcription Quiz. In this exercise, the emphasis is on the language arts rules presented in the program.

The Transcription Warmup is an exercise that will help you boost transcribing speed on the word or phrase level. After you practice transcribing the lines in the Warmup, your instructor will time you for spurts of 10, 15, or 20 seconds on each of the lines. You should try to transcribe as fast as you can without making any errors.

After reading the Transcription Speed-Building Drill letter, your instructor may tell you to practice transcribing the letter for a minute or two or may time you for 15, 20, or 30 seconds on some or all of the lines in the letter. After you are familiar with the content of the letter, your instructor will give you two or three

1-minute timed writings on the letter. You should verify the accuracy of the transcript and compute your 1-minute speed. You might also transcribe the entire letter, noting the time you start transcribing and the time you finish. Divide the number of words by the number of minutes to find your words-a-minute transcription rate.

As you transcribe the Transcription Quiz, you will be expected to insert the missing marks of punctuation. Although the emphasis is on the language arts rules, you should try to maintain the speed you reached during the Transcription Speed Building Drill.

Mailable Letter Production

The third and final segment of each lesson is very much like the Reading and Writing Practice in Part 1. You will read and write the material for homework, but you will also transcribe the letters and memos in mailable format. Inside addresses are provided in the margin. At the beginning you will transcribe from the textbook, but by the end of the program you should be transcribing from your own shorthand notes.

Appendix

The appendix of Part 2 contains a word processing glossary with their corresponding shorthand outline for each term. The glossary will help you understand the terminology associated with an automated or electronic office. Also included is a chart of common shorthand phrases, a chart of the brief forms in alphabetical order, and a chart of brief-form derivatives, the names and addresses to be used in transcribing the letters from *The Dictation Book: Letters and Memos.*

Topical Contents (Lessons 11–50)

Personal and Professional Uses of Shorthand

Listening Skills

Letter Formats

Punctuation Checkup

Communication Checkup

SECTION II

1

This lesson begins your review of the principles of Gregg Shorthand.

The Alphabet

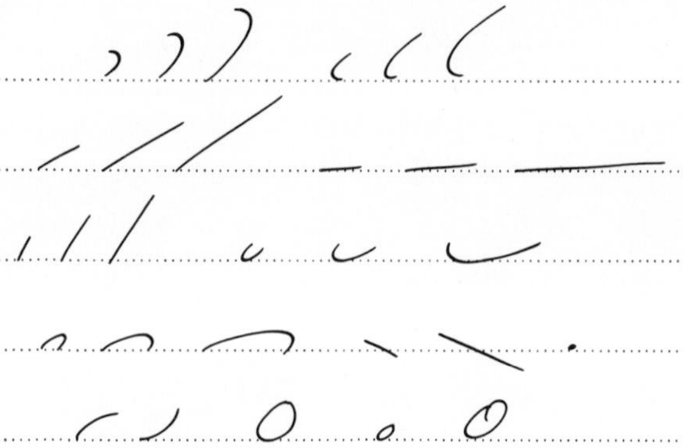

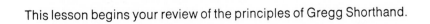

Circles Inside Curves

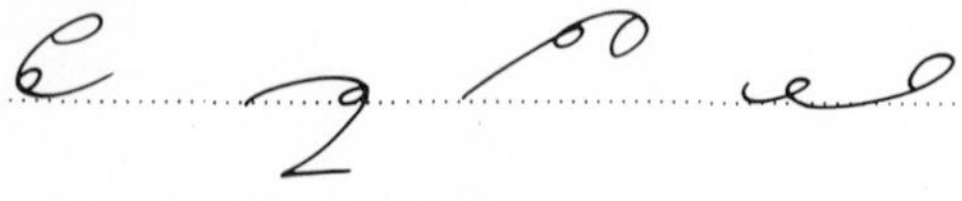

Circles Outside Angles

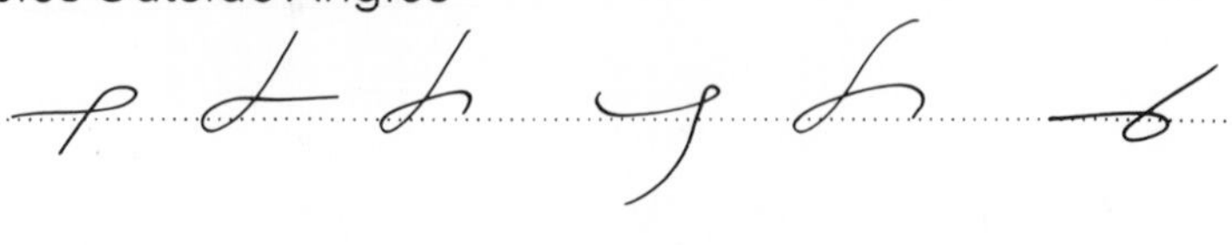

Key to the Shorthand

S, f, v, s, p, b.
T, d, ted, n, m, men.
Sh, chay, jay, o, r, l.
Oo, k, gay, ng, nk, h-ing.
Over th, under th, a, e, i.
Appear, given, decay, relay.
Match, jam, jack, leave, bag, made.

Circles Clockwise at Beginning and End of Straight Stroke

Circles Clockwise Between Straight Strokes

Circles on Back of First Curve of Reverse Curves

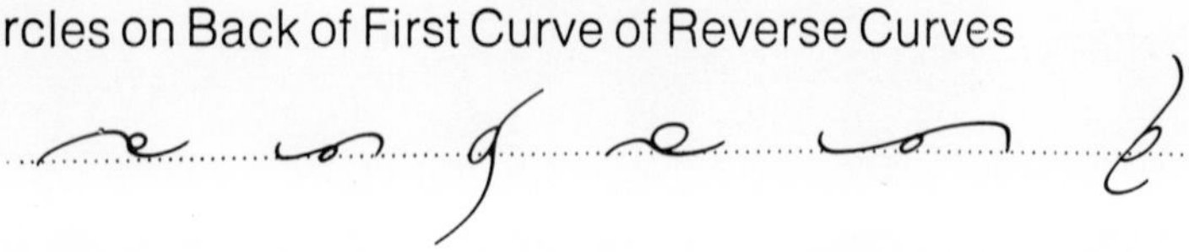

O on its Side Before N M

OO After N M

S and Curves—Continue Direction of Curve

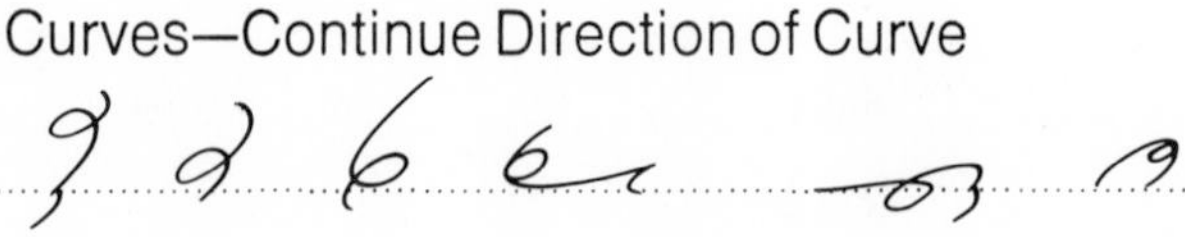

COMMON PHRASES

of Gregg Shorthand

S and Straight Strokes—Make Sharp Angle

Key to the Shorthand

Me, aim, may, stay, day, aid.
Stayed, date, main, name, deed, mean.
Gear, wreck, pave, care, leg, vapor.
Own, known, owner, home, omit.
New, noon, newly, moon, Monday.
Safes, face, base, sales, makes, these.
Stones, homes, stay, needs, snow.

Brief Forms

Brief-Form Derivatives

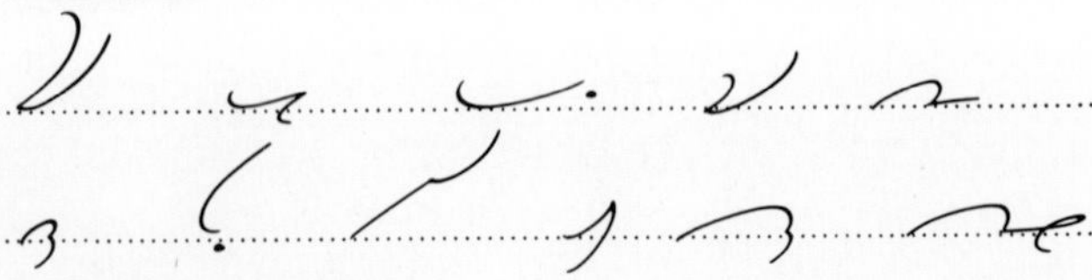

Phrases

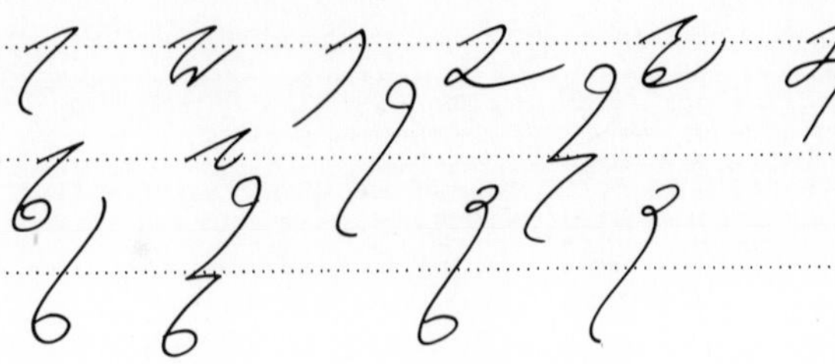

BRIEF-FORM DERIVATIVES

of Gregg Shorthand

Key to Shorthand

I, Mr., have, are-our-hour, will-well, a-an.
Am, it-at, in-not, is-his, the, that.
Haven't, ours-ourselves, willing, isn't, cannot.
Yourself-yours, being, wouldn't, therefore, goods, goodness.
To be, to put, to have, to fill, to spend, to change.
To buy, to show, I have been, I have not been.
Have been able, I have not been able, we have been able, we have been.

Reading and Writing Practice

1 **ar·riv·al**
2 **here**
3 **sup·pli·ers**
4 **ear·li·er**

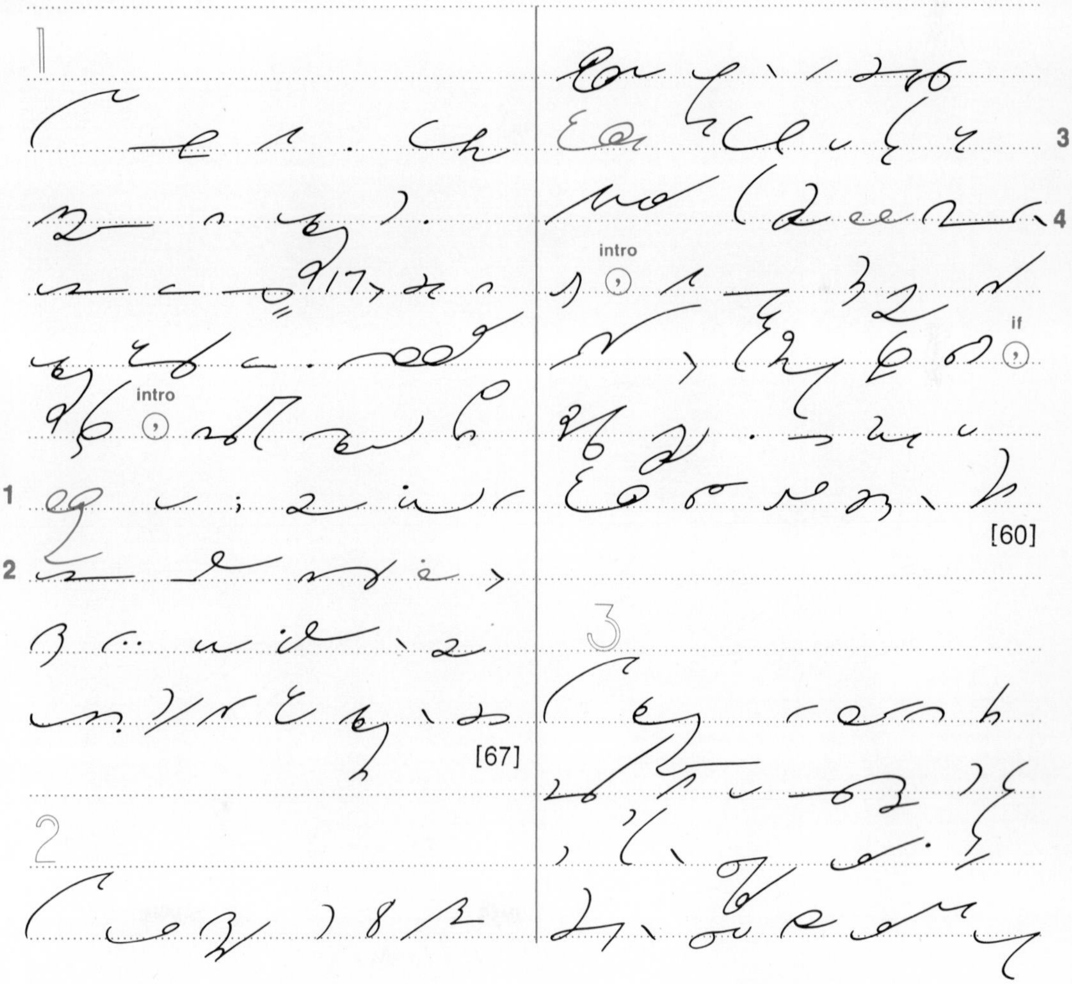

BRIEF FORMS OF GREGG SHORTHAND

in Alphabetical Order

5 too
6 pa·tient
7 ac·cept
8 thor·ough
9 ar·range·ments

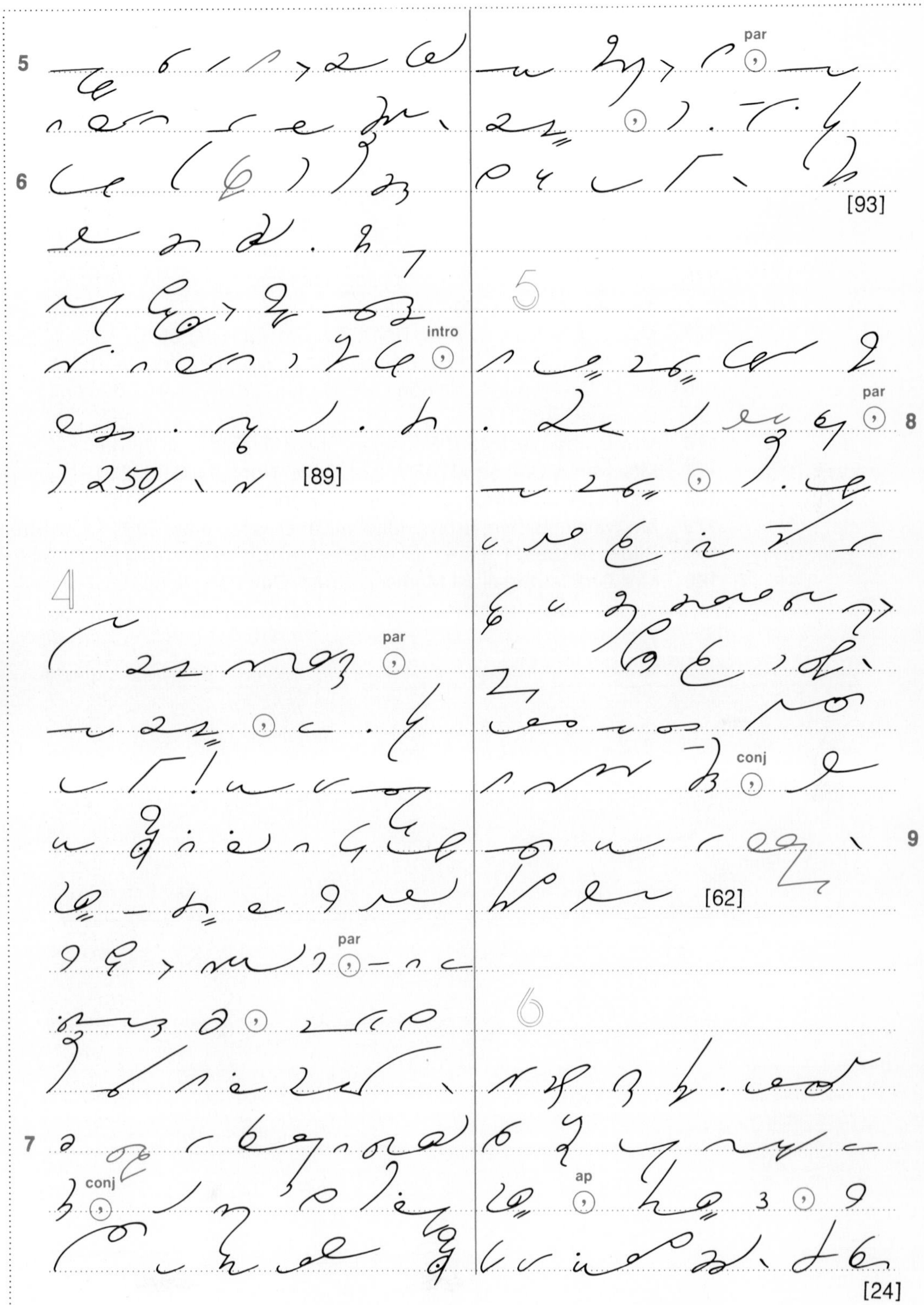

167 Hart Clothiers, Ltd., 16 Healey Plaza, Erie, PA 16511

168 Argyle Shoes, 320 State Street, Sacramento, CA 95811

169 Mr. Warren Green, Western Electric Cooperative, 5920 Tyler Street, Boise, ID 83725

170 Mr. Robert Ames, Director of Marketing, Anderson Electric Company, 716 Fillmore Street, Raleigh, NC 27611

171 Customer Service Department, Public Service Corporation, 75 Snyder Road, Johnson City, TN 37601

172 Mr. Frank Kelly, Kelly, Andre, and Associates, P. O. Box 781, Kansas City, MO 64111

173 Mr. Jerry Nelson, 81 River Road, Bellows Falls, VT 05101

174 Mrs. Anna Green, 7112 Cameron Place, Grand Rapids, MI 49511

175 Mr. G. C. Cooper, Marathon Food Center, 8617 Cleveland Avenue, Denver, CO 80211

176 Mrs. Lynda West, 4201 Roosevelt Street, Trenton, NJ 08611

177 Mrs. Nancy Graham, 1703 Wilson Drive, Norwalk, CT 06250

178 Ms. Kathleen Murray, 812 Knowles Avenue, Peoria, IL 61611

179 Mr. William Brown, Brown, Mitchell, and Associates, 2963 Sears Street, Biloxi, MS 39511

180 Mrs. Charles Small, 51 Madison Street, Oak Park, IL 60311

2

This lesson continues your review of Gregg Shorthand theory.

OO-s Joins Without Angles

 **But** 

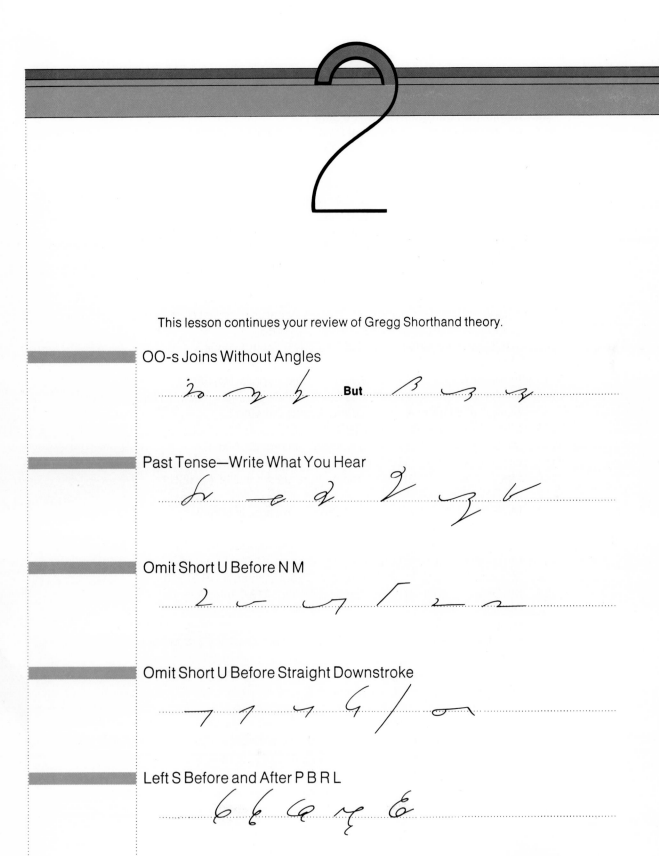

Past Tense—Write What You Hear

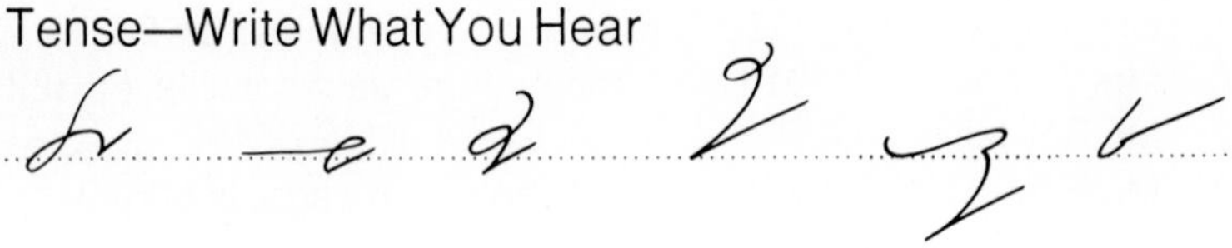

Omit Short U Before N M

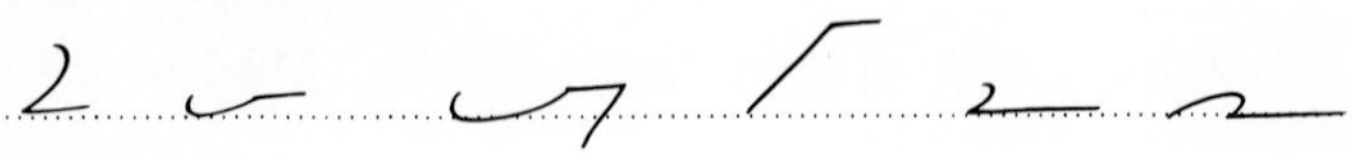

Omit Short U Before Straight Downstroke

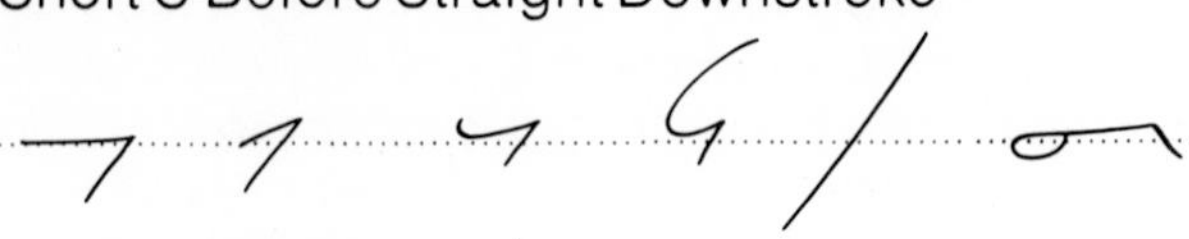

Left S Before and After P B R L

131 Memo from Carol Marvin to The Staff
132 Memo from Carol Marvin to The Staff
133 Mr. Timothy Franks, 416 Forest Drive, Missoula, MT 59801
134 Public Relations Department, United Oil Company, 1435 Sherman Avenue, Wilmington, DE 19811
135 Mr. and Mrs. Michael Troy, 1226 Gold Road, Albany, NY 14500
136 Ms. Vera Savic, Editorial Secretary, American Consumer Magazine, 1027 North Seventh Street, San Diego, CA 92100
137 Smith Van Line, Post Office Box 508, Indianapolis, IN 46211
138 Mr. Aaron Levine, 824 East Grand Avenue, Evansville, IN 47711
139 Memo from Lorraine Williams to Roger Anderson
140 Office of Career Planning and Placement, North Central College, Pittsburgh, PA 15211
141 Miss Janet Young, Business Education Department, West High School, 309 Maywood Avenue, Los Angeles, CA 90015
142 J. R. Lesley, Administration Building, 3130 Tenth Avenue, Minneapolis, MN 55411
143 Miss Ann Chase, 1112 Riggs Avenue, Minneapolis, MN 55411
144 Mr. Charles Hamilton, Business Education Department, Central High School, 419 Grand Avenue, Grand Rapids, MI 49511
145 Memo from Dave James to The Staff
146 Mr. David Johnson, 1244 Mark Street, Chicago, IL 60612
147 Dr. Thomas Miller, 1228 East Street, Los Angeles, CA 90015
148 Mrs. Pat Mitchell, 1016 Madison Avenue, Jacksonville, FL 32211
149 Mr. Roy Miller, 405 Platt Avenue, St. Paul, MN 55100
150 Mr. Robert Nelson, 1105 North Avenue, Chicago, IL 60620
151 Mr. Ralph Samuels, 4711 Third Avenue, Miami, FL 33311
152 Mr. Charles Grant, 1705 Beecher Street, Pittsburgh, PA 15211
153 Mr. Brian Day, 1416 Shore Drive, Milwaukee, WI 53211
154 Mr. Ronald Decker, 4324 North 42nd Street, Ashland, OR 97520
155 Mr. Douglas Smith, Ramsey Medical Center, 418 Center Avenue, Richmond, VA 23211
156 Miss Elsa Turner, Apartment 24, 1780 Pine Place, Little Rock, AR 72200
157 Miss Carla Grace, 7841 California Boulevard, Pasadena, CA 91104
158 Mr. George Stone, 163 Center Street, Monroe, LA 71200
159 Ms. Janet Mason, 801 Donald Avenue, Monroe, LA 71200
160 Ms. Wendy Jones, 16 Star Avenue, Orlando, FL 32800
161 Mr. Charles Banks, 783 Oak Drive, Sidney, NE 69162
162 Mr. Robert Alan, 167 Wilson Street, Portsmouth, OH 45662
163 Mrs. Ella Glass, 63 Business Plaza, Buffalo, NY 14211
164 Mr. Glenn Mead, ARCO Manufacturing, 63 Seventh Street, Santa Fe, NM 87501
165 Mr. Brian Holtz, 4121 Green River Road, Laramie, WY 82070
166 Mr. Roger Jones, 1611 East Third Avenue, Pueblo, CO 81011

Left S After T D N M O

Key to the Shorthand

Husky, gust, just, does, loose, rust.
Baked, missed, faced, saved, loved, showed.
Fun, run, lunch, done, some, come.
Much, touch, rush, brush, judge, among.
Base, busy, price, trips, separate.
Hates, needs, claims, boss, finance, cause.

Right S

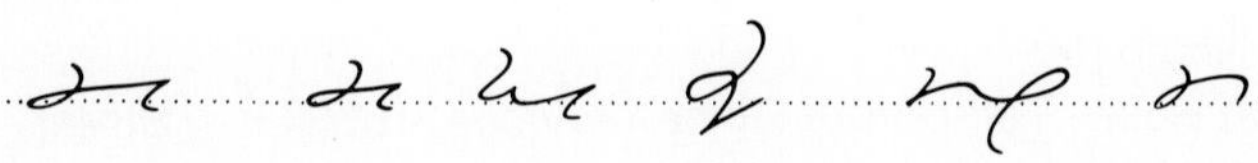

Under Th

Over Th

In- En- Un-

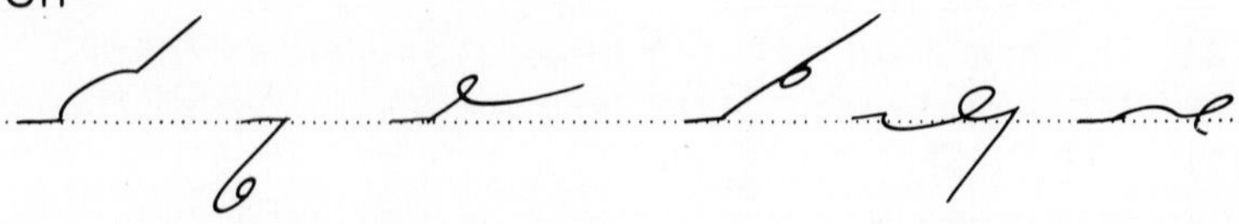

Im- Em-

101 Mr. Charles Henry, 2850 Augusta Street, Burlington, VT 05401
102 Mr. Frank James, 1605 Sunrise Lane, Tacoma, WA 98411
103 Ms. Pam Norton, Tulsa Office Supply Company, 628 Viking Place, Tulsa, OK 74100
104 Mr. Walter North, 2520 Oakridge Drive, Salem, OR 97311
105 Mrs. Paula Fleming, National Credit Card Company, 1823 Virginia Avenue, Richmond, VA 23211
106 Western Star Hotel, 458 Main Street, Durango, CO 81301
107 Lake View Restaurant, 1532 Shore Drive, Burlington, VT 05401
108 Mr. and Mrs. Donald Timm, 1422 Highland Avenue, Cincinnati, OH 45212
109 Mrs. Anna Simms, Professional Business Program, 1611 Churchill Street, New York City, NY 10016
110 Mr. James Bloom, Modern Marketing Associates, 2131 14th Street, Trenton, NJ 08611
111 Mr. Harold Day, Market Research Department, Smith Manufacturing Company, 256 West 14th Street, New York City, NY 10061
112 Mr. Mark Chan, Modern Business Methods, 724 Marshall Avenue, Omaha, NE 68100
113 Mrs. Joan Reilly, Temporary Office Services, 1558 Gary Street, Rockford, IL 61100
114 Mrs. Helen Gates, 620 East Grand Avenue, Springfield, IL 62711
115 Mr. Arthur J. Green, 1407 West Grand Avenue, Madison, WI 53711
116 Dr. Scott Carson, 8219 River Street, Cincinnati, OH 45212
117 Mr. Tom Carpenter, 3340 Riverview Drive, Providence, RI 02911
118 Ms. Margaret Davidson, Ann Logan Corporation, 906 Harris Street, Hartford, CT 06600
119 Mr. John Hoffman, Central Illinois Insurance Association, 515 Clinton Street, Springfield, IL 62711
120 Mr. Edward Ralph, 16 Pine Place, Clear Lake, IA 50428
121 Ms. Elizabeth Otto, 6270 Thurber Road, Grand Rapids, MI 49511
122 Mr. Brian Hoffman, Editor, Wisconsin Sporting Magazine, Post Office Box 2266, Milwaukee, WI 53211
123 Mrs. Mary Drake, Los Angeles Evening College, 608 Charles Avenue, Los Angeles, CA 90011
124 Ms. Ellen Bauer, Performing Arts Manager, Central College, Columbus, NE 68601
125 Dr. Anna Sharp, 1911 14th Street, Lexington, KY 40511
126 Mr. Martin Sanchez, 2712 Shale Road, Los Angeles, CA 90012
127 Mr. Mark Hart, 3158 Lesley Lane, Erie, PA 16511
128 Ms. Sandra Burk, History Department, Southern State College, Reno, NV 89511
129 Mr. Allen Lansing, Post Office Box 1201, Boston, MA 02100
130 Ms. Maria Sanchez, Madison Real Estate Company, 3210 Oak Street, Hartford, CT 06611

But: When In-, En-, Un-, Im-, Em- Precede a Vowel

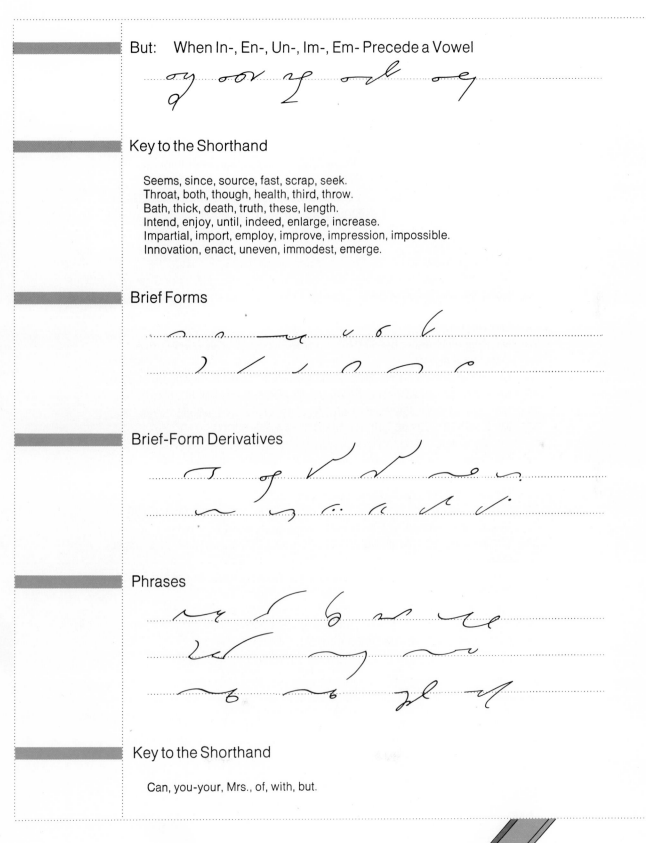

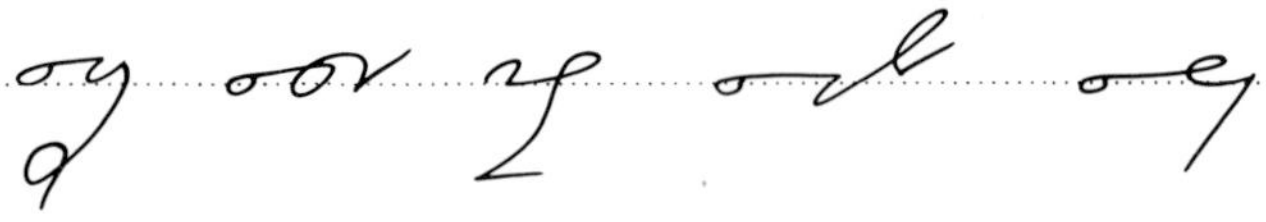

Key to the Shorthand

Seems, since, source, fast, scrap, seek.
Throat, both, though, health, third, throw.
Bath, thick, death, truth, these, length.
Intend, enjoy, until, indeed, enlarge, increase.
Impartial, import, employ, improve, impression, impossible.
Innovation, enact, uneven, immodest, emerge.

Brief Forms

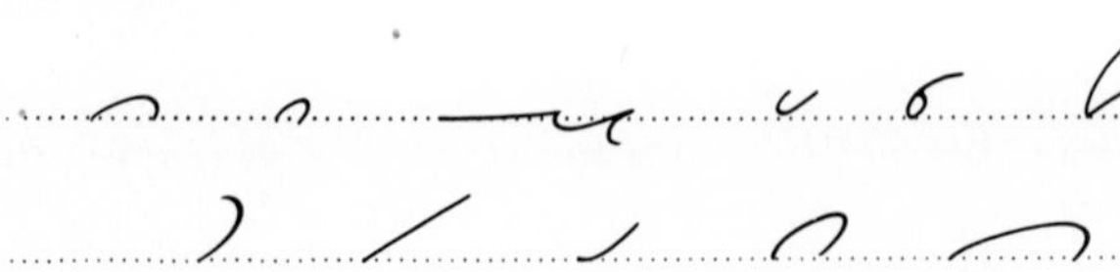

Brief-Form Derivatives

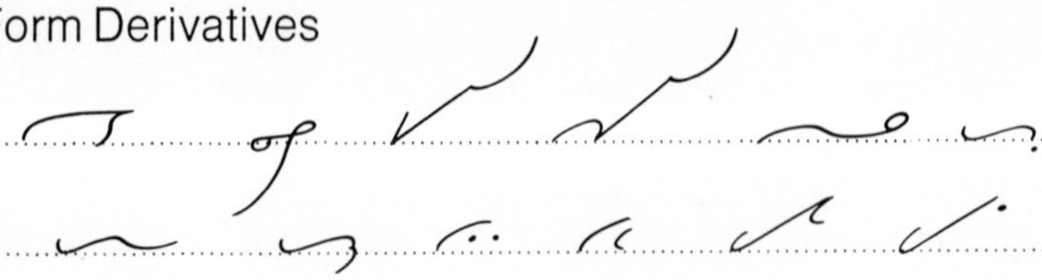

Phrases

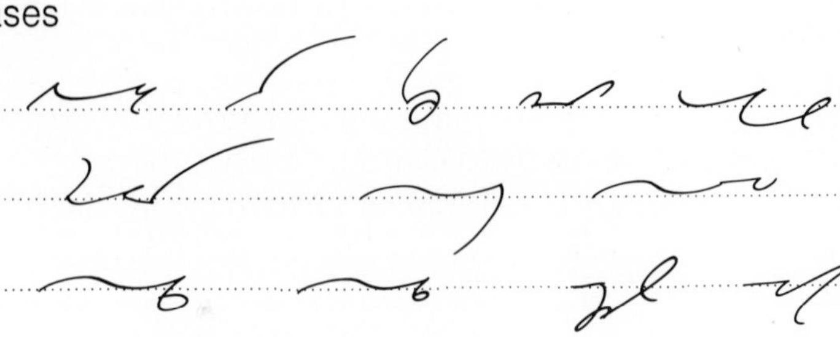

Key to the Shorthand

Can, you-your, Mrs., of, with, but.

68 Ms. Jessie Adams, 1019 Stein Boulevard, Pittsburgh, PA 15211
69 Miss Ellen Brown, Nathan Hale High School, 2620 Fountain Avenue, Duluth, MN 55800
70 Mr. John Green, World Publishing Corporation, 812 Lake Street, Bloomington, IN 47401
71 Ms. Jean Roy, Lake City Printing, 431 Gilbert Avenue, Minneapolis, MN 55411
72 Mr. Ralph Barth, Olson Printing Company, 421 Cleveland Avenue, Buffalo, NY 14211
73 Mr. Lyle Newman, Program Chairperson, National Association of Sales Representatives, 404 Taft Street, Washington, DC 20011
74 Mr. Brad Brenner, Atlantic Floor Coverings, 528 Cameron Street, Newark, NJ 07105
75 Mr. Bruce May, 605 Gray Street, Janesville, WI 53545
76 Mr. Simon Gray, Insurance Associates of California, 312 York Street, Long Beach, CA 90811
77 Ms. Ellen McHenry, Metro Insurance Company, 8151 Loveland Street, Denver, CO 80211
78 Mr. Russell P. Jackson, Detroit Office Products, 817 Walsh Avenue, Detroit, MI 48213
79 Mr. Ralph Jones, Jones Auto, 216 Lakewood Street, Chicago, IL 60625
80 Mr. Abraham, 227 Sherman Avenue, Cleveland, OH 44111
81 Ms. Lynn Green, 238 West Grand Avenue, Oxford, MI 48051
82 Mr. Ralph Clay, 2106 Taft Avenue, Topeka, KS 66610
83 Mr. Myron Harmon, 138 Graham Avenue, Chicago, IL 60621
84 Ms. Edna Pace, 307 Dodge Street, Louisville, KY 40211
85 Ms. Marcia Stern, 3633 Lloyd Avenue, Santa Fe, NM 87501
86 Mrs. Alice West, 1620 Benton Avenue, Minneapolis, MN 55411
87 Dawson Insurance Agency, 1620 Adams Avenue, Boston, MA 02100
88 Mrs. Cathy North, 138 10th Street, Chicago, IL 60611
89 Mr. George Mills, National Tire Corporation, 208 North Michigan Street, Gary, IN 46411
90 Mr. Nick Smith, Reno Auto Imports, 3706 Star Avenue, Reno, NV 89511
91 Mrs. Sheryl Harper, 213 7th Avenue, Pittsburgh, PA 15211
92 Ms. Golda Simmons, 716 Fulton Street, Raleigh, NC 27611
93 Dr. James Klein, 1819 Lynn Drive, Houston, TX 77011
94 Mr. Raymond Tyler, 1910 Water Street, Omaha, NE 68100
95 Mr. Brian Holtz, 2014 Green Tree Road, Las Vegas, NV 89100
96 Mr. Frank Davis, Lexington Service Center, 7009 Walnut Road, Lexington, KY 40511
97 Mr. John Birch, 5821 La Salle, Wheeling, WV 26003
98 Ms. Nancy Parker, 3633 River Drive, Chicago, IL 60611
99 Mr. James O'Neill, 827 Revere Street, Los Angeles, CA 90012
100 Mr. Charles Keen, 527 West 6th Avenue, St. Louis, MO 63111

For, would, there-their, this, good, they.
Themselves, whenever, shouldn't, couldn't, gladly, working.
Worker, works, thinking, things-thinks, orders, ordering.
At a loss, at a time, by the way, one or two, will you please.
For a long time, glad to have, glad to know.
Glad to say, glad to see, in a few days, in order to be.

Reading and Writing Practice

1 an·nu·al
2 se·ri·ous
3 touch
4 past
5 great

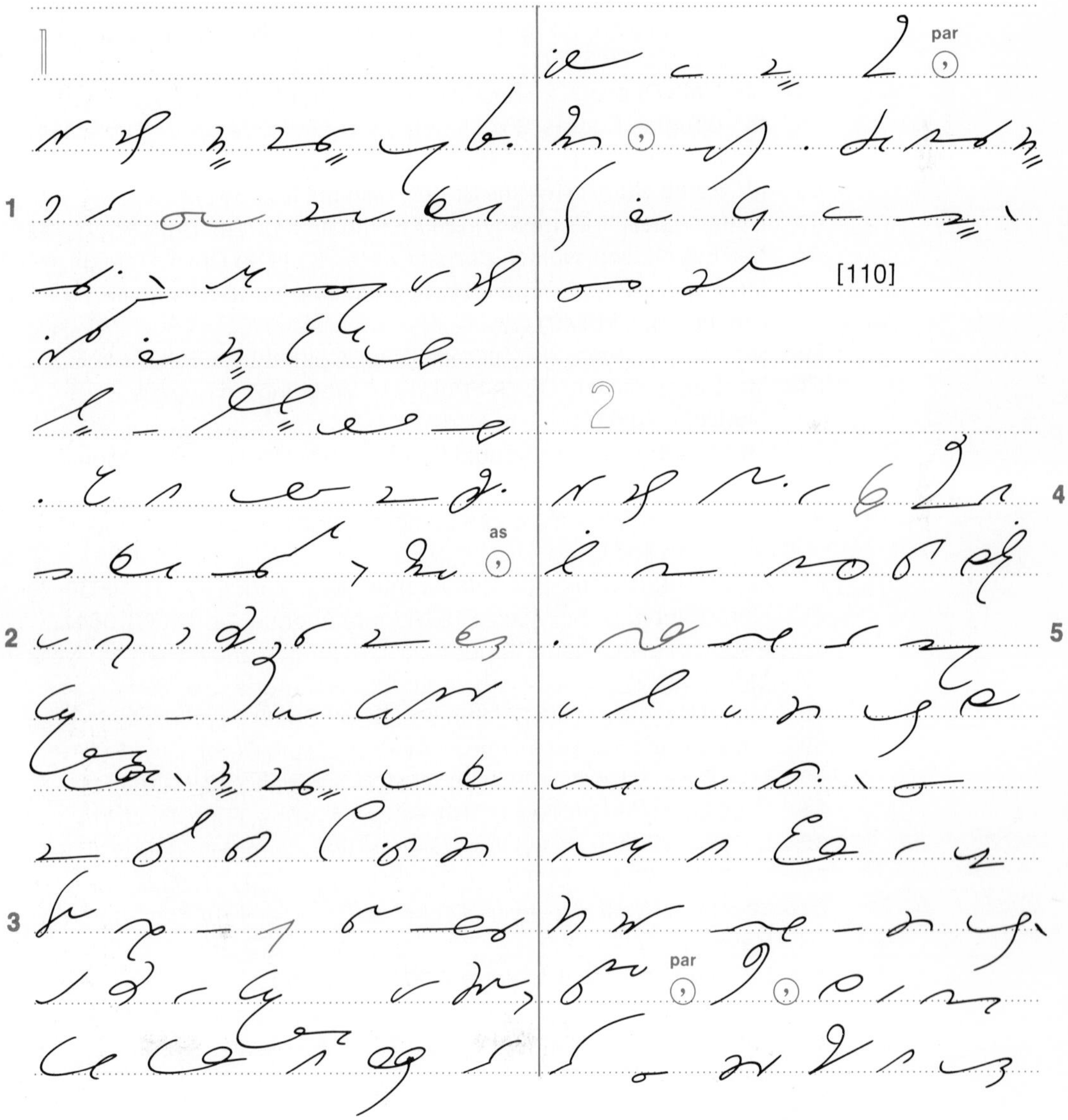

34 Mr. Morgan James, Attorney, 1820 Garfield Avenue, Logan, UT 84321
35 Mr. Martin Hayes, Hayes Sporting Goods, 322 Cameron Street, Wichita Falls, TX 76311
36 Mr. Robert Perry, 1041 Western Avenue, Buffalo, NY 14211
37 Ms. Joan Goff, 206 Williams Drive, Bloomington, IN 47401
38 Husberg's Fine Furniture, 2013 Vine Street, Fresno, CA 93711
39 Mr. Michael Sanchez, Manager, Holiday House Hotel, 420 Putnam Drive, Biloxi, MS 39511
40 Mr. Kevin Nelson, Lakeland Auto Parts, 620 Vine Street, St. Petersburg, FL 33711
41 Miss Mary Jo Andera, Brooks Paper Products, 423 Mead Road, Bangor, ME 04401
42 Mr. Adrian Sanchez, Sanchez Sporting Goods, 930 Cedar Avenue, St. Louis, MO 63111
43 Mr. Mark Direnzio, 29 East Wellington Street, Chicago, IL 60612
44 Mr. Douglas Rogers, 6575 North Shore Drive, Tacoma, WA 98411
45 Mr. David Block, 2220 14th Street, Pittsburgh, PA 15211
46 Mr. Ralph Corsi, 816 Pine Street, Trenton, NJ 08611
47 Buffalo Fuel Oil Company, 1817 South 85th Street, Buffalo, NY 14211
48 Ms. Eve Nelson, Nelson Carpet Center, 814 Lee Drive, Raleigh, NC 27611
49 Mr. Robert Harper, Harper Home Furnishings, 16 Star Plaza, Burlington, VT 05401
50 Mr. Robert Green, 283 Thomas Drive, Columbus, OH 43211
51 Ms. Baker, Quality Quick Print, 1714 Washington Avenue, Madison, WI 53711
52 Mrs. Martha Burton, Arcadia Furniture Company, 415 London Road, Detroit, MI 48213
53 Mr. Brian Shields, Southern Lumber Company, 815 Fremont Street, Miami, FL 33311
54 Central State Bank, 507 Fifth Avenue, New York City, NY 10036
55 Derby Financial Services, 816 Niagara Avenue, Derby, CT 06418
56 Southern Investment Corporation, 112 First Avenue, Raleigh, NC 27611
57 Mrs. Elvira Pace, 431 Hudson Street, Alexandria, VA 23211
58 Mrs. Helen Forest, 3612 Michigan Drive, South Bend, IN 46615
59 Mr. Edward Lee, 1910 Truman Avenue, South Bend, IN 46615
60 Mrs. Beverly North, 109 Tyler Avenue, Kansas City, MO 64111
61 Gary First National Bank, 7161 Fairfax Avenue, Gary, IN 46411
62 Mr. Roger Tracy, 431 Gilbert Avenue, Dearborn, MI 48100
63 Mr. Ralph Simms, 528 Albany Street, Mason City, IA 53211
64 Mrs. Mary White, Nashville Technical College, 1404 Hamilton Avenue, Nashville, TN 37211
65 Mr. and Mrs. Edward Adams, 930 First Avenue, Seattle, WA 98199
66 Mr. Andrew Nelson, 2061 Taft Avenue, Pasadena, CA 91104
67 Mr. Ralph Timm, Timm's Jewelry Store, 368 Austin Street, Fort Worth, TX 76111

6 re·al
7 re·al·ly
8 good·will

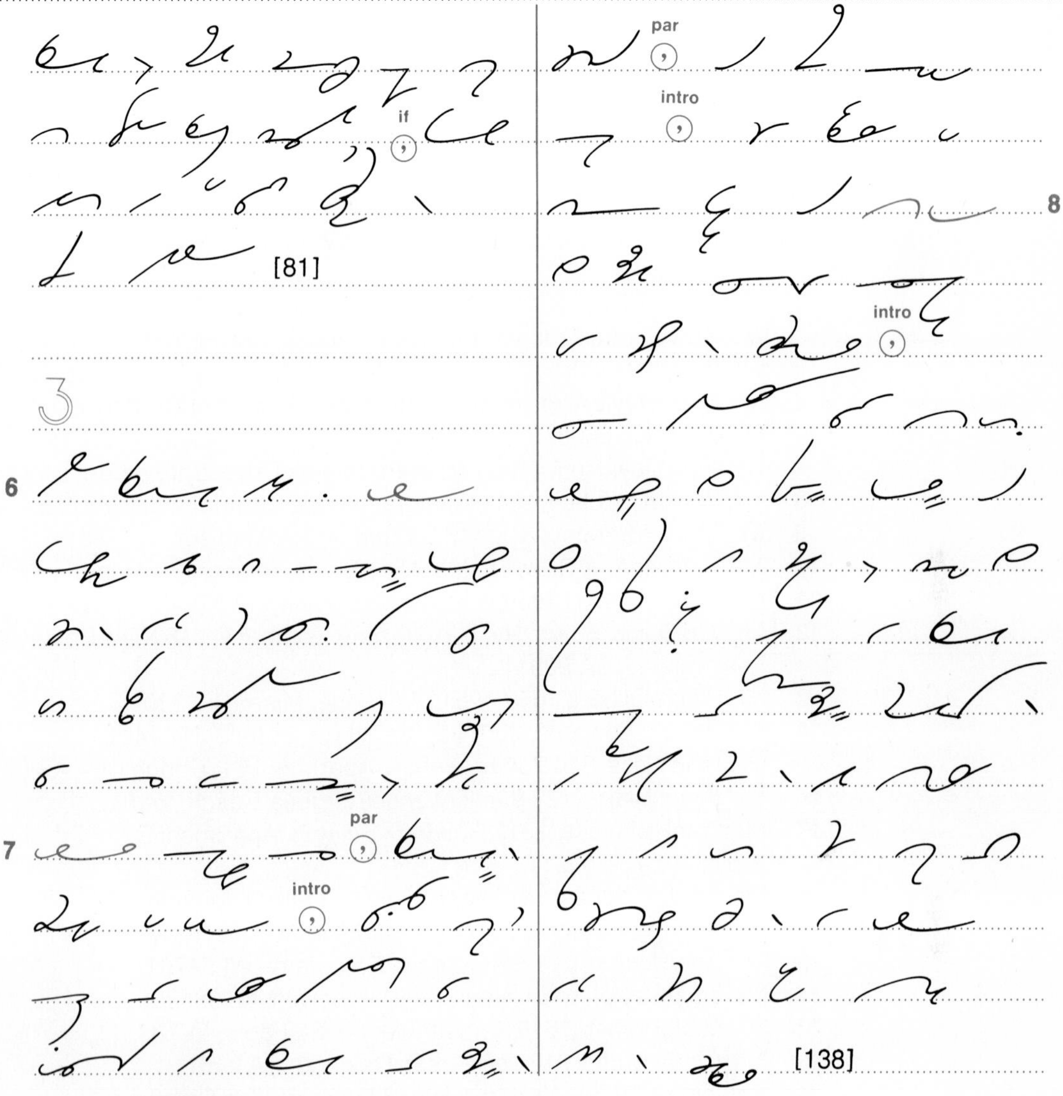

Addresses for Transcription

(The numbers of the following names and addresses correspond to the numbers of the letters in *The Dictation Book: Letters and Memos).*

1 Hotel Rogers, 8511 East 43 Street, New York, NY 10020
2 Mr. Preston Miles, Editor, Travel Today, 1223 State Street, Knoxville, TN 37215
3 Ms. Judy Miller, 850 Oak Street, Bennington, VT 84325
4 Ms. Amy Barth, 1735 Vernon Avenue, Lakeland, FL 33315
5 Mr. Ralph Longstreet, 1433 East Madison Avenue, Sacramento, CA 95811
6 Ms. Jean Doyle, President, Doyle Enterprises, 1221 Brooklyn Street, Hastings, NE 68901
7 Dr. Alvin Davidson, 1132 Meridian Heights Drive, Shreveport, LA 71100
8 Mr. Wilson Mitchell, 1041 Western Avenue, Springfield, IL 62711
9 Ms. Mary Jo Anderson, 1403 Bartlett Street, Madison, NJ 08611
10 Memo from A. J. Brown to Ms. Alice Smith, Accounting Department
11 Ms. Kim Lee, 1617 Blair Avenue, Mason City, IA 52240
12 Mr. Joe Davis, Editor, Ryan Publishing Company, 816 Niles Boulevard, Los Angeles, CA 90011
13 Mr. Ralph Gilbert, 1650 West 27 Avenue, Miami, FL 33054
14 Mr. Donald Edwards, 300 Niagara Street, Buffalo, NY 14211
15 Dr. John Case, 816 Porter Avenue, Apartment 61, Dodge City, KS 67801
16 Ms. Janet Blair, 2122 Black Avenue, Virginia Beach, VA 24211
17 Mr. Frank Melrose, 2312 Golf Park Estates, Apartment D, Providence, RI 02911
18 Ms. Adeline Jones, 1415 East Lexington Street, Muncie, IN 47300
19 United Credit Association, 1401 Madison Avenue, New York, NY 10036
20 Ms. Ann Hollrith, 201 State Street, Eau Claire, WI 54701
21 Ms. Judy Taylor, 616 Union Street, Hopewell, NJ 08525
22 Mr. Scott Homer, 1619 Bartlett Avenue, St. Louis, MO 63111
23 Ms. Cindy Burns, 916 Taft Street, Oakland, CA 94511
24 Personnel Office, Western States Transportation Company, 3420 Maple Avenue, Cheyenne, WY 82001
25 Mr. Jack Jones, 415 South Sumner Street, Bowling Green, OH 43402
26 Dr. James Allen, Madison Clinic, 1424 Park Street, Madison, WI 53711
27 Mrs. Vincent Ryan, 112 Sunset Lane, La Mesa, AZ 85200
28 Ms. Mary Garcia, 138 10th Street, Canton, OH 44711
29 Ms. Elizabeth Howard, 924 Circle Court, Charlotte, WV 26005
30 Mrs. Shelly Gray, 3 Maple Drive, Wilmington, DE 19811
31 Mr. George Day, International Import Company, 824 Grand Avenue, East Lansing, MI 48823
32 Mr. Saul Silverman, Silverman's Department Store, 1414 State Street, Long Beach, CA 90811
33 Ms. Mary Torres, 2940 Milton Road, Long Beach, CA 90811

3

This lesson continues your review of Gregg Shorthand theory.

Inter- Enter- Intr-

-ment

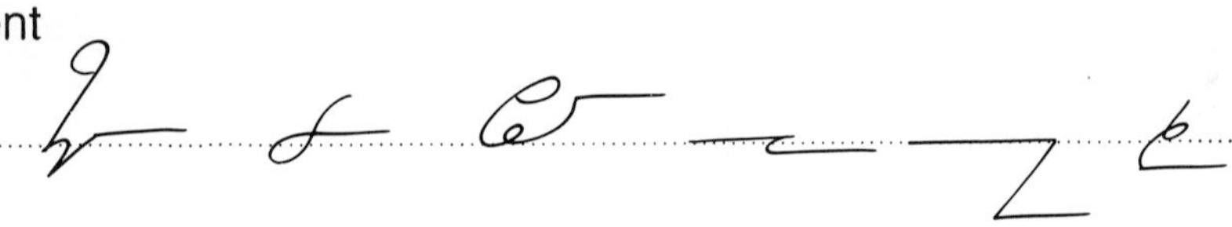

Mis-

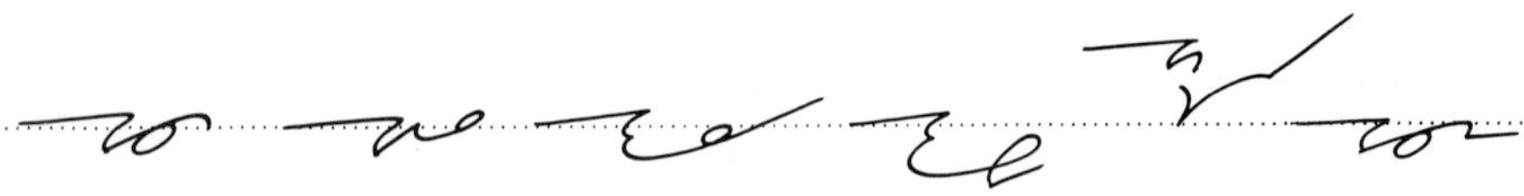

Over

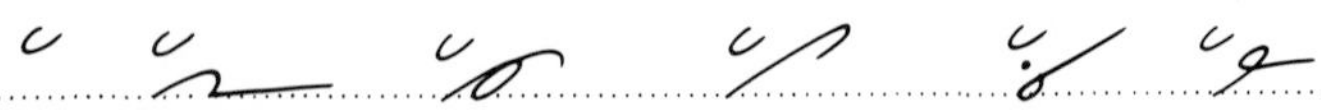

-ulate -ulation

43 Forget, forceful, perform, forecast, informal.

44 Furnish, furnished, furnishings, further, furtive.

45 Turn, return, eastern, determine.

46 Ultimate, ulterior, adult, result, culture, consultation, adulthood, culminate.

Disjoined Word Beginnings

47 Interested, internal, interview, intercept, introduce, introduction, enterprise, entrance, entered.

48 Electricity, electrician, electrical, electric wire, electric fan, electrocute, electric.

49 Supervise, supervision, unsupervised, superhuman, superficial.

50 Circumstance, circumstances, circumstantial, circumvent.

51 Selfish, self-made, self-respect, unselfish.

52 Transit, transport, transact, translation.

53 Understand, undertake, underpaid, underneath.

54 Overcome, overdue, overhead, overpay, oversee.

Phrases

55 To see, to sell, to put, to play.

56 Had been, have been, I have been, have not been, has not been, has been, you should have been, you might have been, I could have been, he would have been.

57 To be able, would be able, had been able, has been able, have not been able, I have not been able, you would be able, should be able, I could be able, you should be able.

58 I want, you want, they want, we want, she wants, who wants, if you want, do you want, if you wanted, they wanted, I wanted.

59 Days ago, weeks ago, months ago, years ago, few days ago, sometime ago.

60 Able to say, able to see, glad to see, in order to be, in order to be able, in order to have, in addition to the, in addition to this.

61 In the past, in the future, for the future, in the world, about the matter, by the way, on the part, upon the subject.

62 Many of the, many of these, many of them, out of date, out of this, one of the, one of them, some of our, some of these, some of them, none of the, none of them.

63 At a loss, as a result, for a few days, for a few minutes, for a few months, for a long time, for a moment, in a position, in a few days, in a few months, at a time.

64 a.m., p.m., C.O.D., Chamber of Commerce, vice versa.

65 Of course, of course it is, as soon as, as soon as possible, to do, I hope, we hope, to us, let me, let us, more than, your order, to me, to make, to know, Dear Mr., Dear Mrs., Dear Ms., Dear Madam, Dear Sir, Yours sincerely, Sincerely yours, Very sincerely, Yours respectfully, Respectfully yours, Very truly yours, Yours very truly, Cordially yours, Yours cordially.

Ul

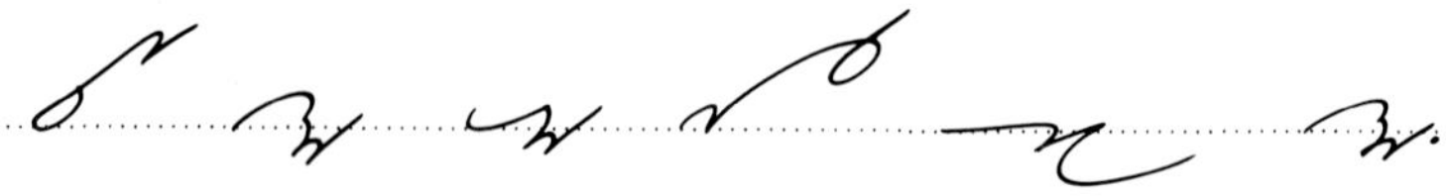

Key to the Shorthand

Interest, introduce, interview, interstate, enterprise, entered.
Adjustment, payment, appointment, moment, management, shipment.
Mistake, mystery, mislead, misplaced, misunderstand, mistaken.
Over, overcome, overtake, overdue, overhead, overturn.
Accumulate, stimulate, tabulate, population, tabulation, speculation.
Adult, consult, result, ultimate, multiple, consulting.

Ye Ya (Write E or A)

-ing

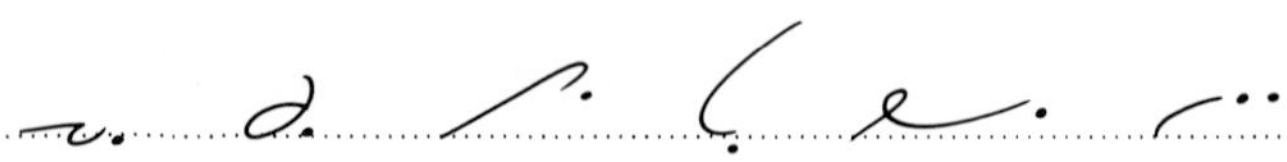

-ings

-ingly

-ly

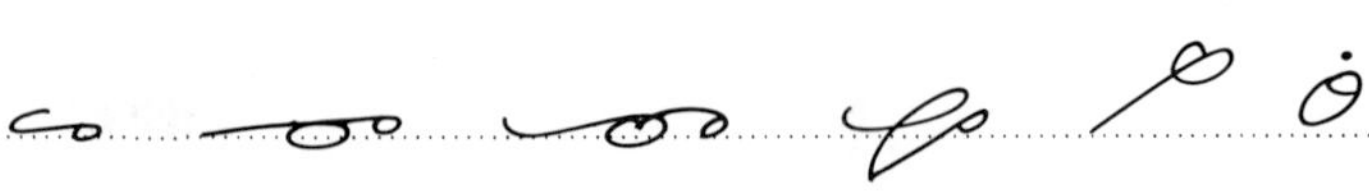

13 Contain, retain, certain, container, attain.

14 Efficient, sufficient, deficient, efficiency, deficiency, proficiency.

Disjoined Word Endings

15 Childhood, motherhood, neighborhood, brotherhood.

16 Reward, onward, afterward, forward, forwarded.

17 Championship, steamship, relationship, authorship.

18 Radical, technical, political, article, logically, periodically, chemically.

19 Congratulate, regulate, stipulate, tabulate, congratulation, regulation, regulations.

20 Grudgingly, unwillingly, knowingly, surprisingly.

21 Readings, mornings, sidings, savings, feelings, drawings.

22 Program, telegram, diagrams.

23 Notification, modification, specifications, classification, gratification, justification, identification.

24 Personality, ability, reliability, durability, facilities, utility, generalities.

25 Faculty, penalty, casualty.

26 Authority, sincerity, majority, minority, clarity, sorority, charity, seniority.

Joined Word Beginnings

27 Permit, perform, perfect, personal.

28 Employ, empower, embroil, embody, embezzle, emphasis.

29 Impress, impression, imply, impossible, impair, impel, impact.

30 Increase, intend, incapable, incapacitate, inclined, inform, informal.

31 Enlarge, enforce, enlist, encourage, encounter, encircled, enrich, enrage.

32 Unkind, unwritten, unwilling, unsuccessful, undue, unpleasant, unpopular, untie.

33 Refer, receive, resign, reform, reorganized.

34 Beneath, believe, belong, before, became.

35 Delay, deliver, deserve, deposit.

36 Dismiss, disappoint, discover, discuss.

37 Mistake, misunderstanding, mistrust, misstate.

38 Explain, excite, extension, excuse, express.

39 Comply, complete, comfort, compose.

40 Condition, conclude, continue, confidence.

41 Submit, substantiate, subdivide, sublease, suburban.

42 Almost, also, already, although, alteration.

But: When two "l's" Occur Together

Key to the Shorthand

Yes, year, yet, yell, yard, yarn.
Knowing, saying, doing, being, telling, thanking.
Sayings, greetings, feelings, readings, settings, trimmings.
Seemingly, exceedingly, increasingly, accordingly, laughingly, knowingly.
Only, mainly, likely, rapidly, daily, highly.
Totally, finally, really.

Brief Forms

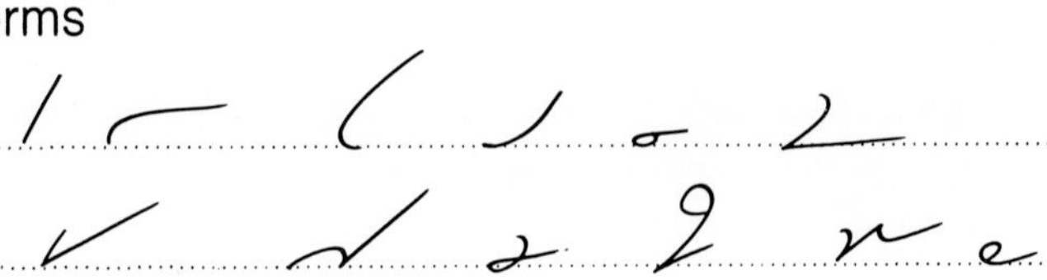

Brief-Form Derivatives

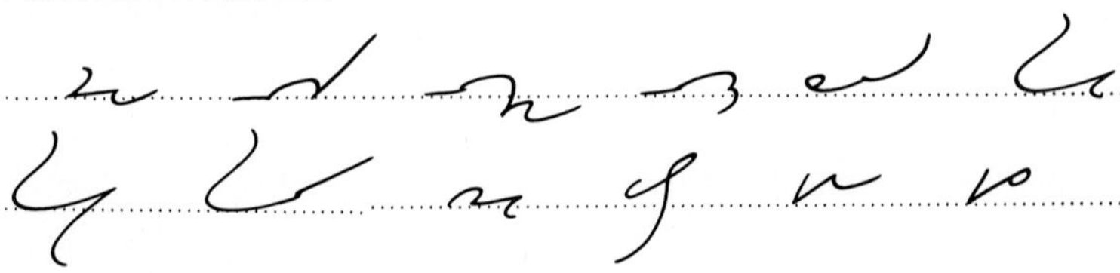

Phrases—Words Omitted

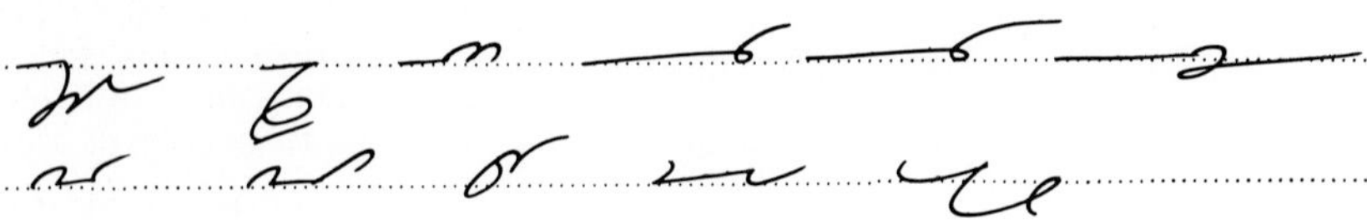

Key to the Shorthand

Which, them, be-by, and, when, from.
Should, could, send, after, street, were.
Sooner, enclosed, enclosure, encloses, weren't, values.
Valuable, valued, once-ones, whatever, shorter, shortly.
In the future, in the past, in the world, many of the, many of them, men and women.
One of the, one or two, out of the, some of our, will you please.

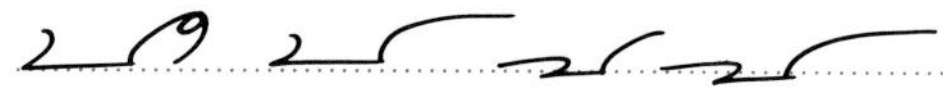

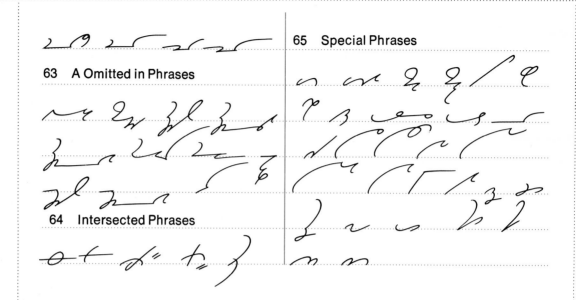

63 A Omitted in Phrases

64 Intersected Phrases

65 Special Phrases

Key to Recall Drills

Joined Word Endings

1 Treatment, alignment, supplement, amusement, moment, basement.

2 Nation, termination, station, operation, inflation, nomination, function.

3 Credential, confidential, essential, commercial, social, official, partial.

4 Greatly, namely, nicely, mainly, only.

5 Readily, speedily, easily, hastily, necessarily, family.

6 Careful, thoughtful, delightful, mindful, useful.

7 Dependable, reliable, profitable, troubled.

8 Gather, together, brother, rather, either, leather, bother, bothered, neither.

9 Actual, gradual, schedule, actually, annual, equally.

10 Furniture, nature, failure, miniature, captured, picture, stature.

11 Yourself, myself, itself, himself, herself, themselves, ourselves, yourselves.

12 Port, support, import, report, deport.

Reading and Writing Practice

1 iden·ti·fy
2 hear
3 Transcribe: 4 p.m.
4 Transcribe: 40
5 wel·come

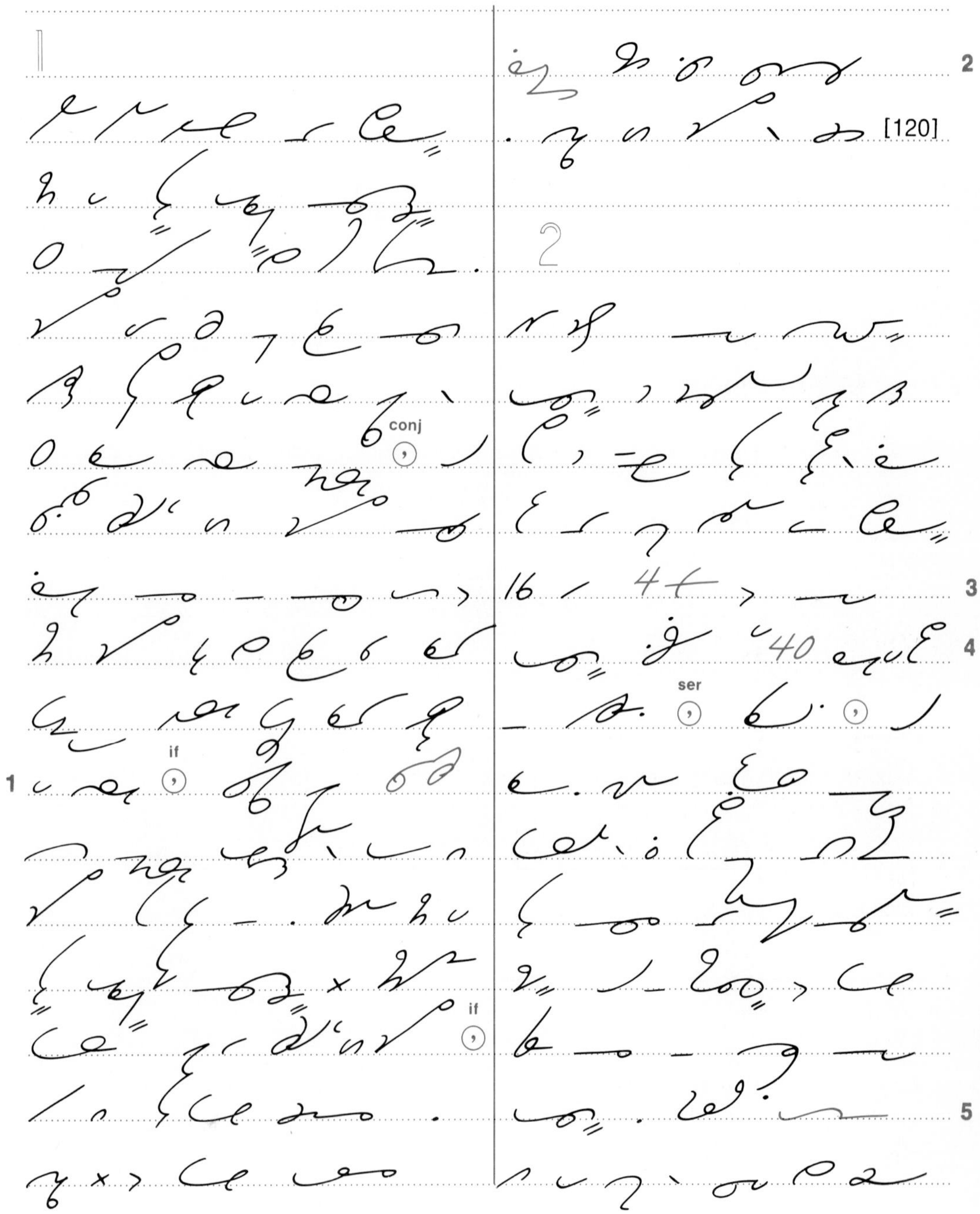

48 Electr, Electric

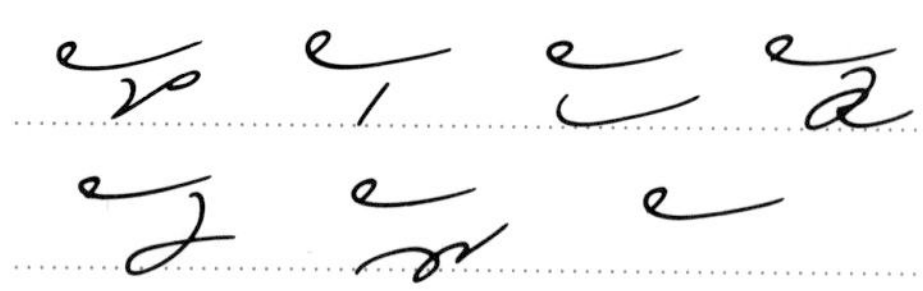

49 Super-

50 Circum-

51 Self-

52 Trans-

53 Under-

54 Over-

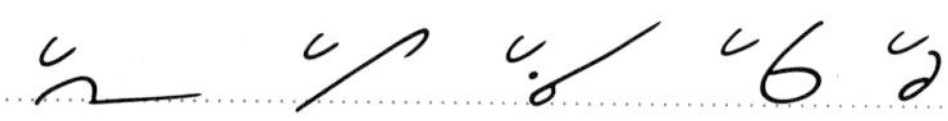

Phrases

55 T for To in Phrases

56 Been Represented by B

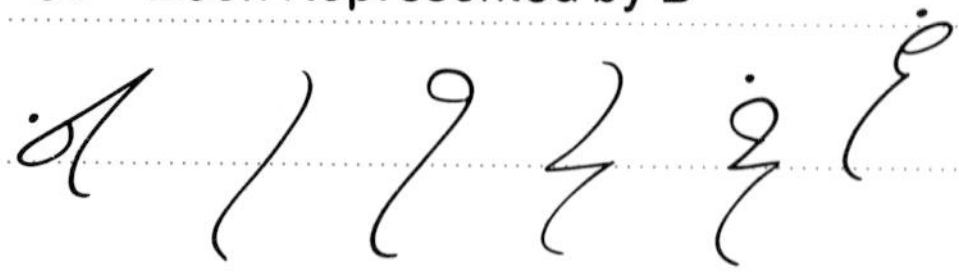

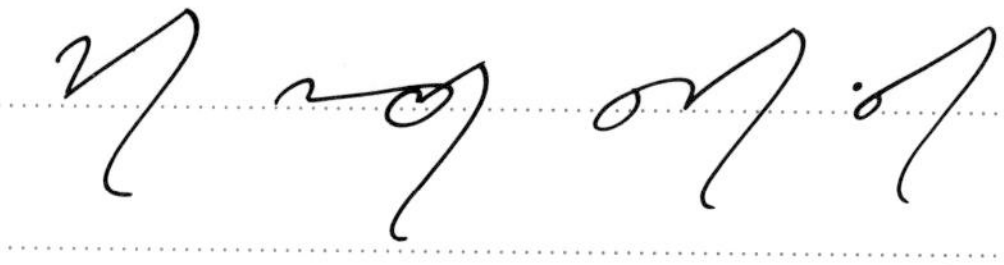

57 Able Represented by A

58 Want Preceded by Pronoun

59 Ago Represented by G

60 To Omitted in Phrases

61 The Omitted in Phrases

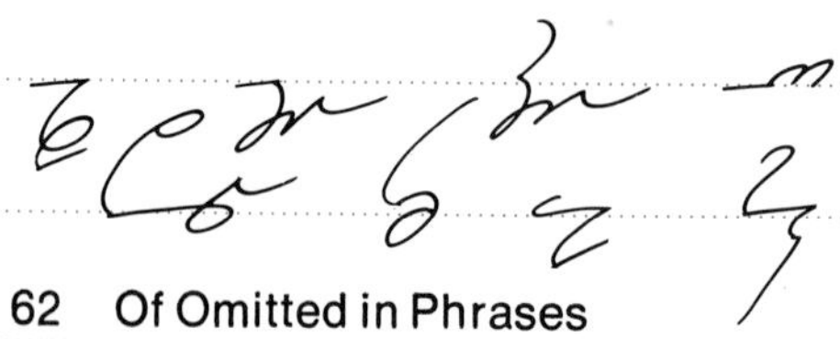

62 Of Omitted in Phrases

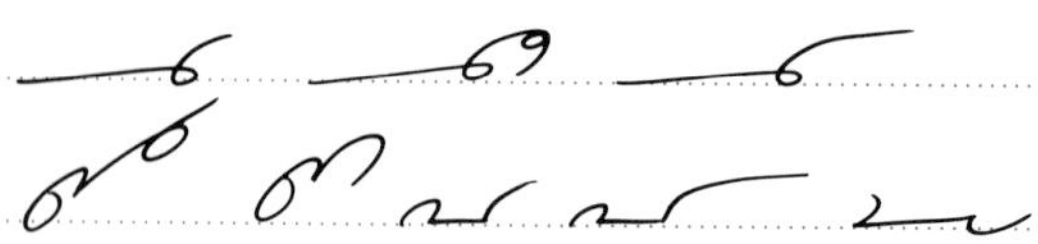

6 wom·en's
7 buy·ers
8 fair

[104]

3

6

intro

7

8

[144]

Executives, when dictating, often derive input from computer-generated reports.

31 En-

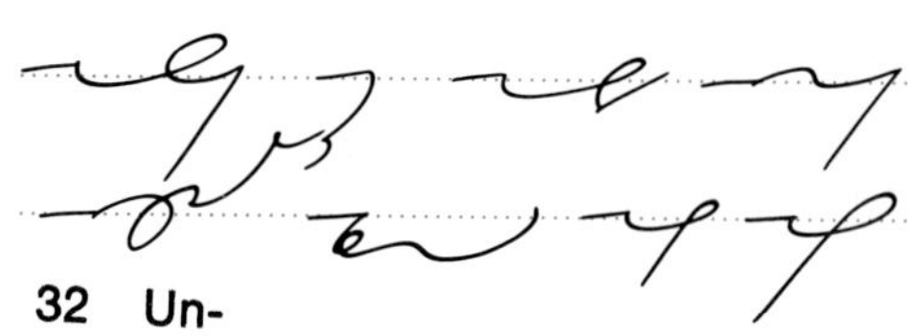

32 Un-

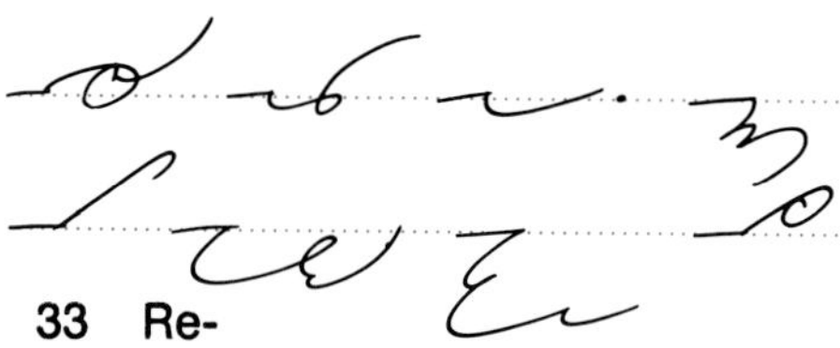

33 Re-

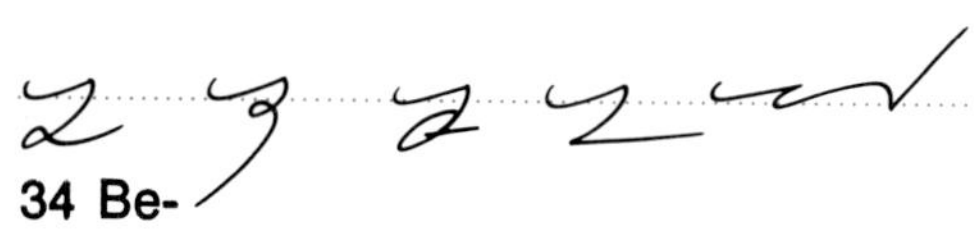

34 Be-

35 De-, Di-

36 Dis-, Des-

37 Mis-

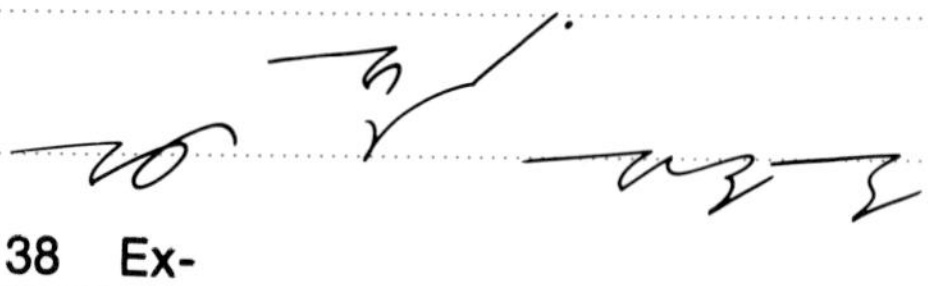

38 Ex-

39 Com-

40 Con-

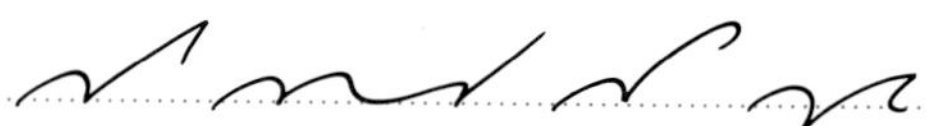

41 Sub-

42 Al-

43 For-, Fore-

44 Fur-

45 Tern-, Etc.

46 Ul-

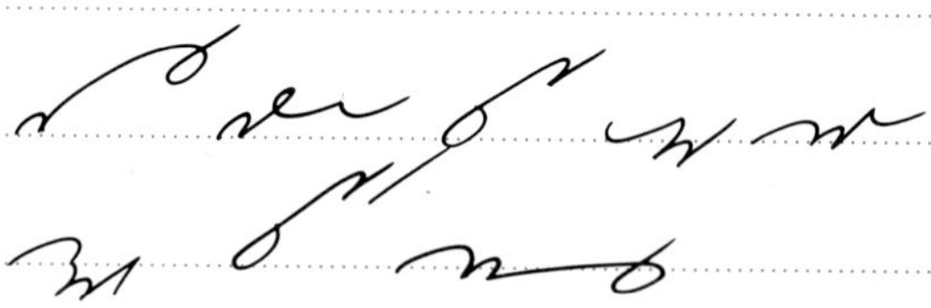

Disjoined Word Beginnings

47 Inter-, Etc.

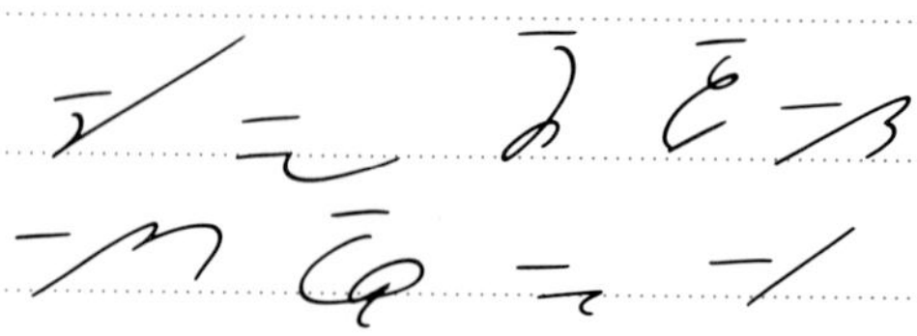

4

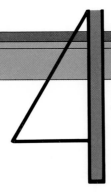

This lesson continues your review of Gregg Shorthand theory.

-ily

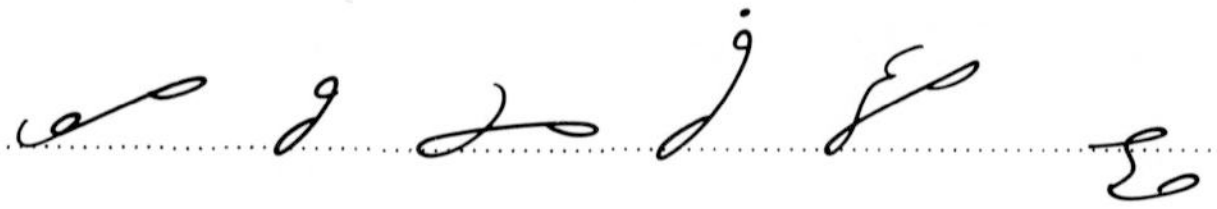

W (oo)

W (dash)

Wh (Write oo)

Sw (s-oo)

16 -ward

17 -ship

18 -cal, -cle

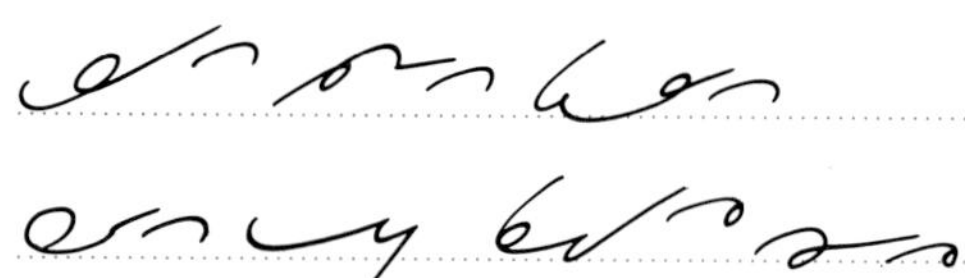

19 -ulate, -ulation

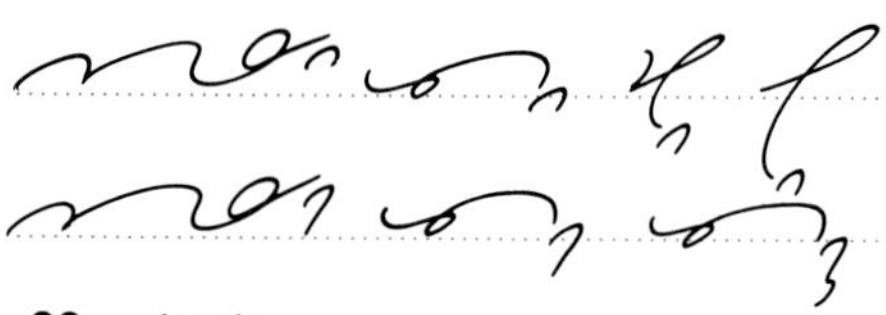

20 -ingly

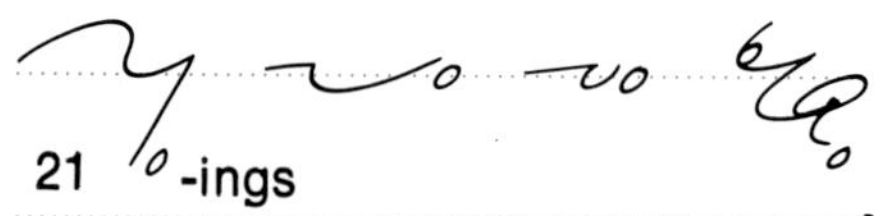

21 -ings

22 -gram

23 -ification

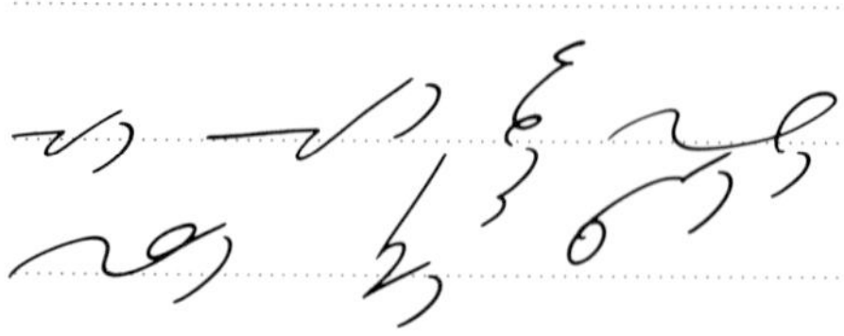

24 -lity

25 -lty

26 -rity

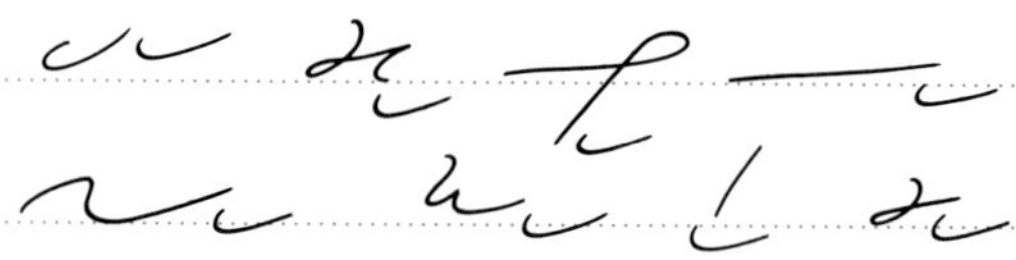

Joined Word Beginnings

27 Per-, Pur-

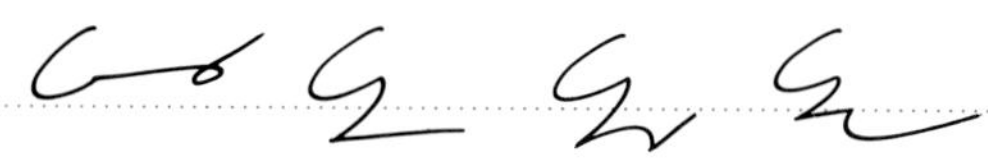

28 Em-

29 Im-

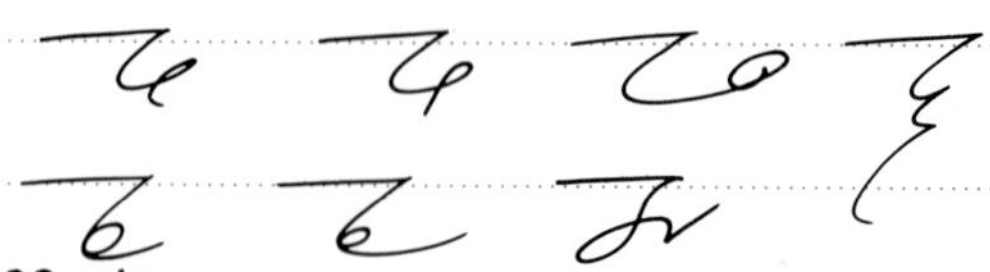

30 In-

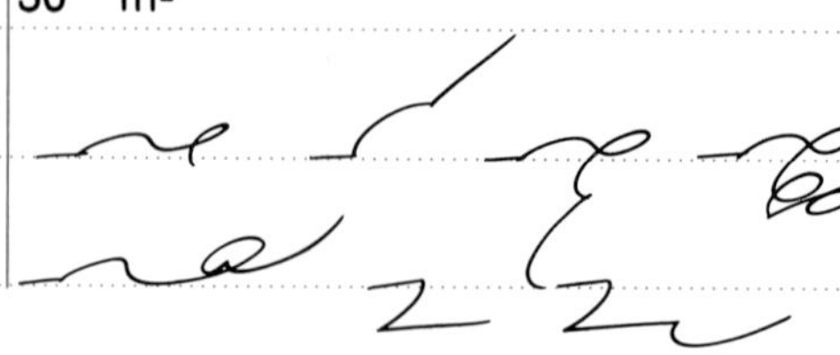

I (Vowel Following)

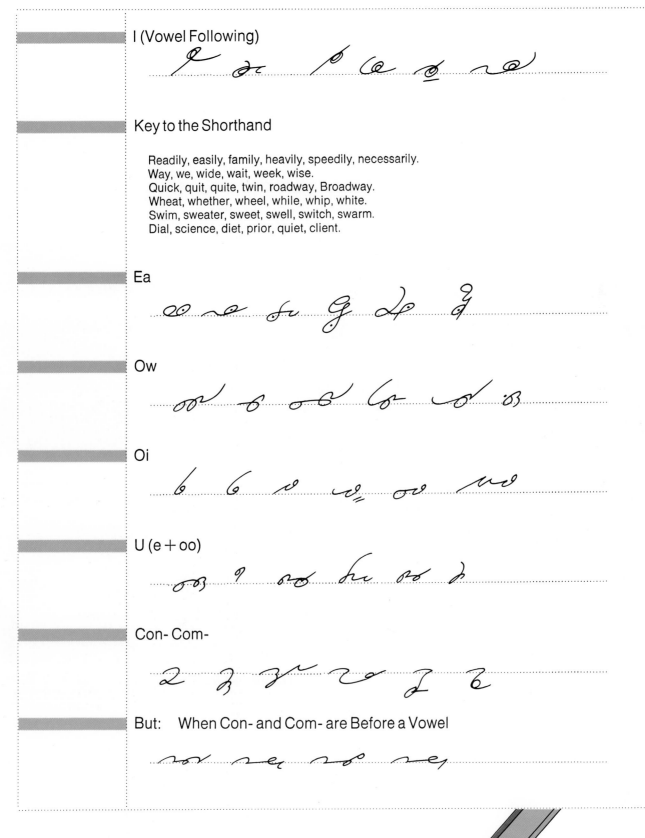

Key to the Shorthand

Readily, easily, family, heavily, speedily, necessarily.
Way, we, wide, wait, week, wise.
Quick, quit, quite, twin, roadway, Broadway.
Wheat, whether, wheel, while, whip, white.
Swim, sweater, sweet, swell, switch, swarm.
Dial, science, diet, prior, quiet, client.

Ea

Ow

Oi

U (e + oo)

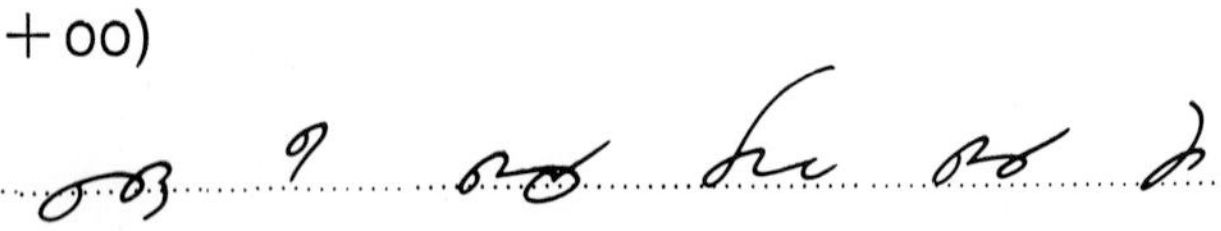

Con- Com-

But: When Con- and Com- are Before a Vowel

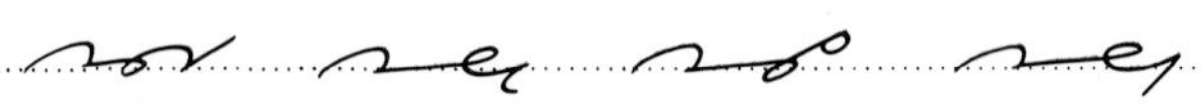

Recall Drills

Joined Word Endings

1 -ment

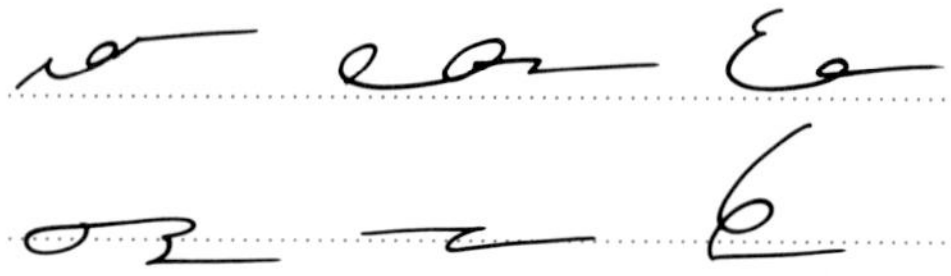

2 -tion

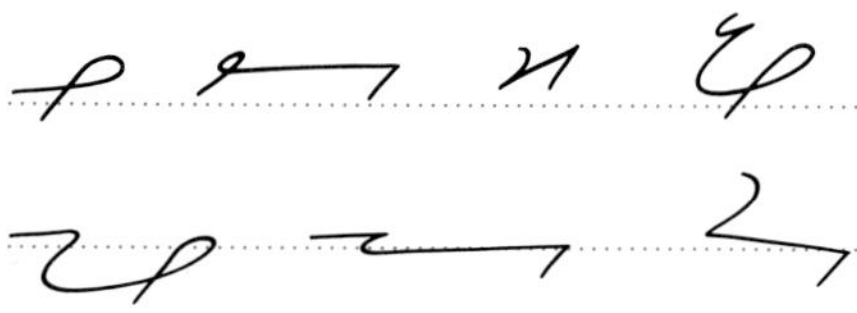

3 -tial

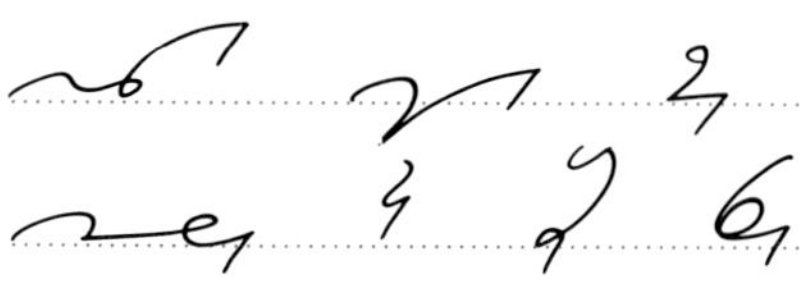

4 -ly

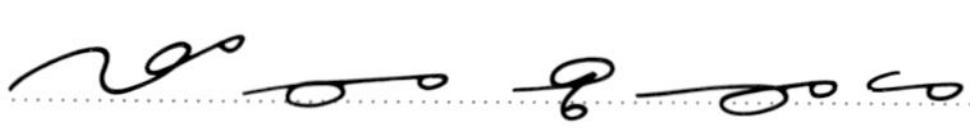

5 -ily

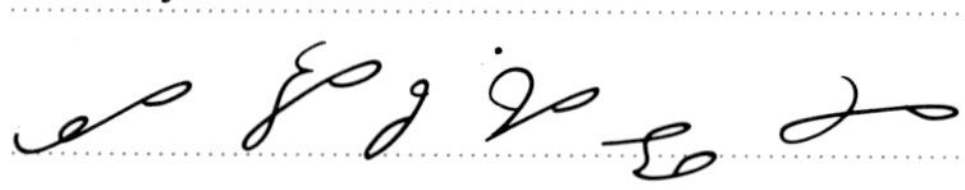

6 -ful

7 -ble

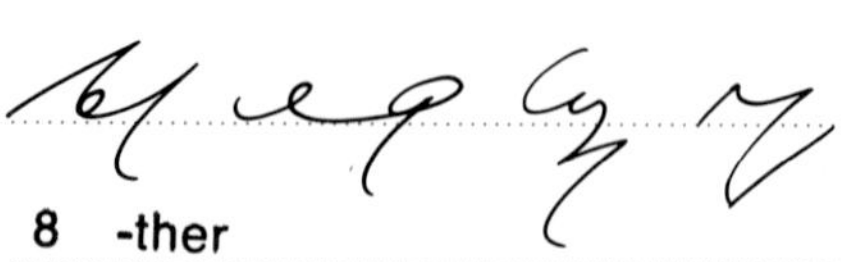

8 -ther

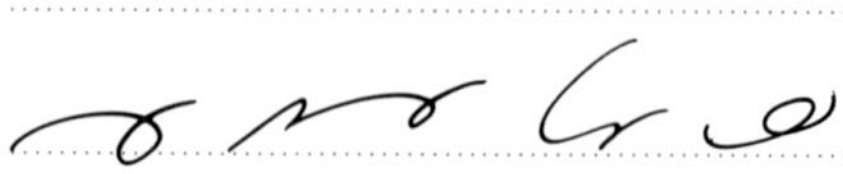

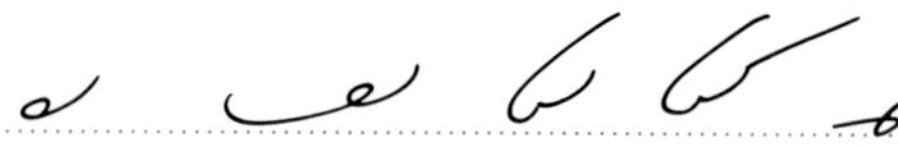

9 -ual

10 -ure

11 -self, -selves

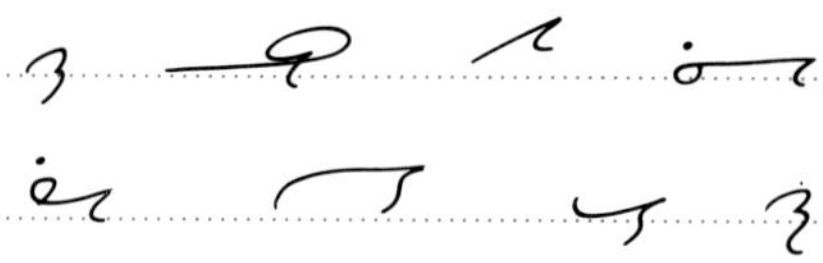

12 -ort

13 -tain

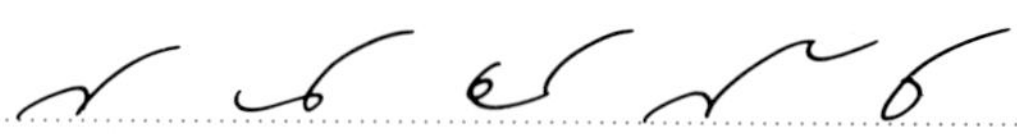

14 -cient, -ciency

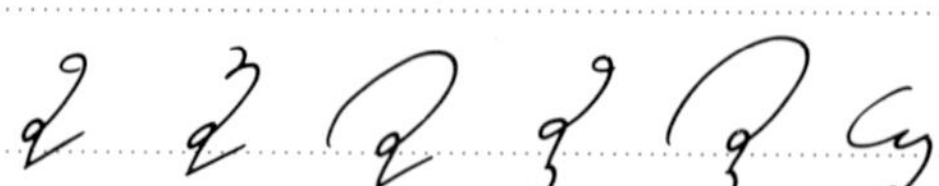

Disjoined Word Endings

15 -hood

Key to the Shorthand

Area, create, piano, appreciate, variation, association.
Account, now, amount, brown, loud, house.
Joy, boy, toy, Roy, annoy, destroy.
Accuse, usual, unite, bureau, unit, few.
Confer, confuse, consider, complete, combine, compare.
Connect, commerce, committee, commercial.

Brief Forms

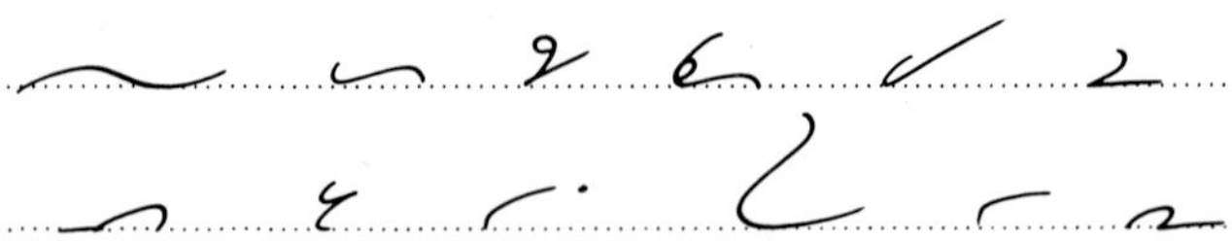

Brief-Form Derivatives

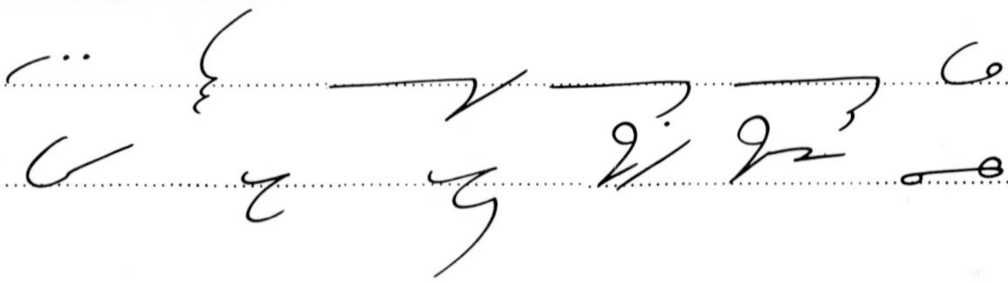

Phrases

Key to the Shorthand

Glad, work, yesterday, circular, order, soon.
Enclose, was, thank, value, than, won-one.
Thanking, businesses, manufactured, manufacturing, manufactures, presently.
Presented, represent, representative, afterward, afternoon, immediately.
Years ago, weeks ago, long ago, some time ago, several months ago.
I want, I wanted, he wants, if you want, we want.

Text Editing — A general phrase referring to a wide variety of word processing systems and procedures.

Turnaround Time — The time it takes to get processed information back to the word originator.

Upgrade — To add to the features or capabilities of a word processor.

Vendor — A supplier of office equipment.

Video Display Terminal — See CRT.

Word Originator — See author.

Word Processing — A system designed to improve the efficiency and effectiveness of business communications through the integration of people, procedures, and equipment.

Word Processing Specialist — A person who operates word processing equipment; may also be called Word Processing Operator, Correspondence Specialist.

Workstation — The place where an employee performs the majority of his or her work; encompasses the desk and any equipment necessary to perform the job, such as a word processor or typewriter.

Reading and Writing Practice

1 Transcribe: $21,530
2 Transcribe: $1,200
3 Fifth
4 Transcribe: 2 p.m.
5 ad•vice
6 in•te•ri•or

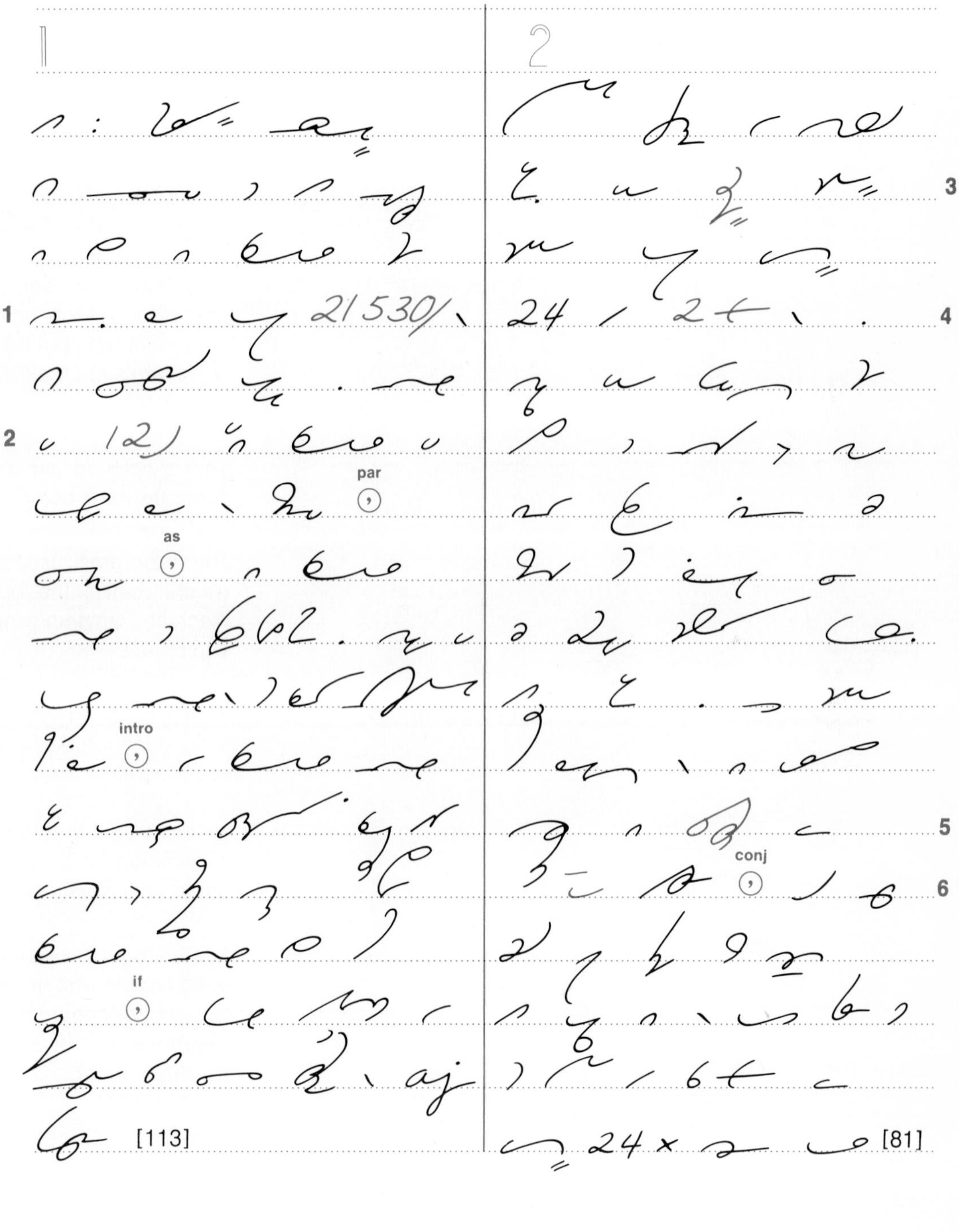

	Principal	See author.
	RAM (Random Access Memory)	Temporary memory.
	ROM (Read Only Memory)	Permanent memory; cannot be altered.
	Shared Logic System	A system comprised of several word processors and one CPU.
	Shared Resource System	A system comprised of several word processors, each having its own internal memory, but which share other peripherals such as a printer or storage system.
	Soft Copy	Text displayed on a video screen; compare hard copy.
	Software	The programs used with hardware which control the operation of the machine; anything not part of the equipment.
	Standalone	A single station word processor that is not connected to any other piece of equipment.
	Telecommunications	An electronic method of transmitting information from one location to another.
	Teleconference	A meeting of geographically separated people who have two-way audio and video communications via the telephone and/or closed-circuit television.
	Terminal	A device equipped with a keyboard which is capable of sending and receiving information to a computer.

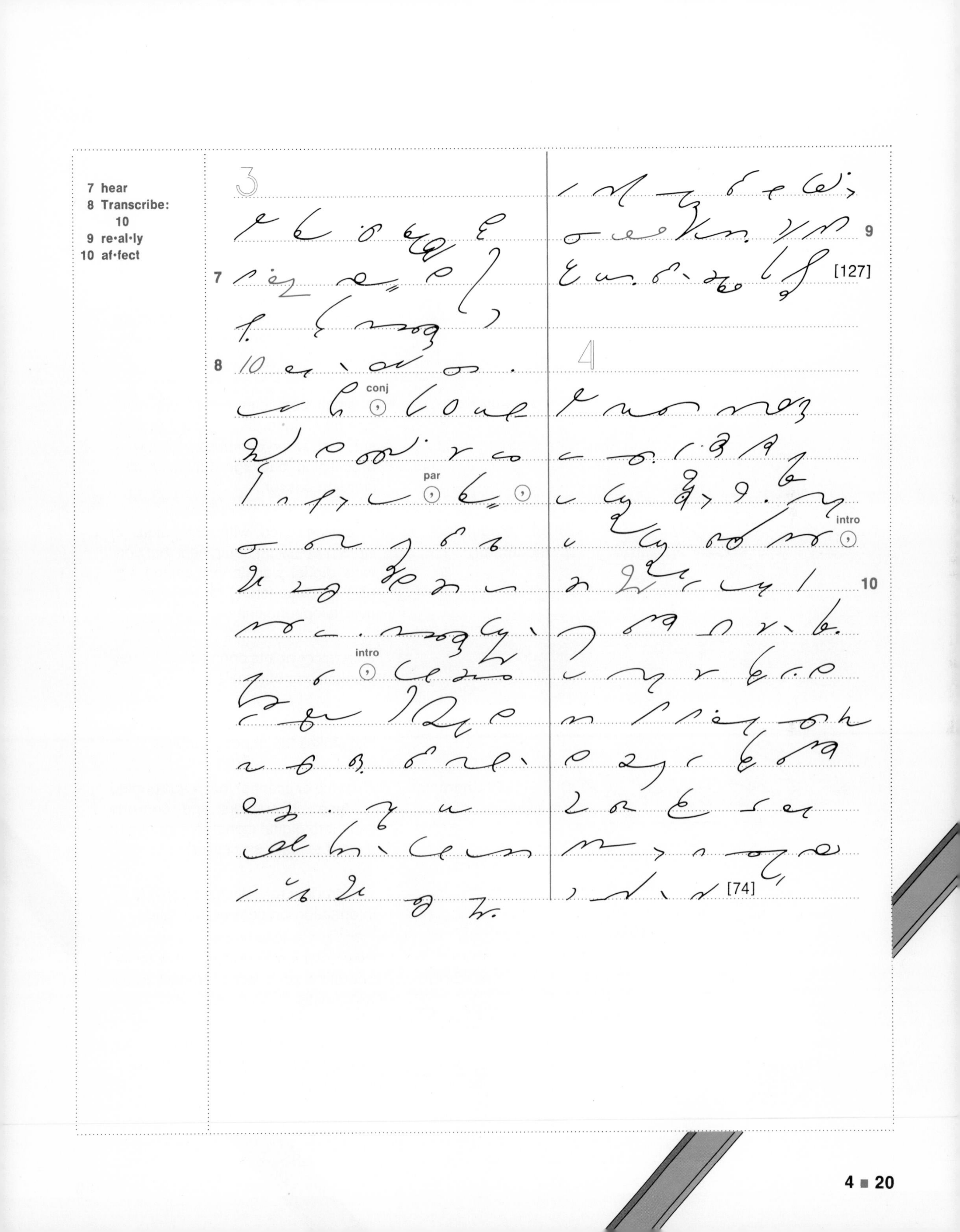

7 hear
8 Transcribe: 10
9 re·al·ly
10 af·fect

3

7

8 10

conj

par

intro

9

[127]

4

intro

10

[74]

	Memory	See internal storage.
	Menu	A list of operator options that can be accessed during the input and processing of information.
	Microform	A miniature image of a document; types include microfilm and microfiche.
	Microcomputer	A small computer, about the same size as a video display word processor, that, when equipped with a word processing package, functions as a word processor.
	MODEM (*Mo*dulator/ *Dem*odulator)	A device used with computers or word processing equipment that converts digital signals into analog signals (such as tones) for transmission over telephone lines.
	Network	A series of points connected by communications channels.
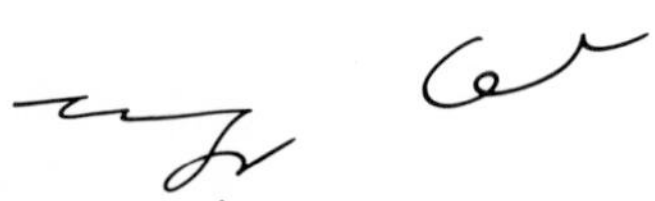	Nonimpact Printer	A printer that has no printing element that strikes the paper or ribbon.
	OCR (Optical Character Reader)	A device or scanner that reads printed or typed characters and converts them into digital signals for input into a word or data processor.
	Output	The product (usually hard copy) of an information processing operation.
	Peripheral	Device which is not essential to the operation of a word processor but which extends its capabilities.
	Playback	The process of printing or displaying material that has been input into a word processor.

5

This lesson continues your review of Gregg Shorthand theory.

-icle

-quent

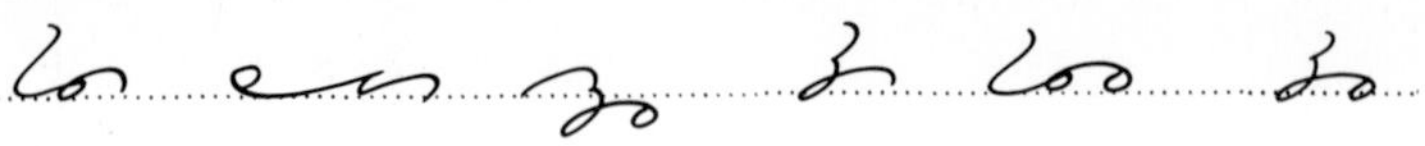

-gram

Re-

But: Before a Forward or Upstroke

	Hardware	Equipment such as a word processor or a computer.
	Impact Printer	Any type of printer that generates characters by striking type through a ribbon onto the paper.
	Information Processing	Coordinating people, equipment, and procedures in order to handle information—both word and data processing.
	Ink-Jet Printer	A nonimpact printer that sprays tiny droplets of ink onto paper which form the alpha/numeric characters.
	Input	The facts or data which are entered into the processing system.
	Intelligent Copier/Printer	A copier or a printer than can manipulate data.
	Internal Processor	See CPU.
	Internal Storage	The storage of data or text within the word processor; also called memory.
	Keyboarding	Entering data into the memory of a word processor by depressing the keys on a keyboard.
	Line Printer	A high-speed printer which prints an entire line at a time instead of a single character.
	Logic	The basic operating instructions for a computer.
	Magnetic Media	Media—software—that records by means of electrical impulses and magnetism. Magnetic media includes cards, cassettes, cartridges, and disks.

-rity

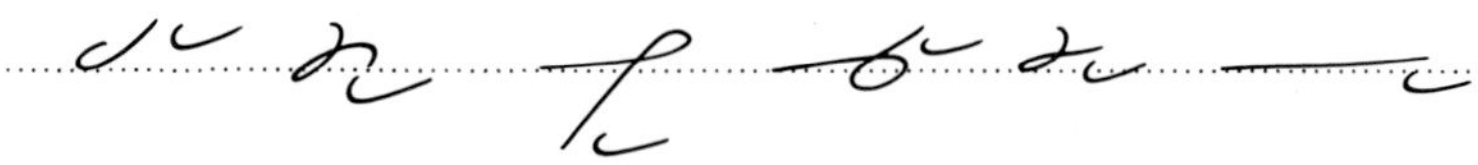

Key to the Shorthand

Article, chemical, medical, particle, mechanical, identical.
Frequent, eloquent, consequently, subsequent, frequently, subsequently.
Program, telegram, diagram, programs, telegrams, diagrams.
Receipt, reason, region, reply, refer, research.
Retake, recall, reduce, relate, reduction, relation.
Authority, security, majority, maturity, seniority, minority.

-lity -lty

-ure

-sure

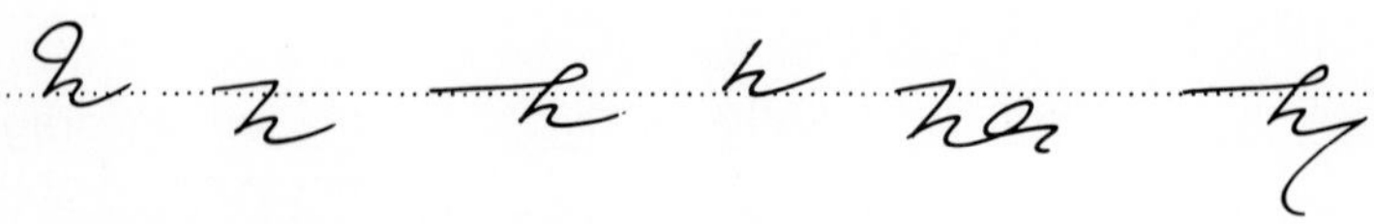

Rd

Ld

	Editing	Changing or rearranging the text by deleting, substituting, inserting, and moving; also includes reformatting.
	Electronic Mail	The transmission and display of business communications via satellites, cables, or telephone wires at very high speeds; no physical movement of paper.
	Electronic Typewriter	A low level blind word processor that houses all components (keyboard, internal processor, storage unit, and printer) in one unit; automates many typing tasks.
	Electrostatic	Type of printing process in which images are burned into paper electrically.
	Facsimile	A copy of a document that is transmitted electronically from one location to another, usually by telephone lines.
	Feasibility Study	A detailed study to determine the company's information processing needs in an effort to increase productivity.
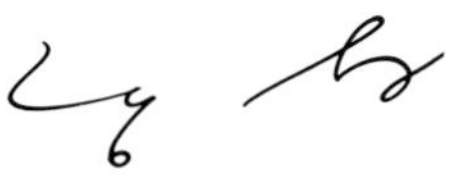	Floppy Diskette	A magnetic storage medium for word processors that looks like a small phonograph record.
	Format	The arrangements of a document on a page.
	Function Keys	Special keys that communicate commands to the internal processor of a word processor.
	Hard Copy	Permanent machine output—such as text printed on paper.

Electric Electr-

Key to the Shorthand

Ability, quality, possibility, facility, personality, penalty, loyalty.
Failure, feature, nature, natural, picture, lecture.
Assure, insure, measure, sure, insurance, measurable.
Tired, hired, assured, record, board, bird.
Build, called, fold, held, hold, told.
Electric, electric motor, electrical, electronic, electricity, electrician.

Brief Forms

Brief-Form Derivatives

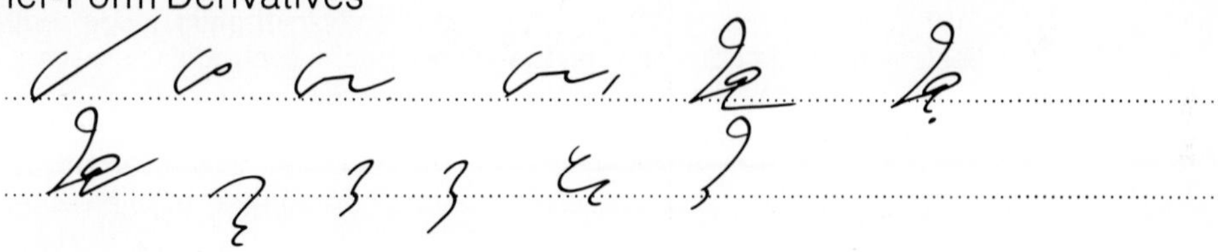

Phrases

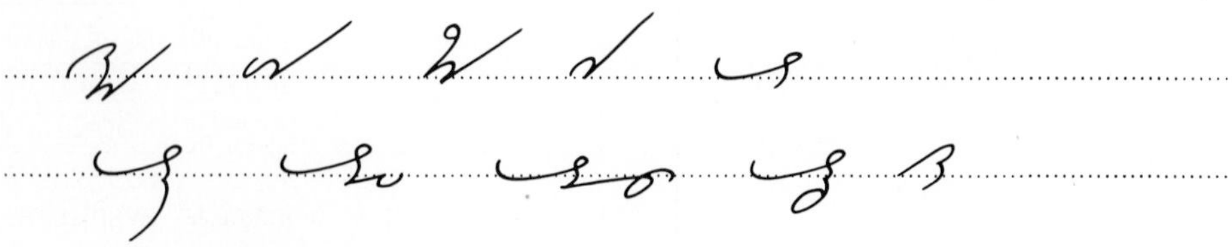

Key to the Shorthand

What, about, thing-think, business, doctor, any.
Gentlemen, important-importance, morning, where, company, manufacture.
Parted, partly, partner, partnership, advertisement, advertising.
Advertised, companies, wishes, wishful, opportunities, advantages.
Thank you for your order, of your order, if your order, your order, let us.
Let us have, let us know, let us make, let us say, to us.

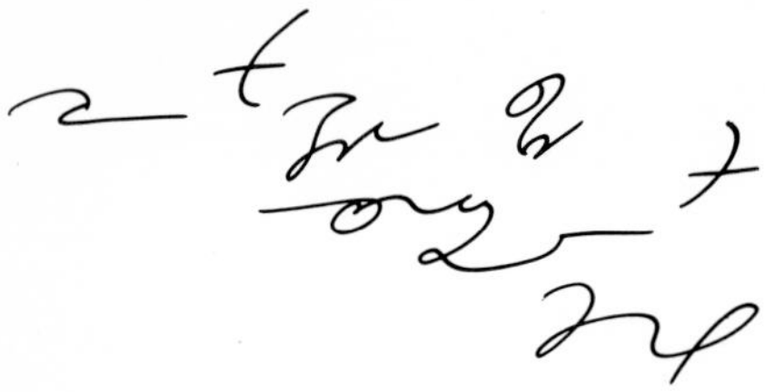	COM (Computer Output Microfilm)	A process by which a computer printout is produced directly on microfilm.
	Configuration	The components and the peripherals which make up a word processing system and the manner in which they are arranged.
	CPU (Central Processing Unit)	The component of a data or word processing system that controls the interpretation and execution of instructions; performs arithmetical and logical functions. The internal processor.
	CRT (Cathode Ray Tube)	An electronic vacuum tube upon which are displayed text and graphics. Also referred to as a video display terminal.
	Cursor	A lighted indicator on a display screen that marks the working position of the operator. Equivalent to the printing point indicator on a typewriter.
	Daisy Wheel	A character printer type element on which the characters are engraved at the end of spokes or bars which resemble a daisy.
	Disk Drive	The unit of a computer or word processor in which the disk is inserted, thereby programming the machine.
	Display Word Processor	A word processor equipped with a video display terminal.
	Document	Any business communication—letter, memo, table, report.
	Dot Matrix	A printing pattern in which closely spaced dots form alpha/numeric characters.

Reading and Writing Practice

1 in·sur·ance
2 ad·di·tion·al
3 arise
4 hear
5 mod·els
6 ear·li·est

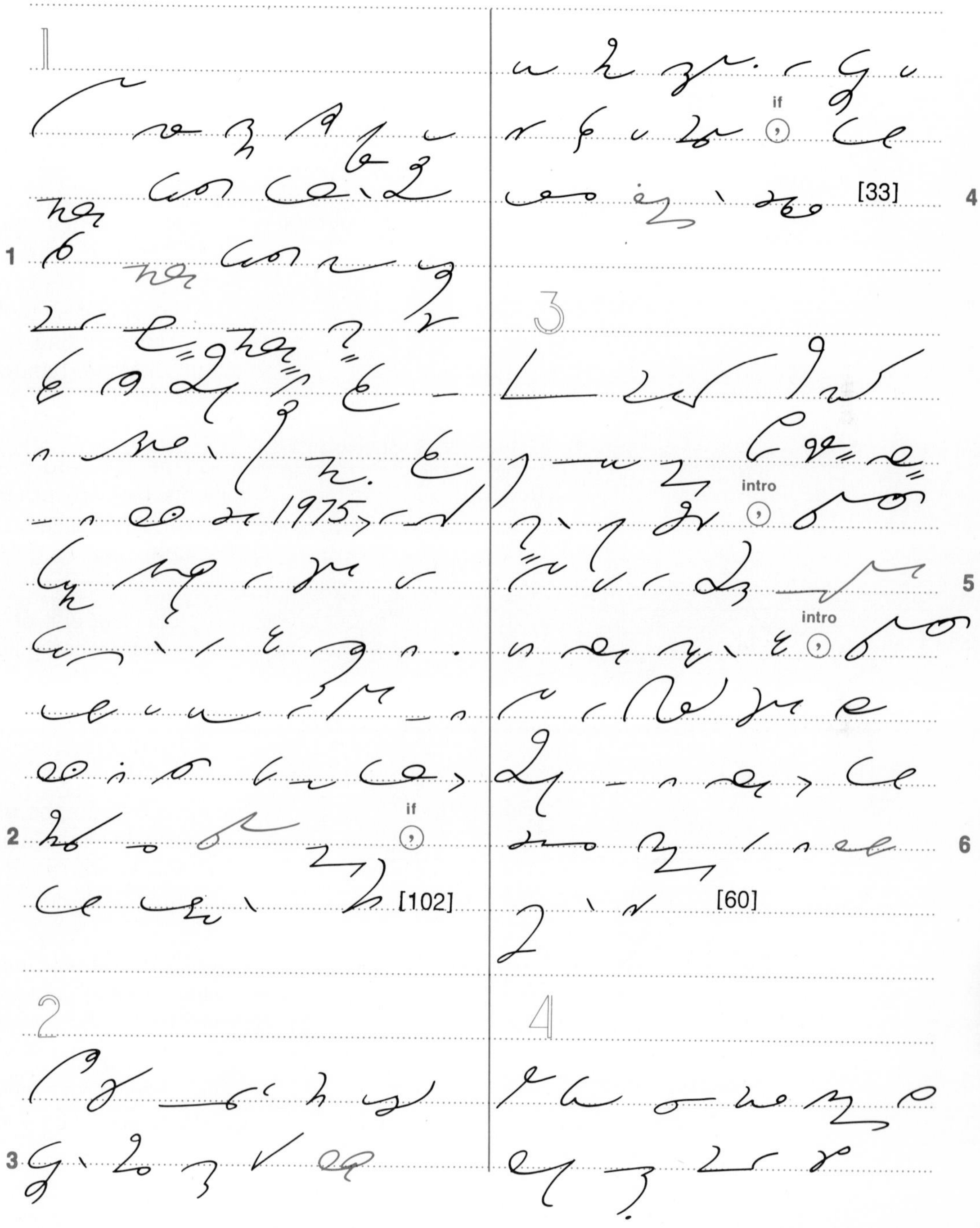

Word Processing Glossary

	Acoustic Coupler	A data communications device that converts data signals to tones which are transmitted over a telephone line using a conventional telephone. (Also reverses the procedures at the receiving end.)
	Administrative Secretary	A support person who performs nonkeyboarding activities: processing mail, answering phones, making reservations, and so forth. May also perform keyboarding activities working from dictated, handwritten, or rough draft input.
	Author	The person who creates the documents that are processed by a WP center. Also called a word originator or a principal.
	Bit	The smallest unit of information recognized by a computer.
	Blind Word Processor	A word processor that does not have a video display.
	Boilerplate	Stored paragraphs that can be combined with each other or with new material to create individualized documents.
	Character Printer	An impact printer that prints a single letter, number, or symbol at one time.
	Communicating Word Processor	A word processor that can transmit and receive text over the telephone lines to and from another word processor.

7 nec·es·sary
8 its
9 page 21
10 quite

7

intro

[84]

5

8

par

intro

21

9

intro

conj

10

[126]

A secretary should make a list of matters to be discussed over the telephone when the traveling manager calls in, checking off each item as it is discussed.

APPENDIX

6

This lesson continues your review of Gregg Shorthand theory.

Trans-

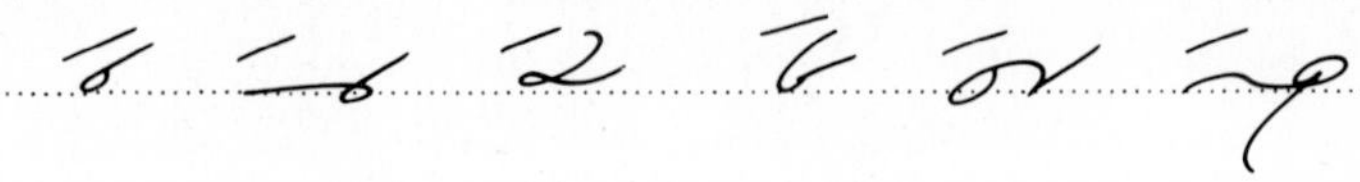

Dis-, Des-

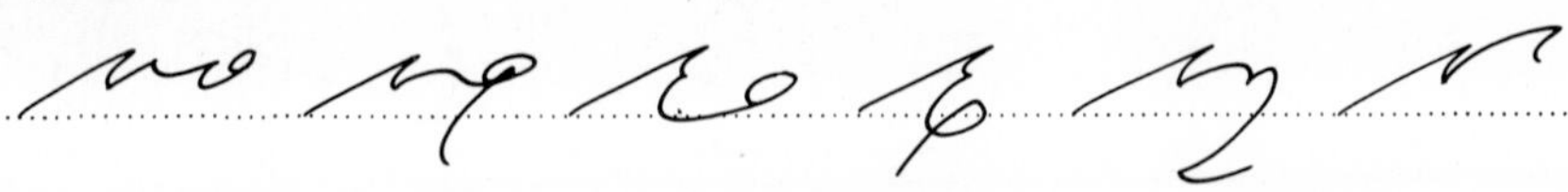

De-

Di-

But: Before an Upstroke

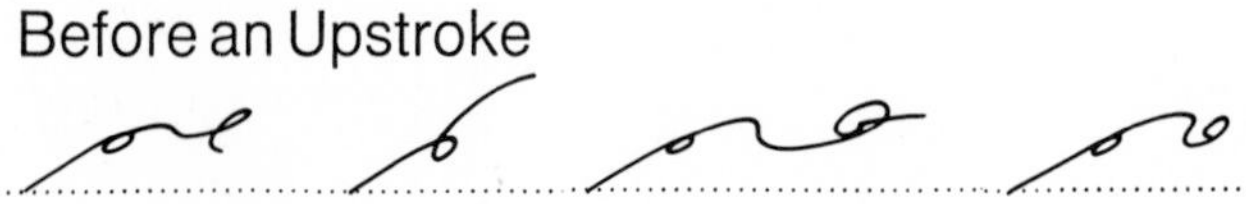

5

Mr. Charles Small
51 Madison Street
Bangor, ME 04401

10 suf·fered
11 wreck
12 fair
13 Transcribe: $400
14 Transcribe: four
15 past
16 Transcribe: six
17 re·ceived

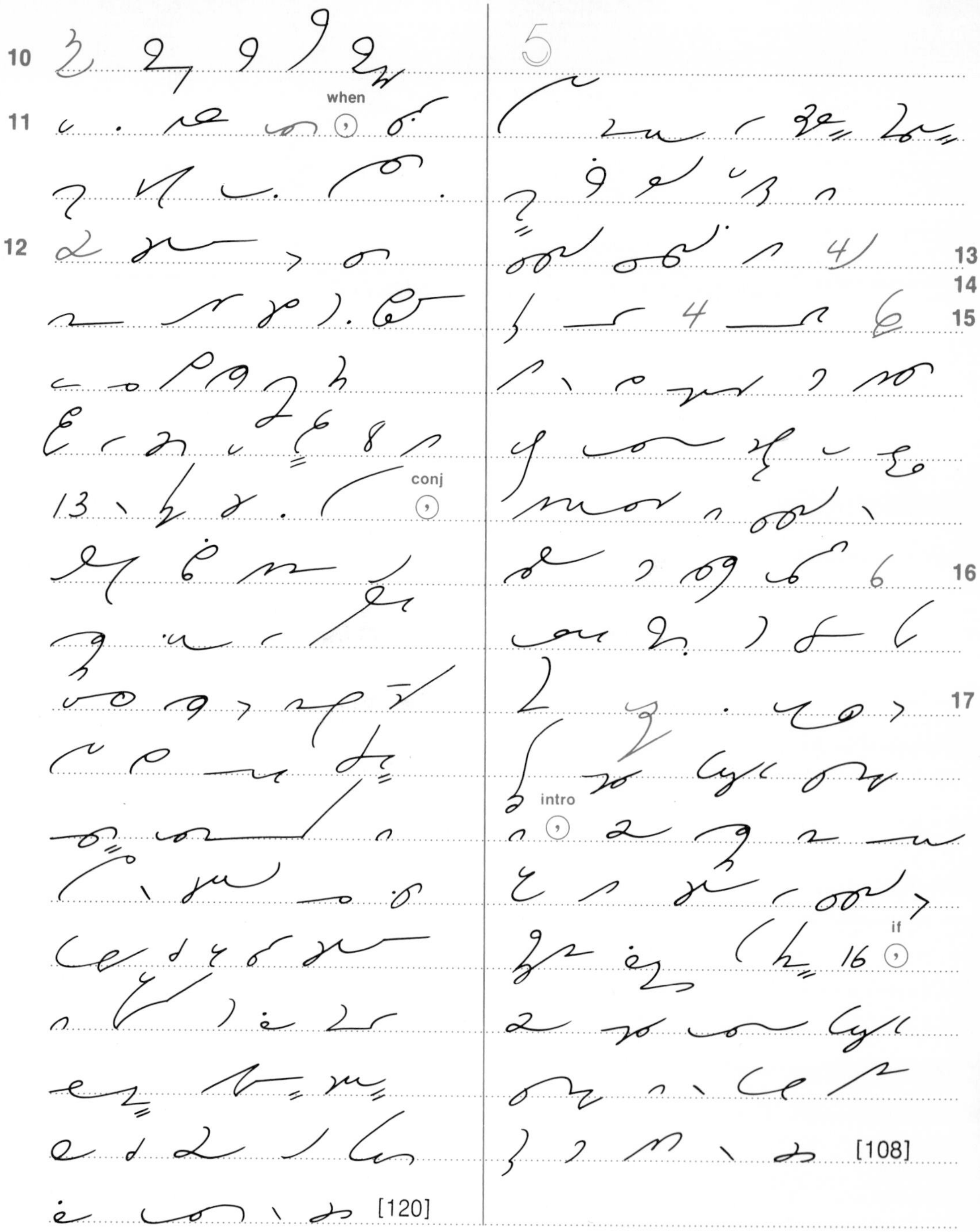

-hood

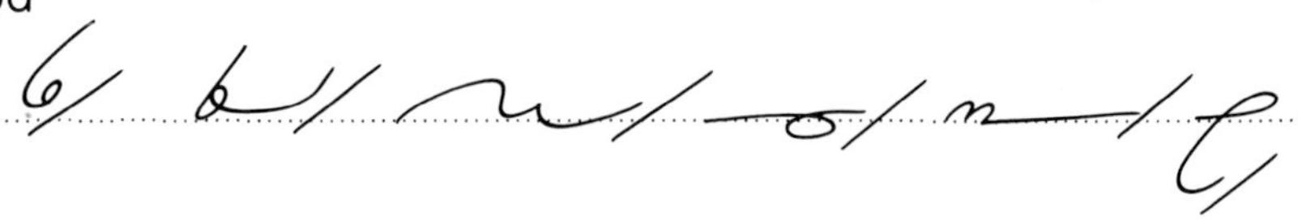

Key to the Shorthand

Transit, transmit, transfer, transport, transact, transcribe.
Destroy, describe, display, dispatch, discover, distance.
Decide, delay, derive, depend, deposit, deliver.
Direct, direction, directions, diploma, diplomacy, digit.
Decrease, detain, decline, decoy.
Boyhood, childhood, girlhood, manhood, womanhood, neighborhood.

-ward

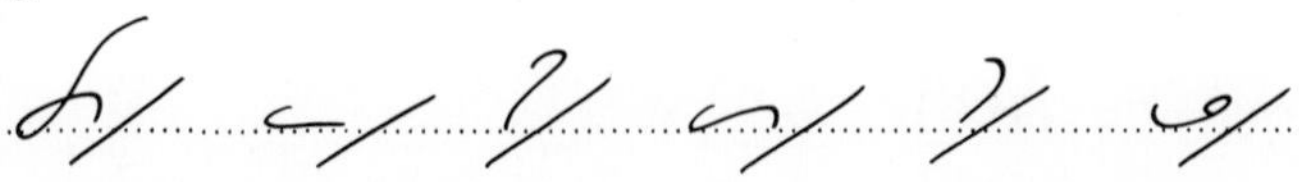

Sub-

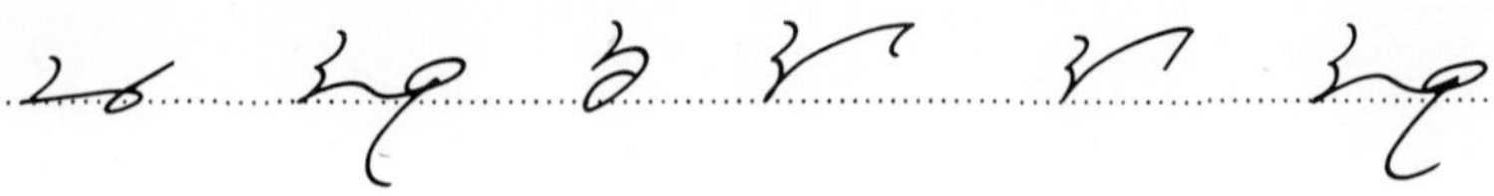

Self-

Circum-

Super-

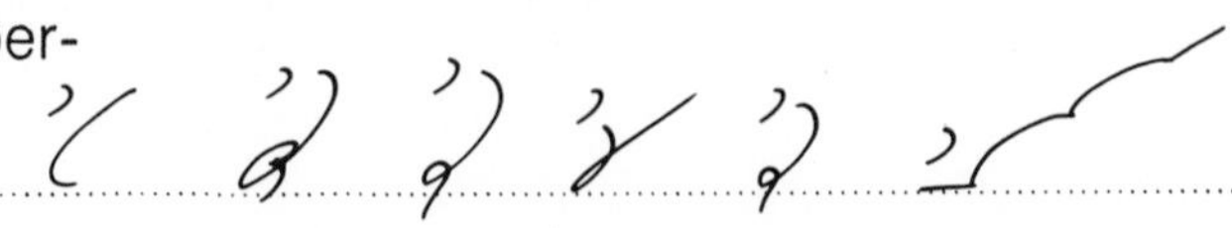

3
Mr. William Ramos
8712 Star Avenue
Houston, TX 77011

4
Mr. William Brown
Brown, Mitchell,
and Associates
2963 Sears Street
Biloxi, MS 39511

3 great
4 Transcribe:
fifth
5 their
6 here·af·ter
7 ca·reer
8 un·der·tak·en
9 any way

3

4

intro

[108]

3

5

6

ser

conj

7

8

if

9

[117]

4

X

Key to the Shorthand

Backward, onward, upward, awkward, forward, reward.
Submit, subscribe, subway, substance, substantial, subscriber.
Self-made, self-evident, self-defense, myself, himself, themselves.
Circumstance, circumference, circumvent, circumstances, circumscribe, circumstantial.
Superb, supervise, supervision, supersede, superficial, superintendent.
Tax, box, fix, taxes, fixture, fixed.

Brief Forms

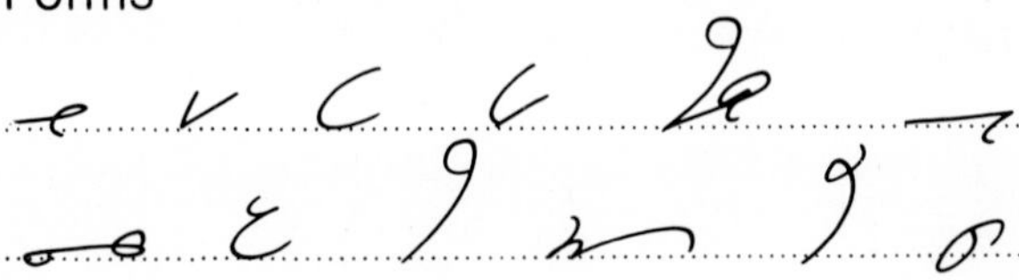

Brief-Form Derivatives

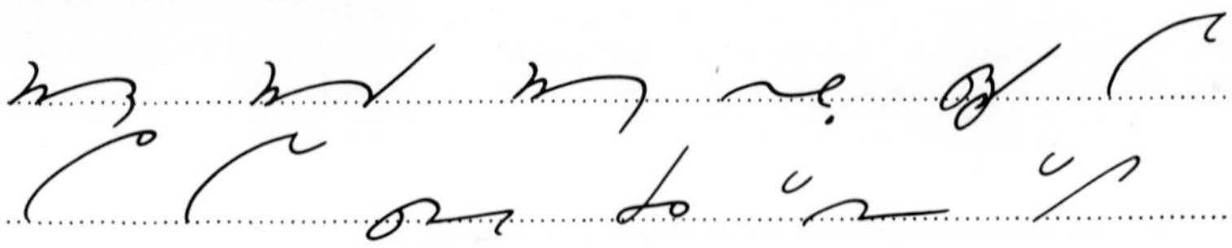

Phrases

Key to the Shorthand

Next, short, present, part, advertise, Ms.
Immediate, opportunity, advantage, suggest, several, out.
Suggests, suggested, suggestion, corresponding, outside, times.
Timely, timer, acknowledgments, generally, overcome, overdo-overdue.
I hope, I hope that, I hope that this, I hope this, I hope to see.
We hope, we hope that, we hope you can, we hope that this, we hope you will.

60

Writing and Transcription Practice

1
Outline For A Letter

2
Ms. Kathleen Murphy
812 Knowles Avenue
Peoria, IL 61611

1 too
2 for·mer·ly

1

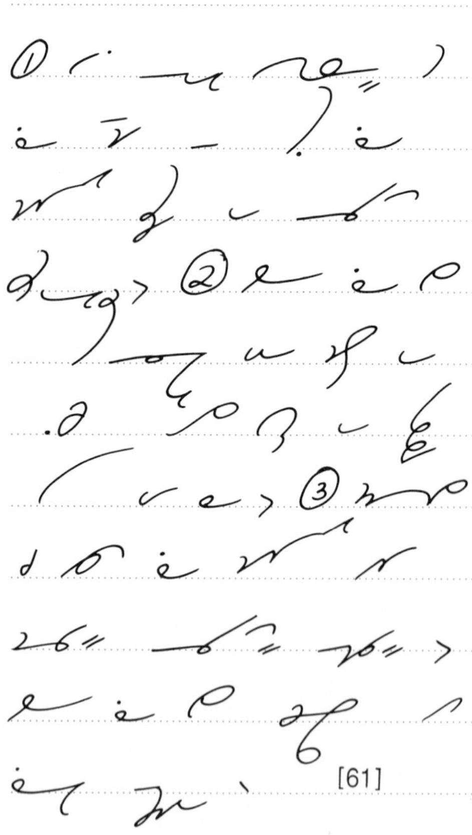

[61]

2

1

2

Reading and Writing Practice

1 some
2 re·al·ize
3 le·gal
4 em·bar·rass·ment
5 typ·i·cal
6 work·day
7 ef·fec·tive

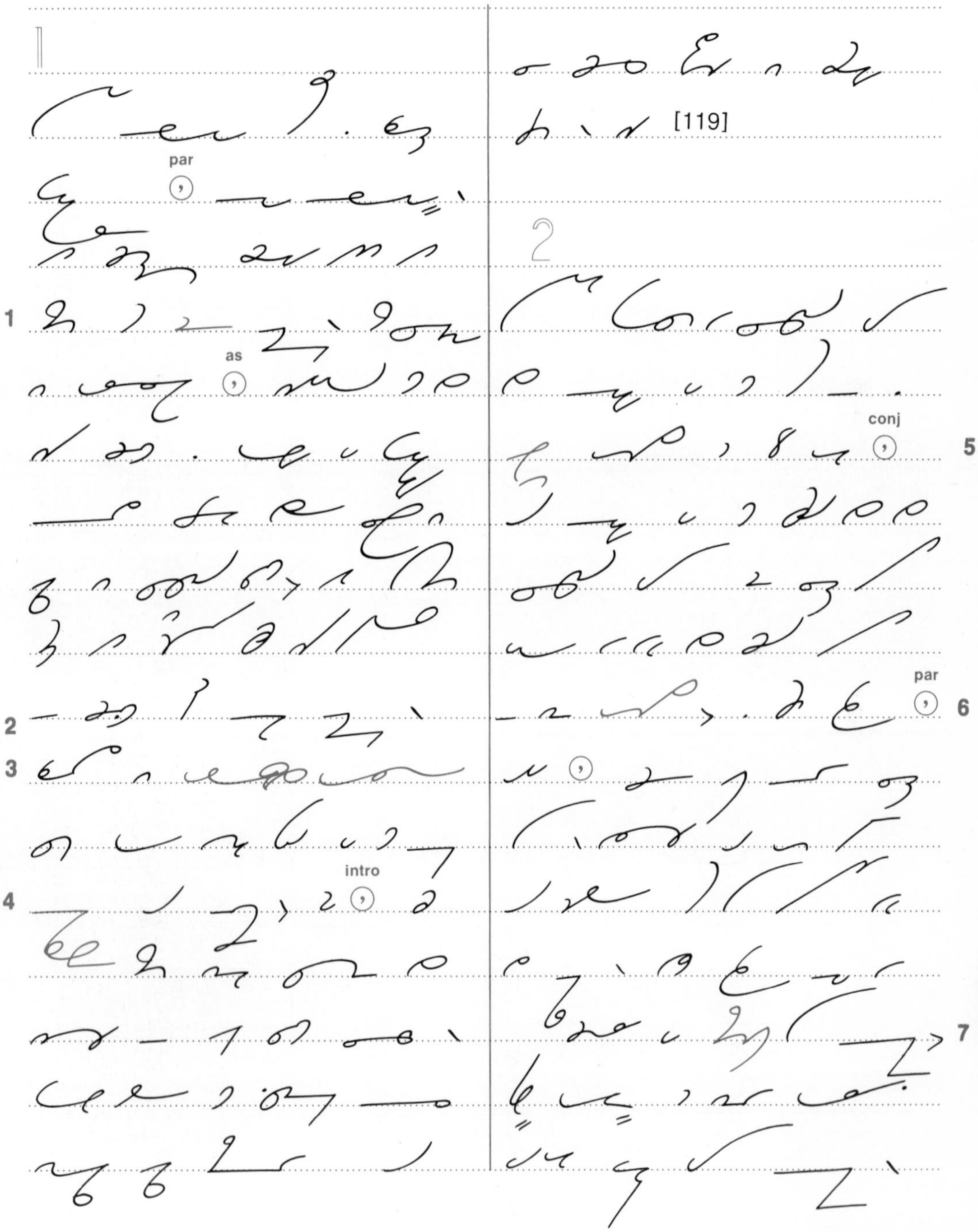

5
Mr. Jonathan Harper
Harper's Country
Market
Box 741
Louisville, KY 40211

8 mod·els
9 suit
10 ap·peared
11 ad·ver·tise·ment
12 edi·tion
13 hu·man be·ings
14 Transcribe: $200
15 Transcribe: 2,000

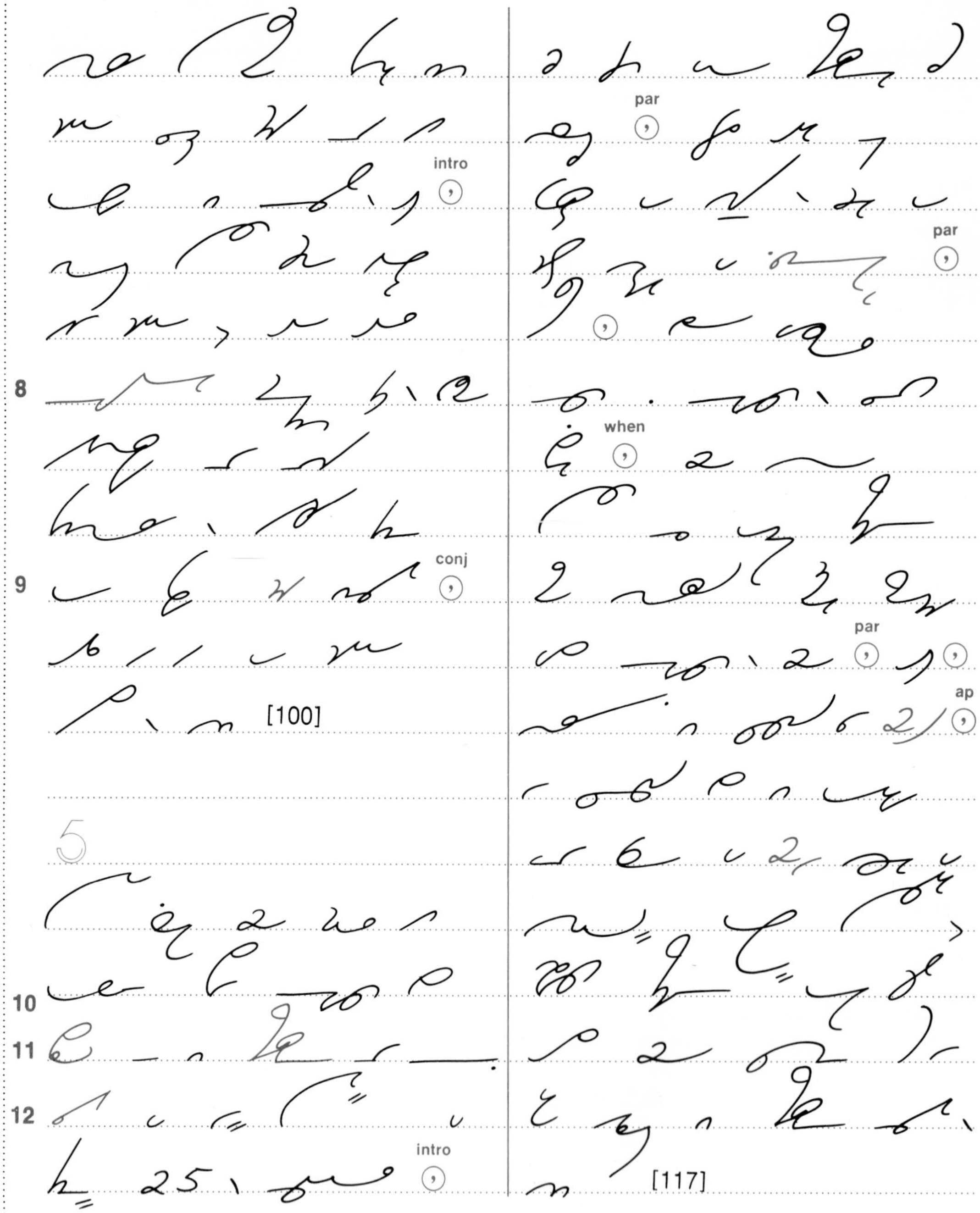

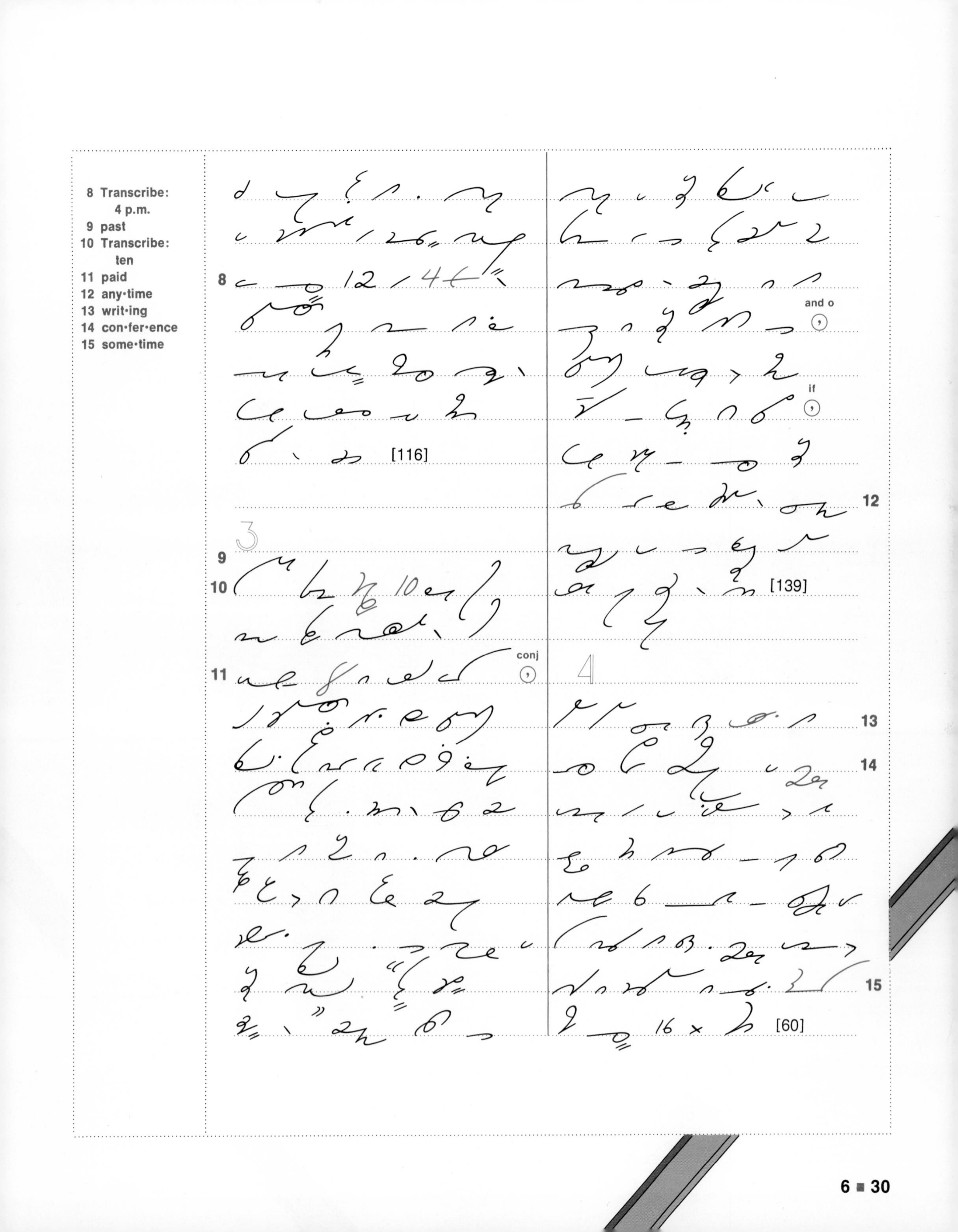

8 Transcribe:
4 p.m.
9 past
10 Transcribe:
ten
11 paid
12 any·time
13 writ·ing
14 con·fer·ence
15 some·time

8

[116]

3

9

10

11

conj

and o

if

12

[139]

4

13

14

15

[60]

3
Mrs. Lynda West
4201 Roosevelt Street
Camden, NJ 08100

4
Mrs. Nancy Graham
1703 Wilson Drive
Norwalk, CT 06611

2 re·ceived
3 Transcribe:
$186
4 co·op·er·a·tion
5 write
6 coun·try
7 any time

[117]

3

when

par

2

3

186

conj

10

if

4

par

5

186

[137]

4

intro

6

7

when

7

This lesson continues your review of Gregg Shorthand theory.

Ex-

Ses Sis Sus

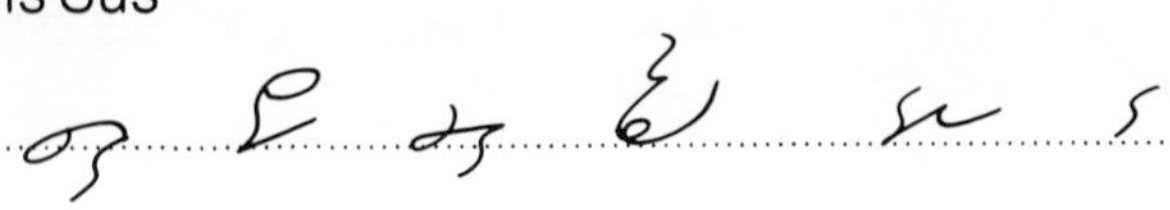

Ort

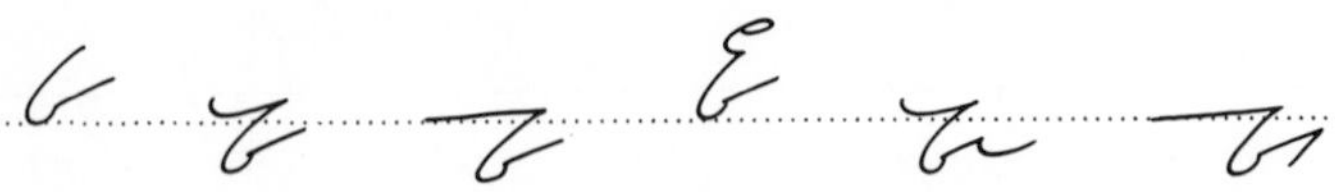

Per-

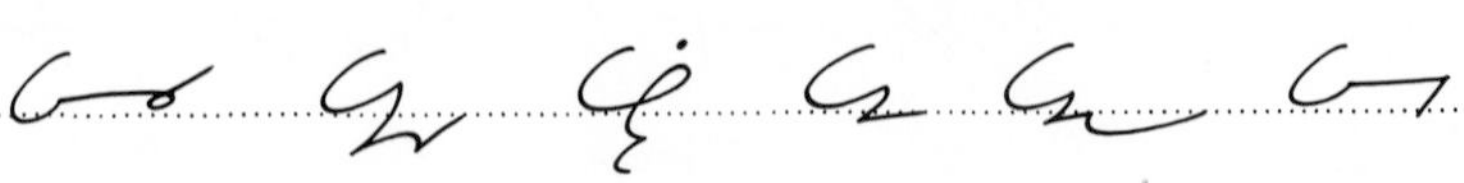

Pur-

59

Writing and Transcription Practice

1
Important Reminder!

2
Mr. G. C. Cooper
Marathon Food Center
8617 Cleveland Avenue
Boulder, CO 80211

1 hear

-ble

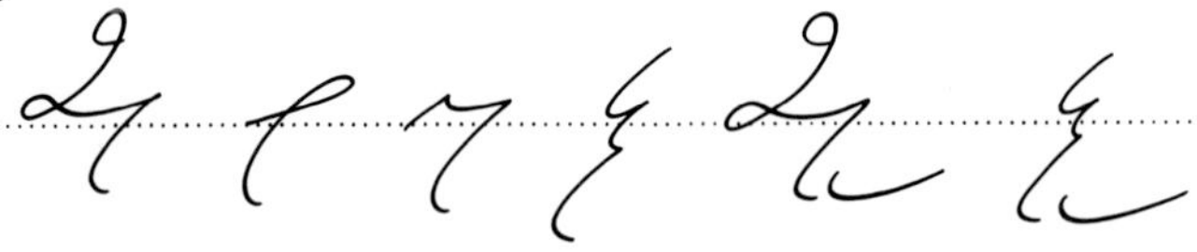

Key to the Shorthand

Express, extend, extra, expect, excellent, exceedingly.
Access, assist, census, suspend, sister, says.
Port, report, import, export, reporter, importation.
Permit, perfect, perhaps, person, personal, permission.
Purple, purchase, pursue, purse, purchased, pursuit.
Available, table, trouble, possible, availability, possibility.

Be-

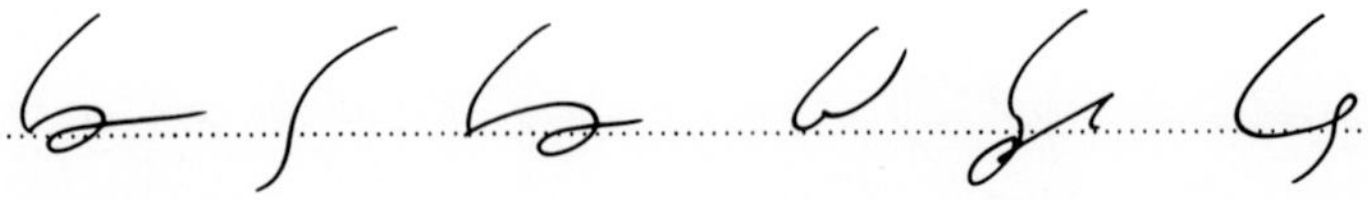

For- Fore- Fur-

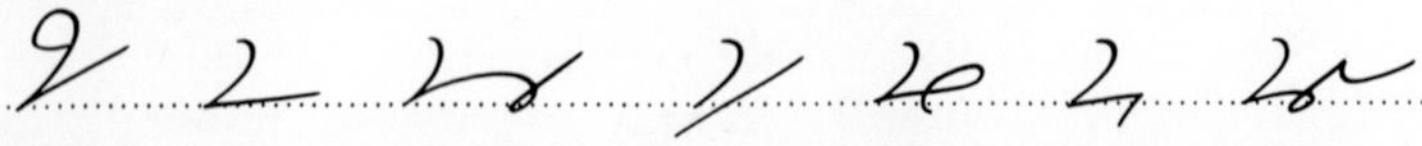

-ful

-ification

-ship

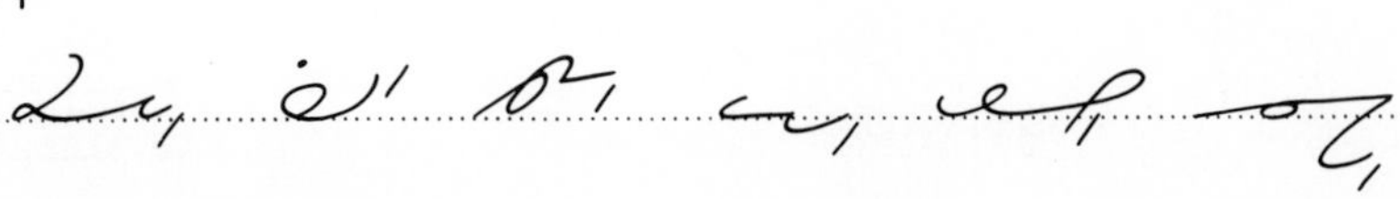

5
Mrs. Anna Green
7112 Cameron Place
Grand Rapids, MI
49511

8 ef•fi•cient

[124]

Attorneys do a great deal of research to support their clients' positions in legal matters. Those attorneys with shorthand skills save valuable time by writing their research notes in shorthand.

-tion

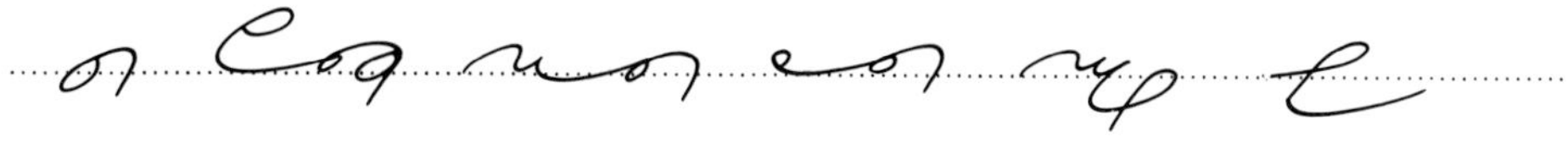

Key to the Shorthand

Became, before, began, beyond, besides, belief.
Afford, form, forget, foreword, furnace, furnish, furniture.
Useful, careful, grateful, faithful, hopeful, delightful.
Classification, modification, notification, justification, qualification, specifications.
Fellowship, hardship, township, ownership, relationship, membership.
Action, application, collection, election, cooperation, national.

Brief Forms

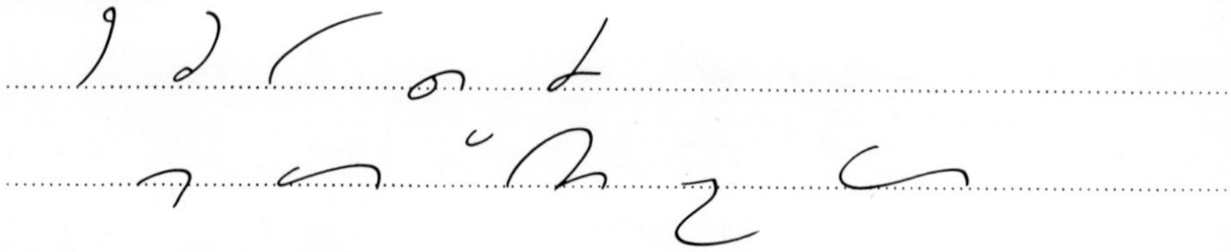

Brief-Form Derivatives

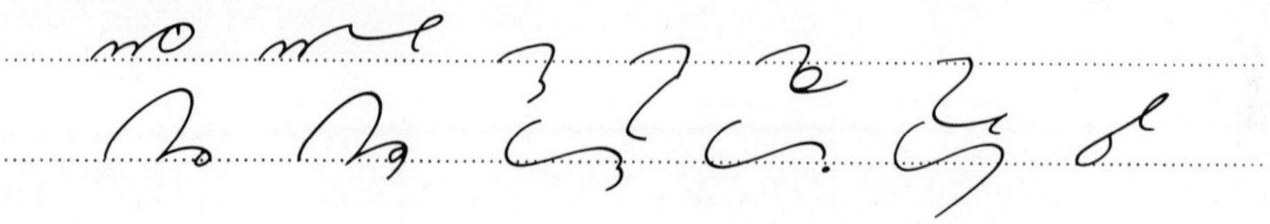

Phrases

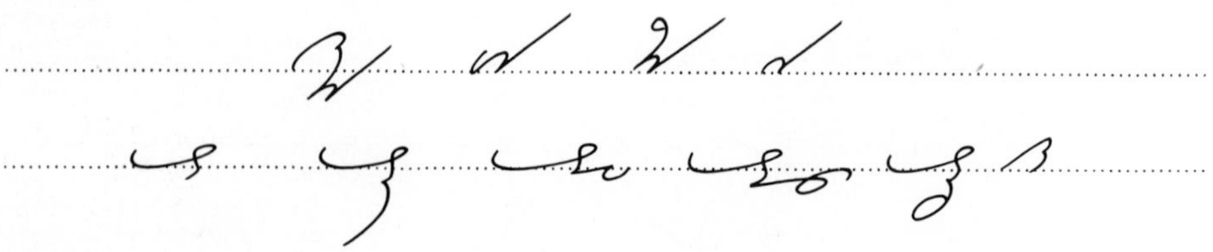

Key to the Shorthand

Ever-every, very, time, acknowledge, general.
question, organize, over, difficult, envelope, progress.
Worthwhile, worthless, questions, questionable, questionnaire, envelopes.
Difficulty, difficulties, progresses, progressing, progressive, ideas.
Thank you for your order, of your order, if your order, your order.
Let us, let us have, let us know, let us make, let us say, to us.

3
Miss Stacy Mills
Apartment C
781 Third Avenue
Lake Worth, FL 33411

4
Mr. Jerry Nelson
81 River Road
Bellows Falls, VT
05101

2 state•ment
3 sum
4 Transcribe:
$11.55
5 oc•curred
6 re•al
7 any way

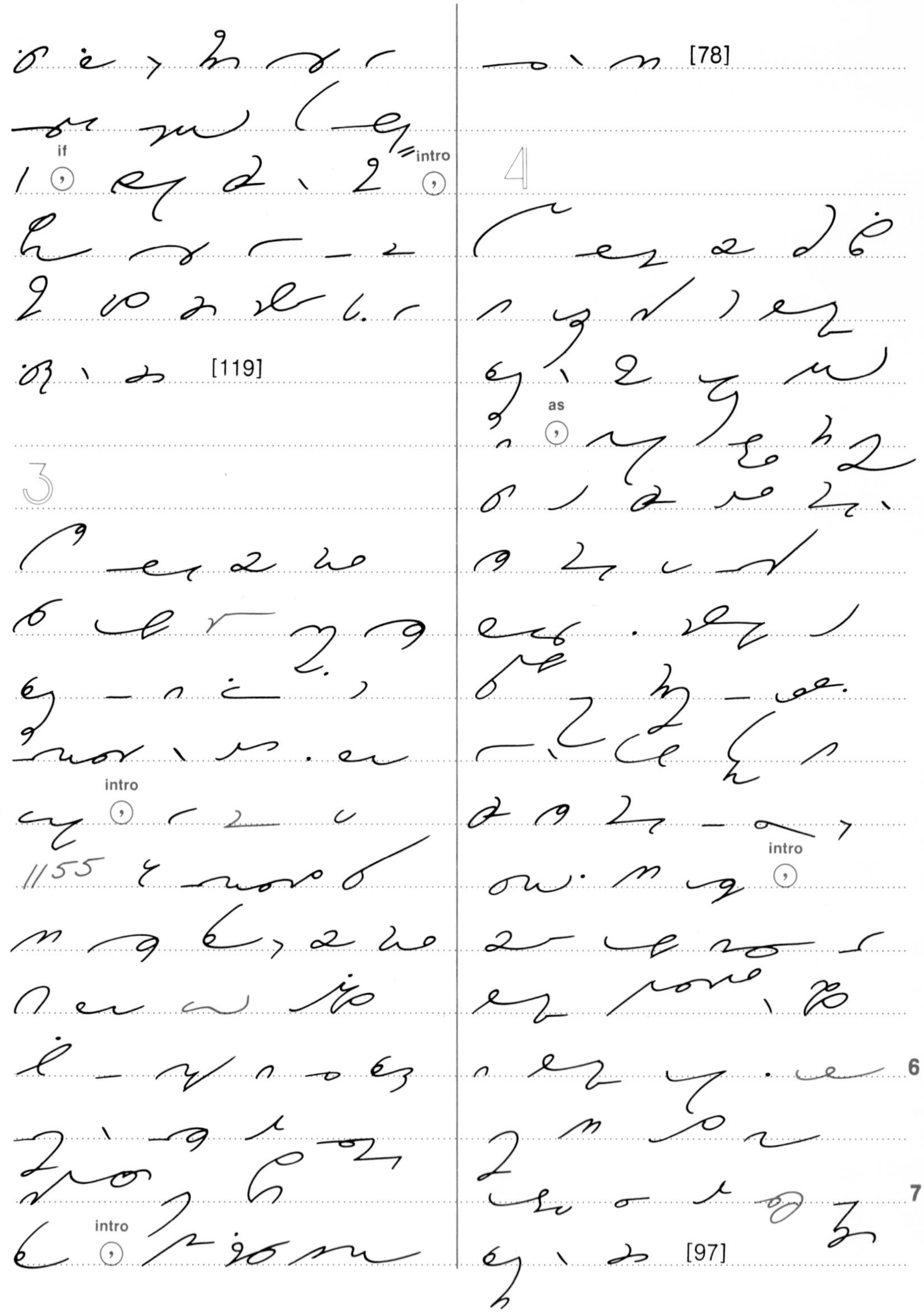

Reading and Writing Practice

1 Transcribe: $18,000
2 ex·ceeds
3 hear
4 passed
5 CPS
6 Transcribe: 1,200
7 sec·re·tar·ies

1

2

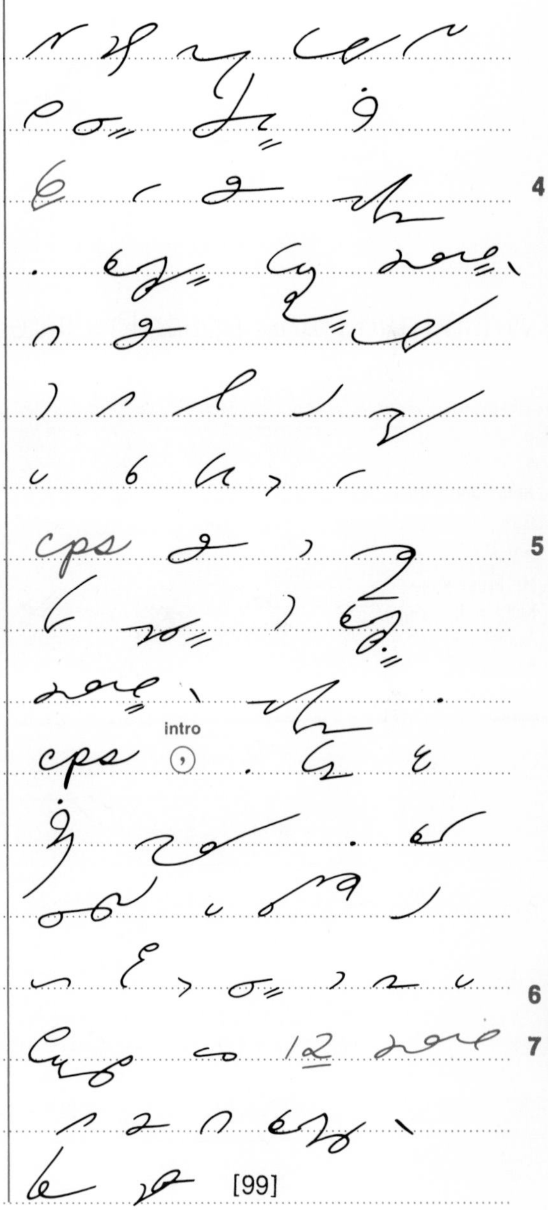

58

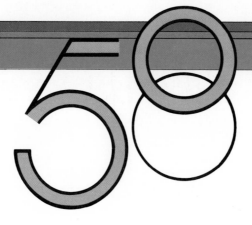

Writing and Transcription Practice

1
Note From Visitor

2
Mr. Frank Kelly
Kelly, Andre, and Associates
P.O. Box 781
Kansas City, MO 64111

1 in·stal·la·tion

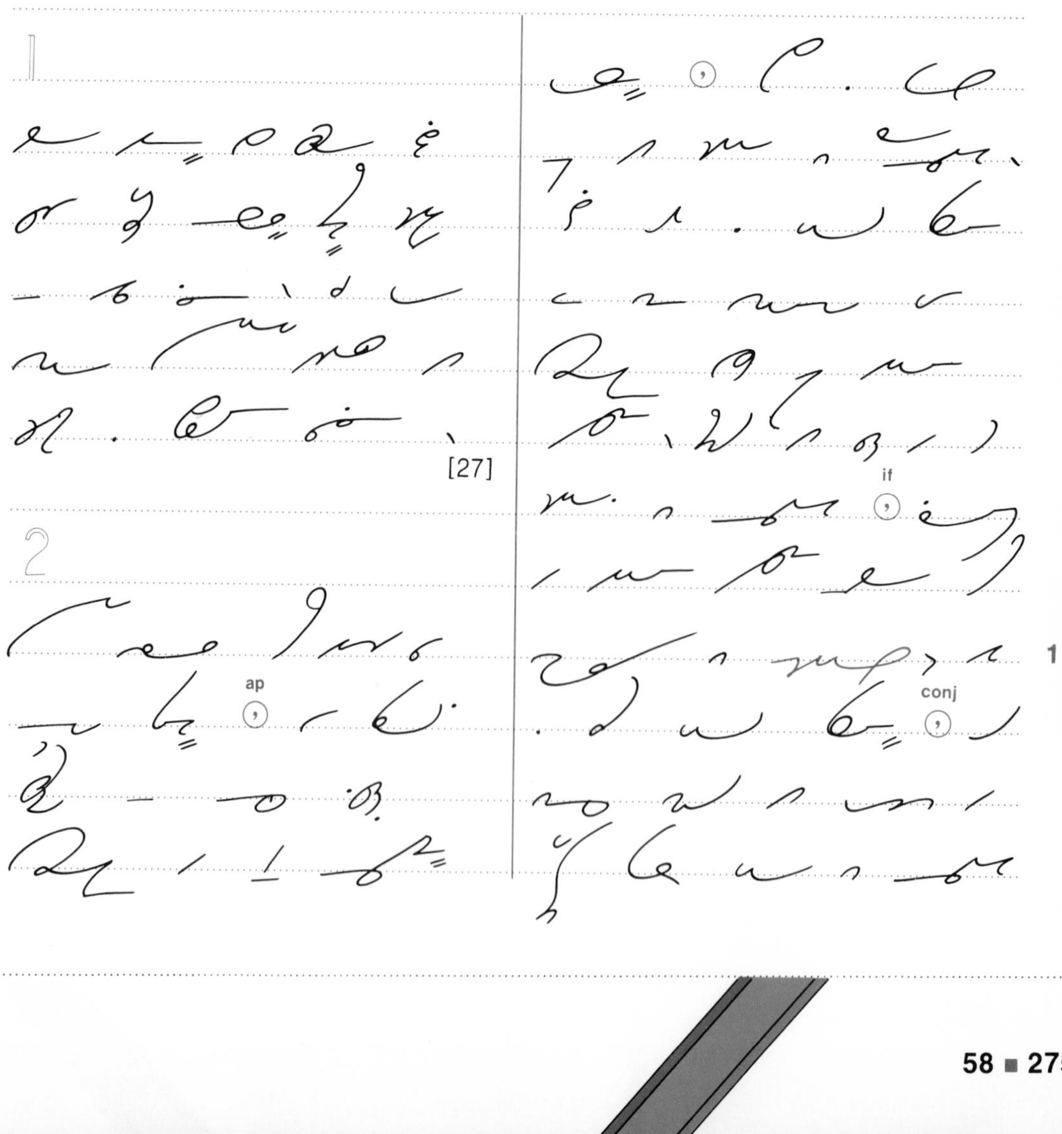

8 ef·fi·cient
9 news·let·ter
10 re·ceiv·ing

3

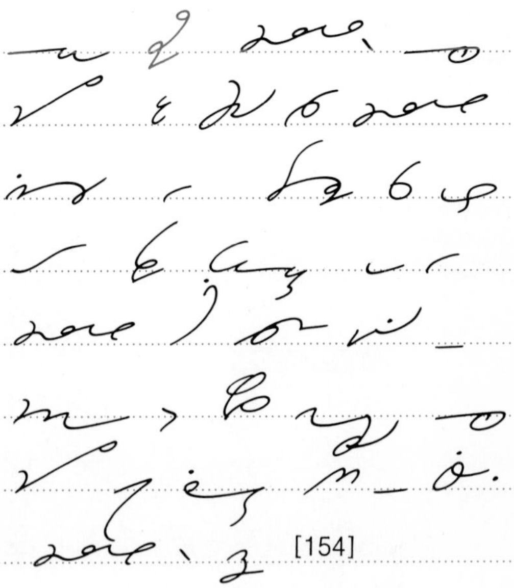

4

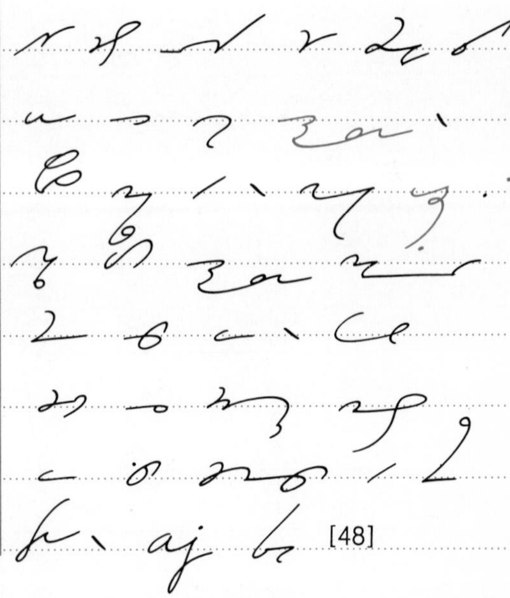

5
Mr. David M. Manski
716 Lancaster Avenue
Dallas, TX 75211

6
Mr. Robert Barns
343 Miller Street
Marietta, GA 30011

6 achieve
7 sched•ule
8 re•viewed

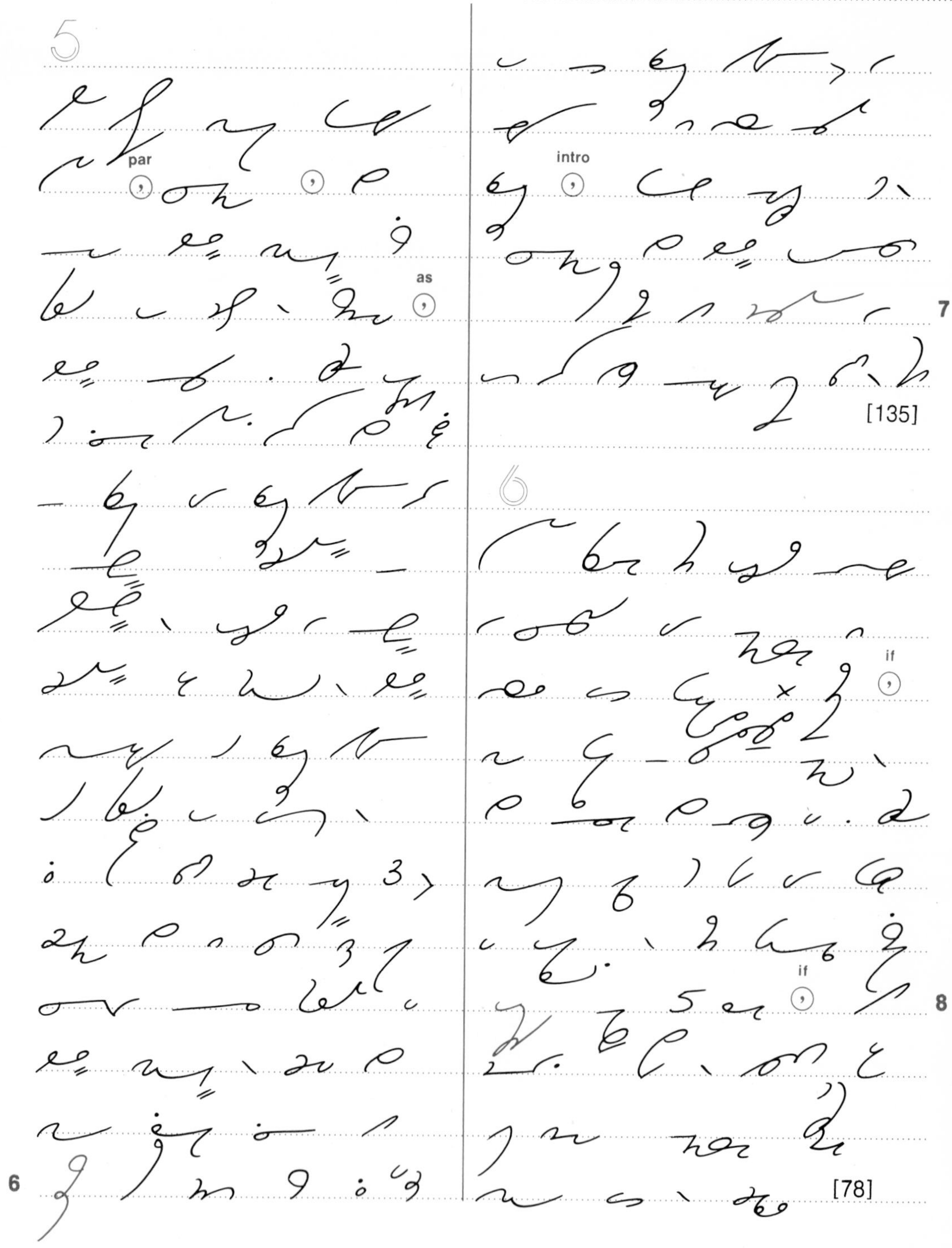

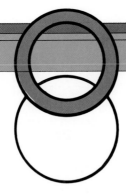

This lesson continues your review of Gregg Shorthand theory.

-tial

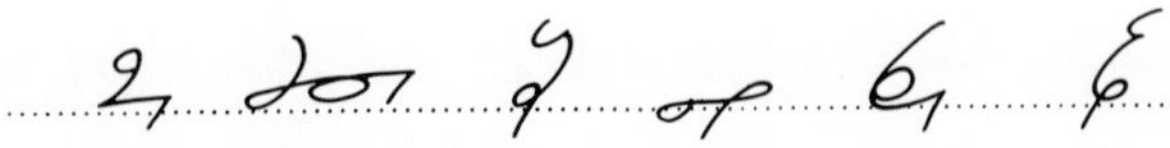

-tient

-ciency

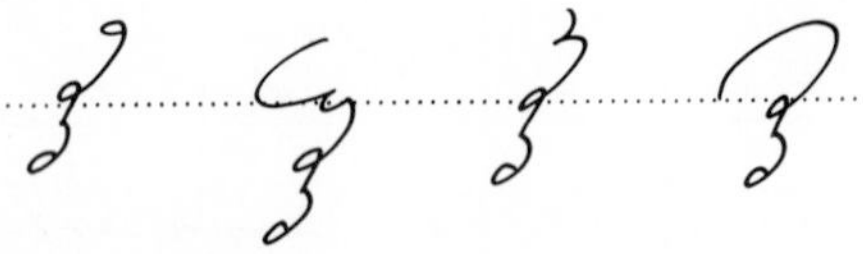

Al-

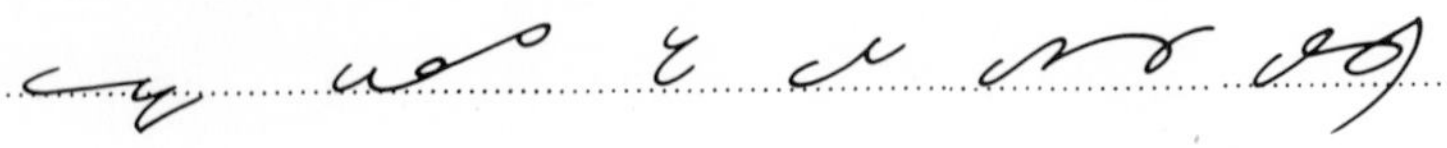

-mission, Etc.

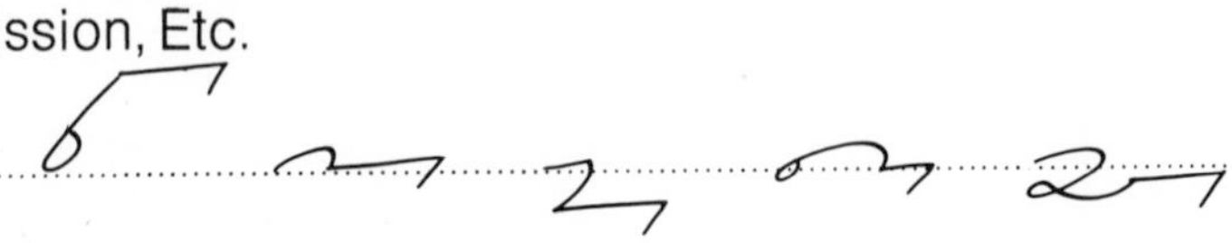

3
Mr. Robert Ames
Director of Marketing
Anderson Electric Company
716 Fillmore Street
Raleigh, NC 27611

4
Customer Service Department
Public Service Corporation
75 Snyder Road
Johnson City, TN 37601

3 ap·pli·ances
4 be·half
5 there

-tition, Etc.

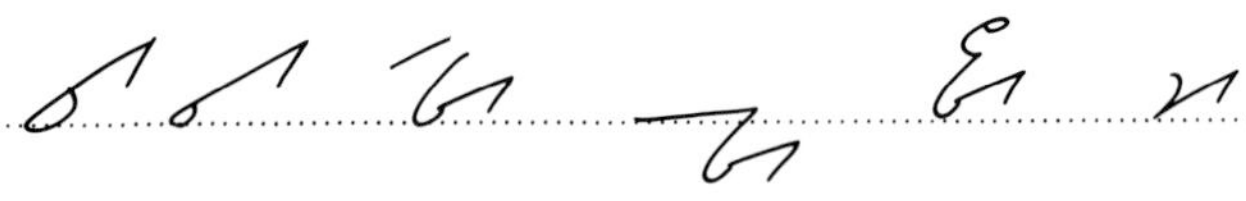

Key to the Shorthand

Essential, financial, official, initial, partial, special.
Efficient, proficient, patient, sufficient, impatient, ancient.
Efficiency, proficiency, sufficiency, deficiency.
Almost, already, also, although, altogether, alternative.
Admission, commission, information, ignition, confirmation.
Addition, edition, transportation, importation, exportation, station.

-ther

Omission of Minor Vowels

-tern, -dern, Etc.

Den, Ten

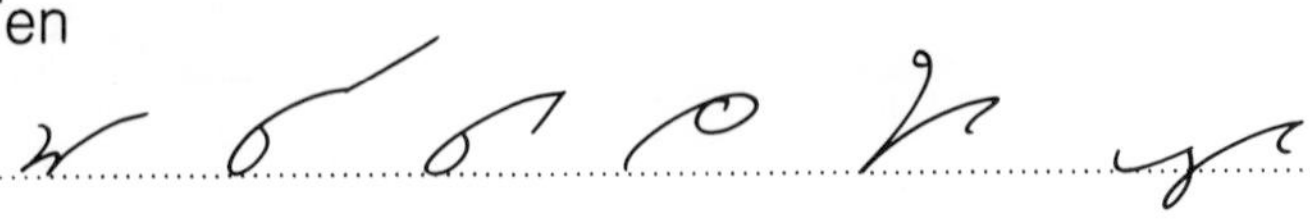

57

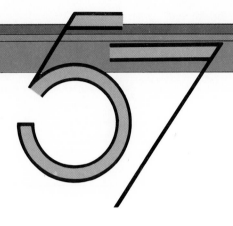

Writing and Transcription Practice

1
Notes From Staff Meeting

2
Mr. Warren Green
Western Electric Cooperative
5920 Tyler Street
Boise, ID 83725

1 fear
2 wheth·er

Key to the Shorthand

Bother, farther, rather, leather, father, neither.
Auditorium, companion, courteous, genuine, ideal.
Graduate, million, previous, radius, serious.
Situate, theory, union, various, graduates.
Return, eastern, southern, pattern, modern, terminal.
Sudden, attend, attention, deny, evidence, residence.

Brief Forms

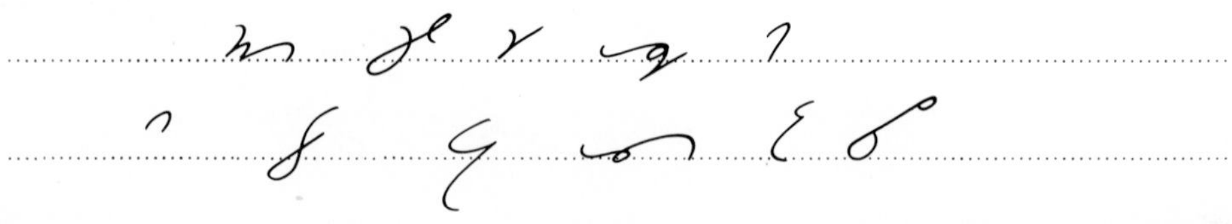

Brief-Form Derivatives

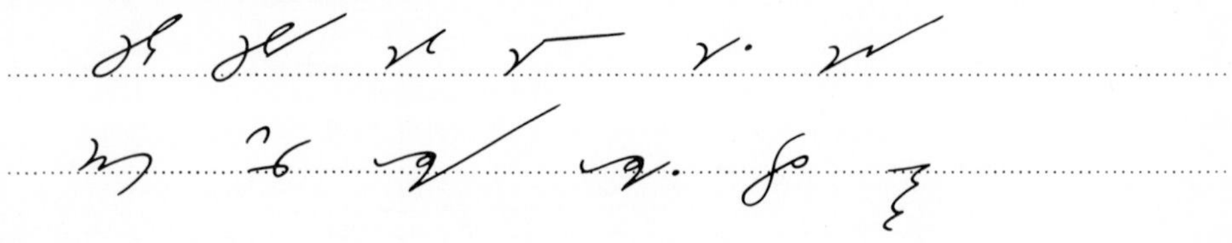

Phrases

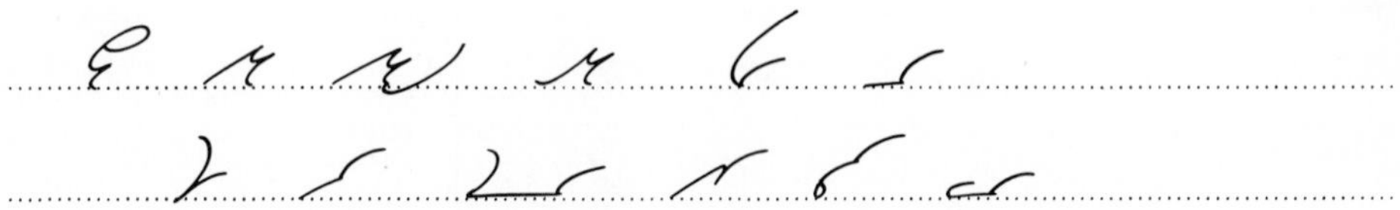

Key to the Shorthand

Success, satisfy-satisfactory, state, request, wish.
Under, particular, probable, regular, speak, idea.
Satisfaction, satisfied, states, statement, stating, stated.
Successful, underneath, requested, requesting, particularly, newspapers.
I was, it was, it wasn't, there was, by the, in the.
For the, at the, from the, to the, with the, on the.

5
Argyle Shoes
320 State Street
Fairbanks, AK 99701

9 shop·ping
10 pair
11 can·celed

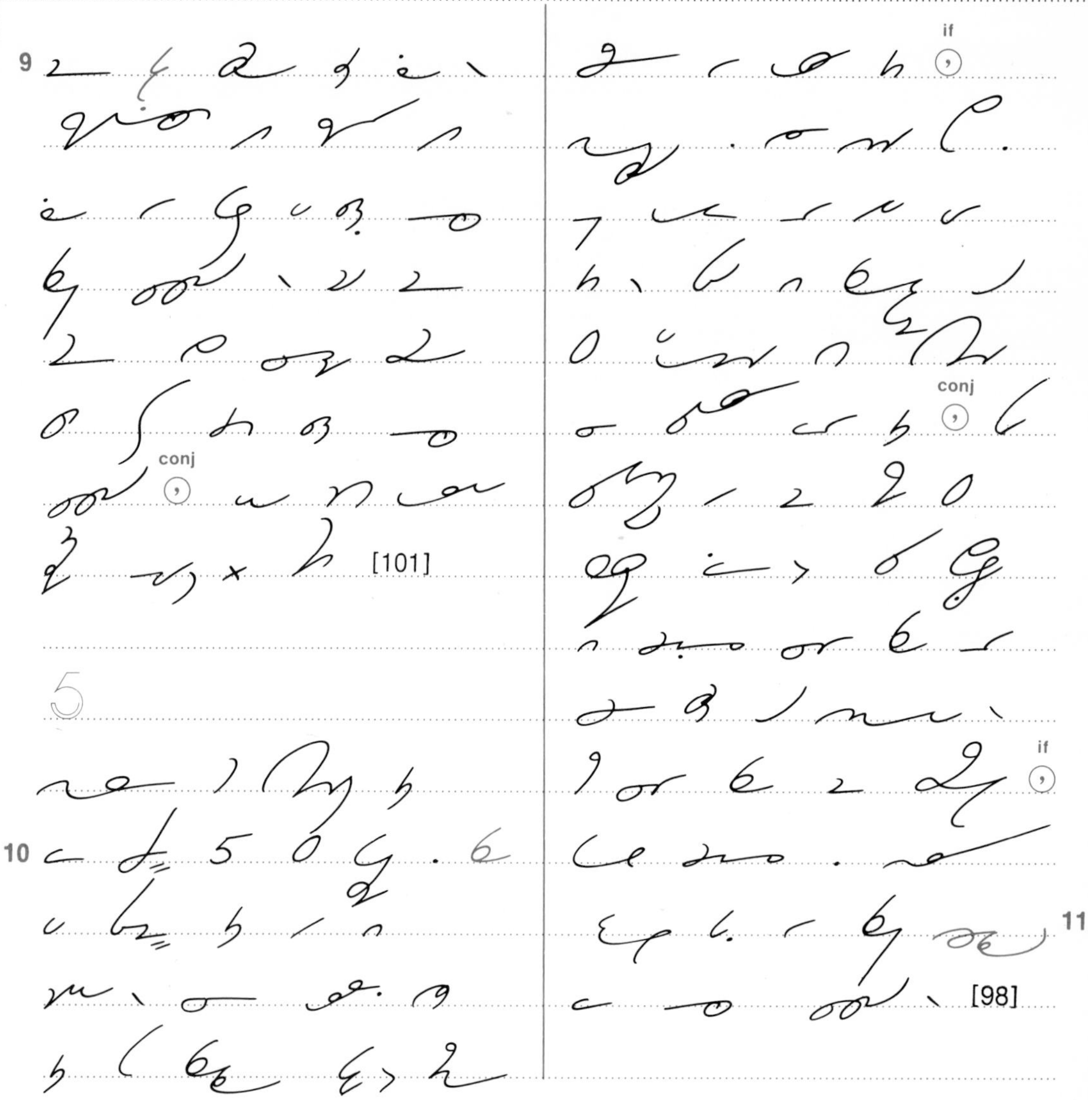

What Do Employers Want:

A recent survey showed that most employers are looking for a secretary with:

1 Ambition.
2 The ability to communicate.
3 A good personality.
4 Neat appearance.
5 Good skills.

Reading and Writing Practice

1 lo·cal
2 east·ern
3 back·yard
4 Transcribe:
8 p.m.

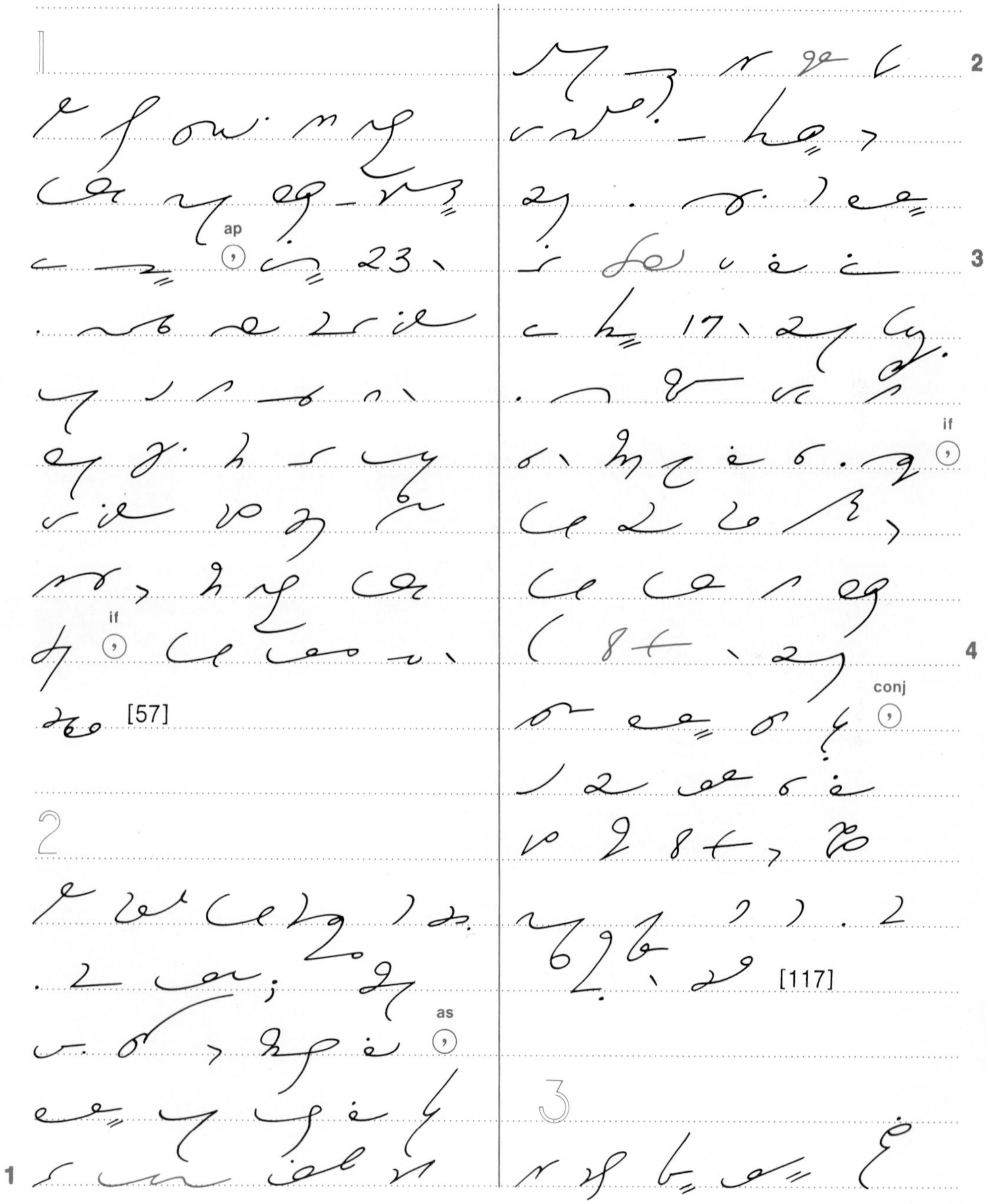

3
Ms. Ann Smth
ARCO Laboratories
1742 Platt Avenue
Charleston, WV 25300

4
Hart Clothiers, Ltd.
16 Healey Plaza
Concord, NH 03301

4 wheth·er
5 great
6 Transcribe:
124
7 al·ready
8 eas·i·er

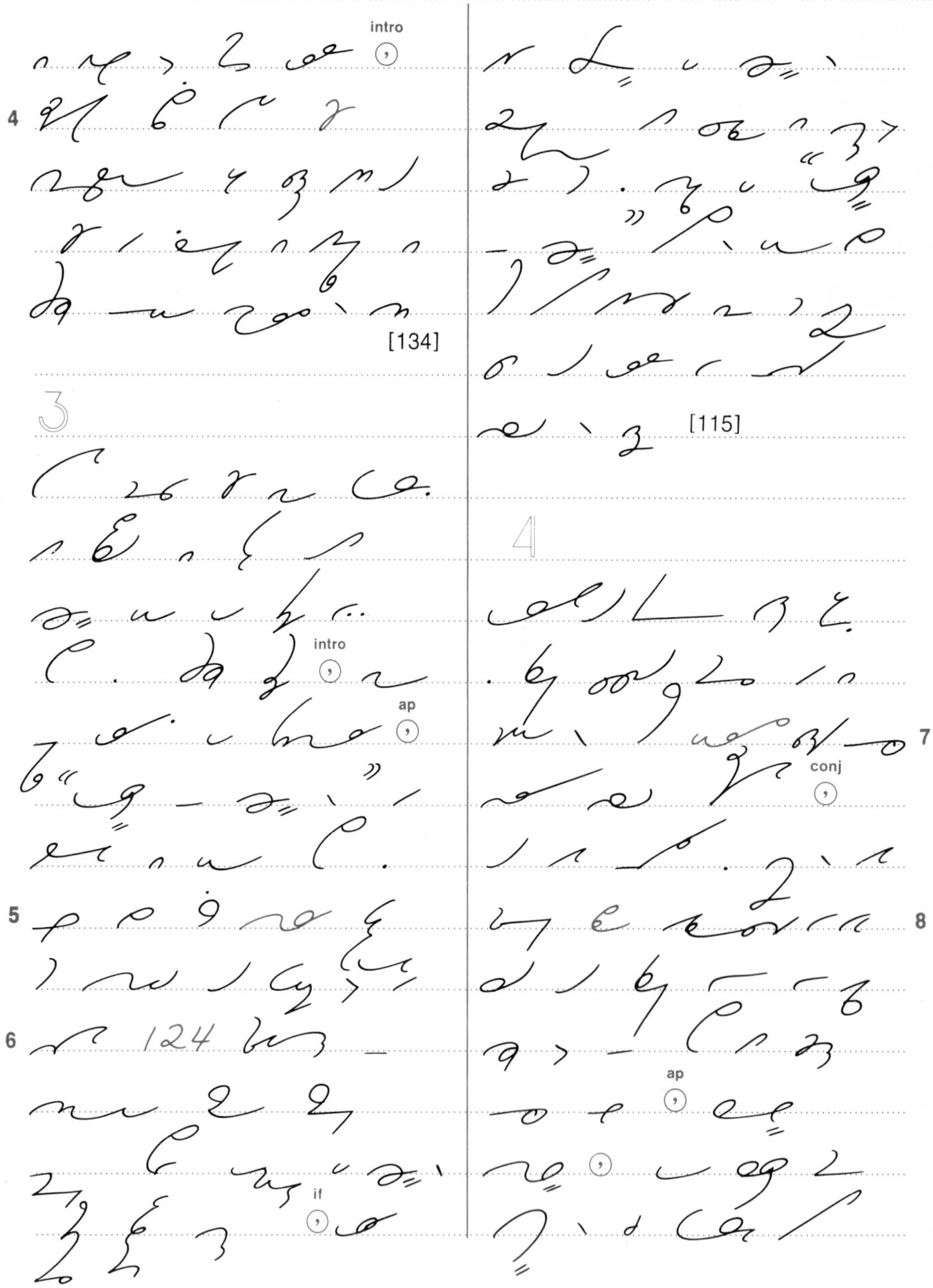

5 ad·mit·ted
6 Room 803
7 Transcribe: three
8 two
9 ap·ply·ing
10 write
11 Transcribe: 7:30 p.m.

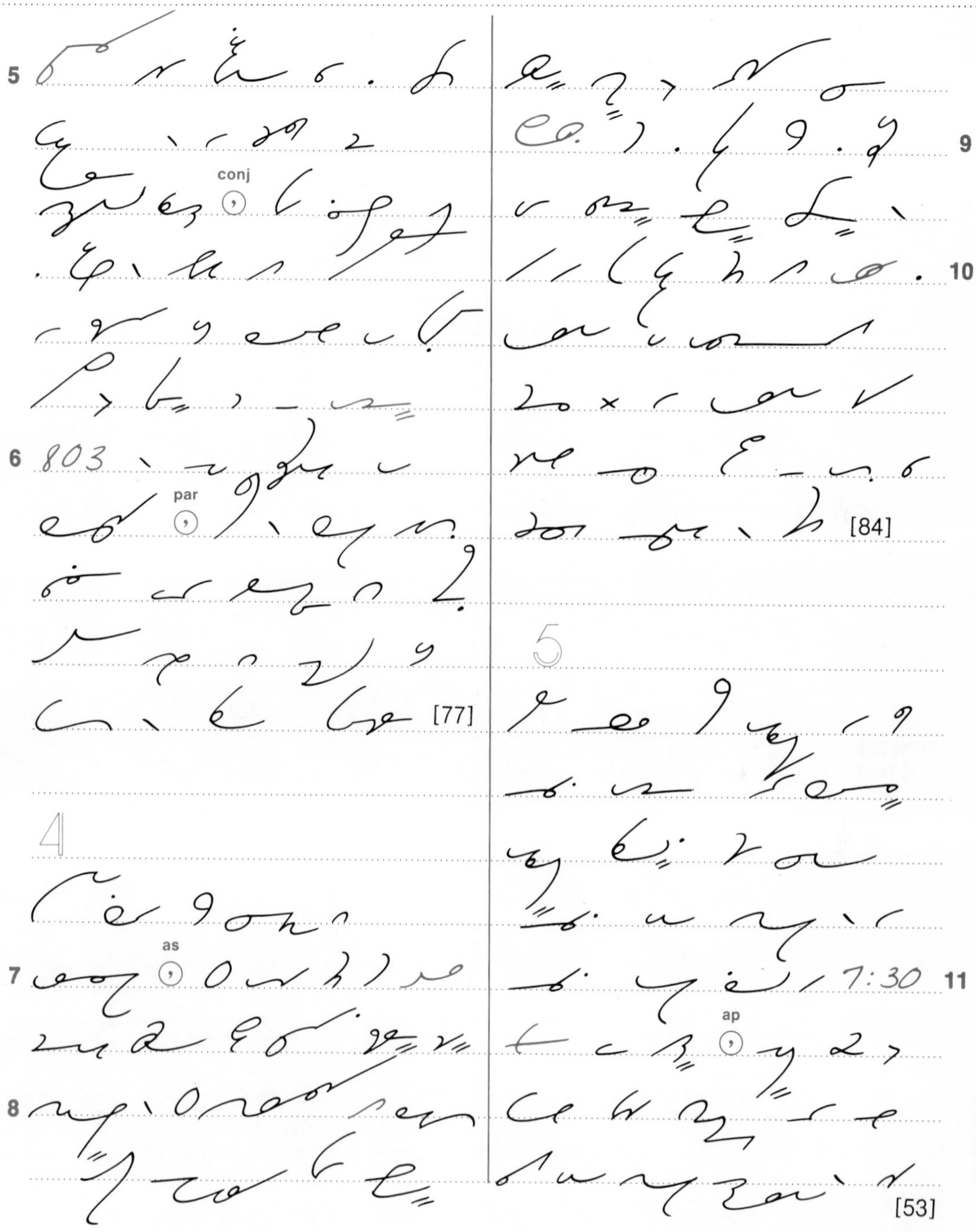

56

Writing and Transcription Practice

1
Reminder For Fred

2
Mrs. Nancy Talbot
1611 East Third Avenue
Pueblo, CO 81011

1 as·sure
2 pleas·ant
3 wher·ev·er

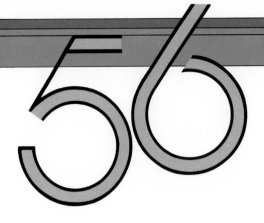

9

This lesson continues your review of Gregg Shorthand theory.

Dem, Tem

-tain

Nd Nt

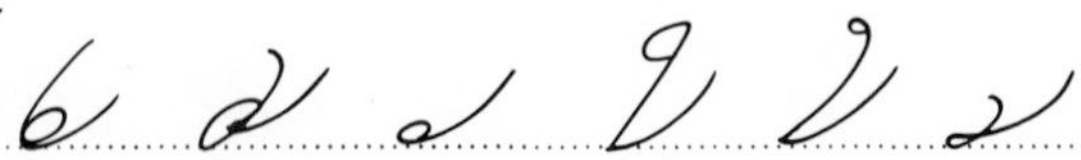

Md Mt

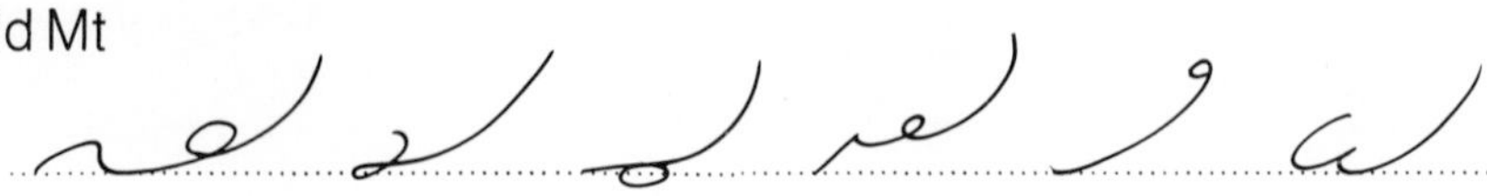

Dif Def, Etc.

5

Mr. Edmond Jones
1411 Starr Avenue
Bennington, VT 03201

4 oc·curs
5 of·fer·ing

5

4

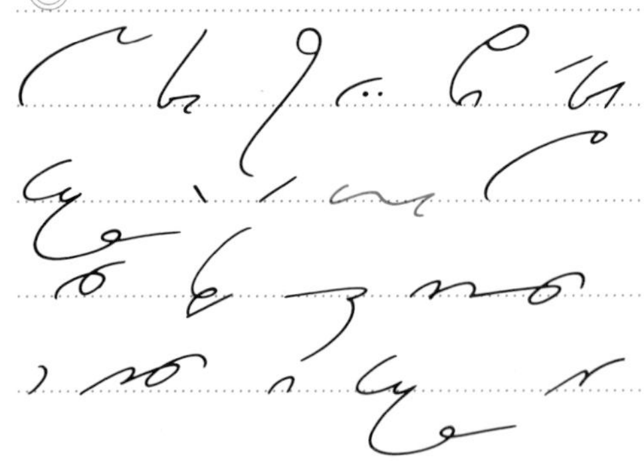

5

-tribute

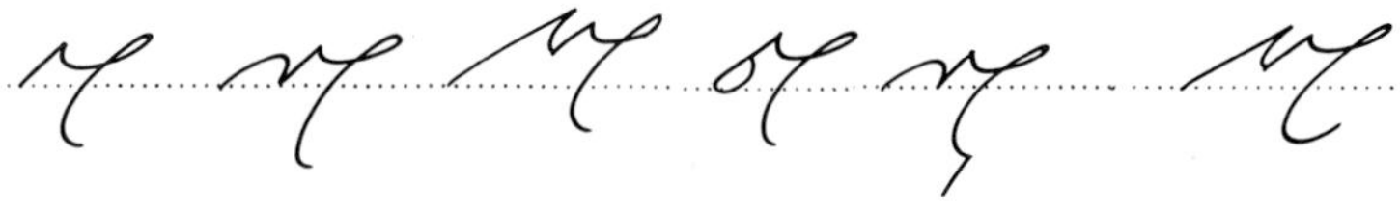

Key to the Shorthand

Freedom, demand, item, attempt, system, temporary.
Certain, contain, obtain, maintain, retain, container.
Band, find, end, agent, event, sent.
Claimed, seemed, named, trimmed, empty, prompt.
Different, divided, definite, defer, develop, defense.
Tribute, contribute, distribute, attribute, contribution, distributor.

-quire

-titute -titude

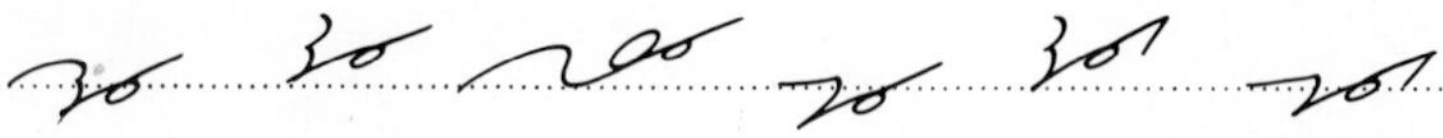

Intersecting Principle

Jog Joining

Compound Words

3
Mr. Glenn Mead
ARCO Manufacturing
63 Seventh Street
Santa Fe, NM 87501

4
Mr. Brian Holtz
4121 Green River Road
Laramie, WY 82070

2 ma•jor
3 freight

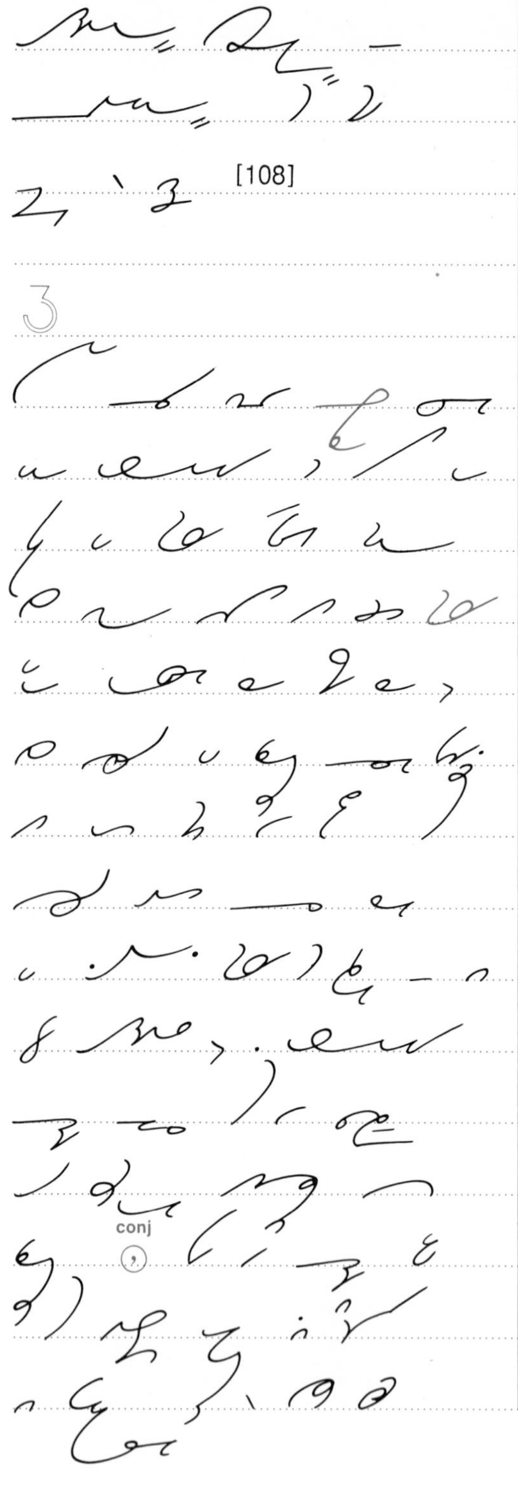

Key to the Shorthand

Inquire, require, acquire, inquiry, required, inquiries.
Constitute, substitute, gratitude, institute, substitution, institution.
Chamber of Commerce, C.O.D., vice versa, a.m., p.m.
Credited, audited, unimportant, unimproved, unimpressive, unintentional.
Anyhow, anywhere, heretofore, however, notwithstanding, inasmuch.
Someone, whatsoever, within, withstand, withstood, worthwhile.

Brief Forms

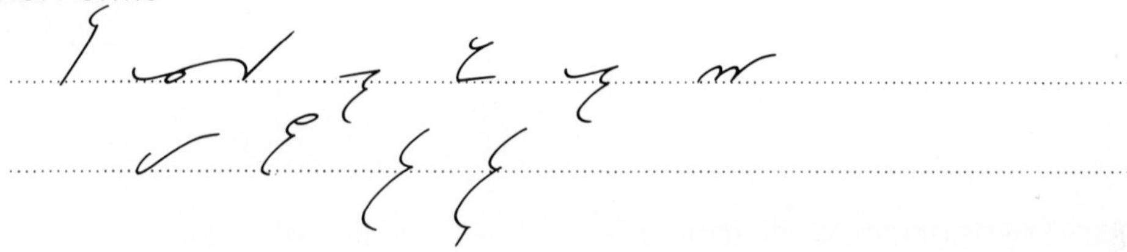

Brief-Form Derivatives

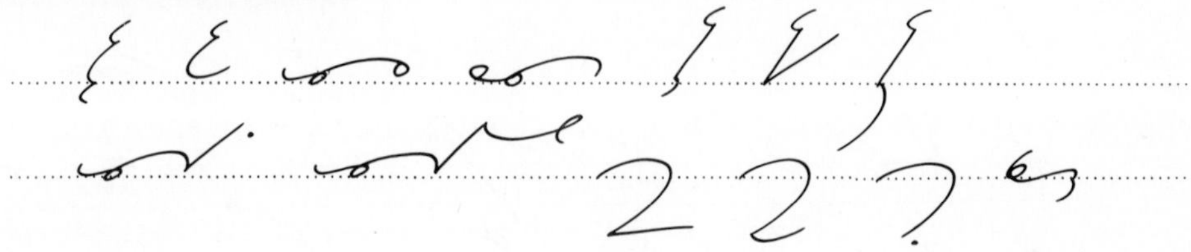

Phrases

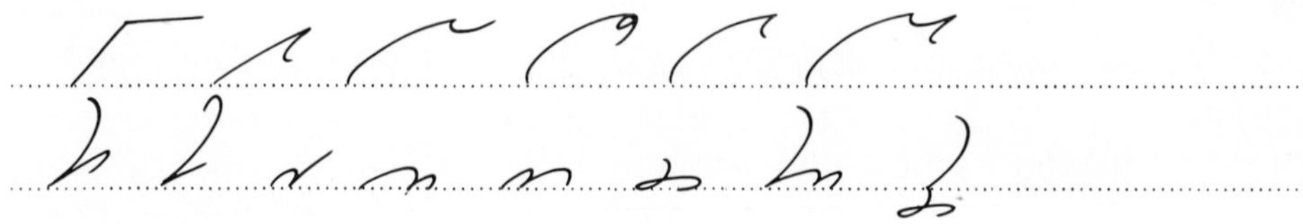

Key to the Shorthand

Subject, regard, newspaper, opinion, responsible, worth.
Ordinary, experience, public, publish-publication.
Speaks, speaker, regularly, irregular, subjects, subjected, subjective.
Regarding, regardless, government, governor, governing, circulars.
Dear Madam, Dear Sir, Dear Mr., Dear Miss, Dear Ms., Dear Mrs.
Very truly yours, Yours very truly, Yours truly, Cordially yours, Yours cordially, Sincerely yours, Very cordially yours, Very sincerely yours.

55

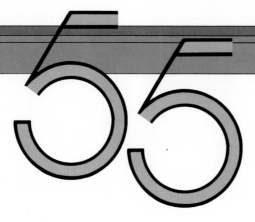

Writing and Transcription Practice

1
Revision To Rough Draft

2
Mrs. Ella Glass
63 Business Plaza
Buffalo, NY 14211

1 sites

Reading and Writing Practice

1 Transcribe:
8 a.m.
2 Cham·ber of
Com·merce
3 Transcribe:
$100

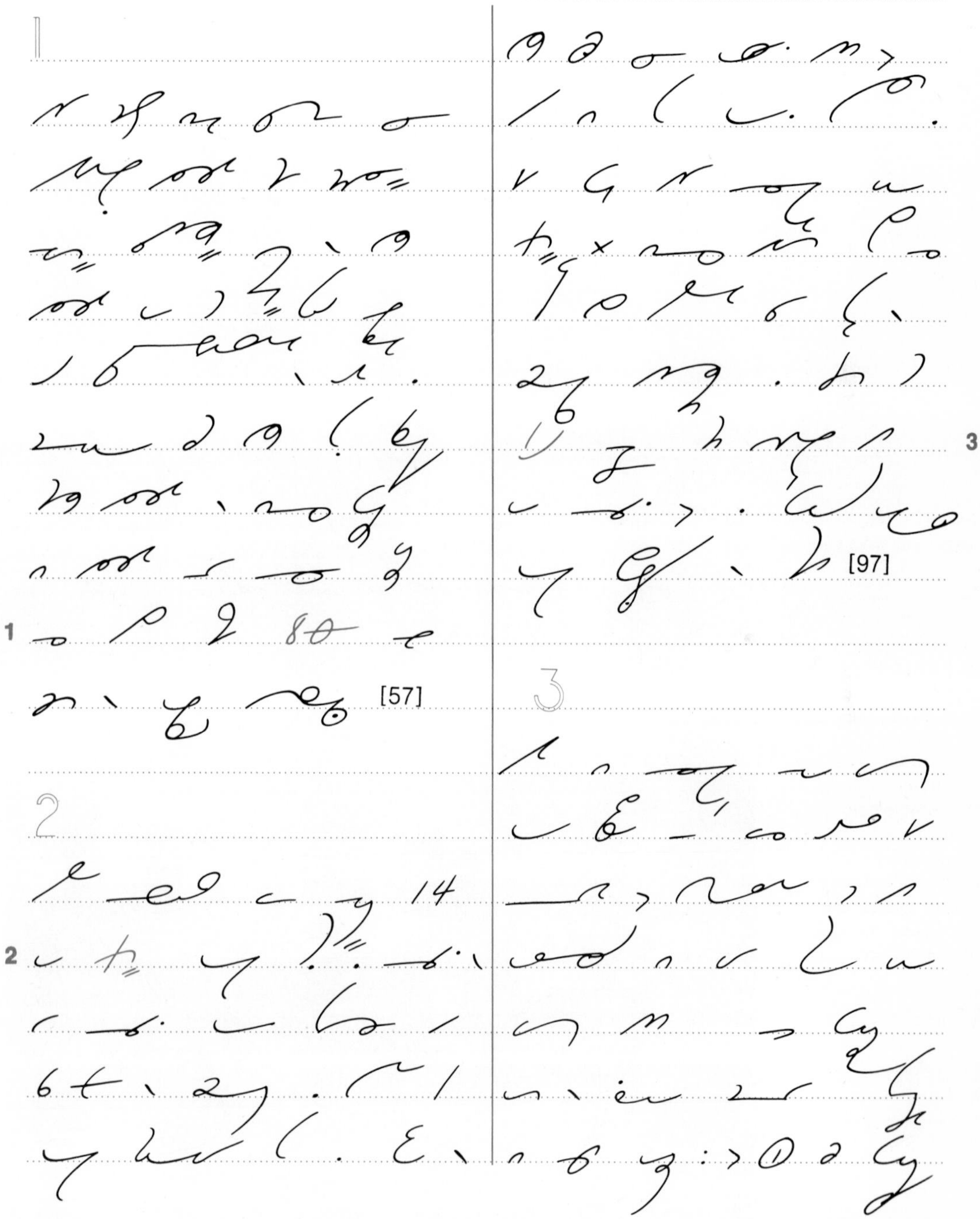

5
Mr. Robert Alan
167 Wilson Street
Portsmouth, OH
45662

8 ex·hib·i·tors
9 re·open·ing
10 wel·come

8

if

[96]

5

24

16

par

9

conj

15

when

intro

10

[110]

Electronic typewriters help to increase transcription efficiency because certain functions—such as centering—are automated.

4 Transcribe: $10,000
5 pol·i·cies
6 cost
7 re·al
8 great
9 re·ceive
10 for·ward

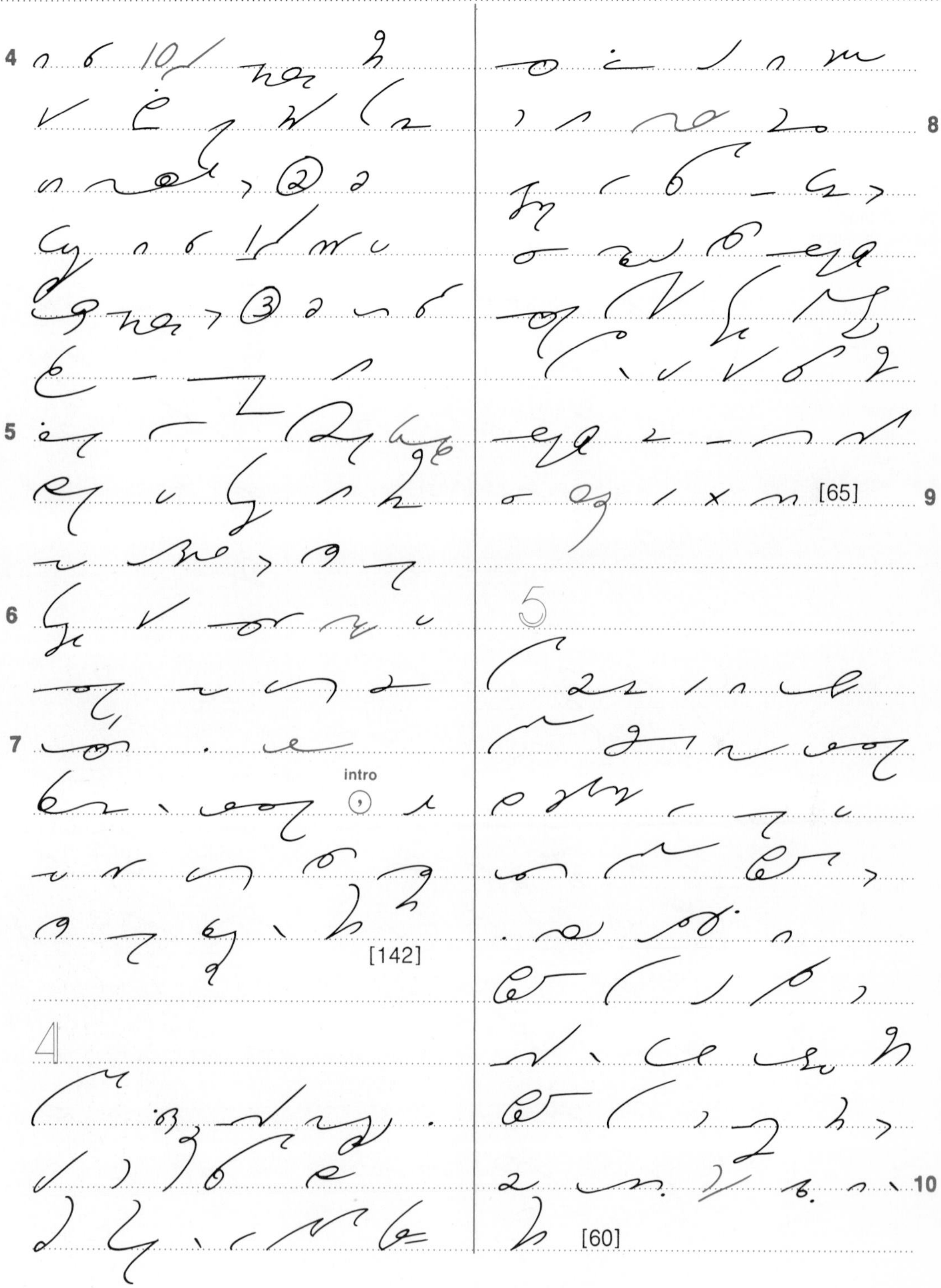

3
Ms. Marcia Stern
Rural Route 2, Box 781
Shreveport, LA 71100

4
Mr. Charles Banks
783 Oak Drive
Sidney, NE 69162

3 op·por·tu·ni·ties
4 al·ready
5 as·signed
6 ex·hib·it
7 re·ferred

3

4
5
6
7

10

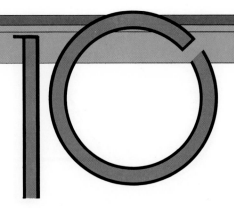

This lesson continues your review of Gregg Shorthand theory.

Omission of Minor Vowels — -ify

Omission of Minor Vowels — -sive, -tive

Omission of Minor Vowels — -age

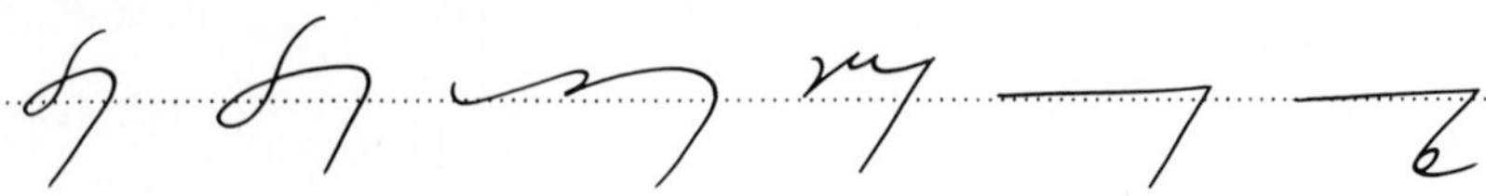

Abbreviated Words

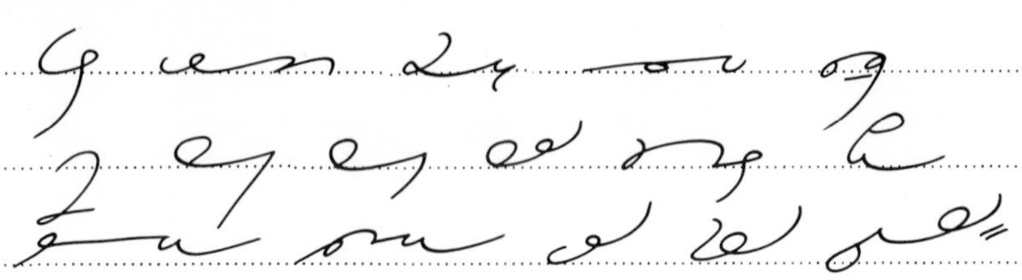

54

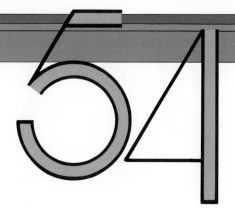

Writing and Transcription Practice

1
Outline For Letter

2
Ms. Wendy Jones
16 Star Avenue
Orlando, FL 32800

1 per·son·al
2 in·cur

Key to the Shorthand

Notify, modify, verify, specify, notified, ratify.
Active, expensive, excessive, defective, activity, extensive.
Package, baggage, luggage, storage, manage, manager.
Privilege, reluctant-reluctance, philosophy, memorandum, equivalent.
Convenient-convenience, algebra, alphabet, arithmetic, significant-significance, apology, terminology, technology, authentic, frantic, Atlantic.

Abbreviated Words

Common Cities

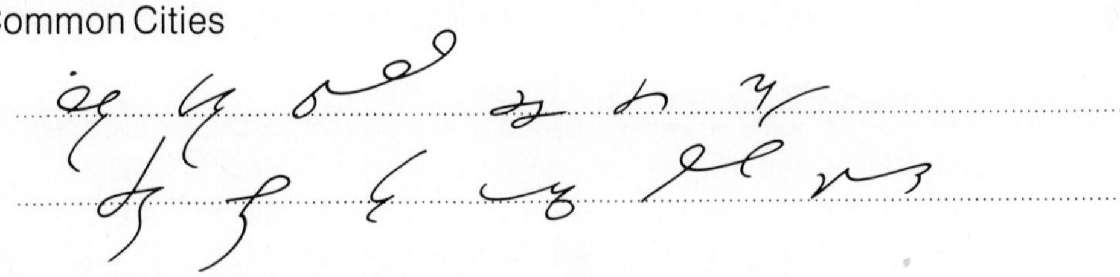

*Common Sound Combinations: Eo Oe

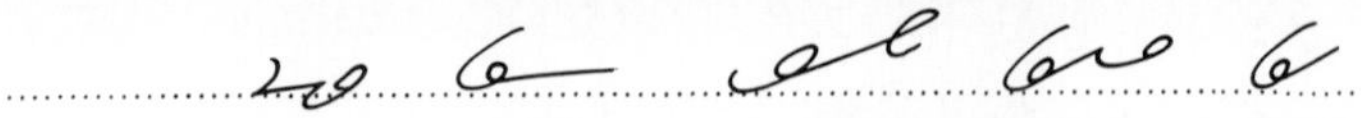

*Common Sound Combinations: Yo Yoo

*Common Sound Combinations: Pre- Pro-

---

*These are not theory principles per se but are combinations of sounds that occur often enough to warrant practice.

5
Mr. Albert Gold
2711 West Cedar Street
Akron, OH 44311

8 ad•vice
9 their

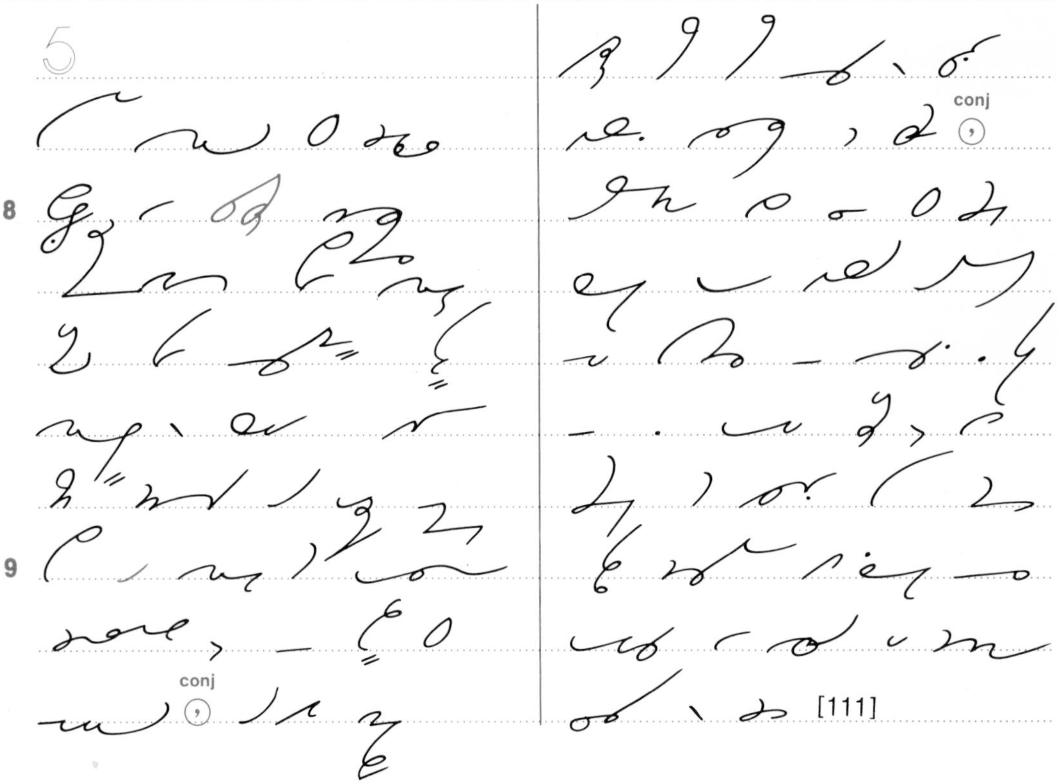

Taking telephone messages can be done quickly by jotting the information down in shorthand.

Key to the Shorthand

Society, variety, propriety, appendicitis, neuritis, arthritis.
Harrisburg, Pittsburgh, Atlanta, Cincinnati, Chicago, Washington.
Janesville, Nashville, Boston, Los Angeles, Dallas, St. Louis.
Snowy, poem, radio, poetry, poet.
Yodel, yawn, yacht, youth, young, yoke.
Prevent, preserve, presume, produce, product, profession.

Brief Forms

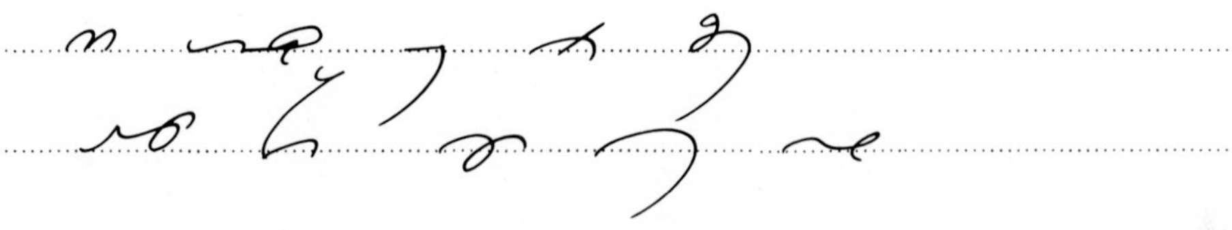

Brief-Form Derivatives

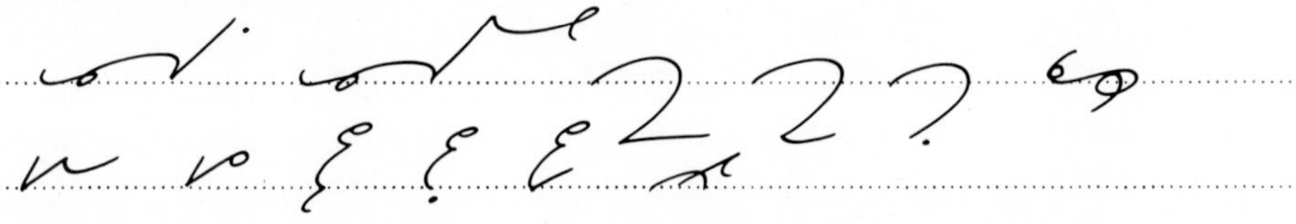

Phrases

Amounts

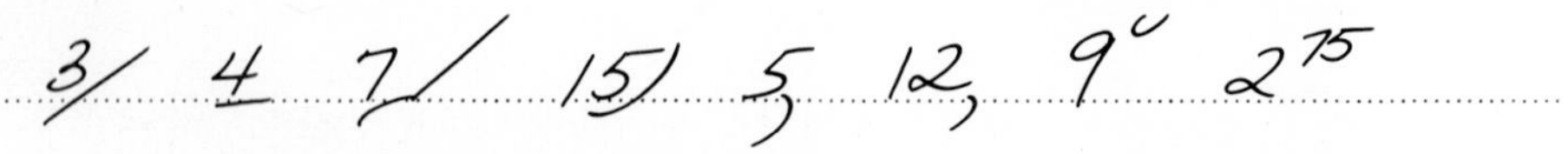

Key to the Shorthand

World, recognize, never, quantity, executive.
Throughout, object, character, govern, correspond-correspondence.
Regarding, regardless, government, governor, governing, circularize.
Shorter, shortly, experiences, experiencing, experienced, quantities.
To me, to make, to know, to do, more than, let me.
$3; 400; $7,000; $1,500; 5 feet; 12 percent; 9 o'clock; $2.75.

3
Mr. Leland Banks
Banks Legal Services
15 Grand Avenue
Wichita, KS 67200

4
Mr. George Stone
163 Center Street
Monroe, LA 71200

3 Transcribe:
$500
4 ad·vised
5 le·gal
6 ef·fec·tive
7 some·time

3

3

4

5

when

par

6

7

[97]

4

conj

conj

conj

if

intro

conj

[111]

Reading and Writing Practice

1 **Transcribe:** five
2 **Transcribe:** $14.75
3 **ship·ment**
4 **bro·chure**
5 **phi·los·o·phy**
6 **Transcribe:** $200

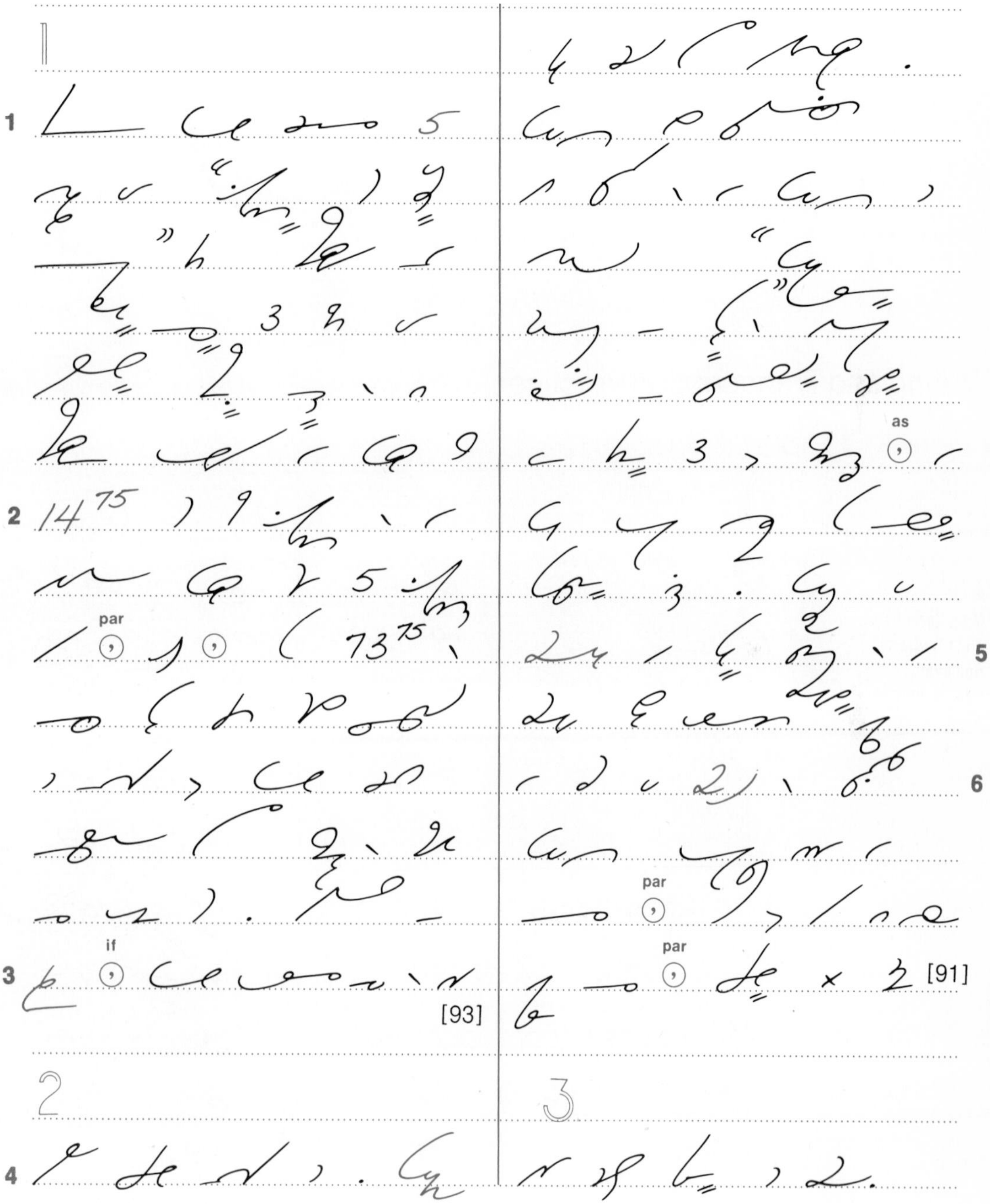

53

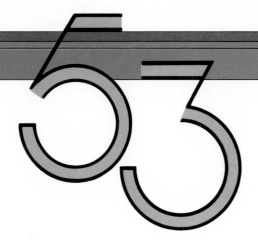

Writing and Transcription Practice

1
Personal To Do List

2
Miss Carla Grace
7841 California
Boulevard
Hilo, HI 96720

1 prin·ci·pal
2 there

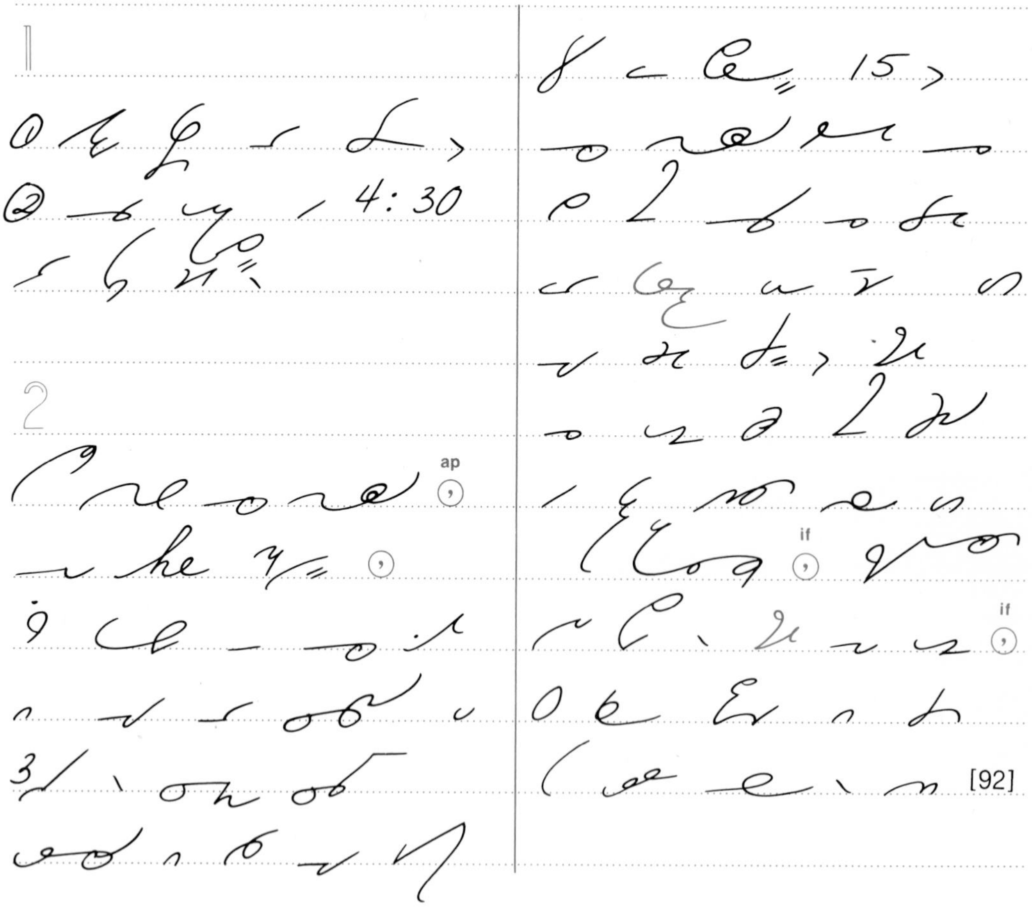

7 sur·gery
8 ap·pen·di·ci·tis
9 ad·di·tion
10 write

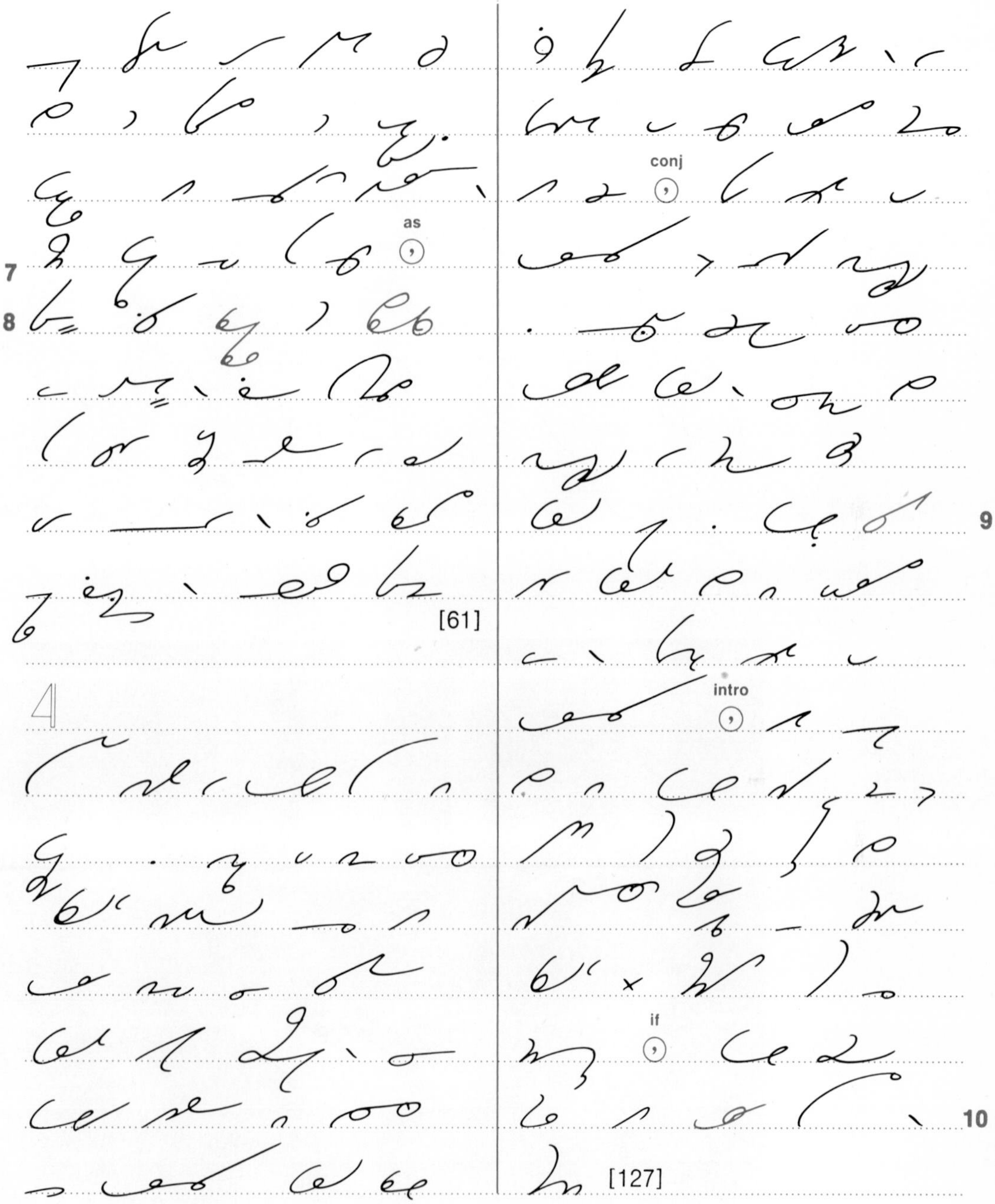

10 X-ray
11 patient's

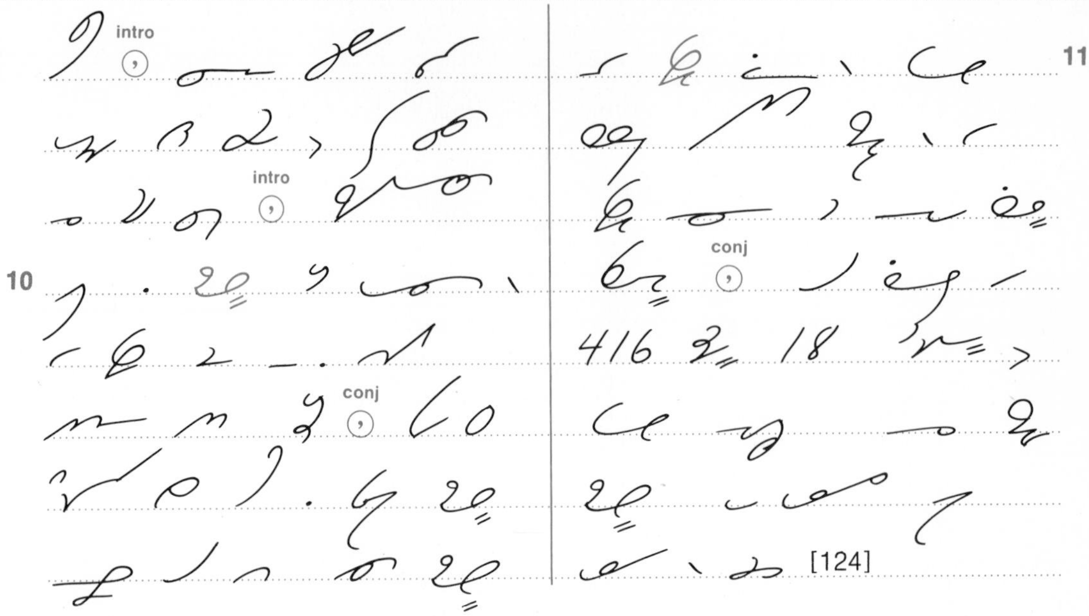

A reporter uses shorthand to obtain a complete and accurate record of the interview.

SECTION 2

4
Mrs. Martha Brown
843 Lexington Parkway
Stamford, CT 06900

5
Mr. Douglas Smith
Ramsey Medical Center
418 Center Avenue
Richmond, VA 23211

6 op·por·tu·ni·ty
7 past
8 pa·tients
9 healed

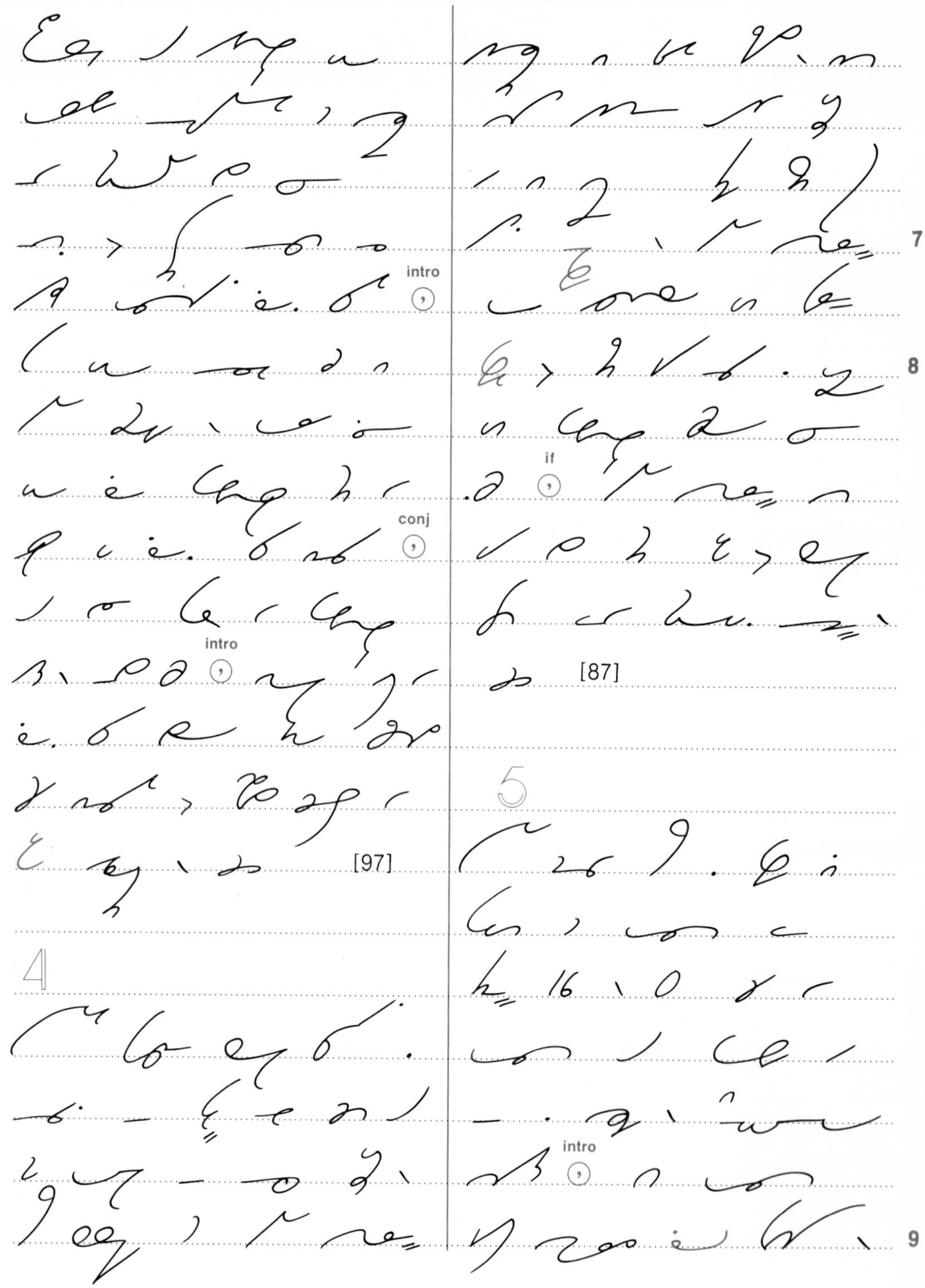

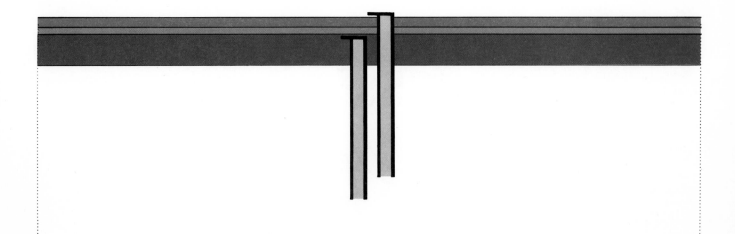

Building Professional Skills

Punctuation Checkup

, parenthetical

Parenthetical expressions are words or phrases that are not needed for the grammatical completeness of a sentence. They are set off by commas. A parenthetical expression occurring at the end of a sentence needs only one comma.

Today is, of course, a holiday.
Tell me, Tom, what time you will arrive.
It is too cold for swimming, as you know.

Communication Checkup

bring ■ take

Because the meanings of the words *bring* and *take* are similar, people sometimes use one of the words when the other word would be correct. Of course, a secretary whose boss makes a grammatical error while dictating corrects that error in the transcript.

bring To carry to the speaker.

Please bring the file to me.

take To carry away from the speaker.

Please take the file to your office.

52

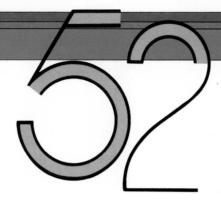

Writing and Transcription Practice

1
Personal To Do List

2
Mr. Ronald Decker
4324 North 42nd Street
Ashland, OR 97520

3
Miss Elsa Turner
Apartment 24
1780 Pine Place
Little Rock, AR 72200

1 cost
2 yours
3 in·qui·ry
4 hear·ing
5 aids

Building Transcription Skill

Transcription Warmup

10
20
32
42

Transcription Speed Building

10
20
31
40
51
60
68
78
82

18 par·tic·u·lar

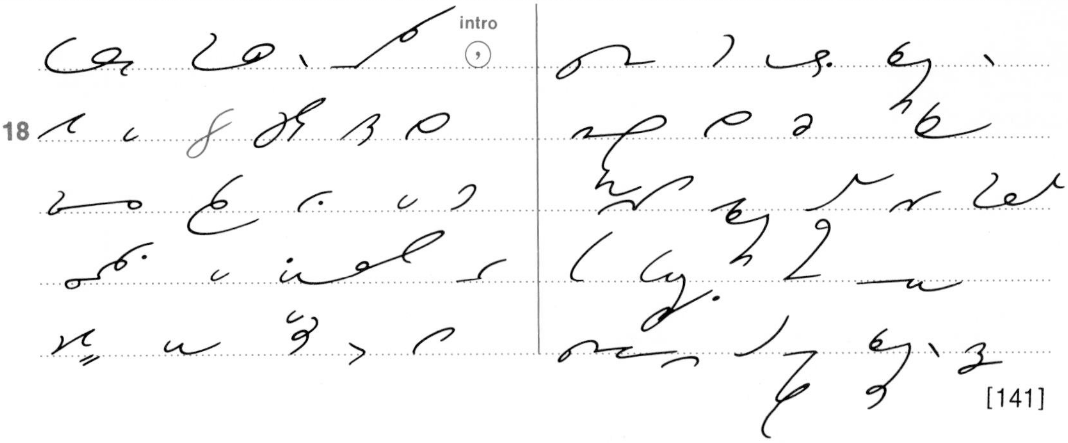

[141]

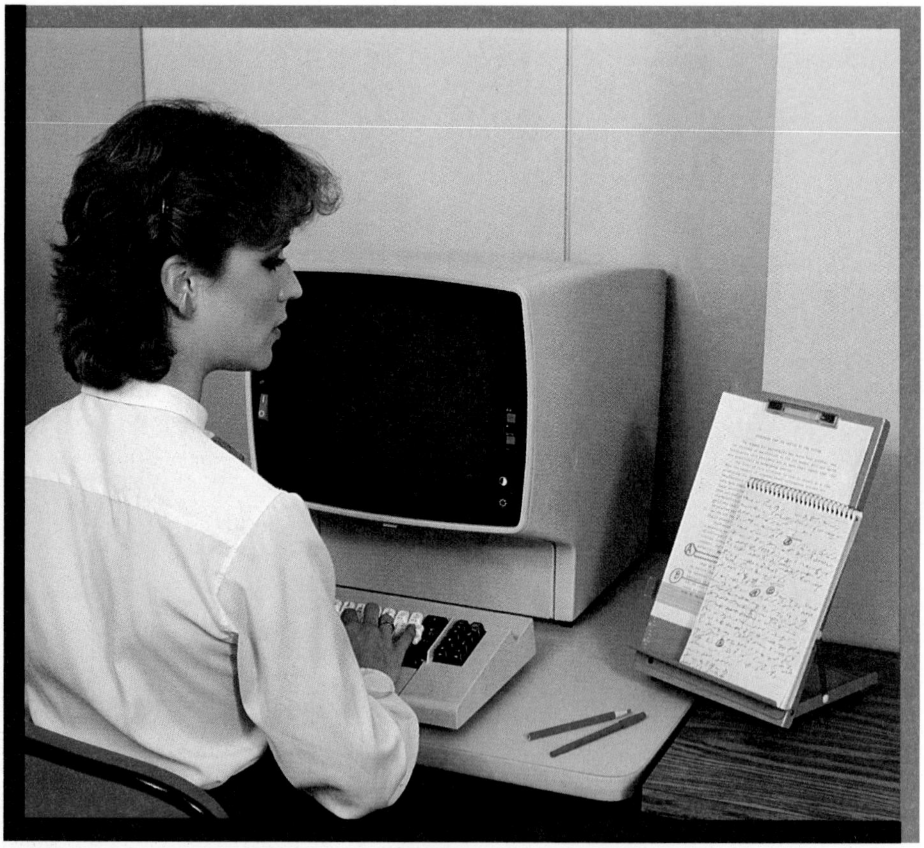

When additions need to be inserted in a typed document, it is possible for the manager to dictate the additions, eliminating the need to write them out in longhand.

Transcription Quiz

Transcribe the following letter, adding the appropriate punctuation to your transcript.

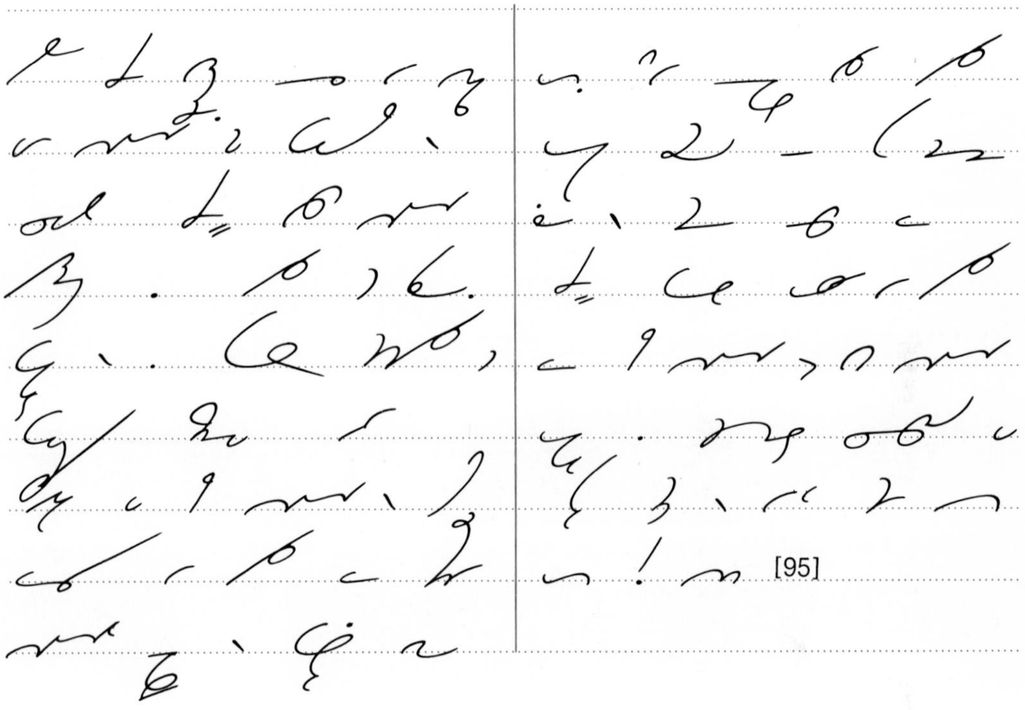

Mailable Letter Production

1
Ms. Sarah Adams
Westport Fashion Shop
815 National Avenue
Westport, NY 12993

1 cop·ies

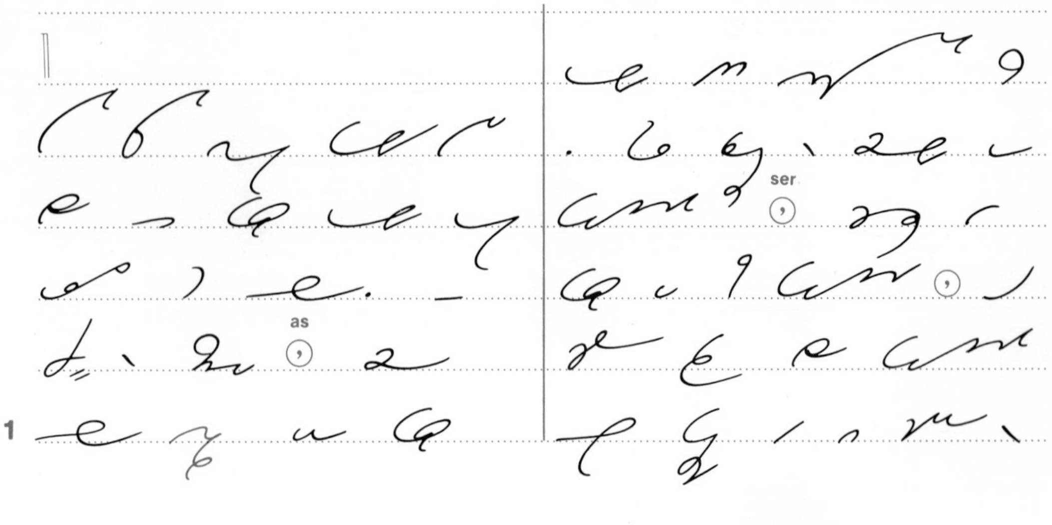

5
Mrs. Raphael Simms
4711 Sunset Boulevard
Natchez, MS 39120

10 un·used
11 ad·just·ment
12 any·one
13 Transcribe: $5
14 hol·i·day
15 ac·cept
16 choos·ing
17 Transcribe: 80

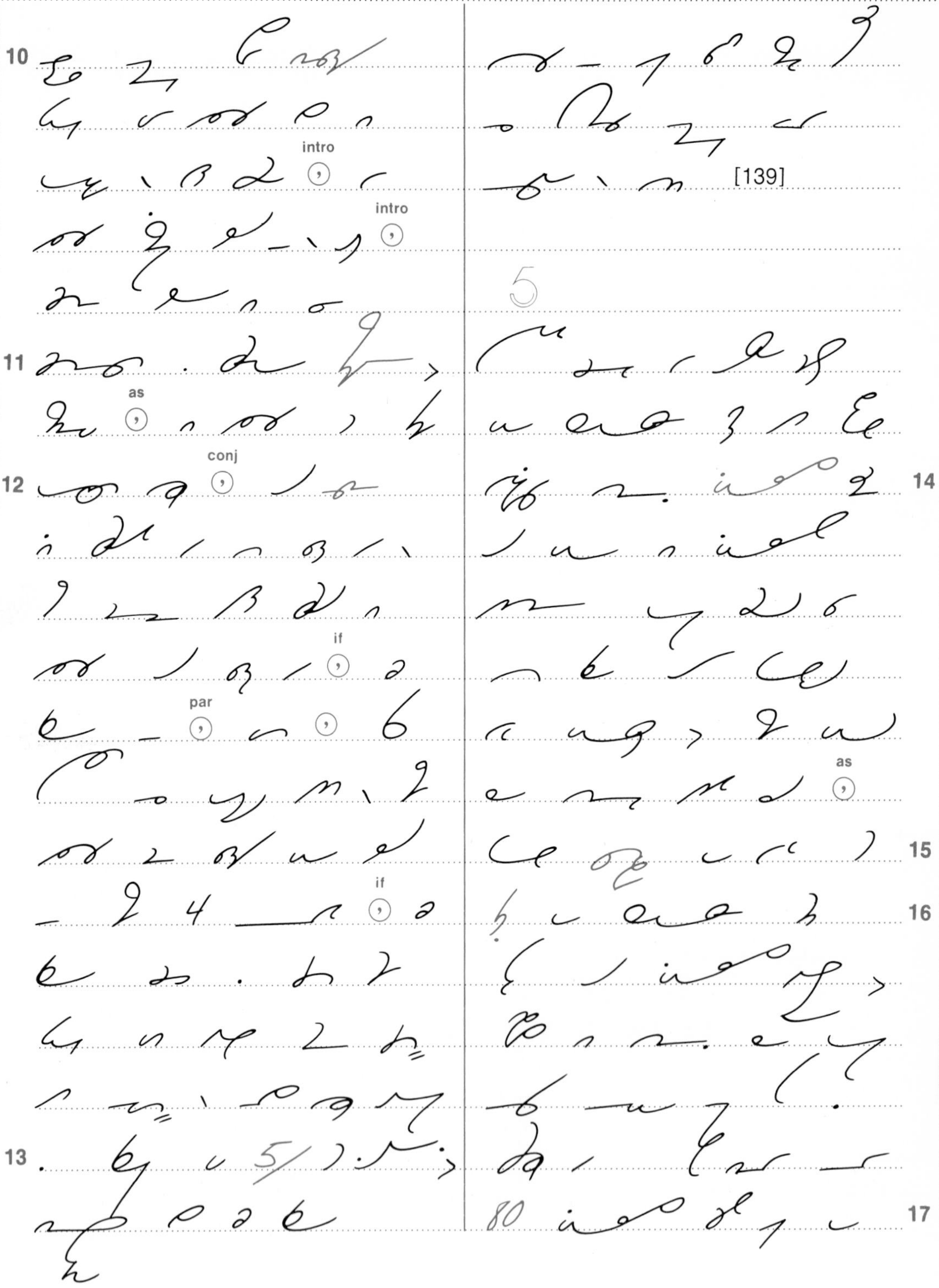

2
Ms. Ann Torres
8611 Cleveland Avenue
Phoenix, AZ 85012

3
Dr. Frank Labarre
167 Oakdale Boulevard
Sacramento, CA 95811

2 ad·ver·tis·ing
3 ea·ger
4 ad·dress·es
5 sales·clerk
6 may be
7 imag·ine
8 fa·mil·iar

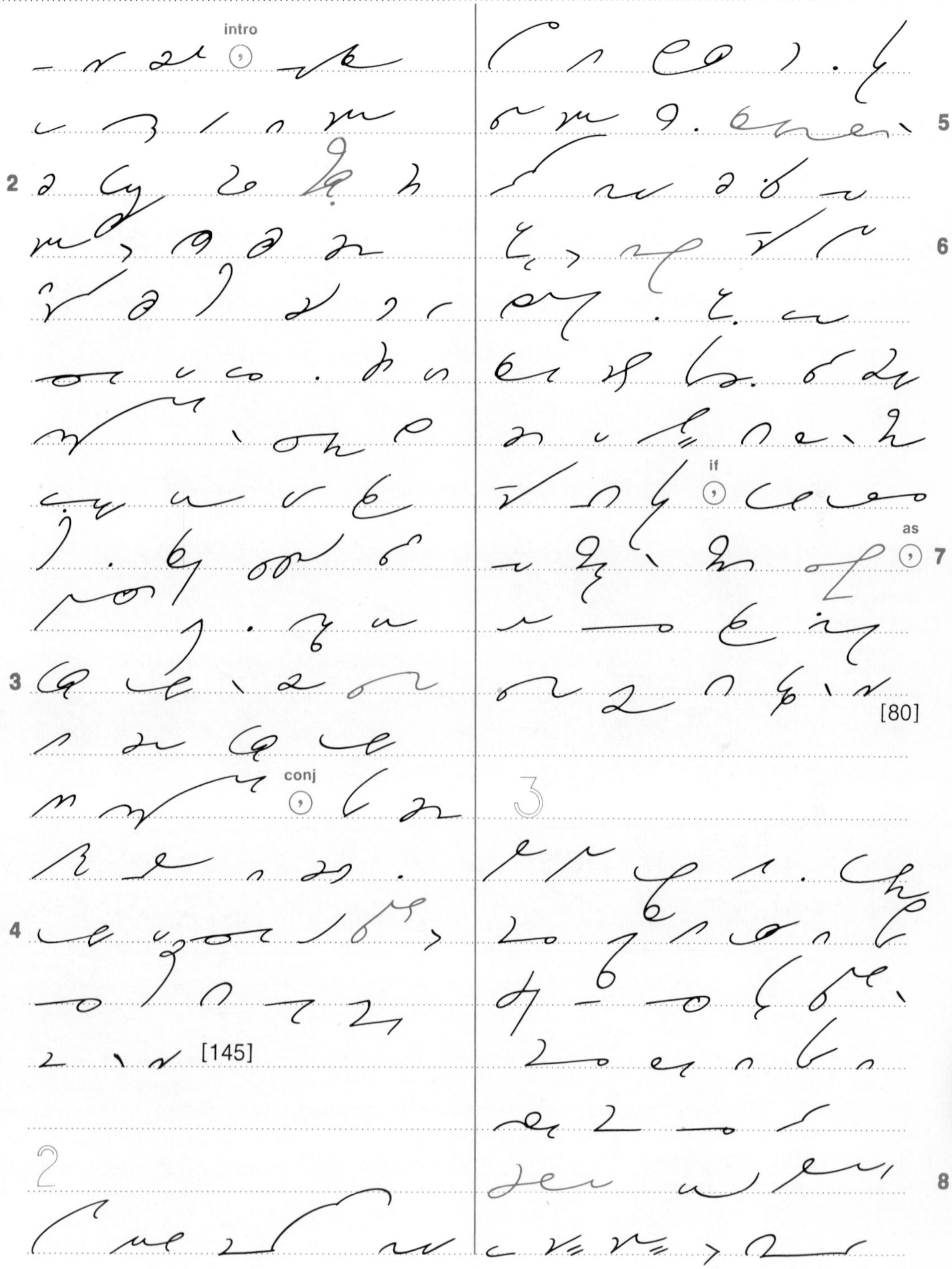

3
Ms. Susan Rogers
Pittsburgh Research
Associates
P.O. Box 1191
Pittsburgh, PA 15211

4
Mr. Brian Day
1416 Shore Drive
Milwaukee, WI 53211

3 sur·vey
4 any time
5 co·op·er·ate
6 ques·tion·naire
7 oc·ca·sions
8 im·prove·ment
9 wait

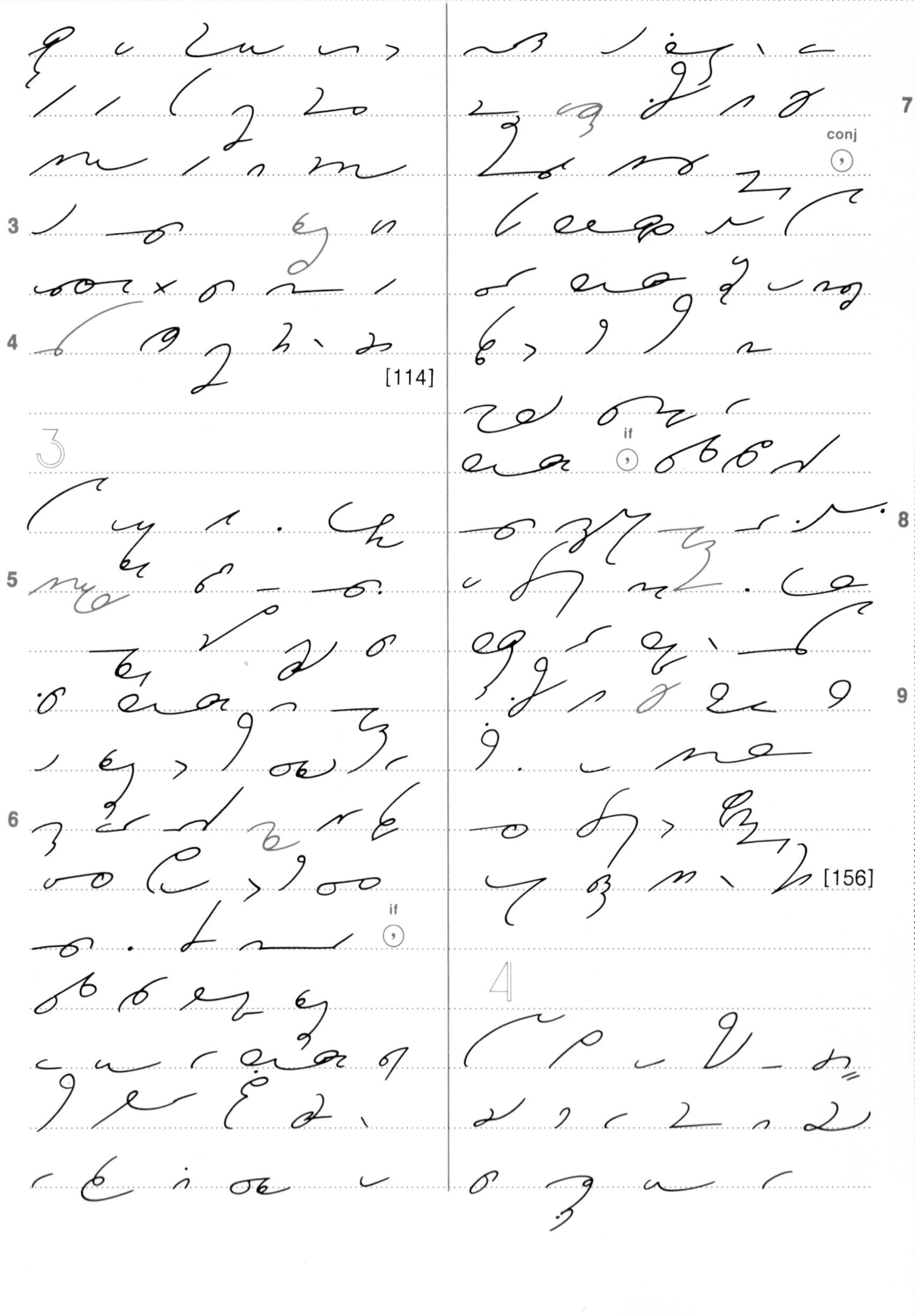

9 con·ve·nience
10 here

9

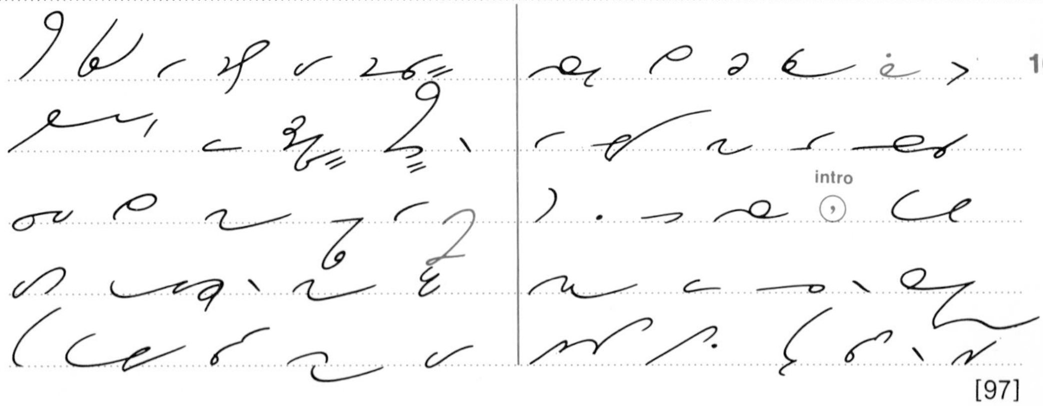

10

[97]

Taking lecture notes in shorthand has two prime benefits—it is faster than longhand and, unlike recording devices, it enables the student to edit so that only the key points are recorded.

51

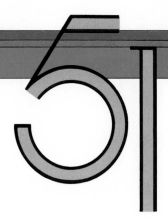

Writing and Transcription Practice

1
Phone Message

2
Mr. Ralph Novak, Principal
Harris Middle School
1718 Tenth Street
Miami, FL 33311

1 priv·i·lege
2 oc·curred

12

Building Professional Skills

Letter Style ■ Modified Block

The most commonly-used letter style in the business office today is the modified block style. As can be seen from the illustration on page 61, the date, the complimentary close, and the signature block all begin at the center of the line of writing. Typically, paragraphs are blocked with this style of letter although they may be indented.

Communication Checkup

either or ■ neither nor

The words *either or* are used to indicate a pair of positive alternatives. The words *neither nor* are used to indicate a negative attitude about a pair of possibilities. Naturally it is not appropriate to pair one of the positive words with one of the negative words.

She neither likes to cook **nor** to do housework.
He either likes skiing **or** swimming.

Building Transcription Skill

Transcription Warmup

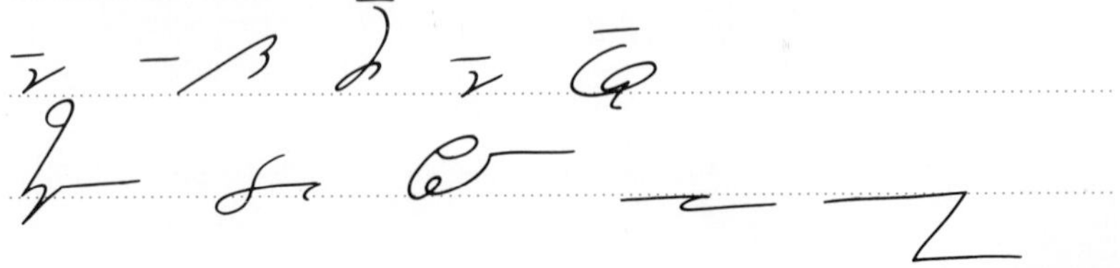

10
20

SECTION 3

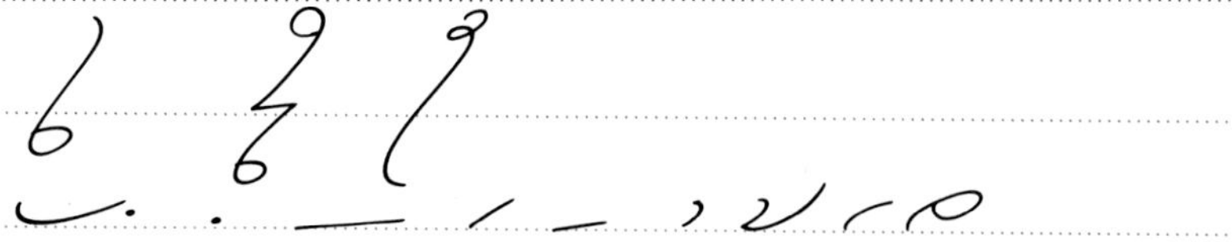

30

40

Transcription Speed Building

11

21

30

43

53

63

73

80

83

Transcription Quiz

Transcribe the following letter, adding the appropriate punctuation to your transcript.

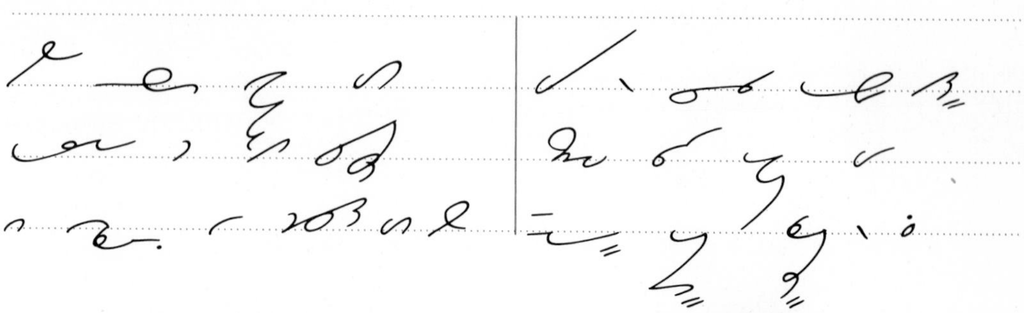

4
Home To Do List

5
Suggestions For Ms. James

6
Outline For A Letter I Will Write

8 ap·pre·ci·ate

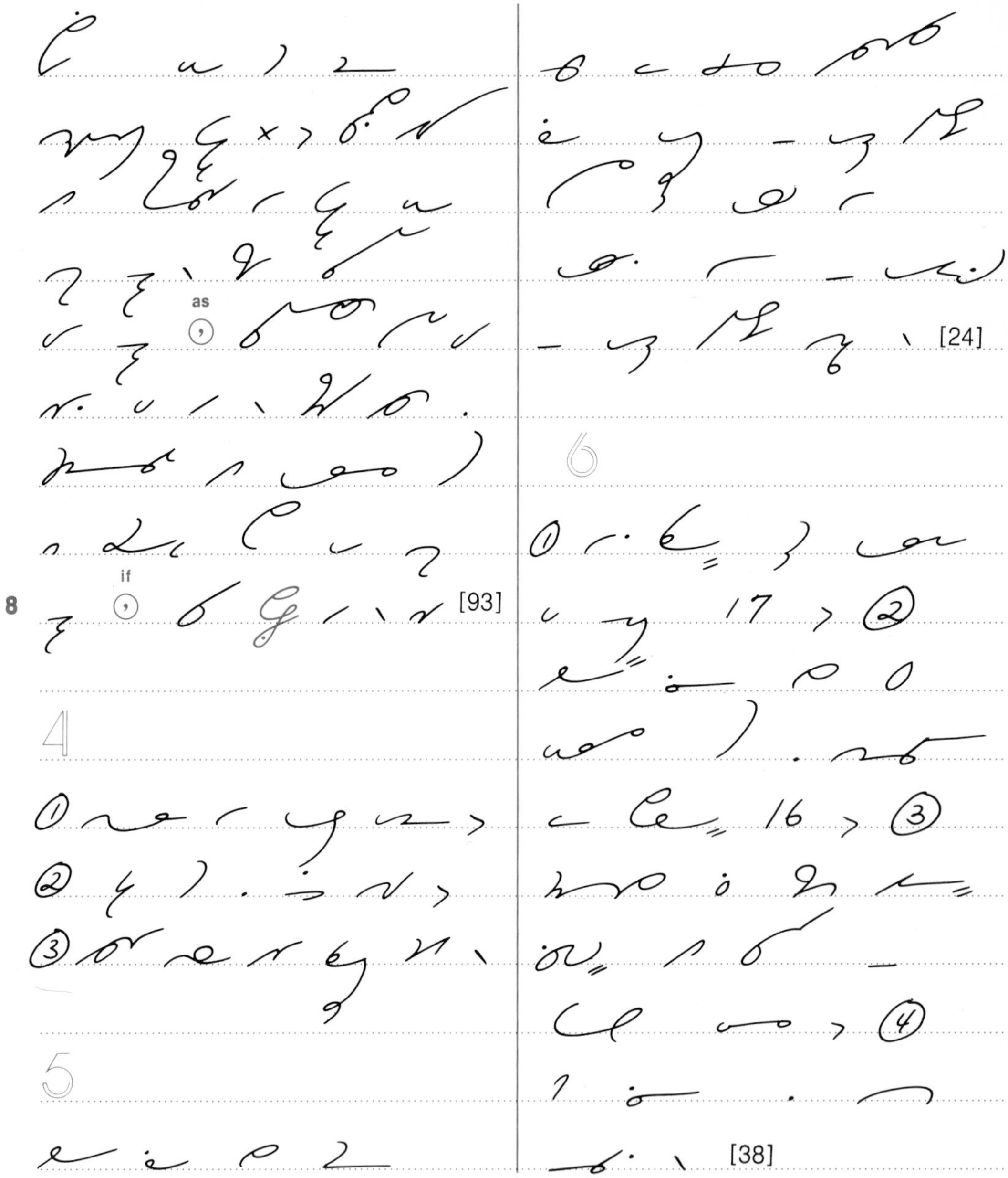

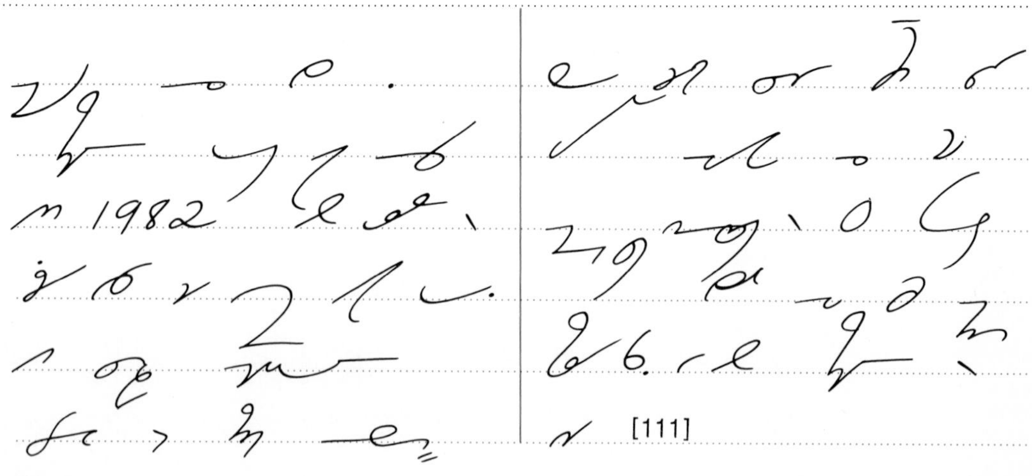

Mailable Letter Production

1
Mr. Ralph Berger
2726 Somona Parkway
Logan, UT 84321

1 paid
2 of·fered
3 sit·u·a·tion
4 le·gal
5 week

2
Mr. Roy Miller
405 Platt Avenue
St. Paul, MN 55100

3
Ms. L. K. Wade
510 Fall Road
Omaha, NE 68100

2 their
3 valu·able
4 ca·reer
5 its
6 wheth·er
7 crit·i·cal·ly

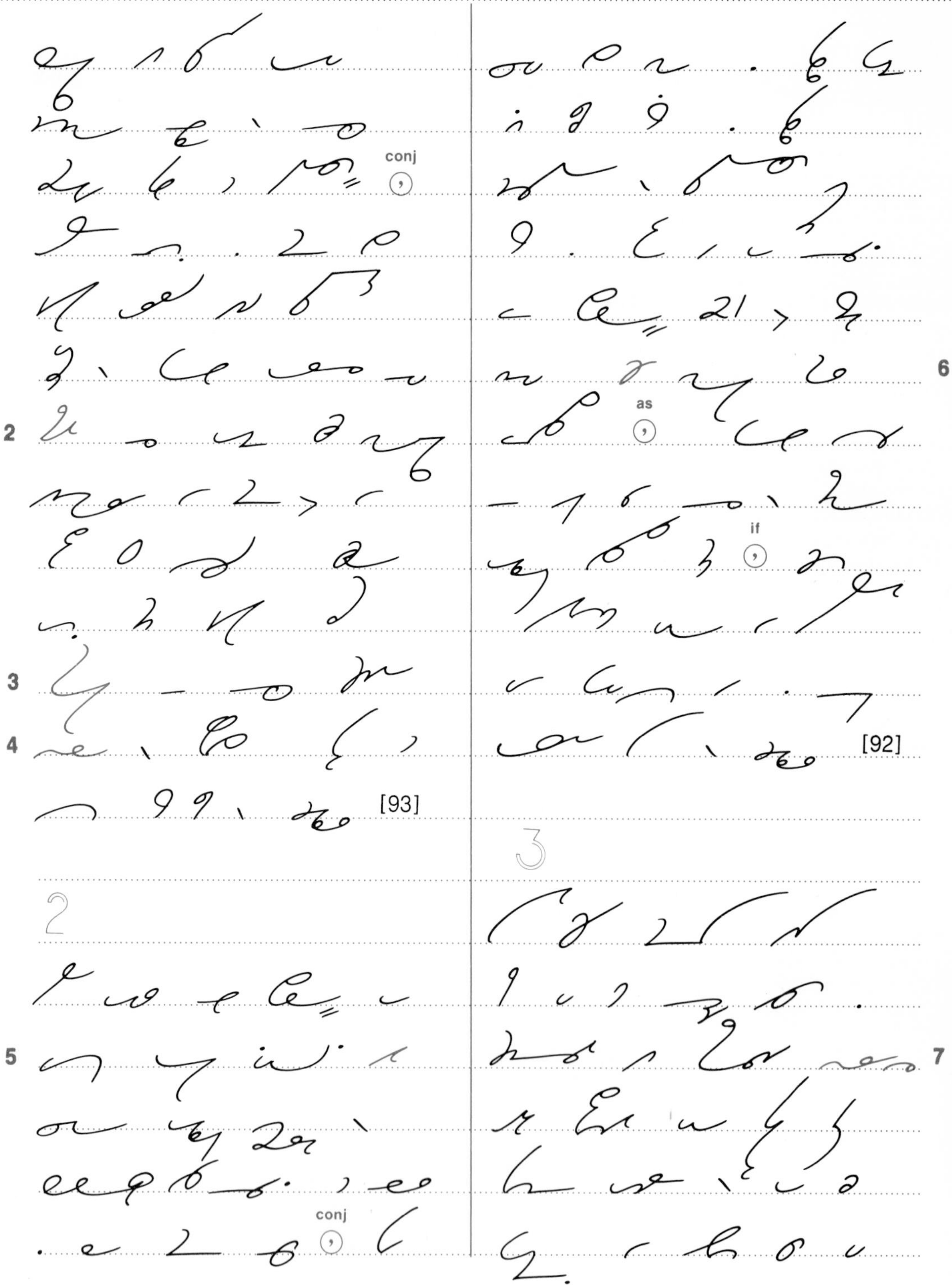

2
Mrs. E. H. Gates
Mason's Department Store
250 Henry Avenue
Memphis, TN 38111

3
Mr. James O'Neill
330 Broadway
Atlantic City, NJ 08411

6 ap·plied
7 ref·er·ence
8 any way
9 in·tro·duce
10 En·ter·prise
11 ca·reer
12 man·age·ment
13 per·son·al

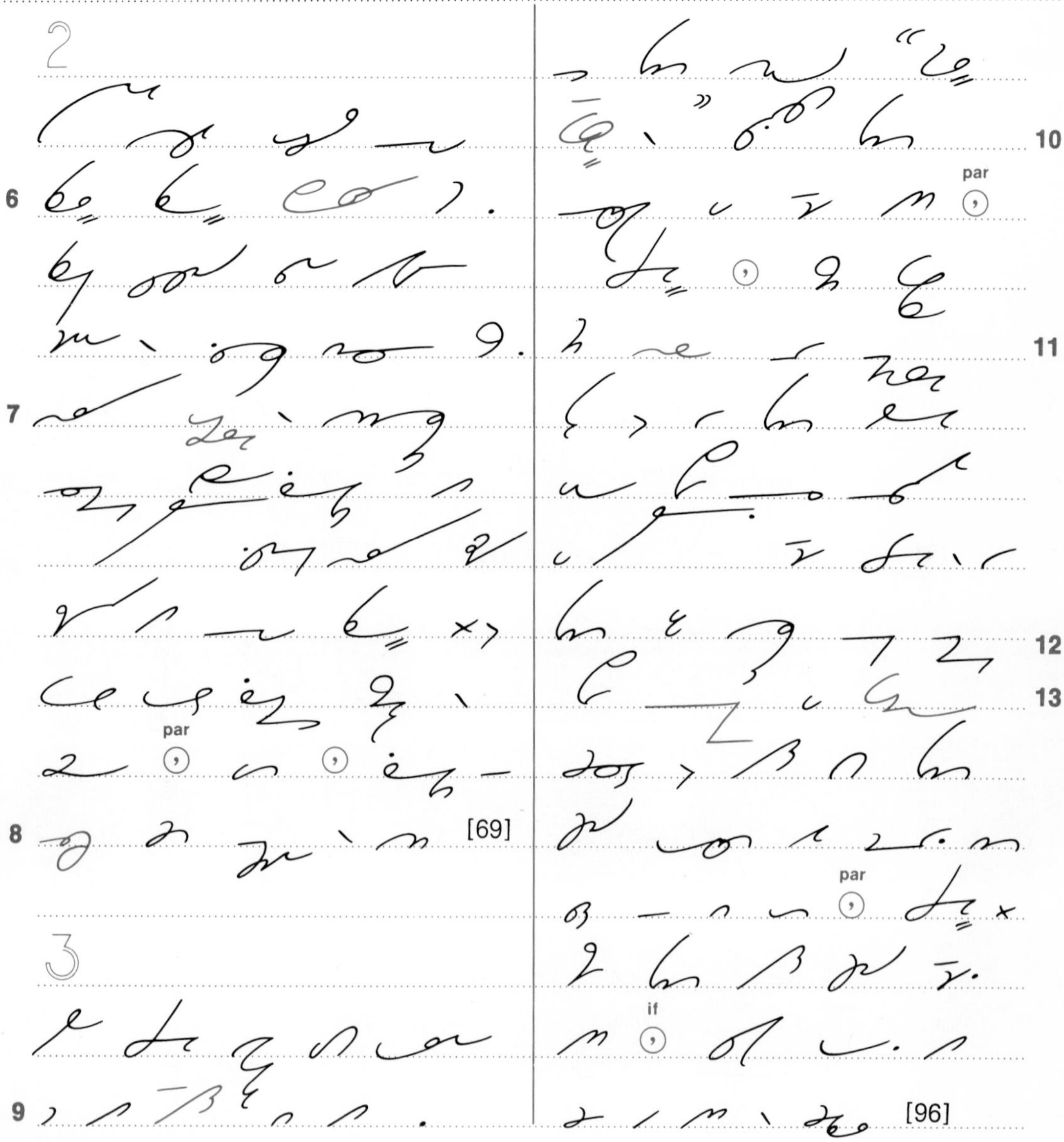

Transcription Quiz

Transcribe the following letter, adding the appropriate punctuation to your transcript.

Mailable Letter Production

1
Mrs. Pat Mitchell
1016 Madison Avenue
Jacksonville, FL 32211

1 write

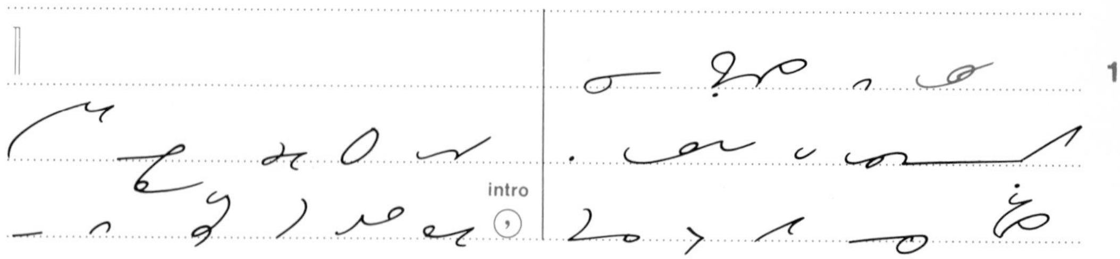

8091 Mission Boulevard **THE JULIAN J CORPORATION** San Diego, CA 92109

April 6, 19XX

Mr. David McAndrew
Westerly Business College
308 Calle Mirador
El Cajon, CA 92021

Dear Mr. McAndrew:

I am delighted to respond to your request for information regarding the skills we require for word processing positions. We believe it is vital that we communicate our needs to the community, particularly the educational institutions, so that future applicants develop the skills we desire. Those skills are as follows:

The ability to type at least 50 words a minute.

The ability to proofread accurately.

Excellent language ability. They need to be able to spell, punctuate, divide words, and recognize proper sentence structure.

The ability to transcribe from dictated shorthand notes, machine dictation, handwritten rough drafts, and edited typewritten copy.

Looking at this list of requirements, you can see that the best people for the job will be those who have studied shorthand, who have excellent typing skills, and who have experience in working with word processing equipment.

If you have any further questions, please call me. My telephone number is 619-555-2073.

Very truly yours,

Fred Samuelson

Fred Samuelson
Director of Employment

The *t* is not doubled when the last syllable is not accented.

credit	credited	crediting
profit	profited	profiting
budget	budgeted	budgeting

Building Transcription Skill

Transcription Warmup

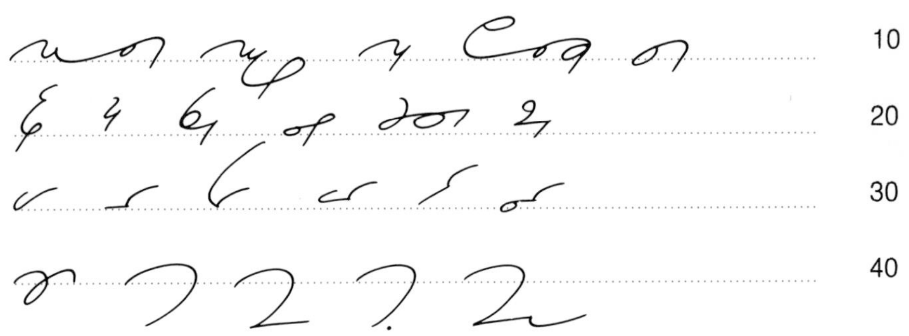

Transcription Speed Building

13

Building Professional Skills

Shorthand for the Professional ■ English Competence

For many people, the study of shorthand is the event that makes them feel that they are really beginning to master the English language. Gregg Shorthand books are filled with spelling tips, word division hints, similar-words drills, and a thorough review of the most frequently used marks of punctuation. Punctuation *along with the reason for punctuation* is ever present. Students cannot help but improve their knowledge of the English language by studying the Gregg Shorthand books, and they apply that knowledge when transcribing their shorthand notes.

It is not surprising that many secretaries attribute a significant part of their language competence to their study of Gregg Shorthand. Moreover, employers recognize the value of the study of shorthand in a secretary's background. In a recent survey, an overwhelming majority of business executives stated that they believe the study of shorthand makes a better secretary, whether the secretary takes dictation on the job or not.

Because of the English competence gained through the study of Gregg Shorthand, people who have studied Gregg Shorthand make better typists, better word processing operators, better editors of their bosses' correspondence, and better writers of communications that are delegated to them for composition. Best of all, employers appreciate these advantages.

A secretary who has studied Gregg Shorthand has the best chance of being hired, being promoted, and of having self-assurance on the job.

Communication Checkup

fewer ■ less

fewer A smaller number.

Shorthand students make fewer spelling errors.

less A smaller extent or amount.

50

Building Professional Skills

Shorthand for the Administrative Assistant

The number of secretarial jobs is growing by leaps and bounds. In fact, the secretarial job is the single fastest-growing occupation in the United States today. As the number of secretaries dramatically increases, new administrative levels are being added to the ranks of office workers. Many secretaries who have been promoted to work as administrative assistants with their executive partners have secretaries who report to them. More and more executives are delegating the creation of their routine correspondence to their administrative assistants. These administrative assistants, in turn, dictate correspondence to other secretaries.

Whether the person dictating a letter is an administrative assistant who was once a secretary, or a junior executive who studied shorthand, the shorthand skill is a vital component of the dictation process. The best way for anyone to dictate effectively is to jot down (in shorthand, of course) a list of points that the letter may include. The list is then scanned for omissions and redundancies. Finally, the items in the list are numbered in their best order of presentation in the letter. Using this list as an outline for dictation, the dictator then simply "tells the story" about each of the points that appear in the shorthand draft.

Communication Checkup

adding -ed, -ing to words ending in t

When a word ends in a single accented vowel followed by *t,* the *t* is doubled in forming *-ed* and *-ing* derivatives.

permit	permitted	permitting
transmit	transmitted	transmitting
submit	submitted	submitting

I like Jim less than Joe.
The tickets cost less than $20.

Building Transcription Skill

Transcription Warmup

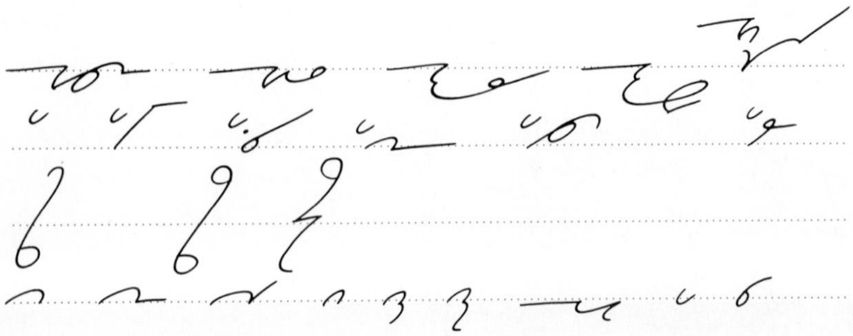

10
20
30
40

Transcription Speed Building

9
17
27
35
46
55
63
73
83

4
Office To Do List

5
While You Were Out

100 [26]

[71]

5

4

26

11:15

[20]

Before dictating a letter to the secretary, an administrative assistant uses shorthand to outline the points to be covered.

Transcription Quiz

Transcribe the following letter, adding the appropriate punctuation to your transcript.

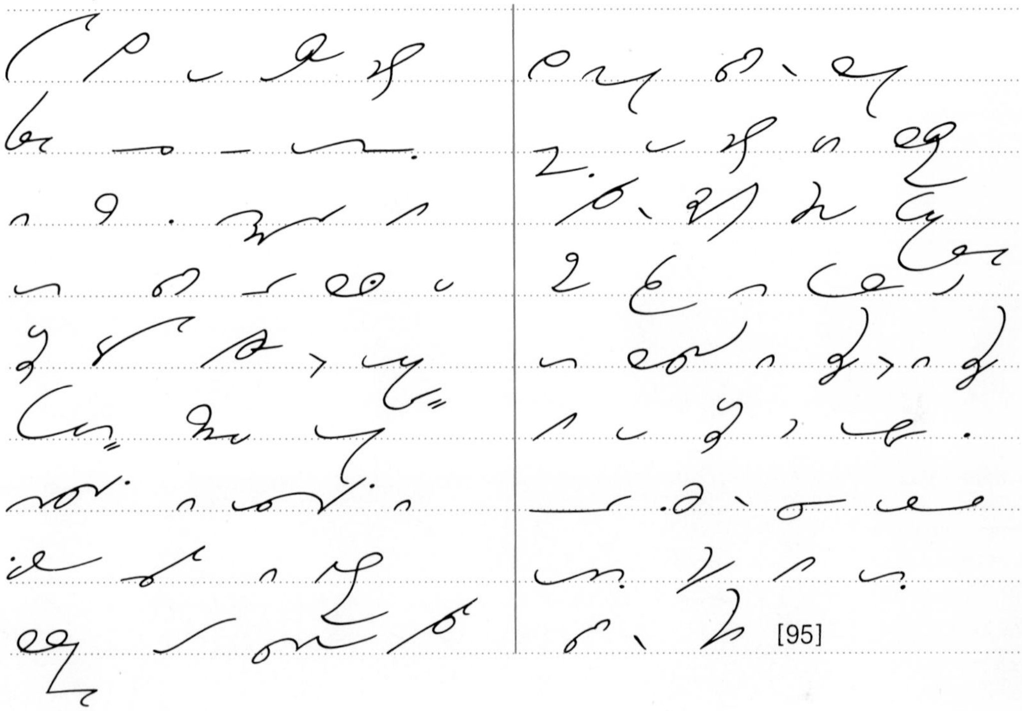

[95]

Mailable Letter Production

1
To: All Managers
From: A. R. DeLong
Subject: Company Library

2
Mrs. Edna Gordon
Credit Manager
Golden's Store
807 West Clairmont Avenue
Bloomington, IN 47401

1 li•brary
2 ma•jor
3 an•nu•al

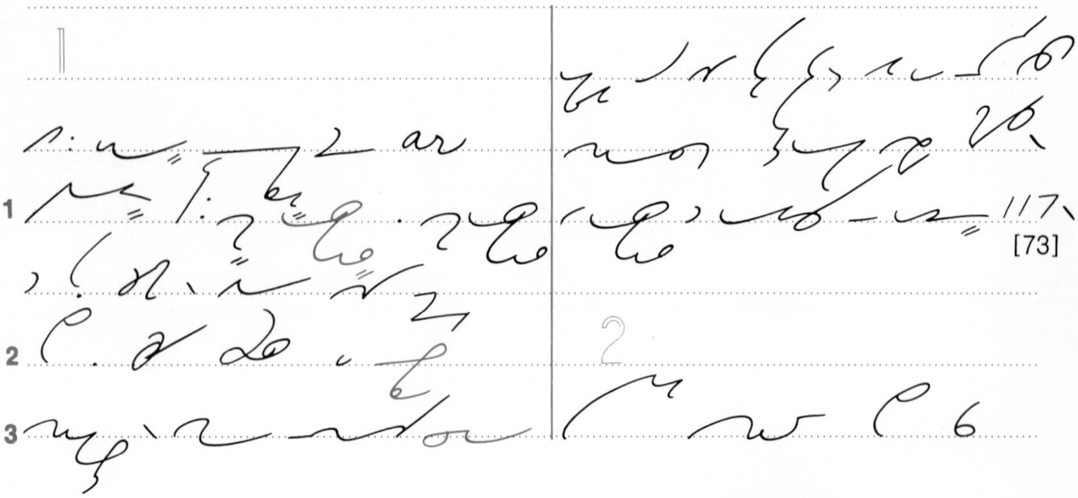

[73]

2
Mrs. Mary Green
4705 Maple Street
Boston, MA 02100

3
Mr. Fred Klein
Post Office Box 439
Mobile, AL 36600

1 per•son•al
2 clar•i•fy
3 com•pa•ny's
4 ar•rive
5 de•vel•op•ment
6 al•ready

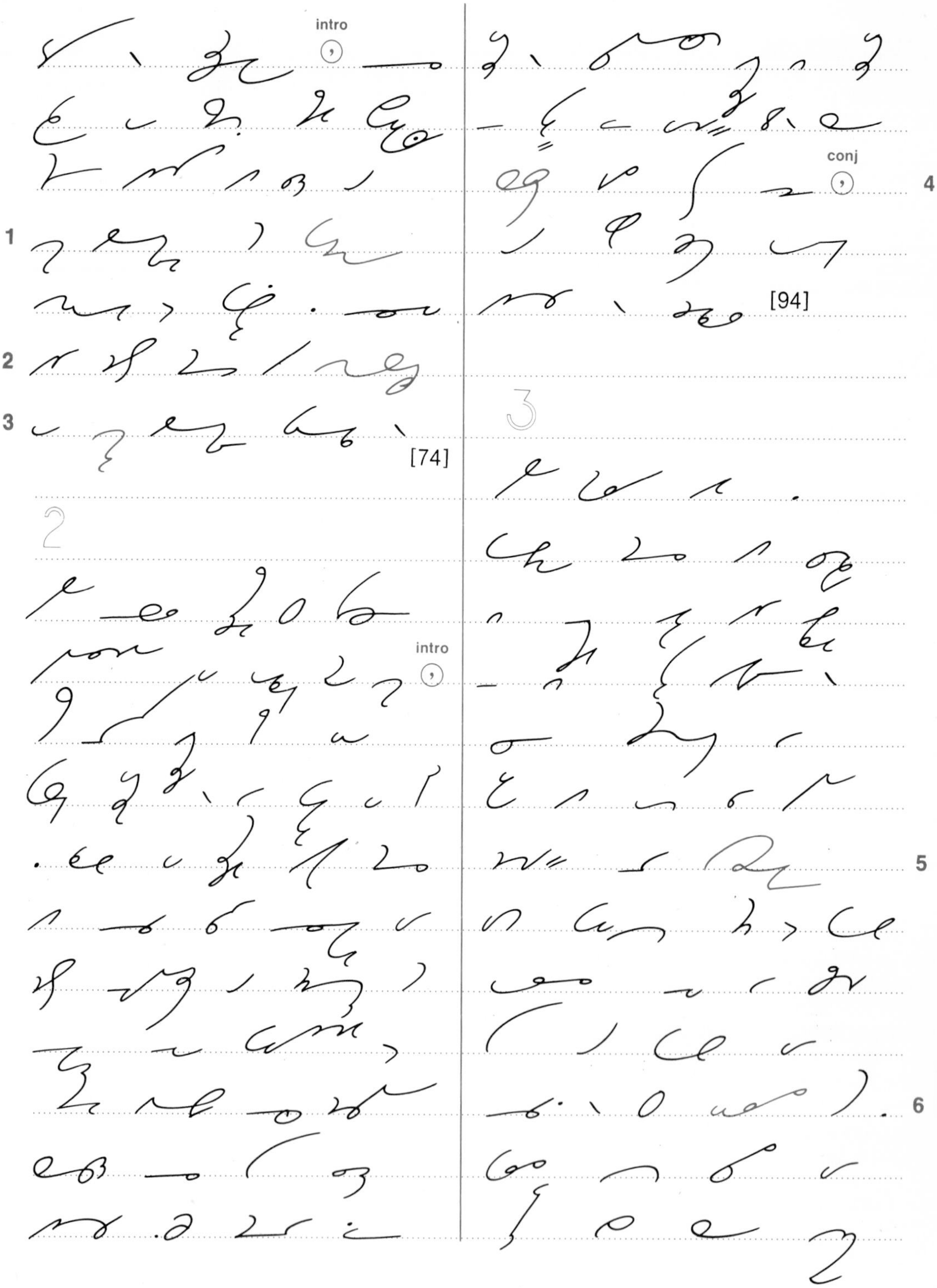

3
Dr. Myron Goldhammer
925 Addison Boulevard
Portland, ME 04100

4 paid
5 past
6 sim·ply
7 over·looked
8 hear
9 of·ten
10 write
11 awk·ward
12 over·due
13 ex·cel·lent

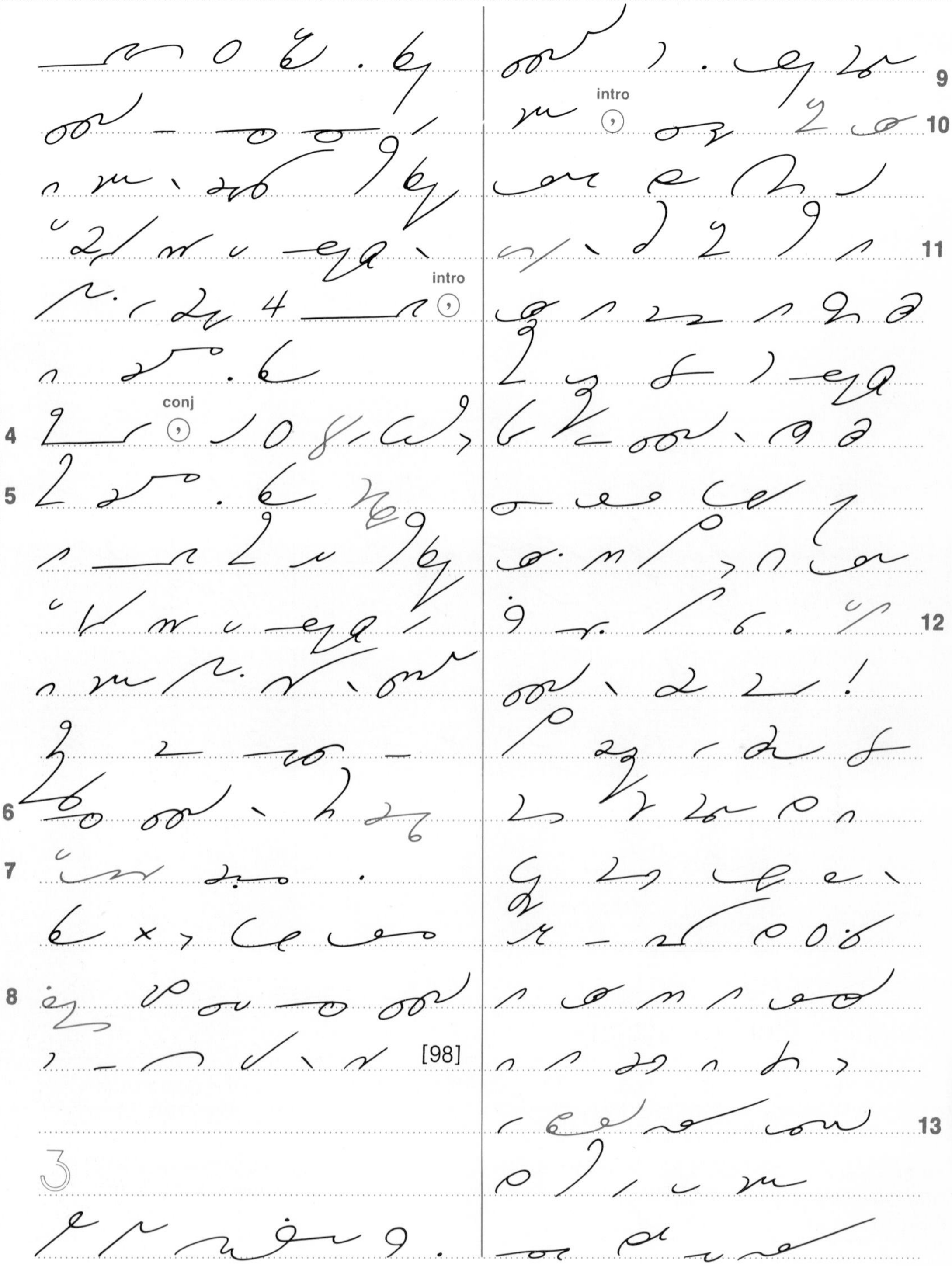

Transcription Quiz

Transcribe the following letter, adding the appropriate punctuation to your transcript.

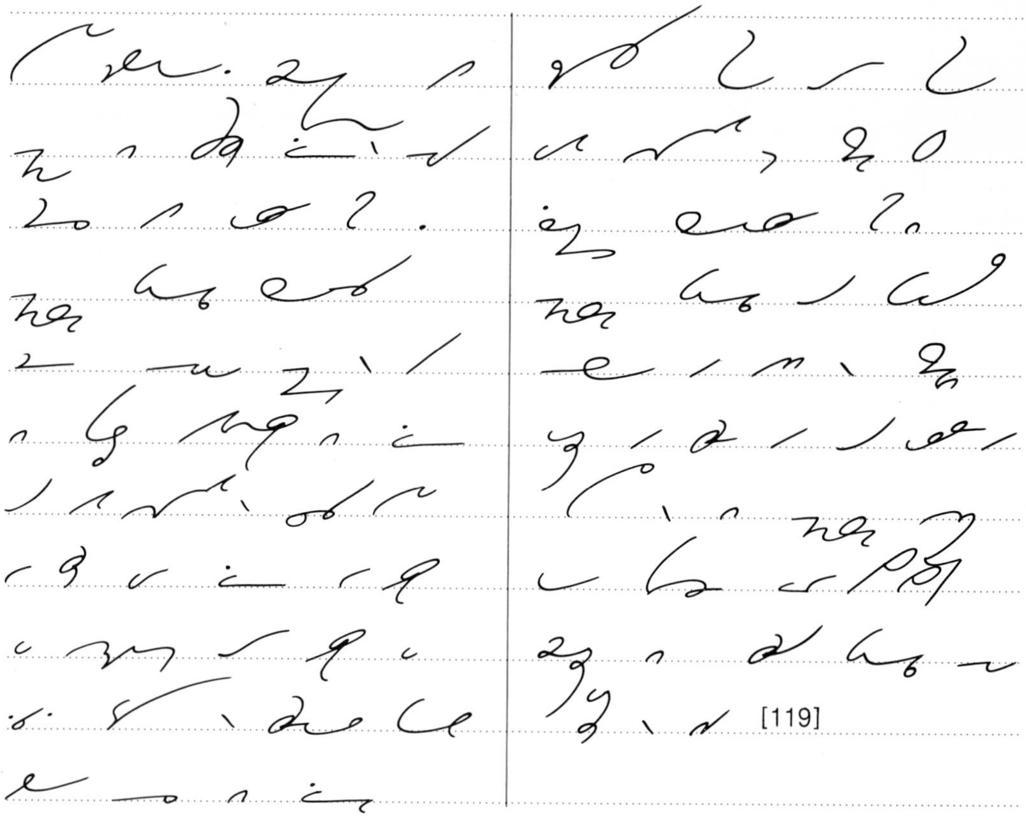

[119]

Mailable Letter Production

1
To: Dave James
From: Betty North
Subject: Telephone Policy

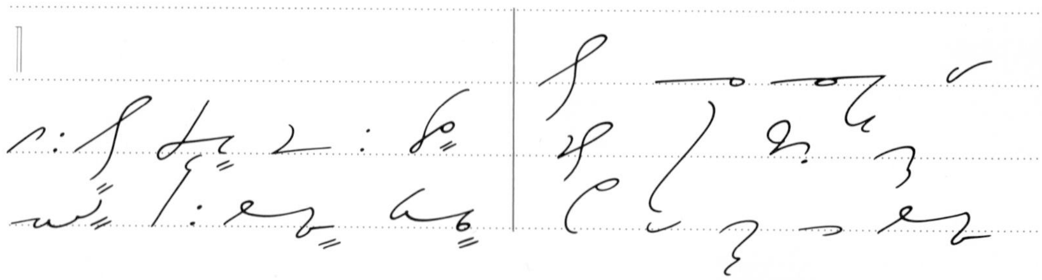

4
To: Fred Samuelson
From: Phyllis Morris
Subject: Requirements For Word Processing Operators

14 lim·it
15 ref·er·ence

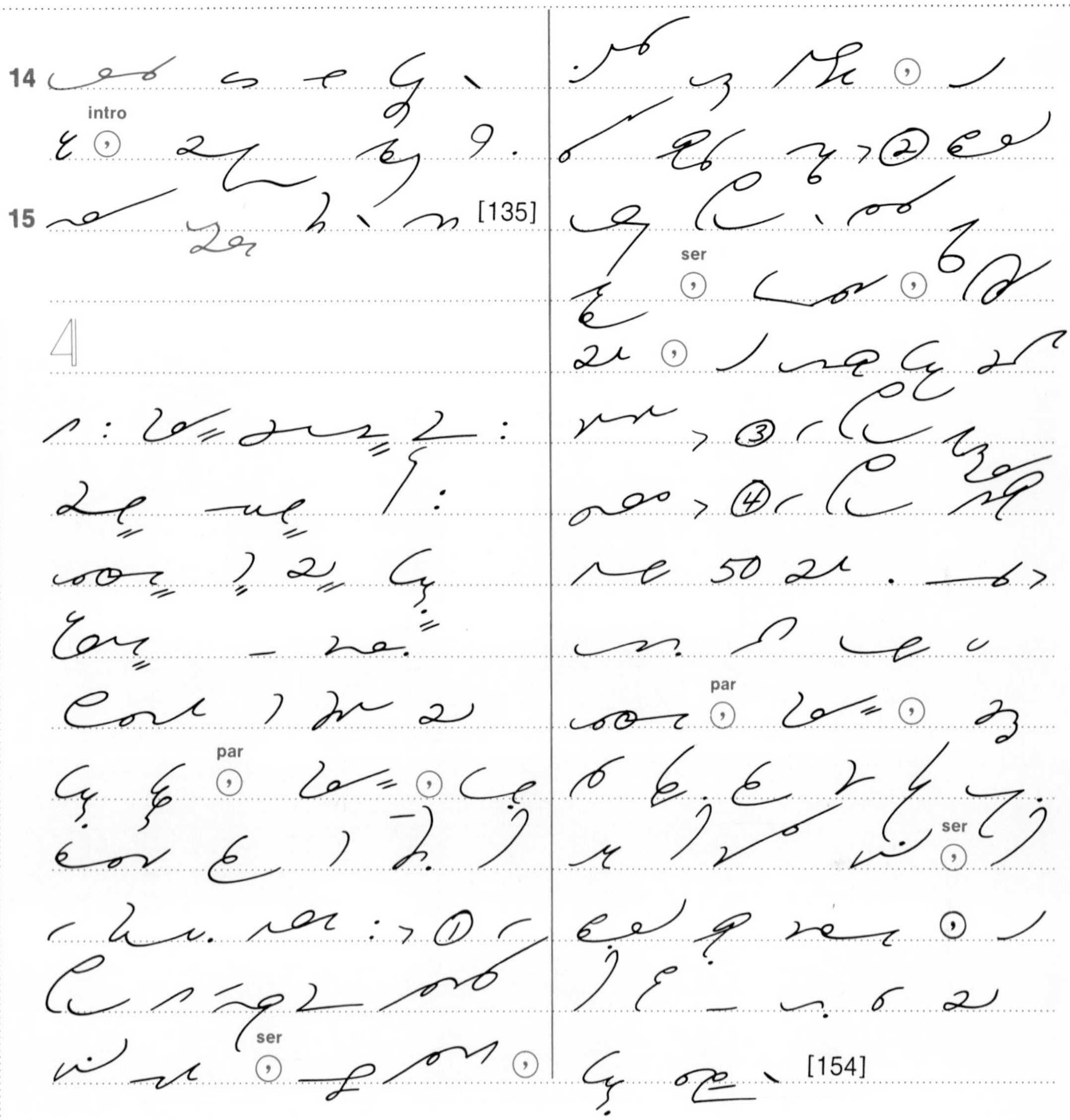

Success:

Are you waiting for your treasure ship to come in? Have you sent one out?

Building Transcription Skill

Transcription Warmup

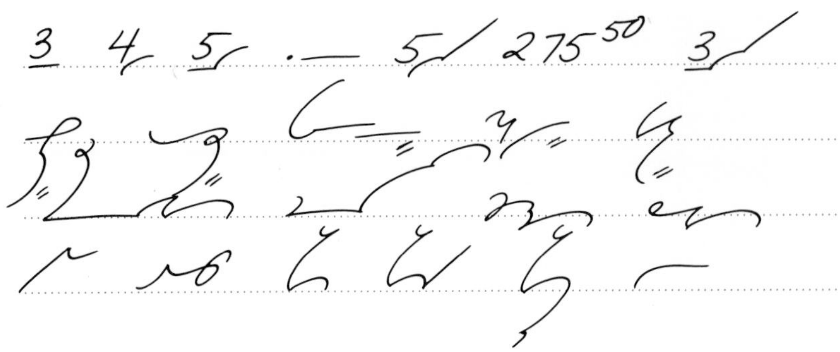

11
20
33
43

Transcription Speed Building

10
19
28
37
46
55
64
74
80

14

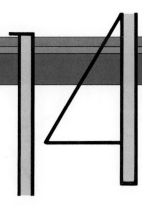

Building Professional Skills

Listing as Communication

Few people think of listening as a communication skill. Most of us who have good hearing think of listening as something that merely happens when another person speaks. But just as there are certain characteristics that a person must possess in order to be a good speaker, there are also certain traits that one must have in order to be a good listener.

Remember, effective communication means that one person comes to understand the thoughts and feelings of another person. That process of face-to-face conversation is a two-way street. For communication to happen, one of the people must be an effective speaker or writer. The other person must be an effective listener.

Communication Checkup

may ■ can

may Having permission to do something.

May I leave the room?
Sue may be absent tomorrow.

can Having the ability to do something.

Wendy can water ski very well.
Can you speak Spanish?

49

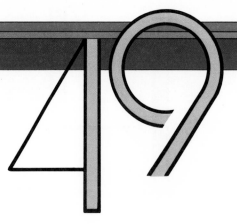

Building Professional Skills

Punctuation Checkup

apostrophe, possessive

The possessive form of most words is indicated by adding *apostrophe s* to those words.

The cat's food is in the dish.
My son's class is interesting.
Steve's keys are lost.

Plural words ending in *s* show possession only by the addition of an apostrophe.

The employees' time cards are on the table.
The skis' bindings are too tight.
The boys' coats are all in a pile.

Communication Checkup

adding -ed, -ing to words ending in r

When a single accented vowel followed by *r* ends a word, the *r* is doubled in forming *-ed* and *-ing* derivatives.

occur	occurred	occurring
refer	referred	referring
prefer	preferred	preferring

Do not double the *r* if the last syllable is not accented.

offer	offered	offering
differ	differed	differing
flatter	flattered	flattering

Building Transcription Skill

Transcription Warmup

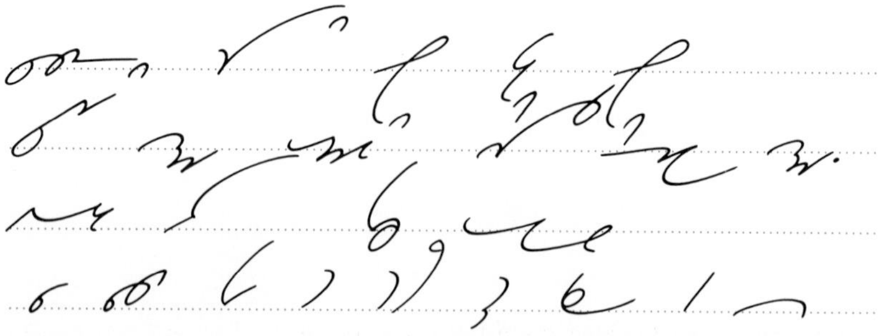

10
20
30
41

Transcription Speed Building

10
20
30
38
48
58
70
77
81

3
Mr. Fred Dorf
6161 King Drive
Detroit, MI 48210

4
Personal Shopping List

8 any time
9 typ·ing
10 cat·a·log

When the manager is not available to meet with an unexpected visitor, the secretary should get as much information as possible in order to arrange a future appointment.

Transcription Quiz

Transcribe the following letter, adding the appropriate punctuation to your transcript.

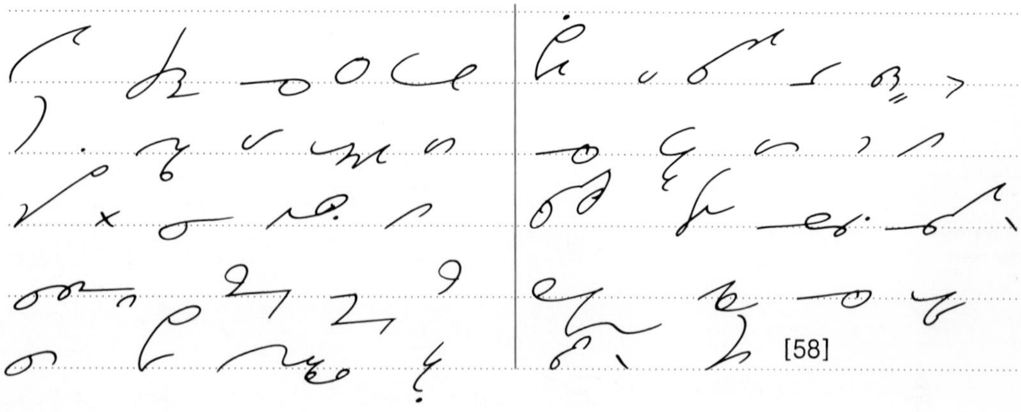

Mailable Letter Production

1
Mrs. Martha Worth
Lakeland Auto Parts
1517 Shore Drive
Chicago, IL 60611

1 eas·i·er
2 edi·tion
3 cat·a·log
4 Here's

2

Miss Ann Chase
1112 Riggs Avenue
Minneapolis, MN
55411

4 sal·a·ry
5 hear·ing
6 en·joy·able
7 cop·ies

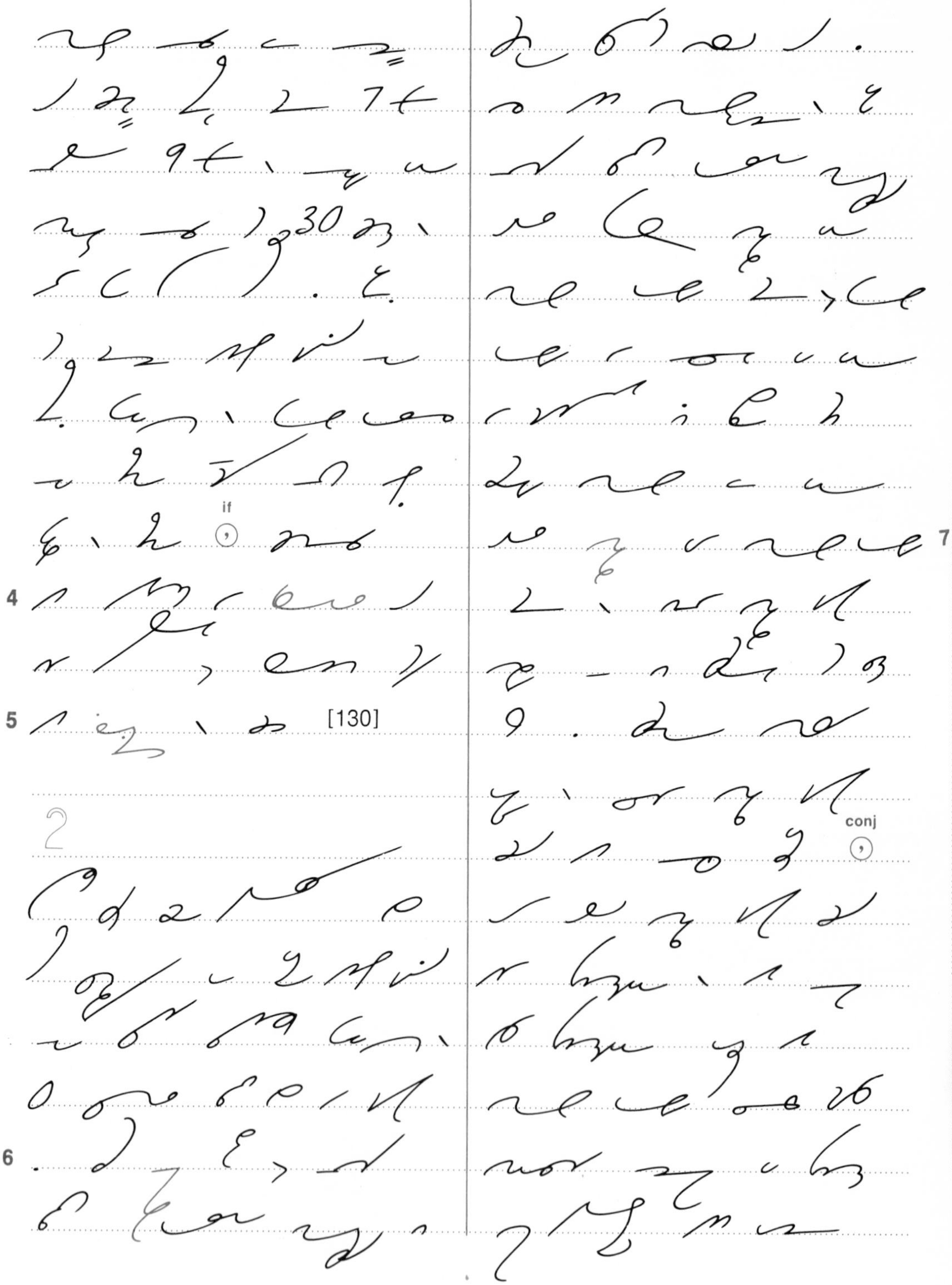

2
Ms. Angela Brooks
Brooks Stationery
2333 14th Street
Providence, RI 02911

3
Mr. Paul Andretti
Andretti Business Services
2510 West Madison Avenue
Baltimore, MD 21200

5 re·ceive
6 han·dle
7 for·ward
8 com·put·er
9 in·stalled
10 too

Transcription Quiz

Transcribe the following letter, adding the appropriate punctuation to your transcript.

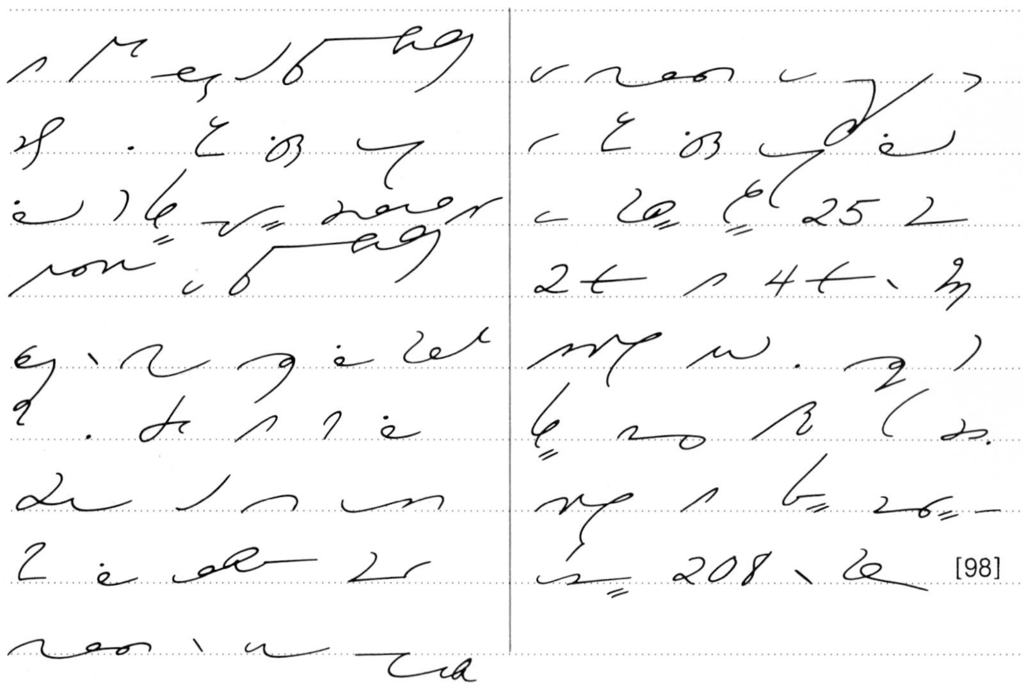

Mailable Letter Production

1
Miss Ann Chase
1112 Riggs Avenue
Minneapolis, MN 55411

1 ex·celled
2 cit·ies
3 Transcribe: 1,000

15

Building Professional Skills

Punctuation Checkup

, apposition

A word or phrase used in apposition is one that explains or identifies other terms. When it occurs within a sentence, it is set off by two commas. When it occurs at the end of a sentence, only one comma is used.

Our auditor, Mr. Santiago, is ill today.
I would like you to meet my mother, Elise Smith.
The meeting will be held on **Tuesday,** September 8.
The book, *Introduction to Business,* is out of print.

Communication Checkup

Preposition at the End of a Sentence

Generally a good writer tries to avoid ending a sentence with a preposition.

Poor Wording What class did you receive a poor grade in?

Better Wording In what class did you receive a poor grade?

Building Transcription Skill

Transcription Warmup

9
19

The *l* is not doubled when the last vowel is not accented.

signal	signaled	signaling
travel	traveled	traveling
level	leveled	leveling

Building Transcription Skill

Transcription Warmup

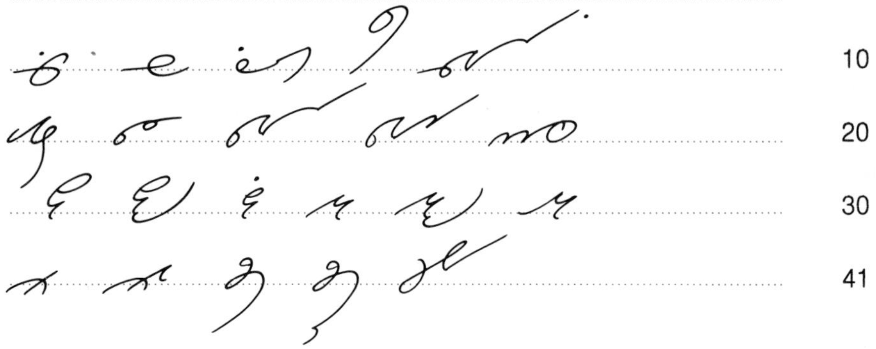

Transcription Speed Building

27

38

Transcription Speed Building

13

21

28

36

42

50

60

70

80

Transcription Quiz

Transcribe the following letter, adding the appropriate punctuation to your transcript.

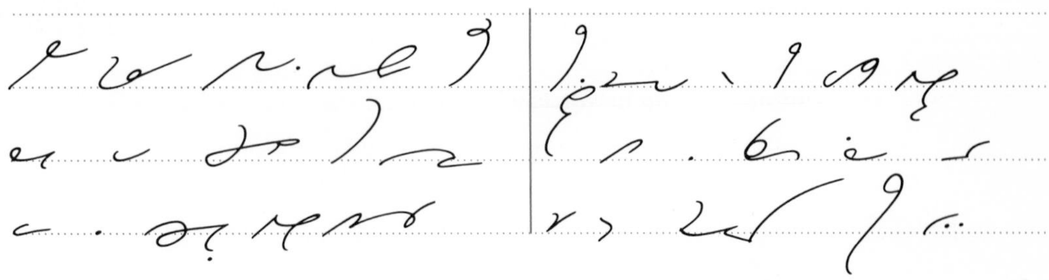

48

Building Professional Skills

Listening ■ Be "You" Oriented

One of the best ways to become an effective listener is to take a sincere interest in other people. For most of us this requires a conscious effort. It is all too easy to be *me* oriented. We like to approach our friends with the attitude, "Do I have a story to tell you!" We like to top our friends' stories with even bigger stories of our own, and we like to be the person in the group who has the funniest joke.

Listening with the *you* approach, however, makes us a far more enjoyable companion for other people to be around, and we learn more. By employing the *you* approach in our face-to-face conversations, we make a conscious effort not to monopolize the conversation. Rather, we provide ample opportunity for the other person to speak at least half the time.

When we are part of a group listening to a speaker, the *you* approach can be used just as effectively. By determining to be interested in both the topic and the speaker, we support the speaker by our eye contact, facial expressions, and other elements of body language.

Communication is a two-way street. Remember, for effective communication to take place, there must be good speaking and good listening in equal proportions.

Communication Checkup

adding -ed, -ing to words ending in l

In order to form an *-ed* or *-ing* derivative of a word ending in a single accented vowel followed by *l*, double the *l*.

excel	excelled	excelling
propel	propelled	propelling
compel	compelled	compelling

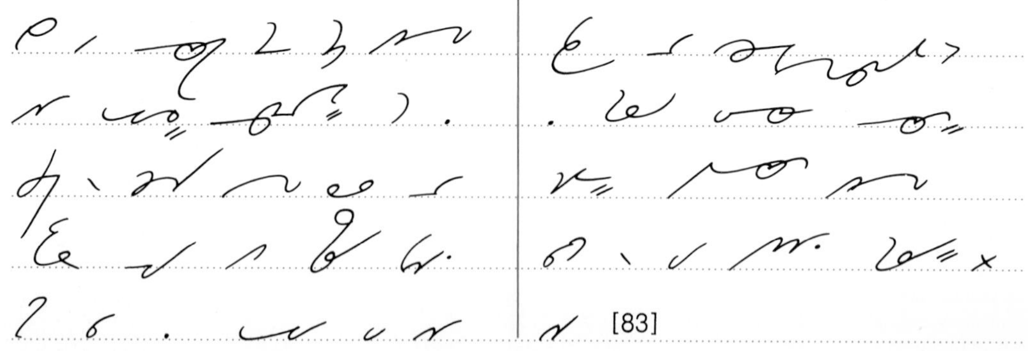

Mailable Letter Production

1
Mr. Thomas Casey
320 Monteray Boulevard
Denver, CO 80211

2
Mr. Alan Henry
603 Franklin Street
Tacoma, WA 98411

1 friend
2 know
3 de·vel·oped
4 any time

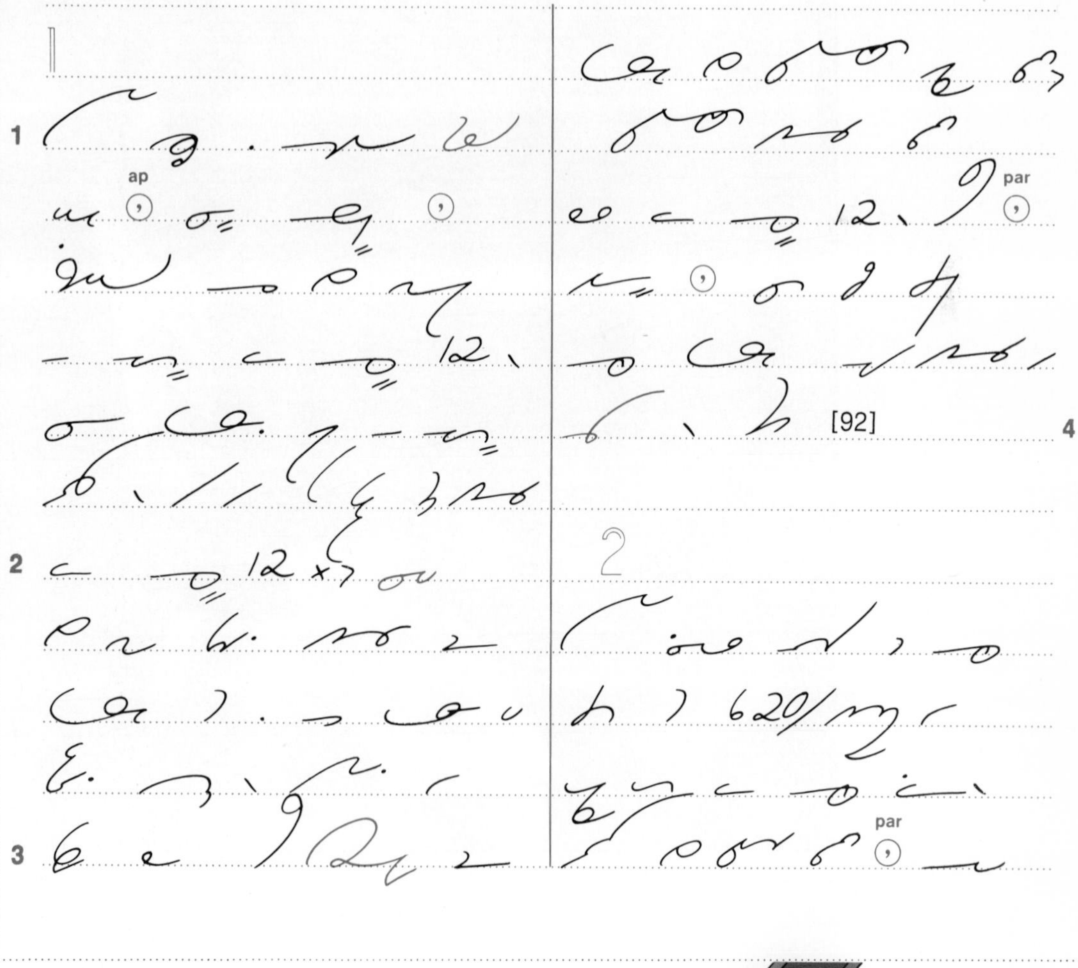

4
Telephone Message

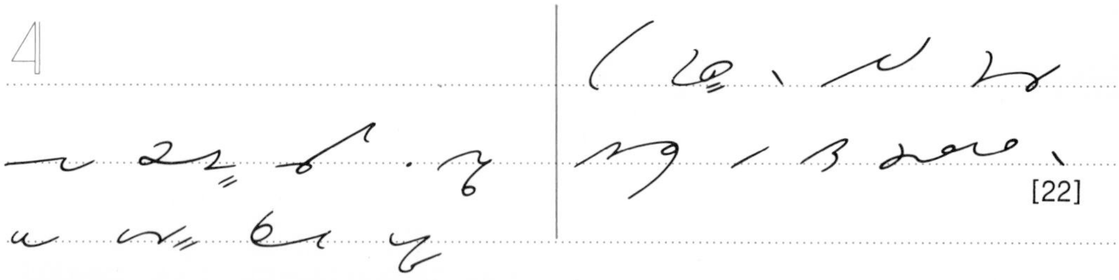

When you go for a job interview, be prepared to take a dictation and transcription test.

3

Mr. David Block
2220 14th Street
Pittsburgh, PA 15211

4

Note For Roger Ames

5 sid·ing
6 em·ploy·ees
7 be·lief
8 fam·i·ly
9 week
10 too
11 on·to

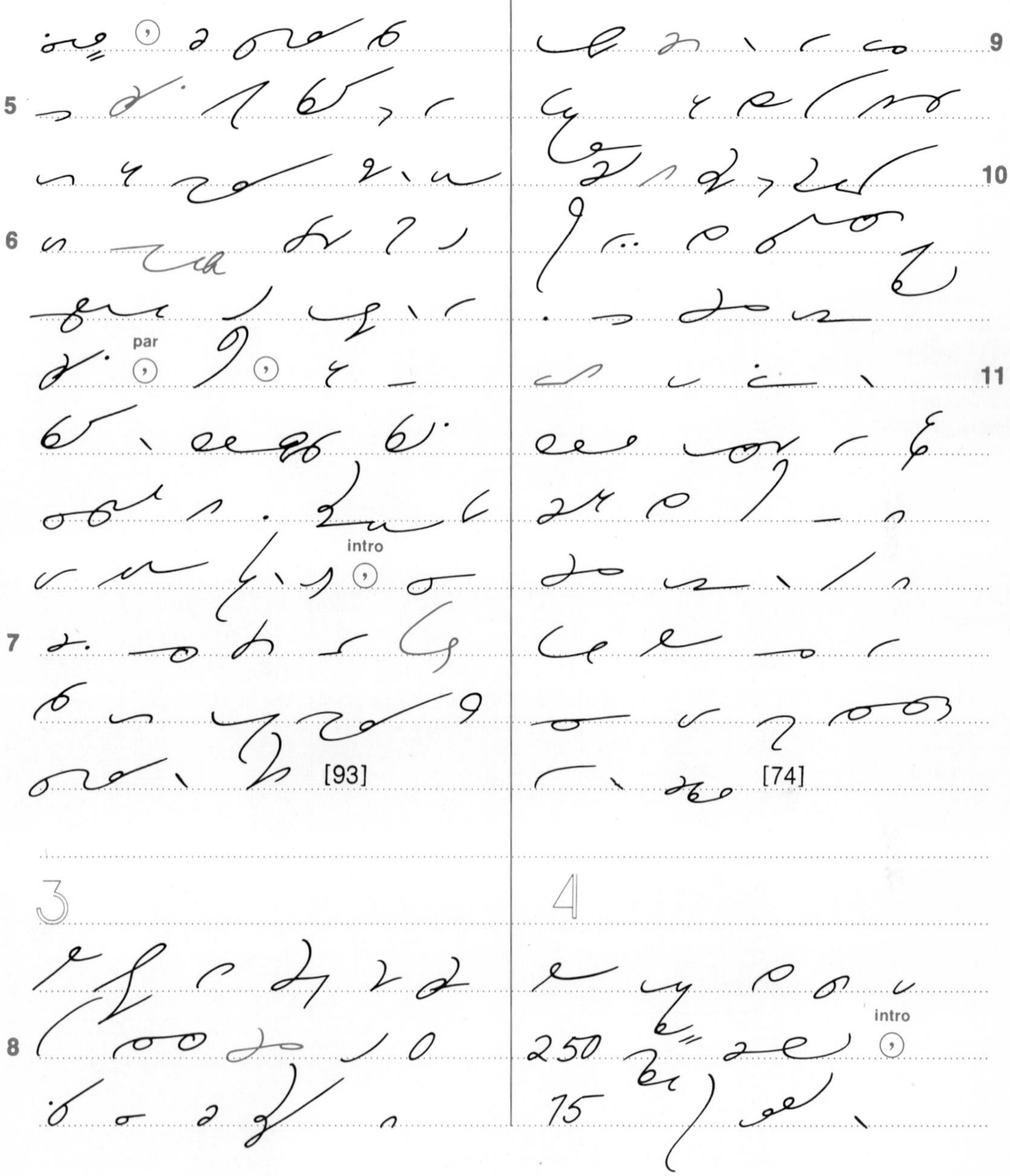

2
Dr. Sara Troy
Department of
Business Education
North Central College
Rapid City, SD 57701

3
Business
Communications
Editor
King Publishing
Company
622 Congress Avenue
Decatur, IL 62500

2 grad·u·ate
3 write
4 rec·om·men·da·tion
5 Ca·reer
6 of·fered
7 gram·mar
8 for·ward

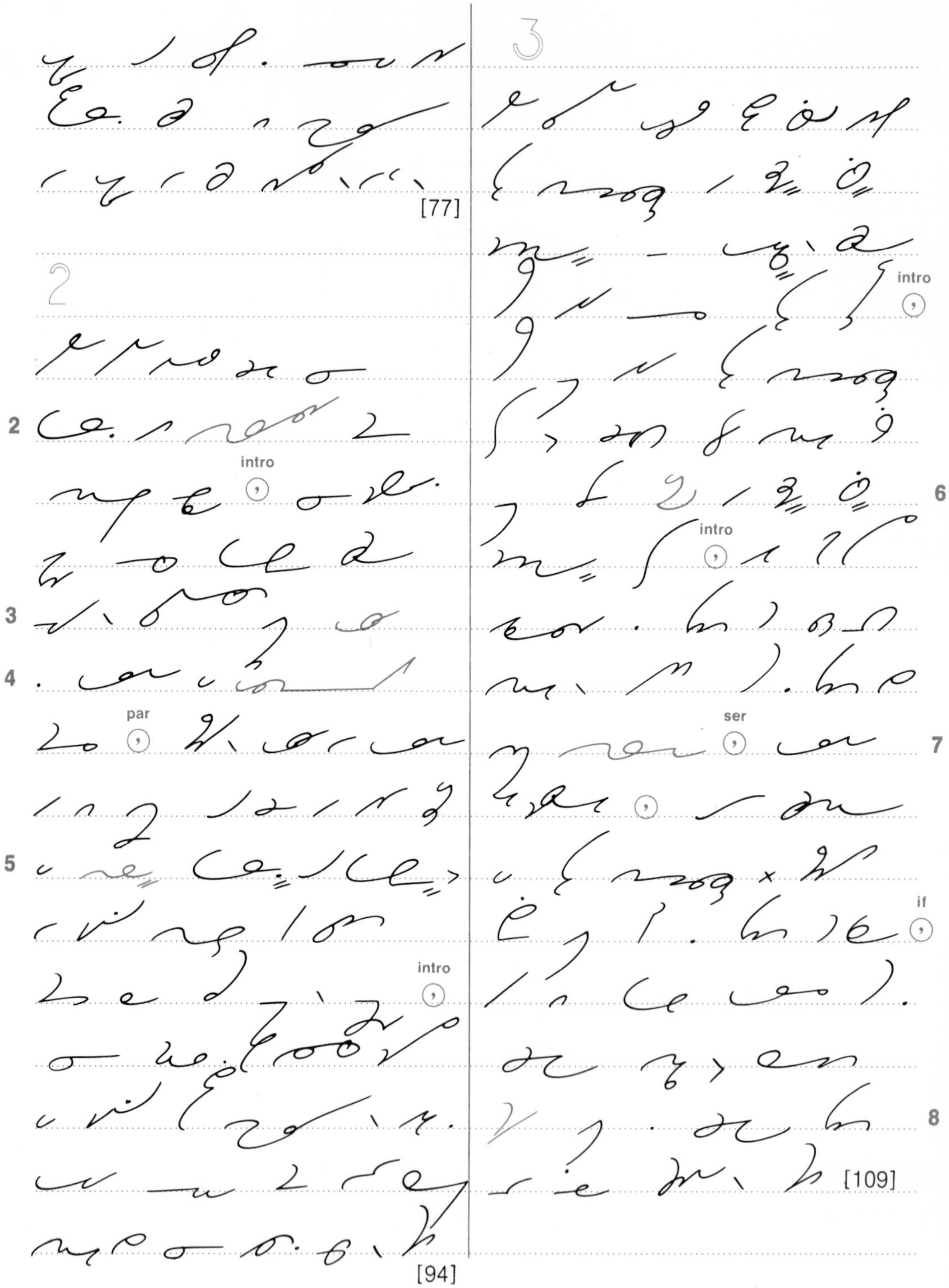

16

Building Professional Skills

Shorthand As Input For Word Processing

When most people think of word processing, they think of a display word processor. The distinguishing feature of a display word processor is, of course, a CRT display screen, accompanied by a standard typewriter keyboard to which has been added some special function controls. Functionally, the display word processor provides for editing and error correction on the CRT screen so that a perfect typed copy can be produced on the printer.

Text in the word processor comes from several sources, just as it does when documents are created at a traditional electric typewriter. Dictation of correspondence to a secretary who takes shorthand and then transcribes the notes while seated at a CRT is one type of input. Of course, many documents are typed as rough drafts for the executive to edit for a second typing. While some editorial changes are best effected in writing, other changes can better be dictated to the secretary. For example, the secretary might write such editorial instructions from the executive as, "Let's use leader lines in the table on page 3, reverse the order of the last two paragraphs on page 6, and number all the footnotes consecutively with a cumulative list at the end of the report."

Even with the word processor available to speed up the job of typewriting, many executives still write their copy in longhand. The secretary who has good dictation skills can do much to help the executive improve office productivity.

Communication Checkup

accept ■ except

accept To receive.

Our committee accepts your report.
You have been accepted for membership.

Transcription Quiz

Transcribe the following letter, adding the appropriate punctuation to your transcript.

Mailable Letter Production

1
To: Lorraine White
From: Roger Anderson
Subject: Late Expense Report

1 filled

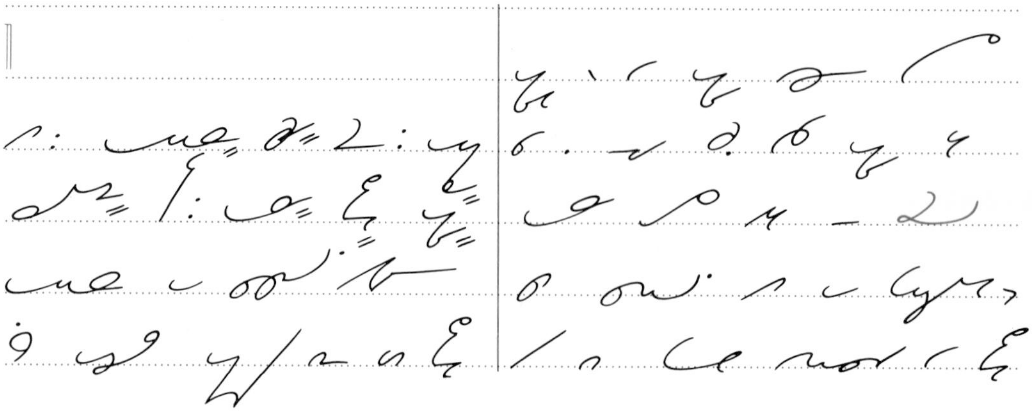

1

except To omit.

All may enter the contest **except** John.
All who have not paid their dues will be **excepted** from membership.

Building Transcription Skill

Transcription Warmup

10
20
31
42

Transcription Speed Building

10
18
27
36
44
52
60
70
80
82

Building Transcription Skill

Transcription Warmup

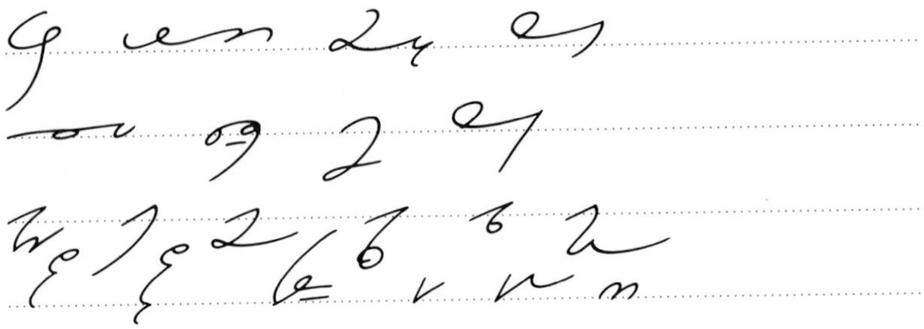

10
20
30
41

Transcription Speed Building

12
20
30
41
50
60
72
80
82

Transcription Quiz

Transcribe the following letter, adding the appropriate punctuation to your transcript.

[97]

Mailable Letter Production

1
Hopewell Heating Systems
18 Washington Avenue
Trenton, NJ 08611

1 past
2 com·fort·able
3 weath·er

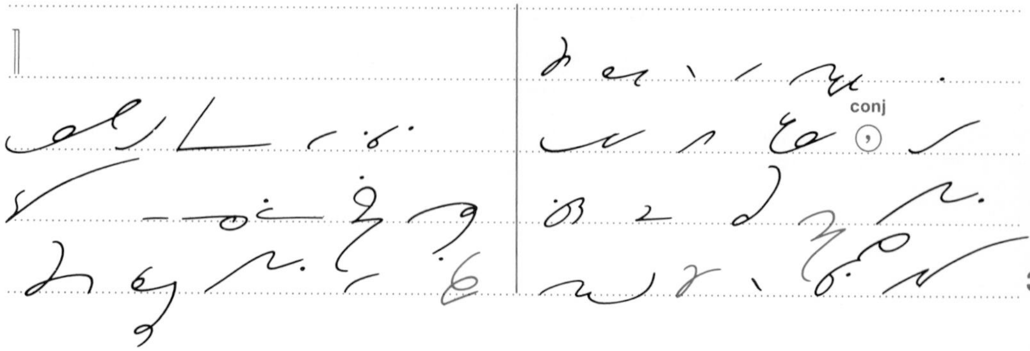

1 2 3

47

Building Professional Skills

Punctuation Checkup

apostrophe, contraction

An apostrophe is used to indicate that letters have been left out of the second part of a compound word in order to form a contraction.

it is it's could not couldn't were not weren't

Communication Checkup

correspondence ■ correspondents

correspondence Written communications.

Will you handle some of my routine correspondence?
It takes less time to dictate correspondence.

correspondents People who correspond.

I have several interesting articles from newspaper correspondents.
Our company has several correspondents in Europe.

2
Mr. Scott Todd
1516 Pine Street
Buffalo, NY 14211

3
Mr. and Mrs.
John Barnes
200 Plant Street
Raleigh, NC 27611

4 fu•el
5 ad•vise
6 touch

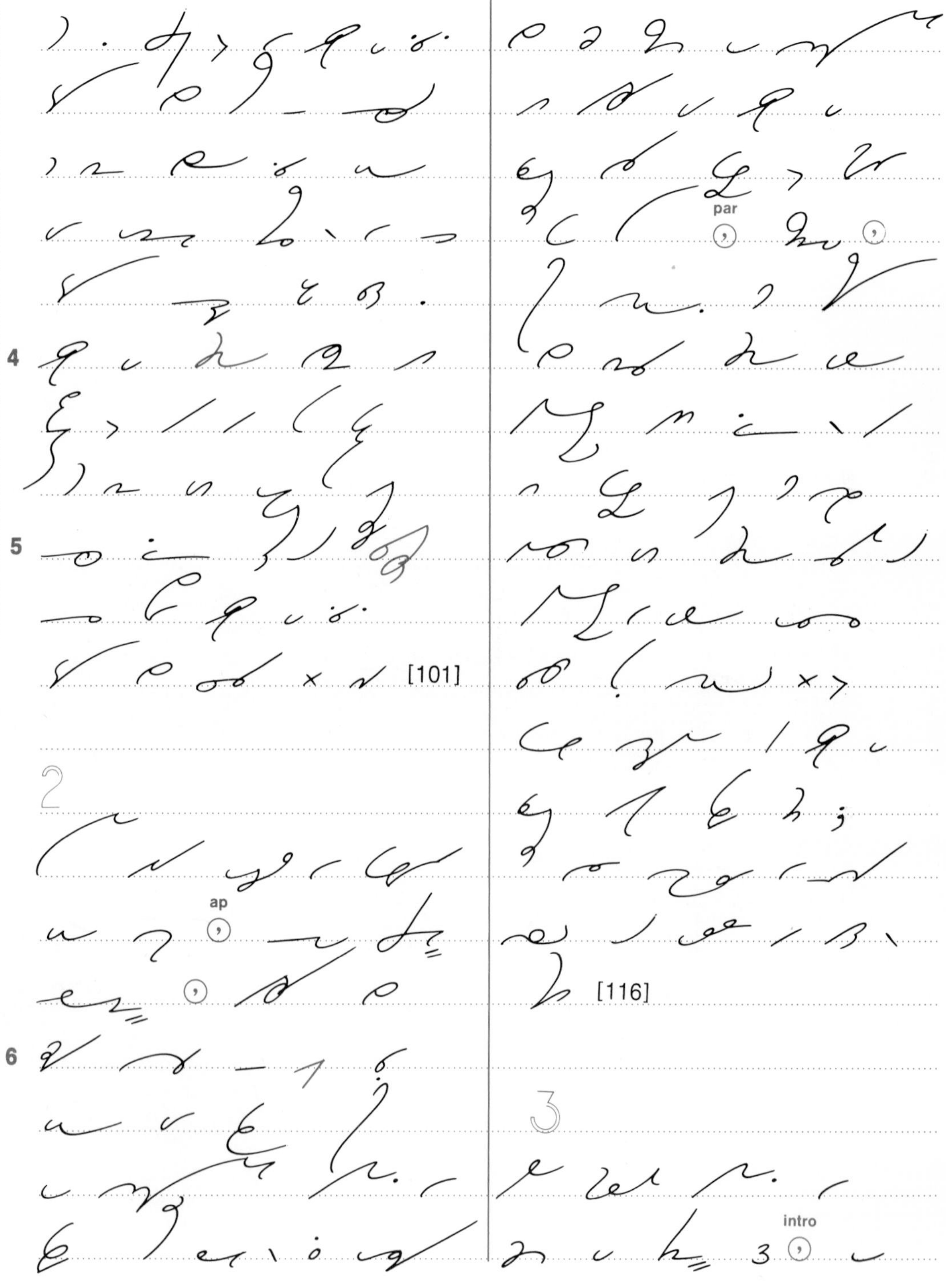

8 ad·min·is·tra·tive
9 dig·it
10 be·lieve

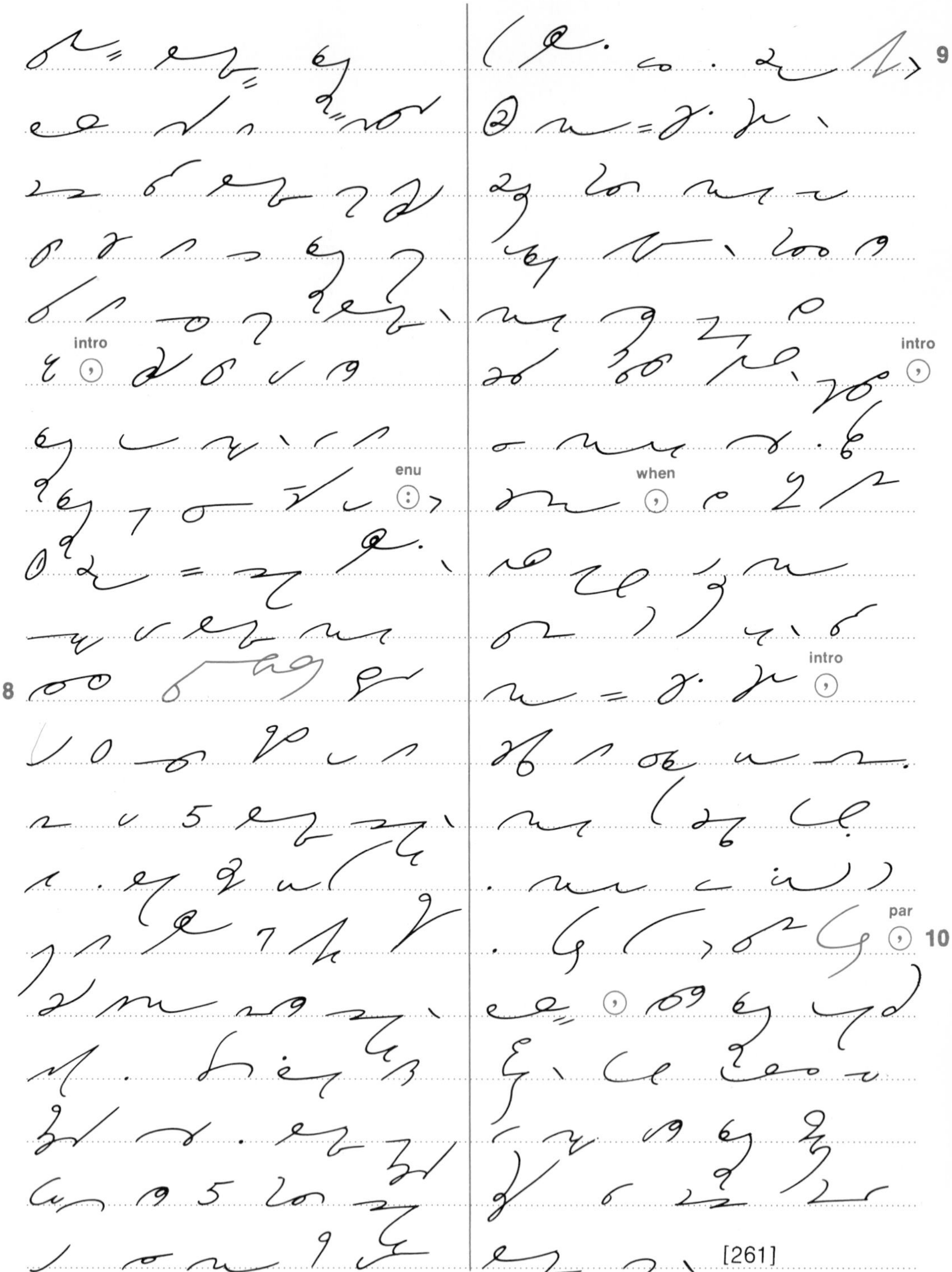

4

To: Maria Perez, Word Processing Center
From: Sara Leary, Director of Marketing
Subject: Monthly Sales Report

7 big·gest
8 rolls
9 in·stal·la·tion

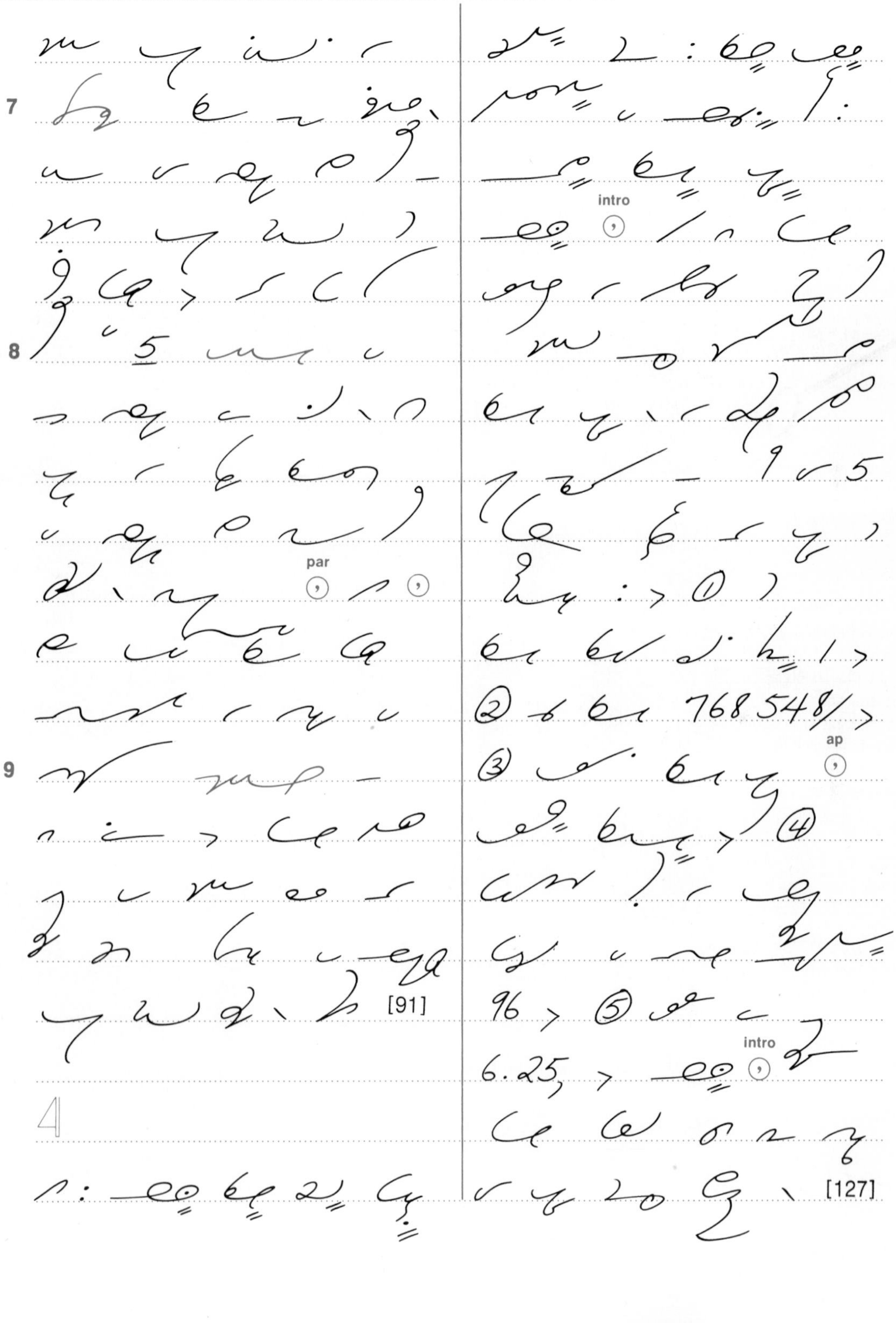

2
To: Purchasing Department
From: Dan Jones
Subject: Problems With Moving Company

3
Roger J. Johnson and Associates
101 East Milwaukee Street
Suite 403
Evansville, IN 47711

4
Ms. Jean Jones
109 West Truman Avenue
Anchorage, AK 99500

5
To: Elaine Olson, Administrative Services
From: Charles Green, Research and Development
Subject: Request For Additional Telephone Services

5 priv·i·lege
6 phi·los·o·phy
7 lib·er·ty

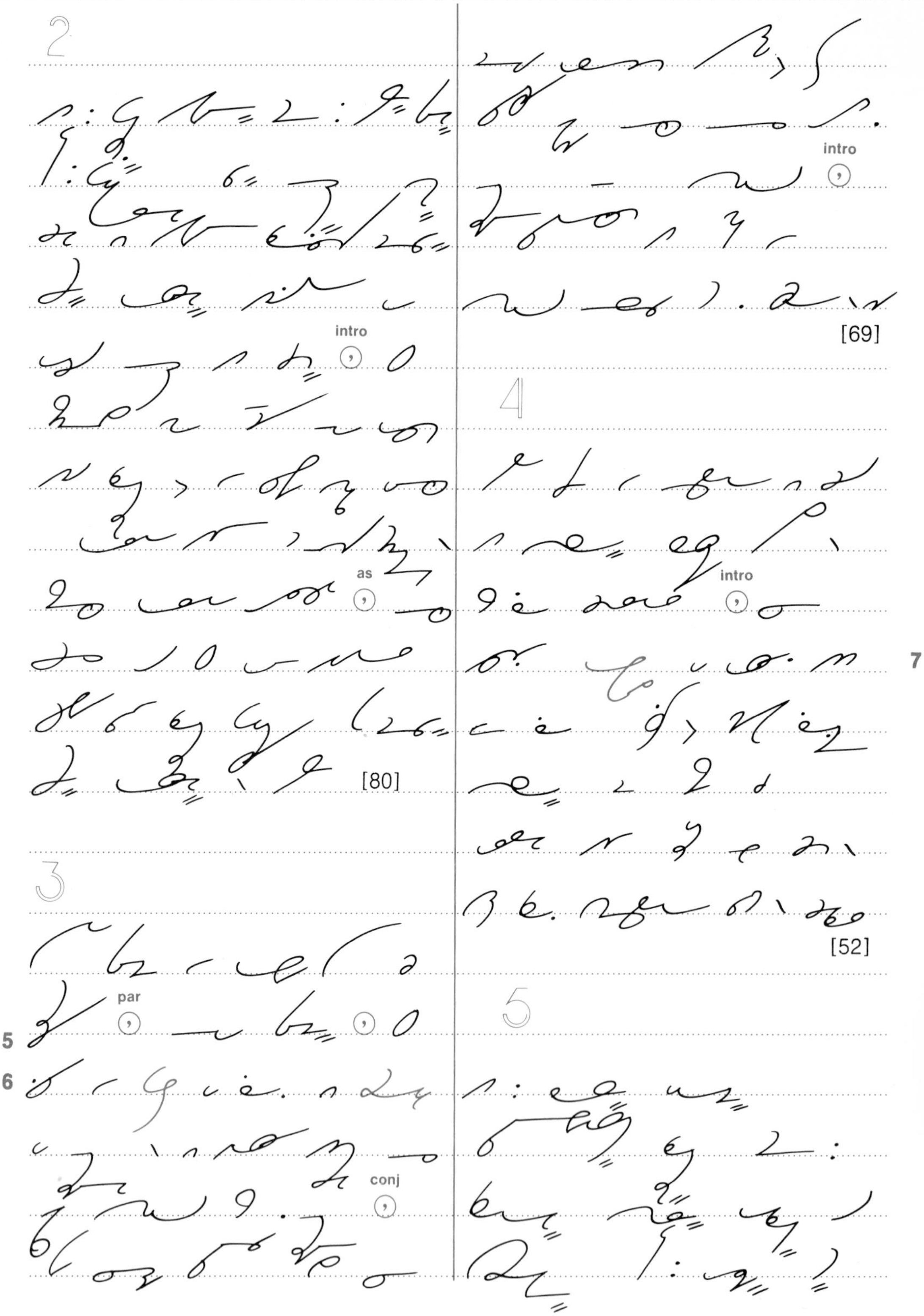

17

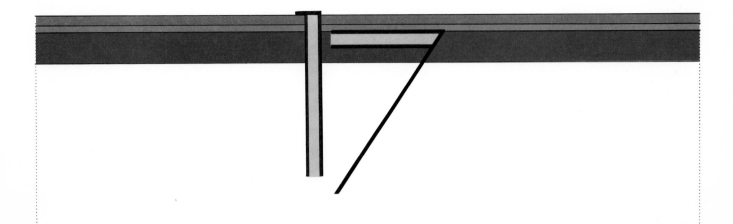

Building Professional Skills

Punctuation Checkup

, if

Introductory phrases beginning with the word *if* are followed by a comma.

If you are early, wait in the lobby.
If it rains, we will stay home.
If the price is too high, don't buy one.

Communication Checkup

adverse ■ averse

adverse — Negative result.

The sale had an adverse effect on profits.
The advertisement produced adverse results.

averse — Opposed to something.

Mary is not averse to Charles' candidacy.
I am not averse to having a party.

Building Transcription Skill

Transcription Warmup

 10

Transcription Quiz

Transcribe the following letter, adding the appropriate punctuation to your transcript.

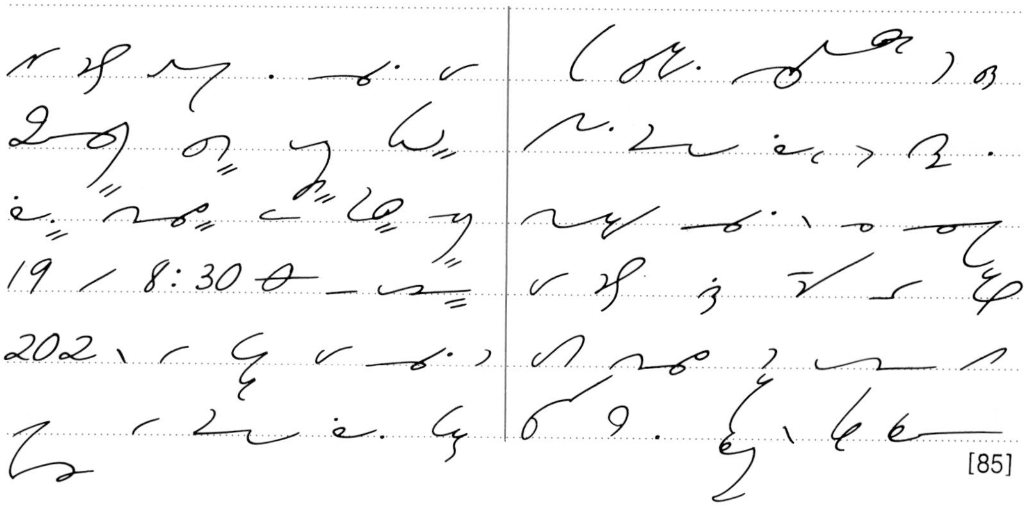

Mailable Letter Production

1
Mr. Douglas Henry
3633 Fairfax Court
St. Louis, MO 63111

1 ar•ti•cle
2 re•ceived
3 prin•ci•ple
4 ar•range•ments

1 2 3 4

20
30
41

Transcription Speed Building

10
18
30
38
45
56
67
78
80

Transcription Quiz

Transcribe the following letter, adding the appropriate punctuation to your transcript.

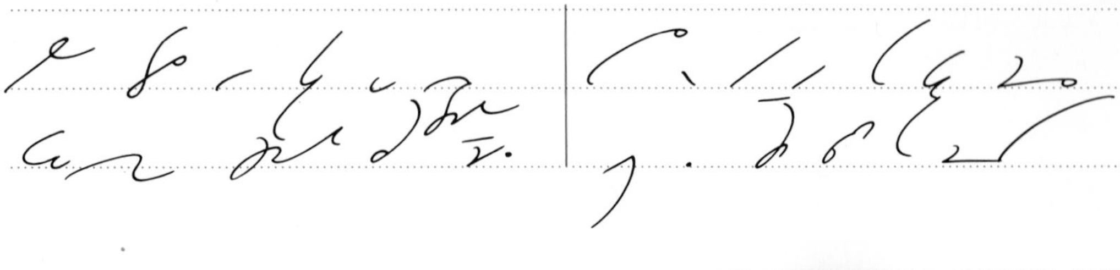

Building Transcription Skill

Transcription Warmup

10
20
32
42

Transcription Speed Building

9
18
29
40
50
60
70
81

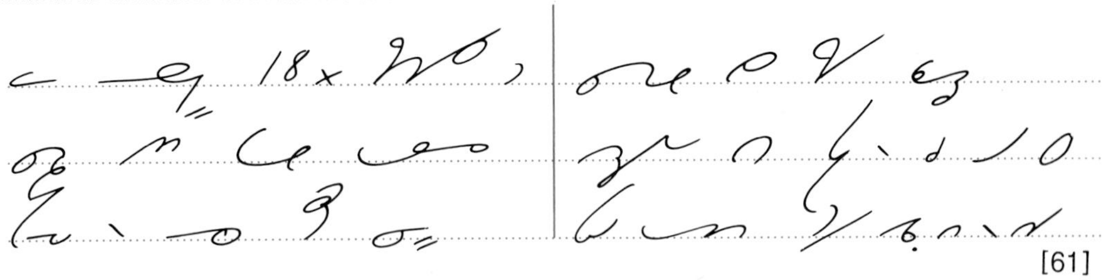

[61]

Mailable Letter Production

1
Ms. Joyce King
521 Home Avenue
Burlington, VT 05401

2
Redford Tree Service
1204 Birch Street
Columbus, OH 43211

1 buy·ing
2 cost
3 against
4 hear
5 any time
6 great

46

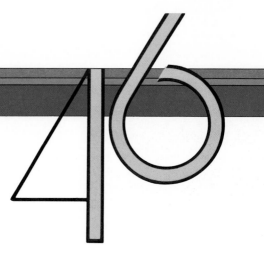

Building Professional Skills

Shorthand for the Professional ■ Phone Calls and Visitors

One of the very valuable uses for the shorthand skill is the recording of information from visitors to the office or people who call on the telephone. We know that people talk several times faster than we can write in longhand. Without shorthand skill, we are forced to ask visitors and callers to repeat information where we fail to make complete notes. Either way, the situation is embarrassing and represents poor practice.

Combining the shorthand skill with good listening habits, we can write down all of the important facts that visitors and telephone callers give us. In this way information is complete, facts are accurate, and commitments may be kept. Moreover, we give every evidence of being competent professionals and create the best possible image for our company.

Communication Checkup

principle ■ principal

principle A rule or generally accepted statement of truth.

The book contains several principles by which to live.
The class is beginning to understand the principles of accounting.

principal Money upon which interest is paid. Also, someone or something that is the leader.

Mrs. Hislip is the principal of the grade school.
New York is one of the principal seaports in the United States.
The accounting students were working problems dealing with principal and interest.

3
Mr. Roger Ames
182 State Street
Madison, WI 53711

7 right
8 cop·ies
9 con·ve·nience
10 di·a·grams

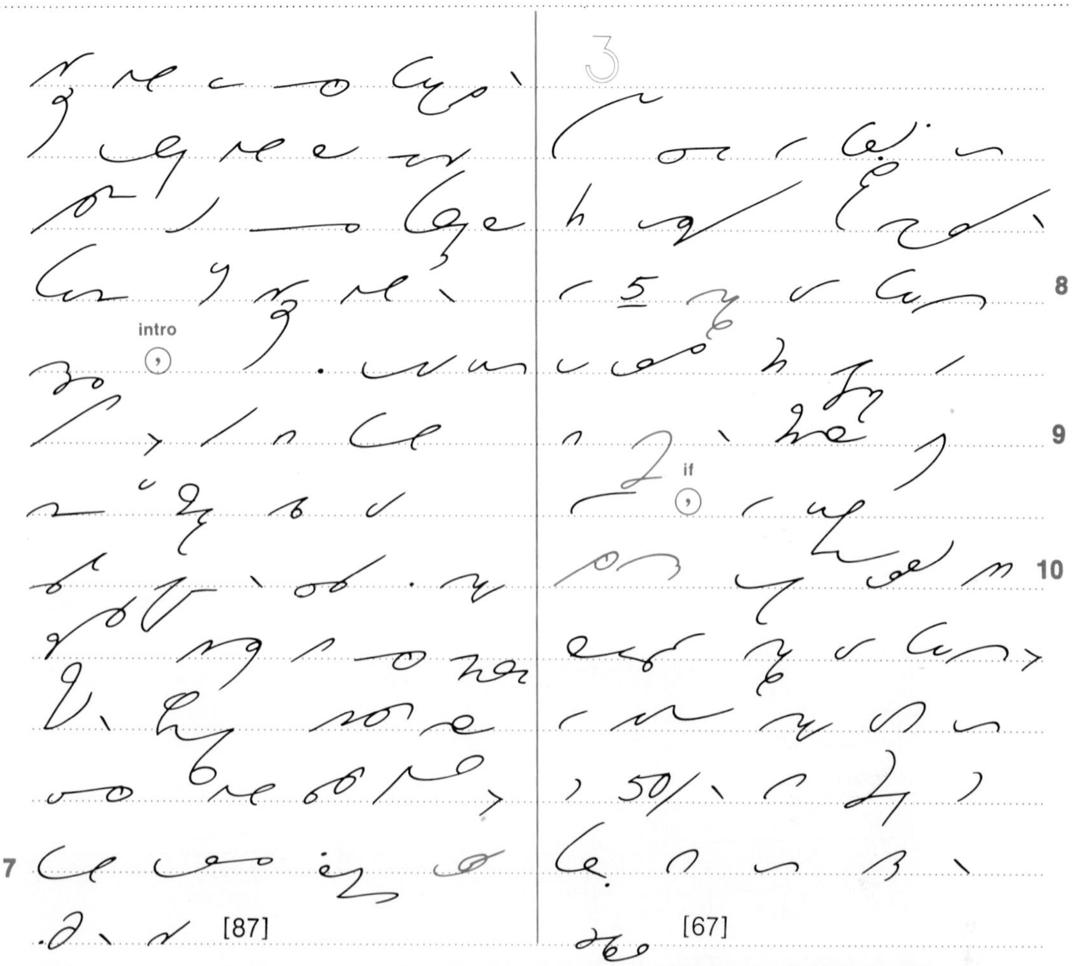

Revisions are often made in a document after it has been typed. If the original document was typed on a word processor and the data stored on magnetic media, it isn't necessary to retype the entire document—only the revisions need to be keyboarded.

4
New Meeting Schedule

12 Transcribe:
7 o'clock
13 pol·i·cies

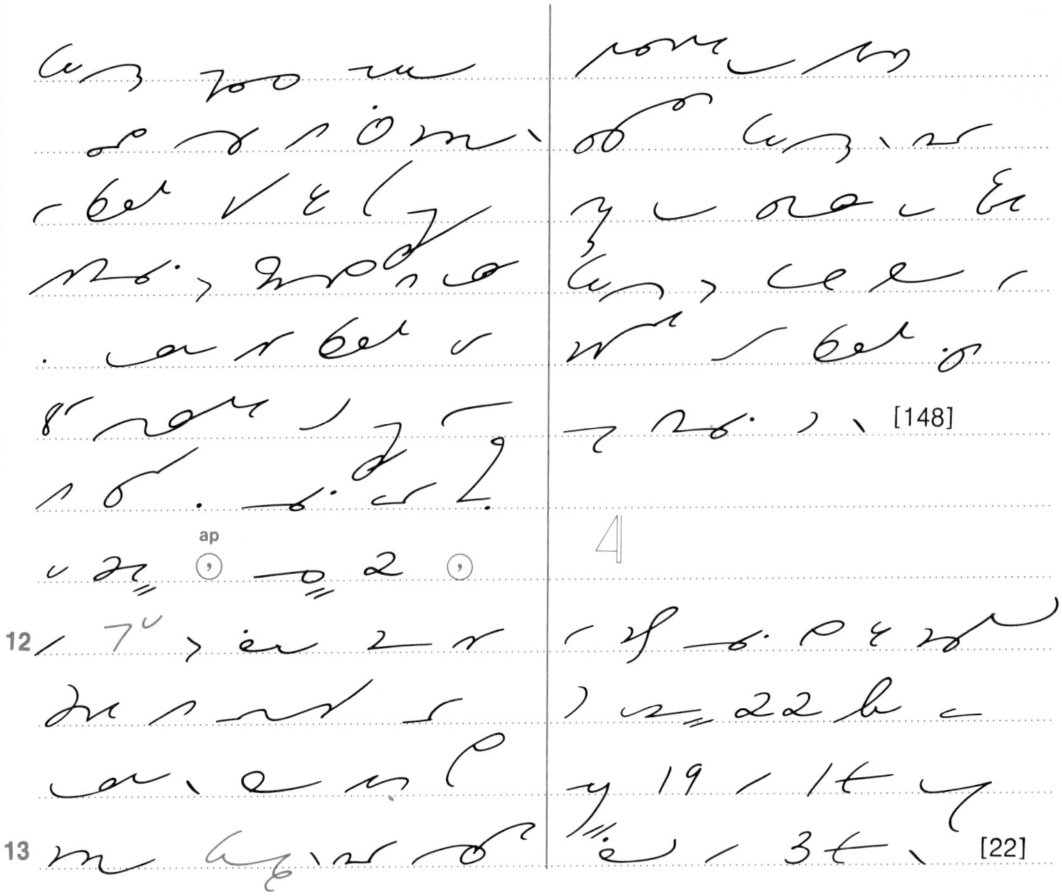

What Makes for Success:

A recent study showed that the people who get job promotions and pay raises are people who:

1 Have a concern for productivity.
2 Take pride in their work.
3 Are dependable.
4 Have a positive attitude.
5 Have the ability to follow instructions.

18

Building Professional Skills

Listening ■ Keep an Open Mind

"I know what you're going to say and I don't want to hear it!" That is a statement that we have all heard. And whenever we hear a statement like this, we know that we have a tough job of communicating ahead of us.

Part of being a good listener is a willingness to hear what other people have to say, a tolerance for ideas that differ from our own. We cannot learn without being exposed to new ideas. Some new ideas we accept and some new ideas we reject, but we must always be willing to listen. A mind is like a book: we learn only when it's open.

Communication Checkup

advice ■ advise

advice — Suggestions given to us by another.

Can you give me advice on which college to attend?
Thank you for the advice, Mary.

advise — To make suggestions to another.

Let me advise you as to what courses to take.
John advised me to stay home.

2
To: Arlene Milton
From: George Day
Subject: Publication of Transportation Costs

3
To: Ann Masters
From: Helen Boyd, Principal
Subject: Meeting With Eighth-Grade Parents

3 qual·i·ties
4 poor
5 ac·cept·able
6 ef·fi·cien·cies
7 wheth·er
8 rights
9 al·ready
10 en·rolled
11 Transcribe: eighth

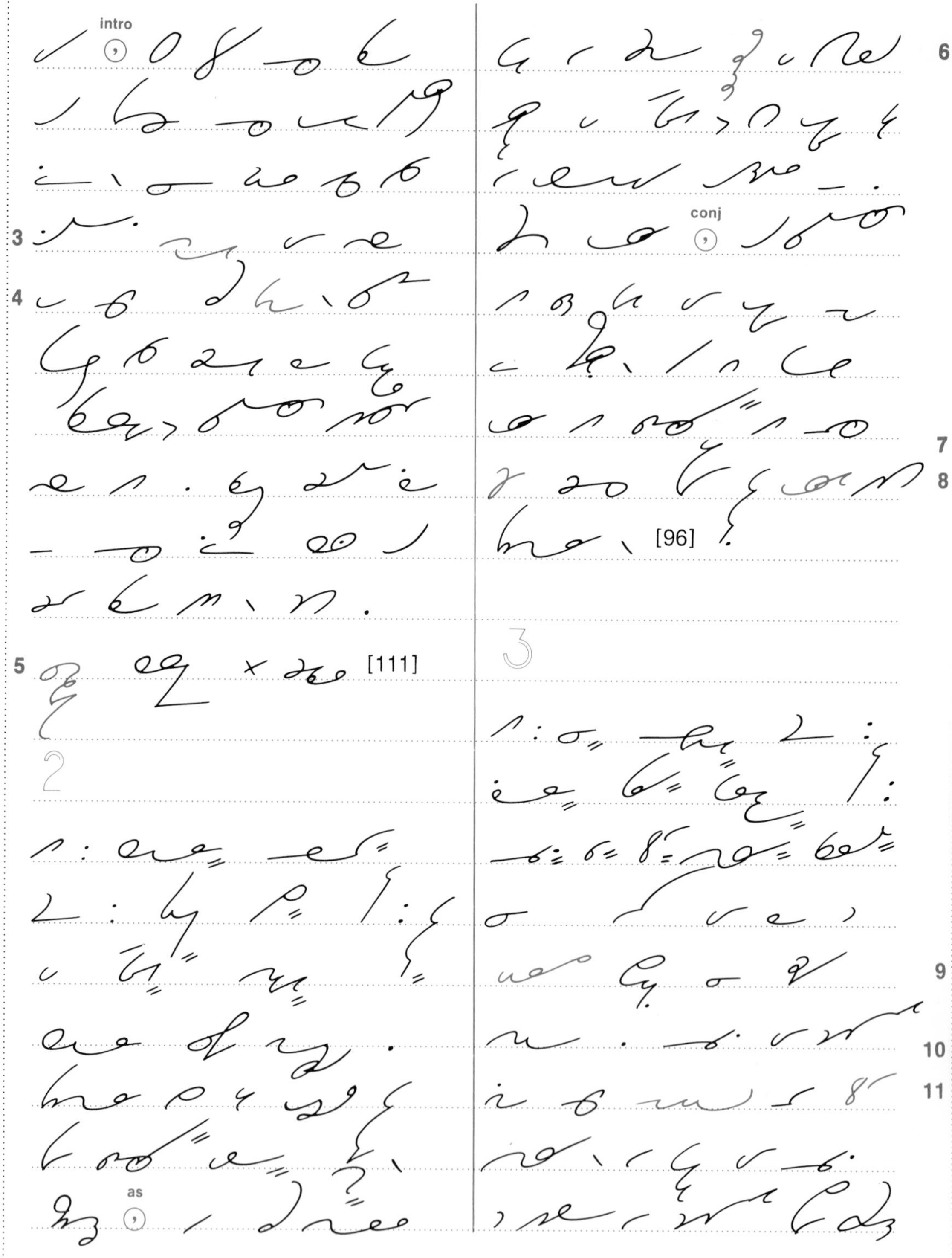

Building Transcription Skill

Transcription Warmup

10 20 31 41

Transcription Speed Building

10 20 30 40 49 60 69 75 81

Transcription Quiz

Transcribe the following letter, adding the appropriate punctuation to your transcript.

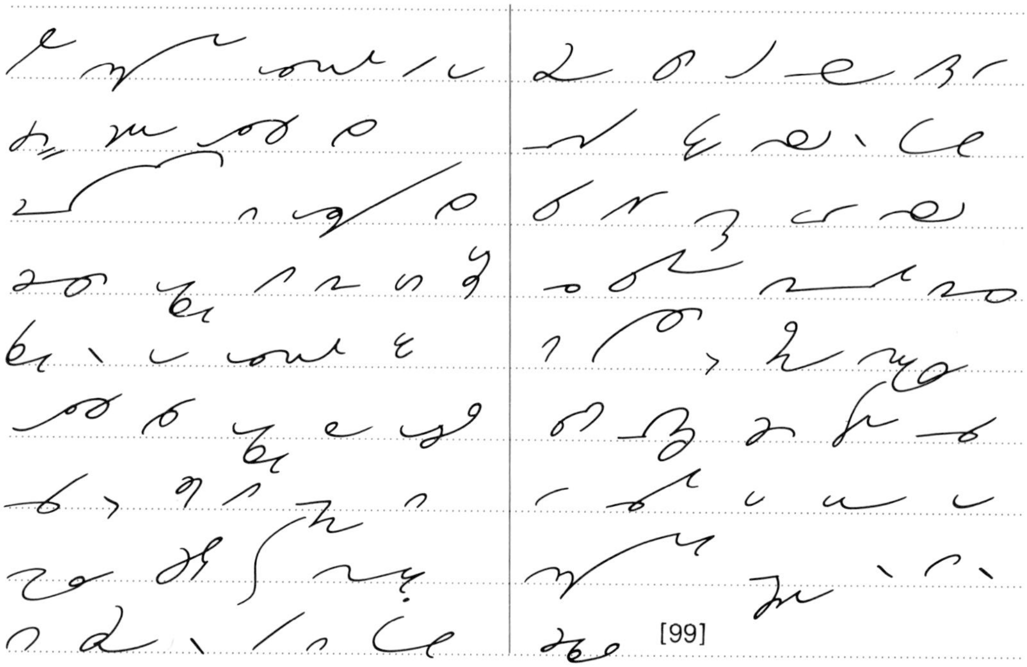

Mailable Letter Production

1
National Tire Center
3340 South Third Avenue
Great Falls, MT 59411

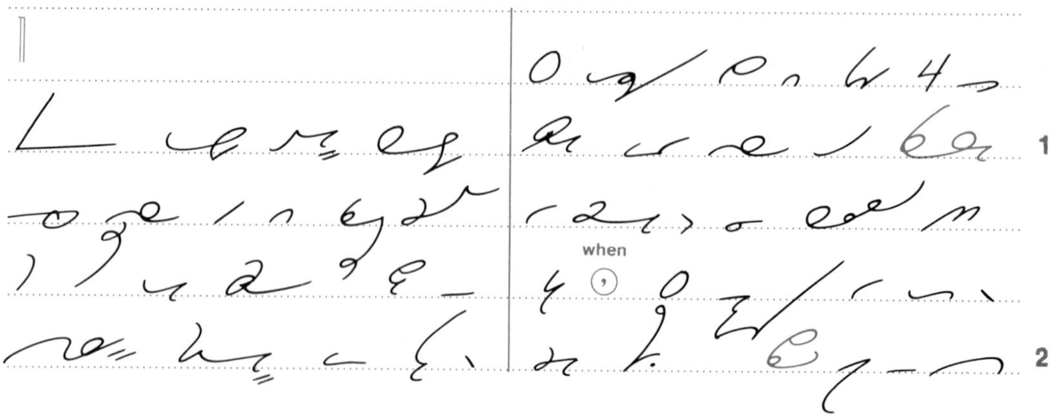

1 bal·ance
2 ap·peared

Transcription Quiz

Transcribe the following letter, adding the appropriate punctuation to your transcript.

[126]

Mailable Letter Production

1
Mr. Edward Harris
17 West Webster Place
Richmond, VA 23211

1 rea·son
2 sup·pli·ers

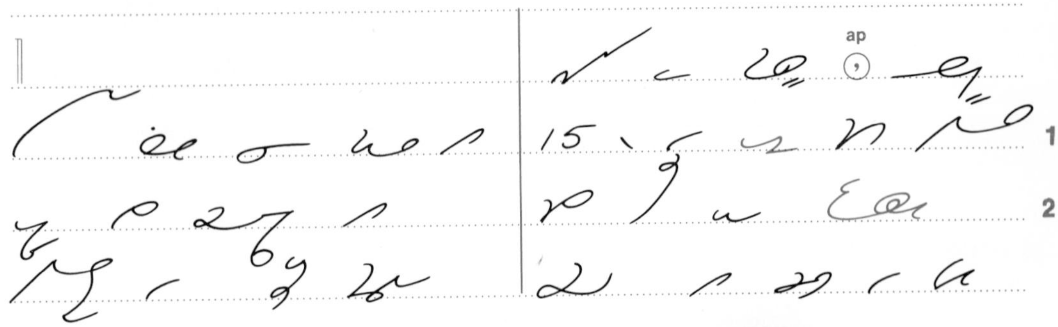

Building Transcription Skill

Transcription Warmup

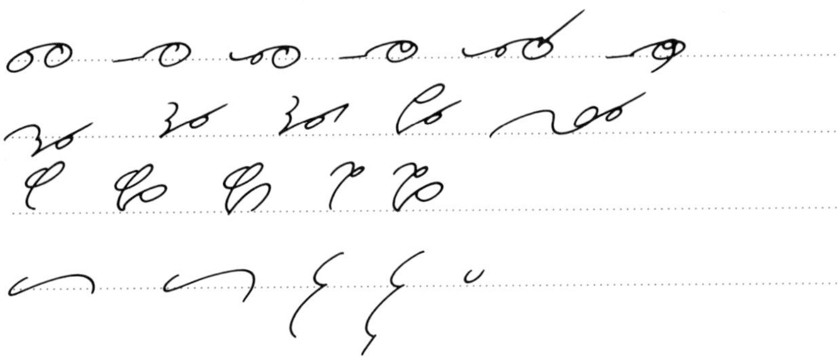

10
21
32
43

Transcription Speed Building

9
21
30
40
50
60
70
80

2

Mr. Charles Burn
1854 Fifth Avenue
New York, NY 10020

3 nec·es·sary
4 ma·jor·i·ty
5 ad·vice
6 neigh·bor·hood
7 fa·cil·i·ties
8 per·son·al

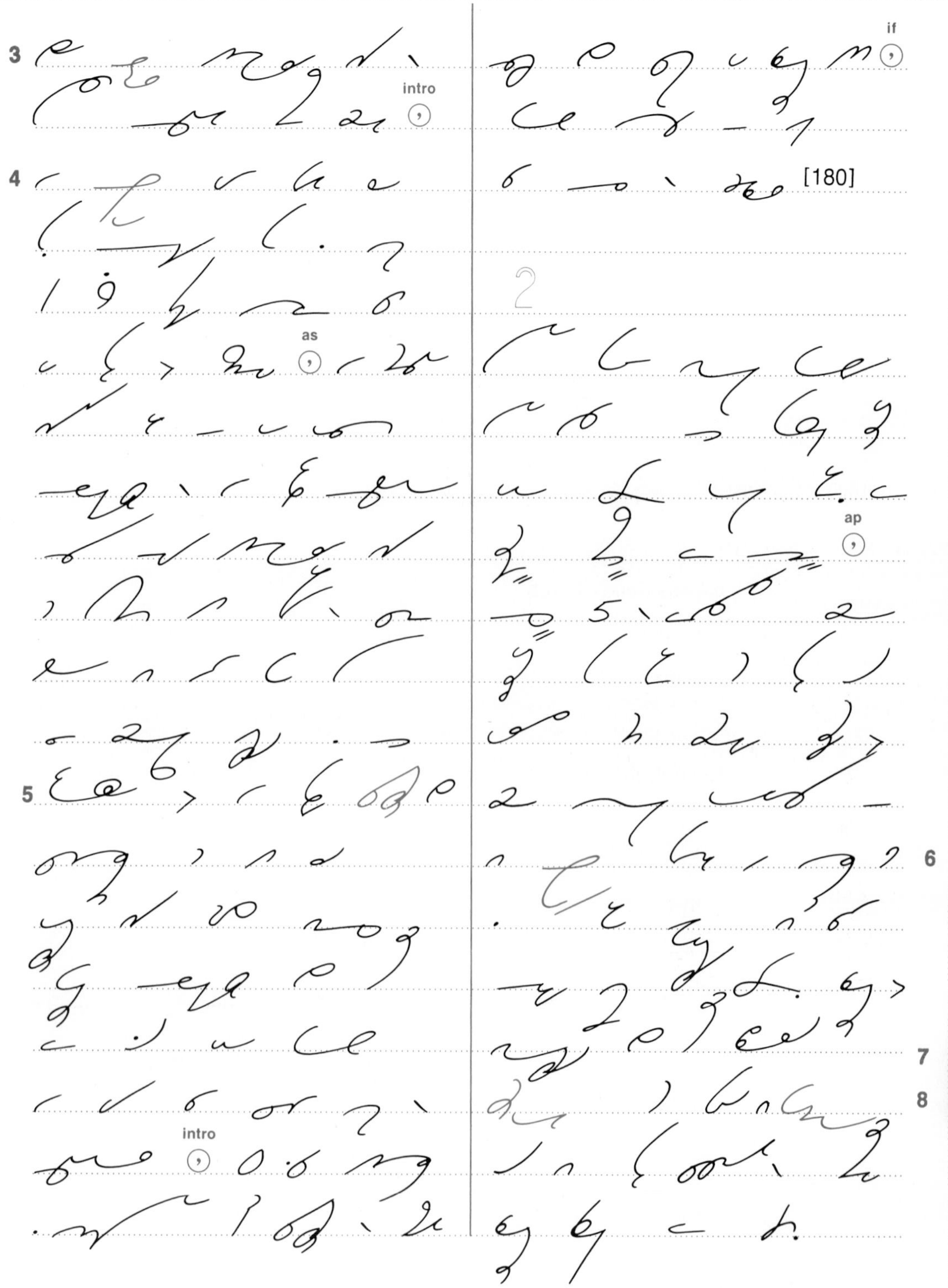

45

Building Professional Skills

Number Usage Checkup

expressions of time

Use figures in expressing time with *o'clock, a.m.,* and *p.m.*

They arrived at 9 oclock.
The meeting began at 8 a.m.
The show will start at 9 p.m.

Exception: In invitations and other formal writings, spell out time with o'clock. When time is expressed without o'clock, a.m., or p.m., spell the time.

Our program will begin promptly at four.

Communication Checkup

all ready ■ already

all ready Everyone in a state of readiness.

The members are all ready for the meeting to begin.
The copies of the report are all ready for distribution.

already Now.

Our guests have already arrived.
The snow has already begun to accumulate.

3
Mr. George Gates
Miami Central Bank
1212 Tampa Boulevard
Miami, FL 33311

9 se·cu·ri·ty
10 re·ceipts
11 here
12 prof·it·able

[158]

[79]

4
Personal Notes

9 re·ceiv·ing

9

par

[133]

4

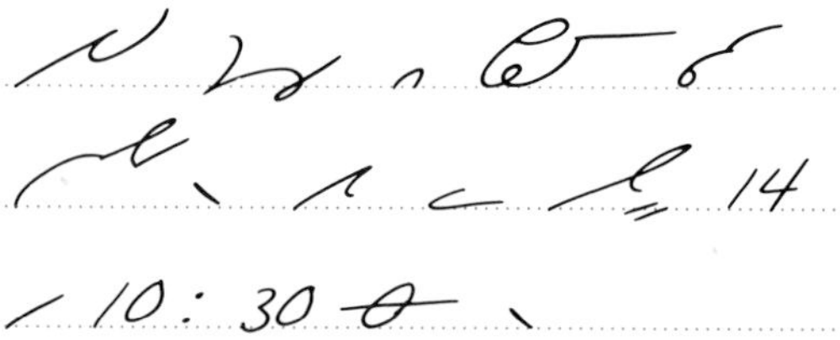

Secretaries often use shorthand when composing responses to mail.

19

Building Professional Skills

Punctuation Checkup

, as

Introductory phrases that begin with the word *as* are followed by a comma.

As you know, the game was delayed.
As you can see, it is raining.
As I said before, finish by 5 p.m.

Communication Checkup

may be ■ maybe

may be — Indicates possibility.

Today may be nice after all.
John may be late for class.

maybe — Indicates doubt.

We will go tomorrow, maybe.
Maybe you didn't hear me right.

2
Ms. Carol Marvin,
Personnel Director
Olson Corporation
915 Mission Drive
Tucson, AZ 85300

3
Mr. Roy Webb
1727 Porter Avenue
Bloomington, IN 47401

3 chair·per·son
4 greater
5 pledge
6 co·op·er·ate
7 ar·ti·cle
8 ac·cept

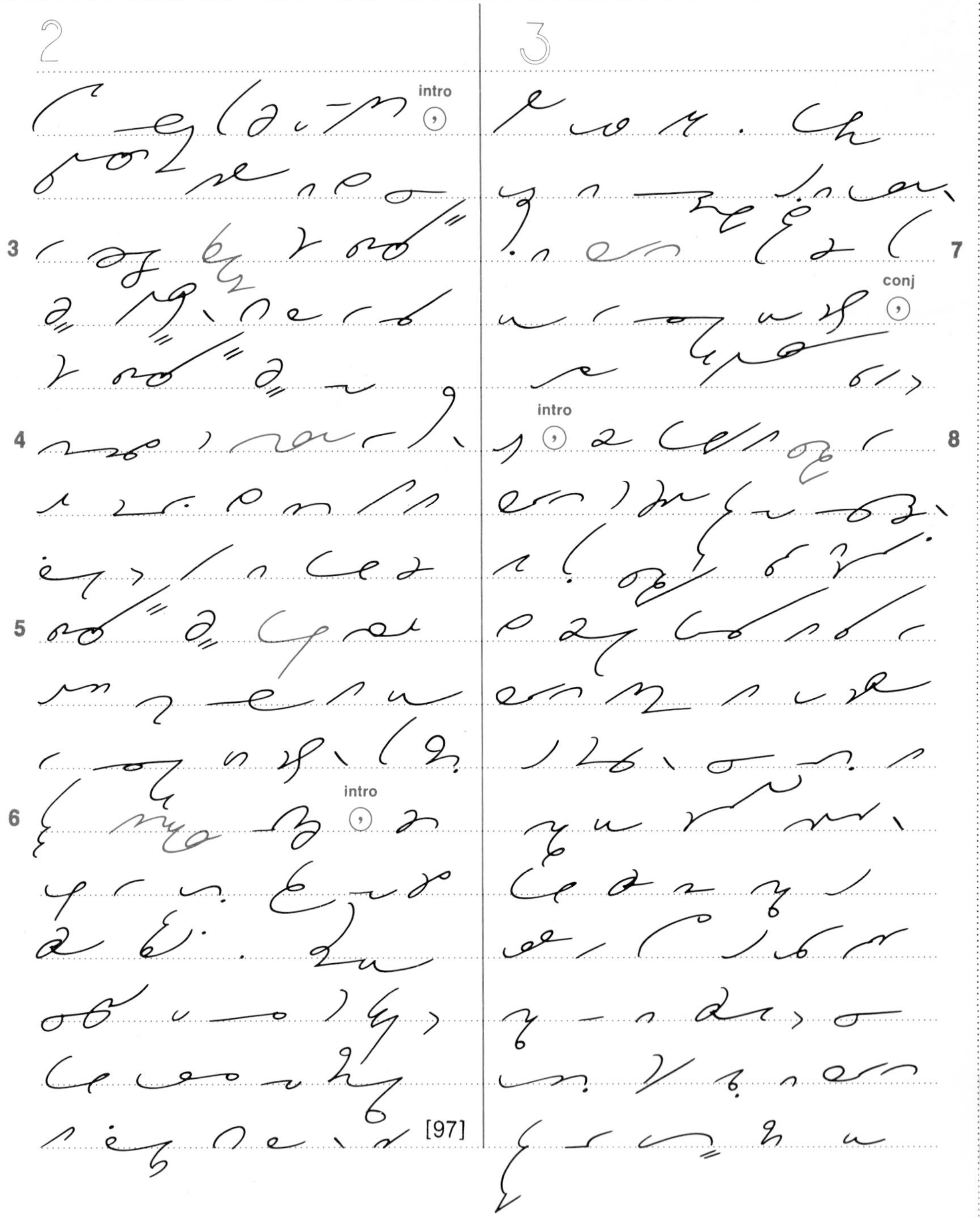

Building Transcription Skill

Transcription Warmup

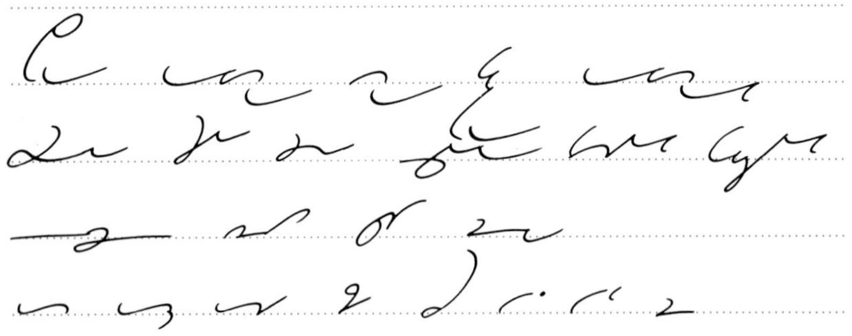

10 20 30 40

Transcription Speed Building

10 20 30 42 50 58 66 74 83

Transcription Quiz

Transcribe the following letter, adding the appropriate punctuation to your transcript.

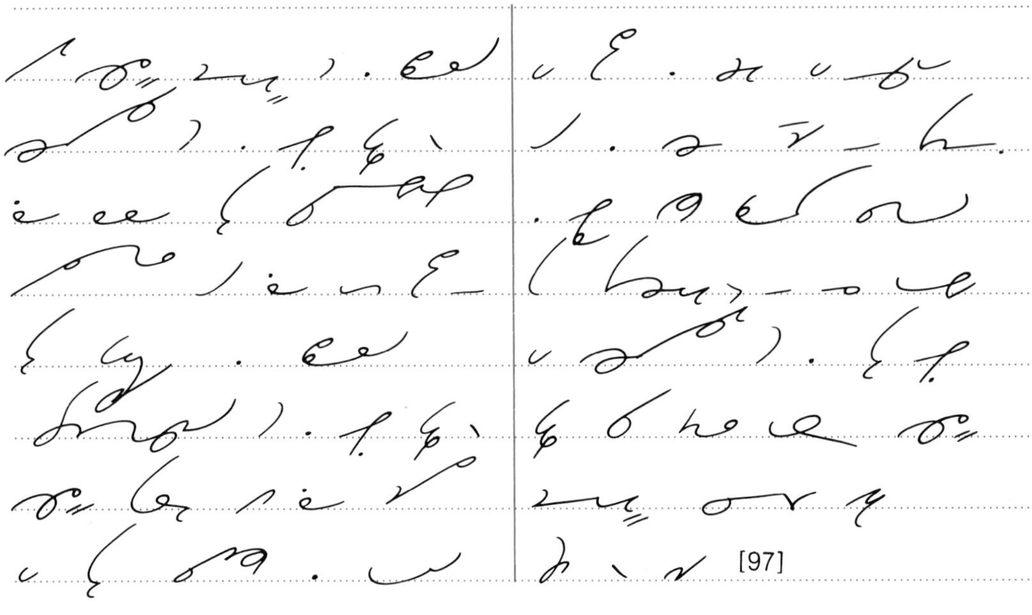

Mailable Letter Production

1
Mr. Roger Day
Post Office Box 1444
Newport, RI 02840

1 ref·er·ence
2 re·ply·ing

1

2

Transcription Quiz

Transcribe the following letter, adding the appropriate punctuation to your transcript.

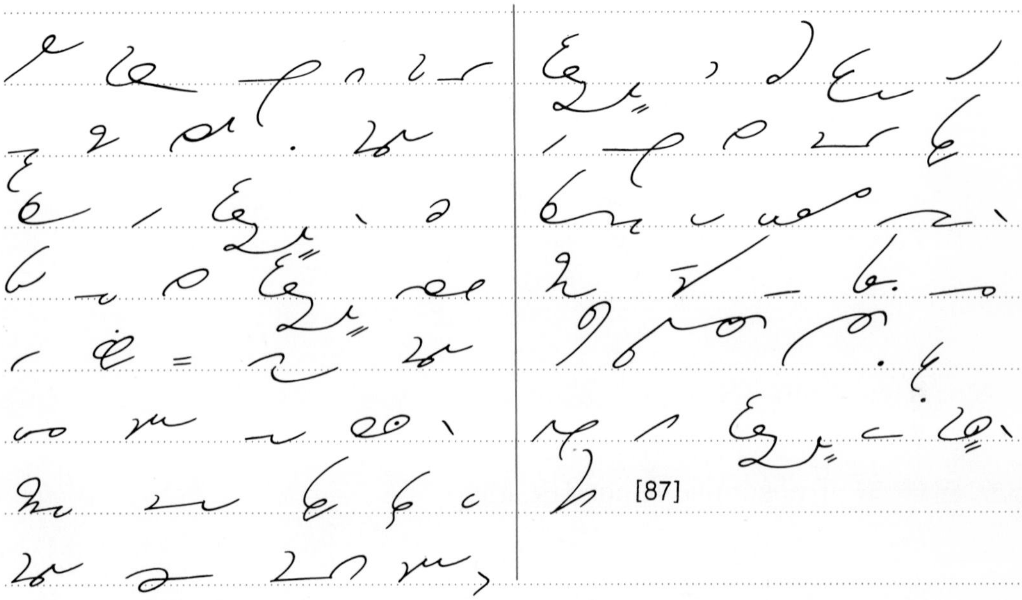

Mailable Letter Production

1
Mrs. Jane Ramsey
3440 Anderson Drive
Derby, CT 06418

1 cli·ents
2 there

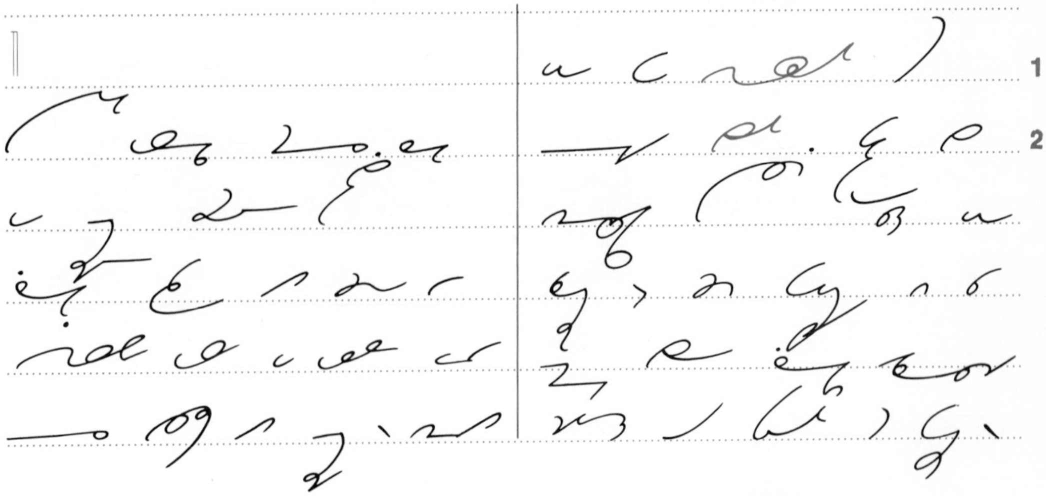

Building Transcription Skill

Transcription Warmup

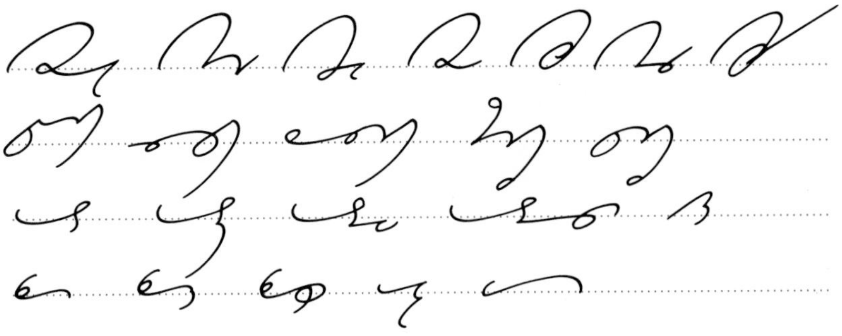

10
20
30
41

Transcription Speed Building

14
24
33
42
52
60
69
80

2
Mr. John Baker
718 Broadview
Boulevard
Winston-Salem, NC
27100

3
Ms. Cordova
Richmond Investment
Company
8080 Mall Drive
Roanoke, VA 24011

3 ad•vise
4 hear
5 in•quir•ing
6 as•sets
7 owe
8 then

3
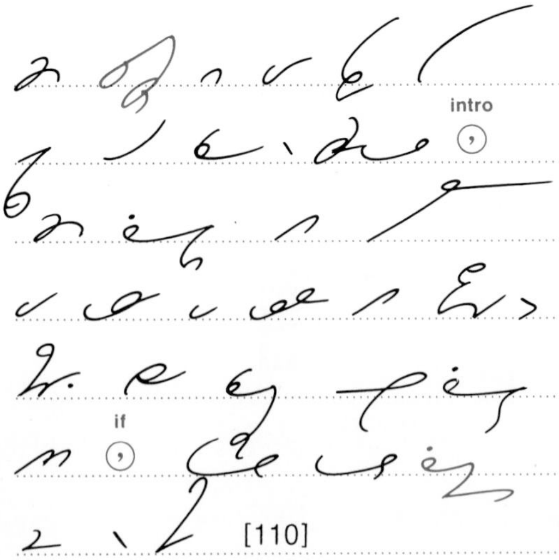

2

5

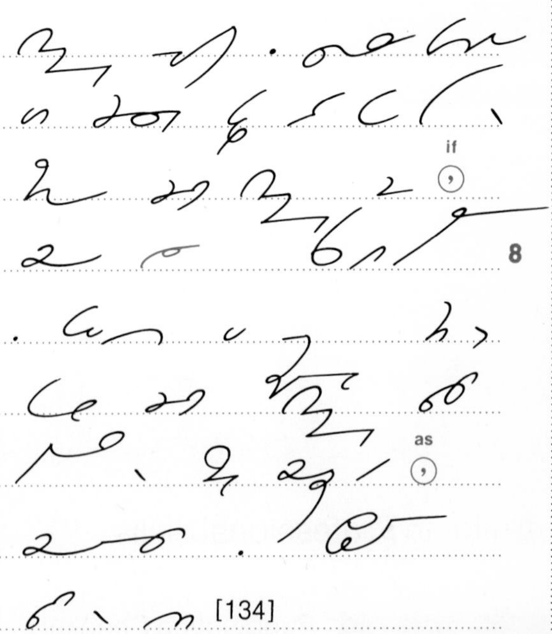

3

44

Building Professional Skills

Punctuation Checkup

period ■ courteous request

Sometimes a request is stated in the form of a question so that it will sound more tactful and less harsh. Such courteous requests are followed by a period rather than a question mark, because they really are not questions for which the writer will accept a variety of answers.

Will you please arrive on time.
May I have your check by the end of the week.
May our meeting now come to order.

Communication Checkup

adding -ly to words

Adding *ly* to words already ending in *l* results in a double *l*.

nearly	sincerely	finally
fairly	really	totally
equally	annually	visually

20

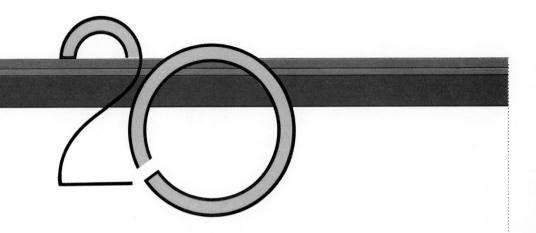

Building Professional Skills

Shorthand ■ "To Do" Lists

Many people think of shorthand as having only one use—that is, for a secretary taking dictation of letters from an executive. In reality, shorthand has many valuable uses both on the job and in one's personal life. Instructions about projects that need to be done, shopping lists, lists of appointments, and other personal reminders can all be easily written in shorthand.

A famous health instructor recently coined the slogan, "Use it or lose it" to encourage people to exercise in order to keep their bodies strong and healthy. That same phrase can be applied to your knowledge of shorthand. In order to really learn shorthand, you must write it all the time. Once you have acquired the habit of using shorthand for all your personal notes, you will become so proficient in its use that you will wish you never had to write longhand again!

Here's an example of a personal "To Do" list:

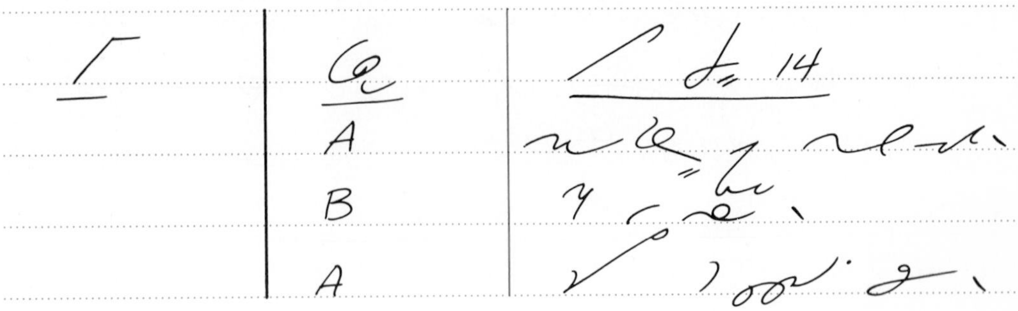

4
Eastern Telephone Company
1732 Fifth Avenue
Springfield, MA 01105

5
To Do List

8 in·ex·pen·sive
9 cop·ies
10 adopt
11 their
12 wheth·er
13 agen·cy

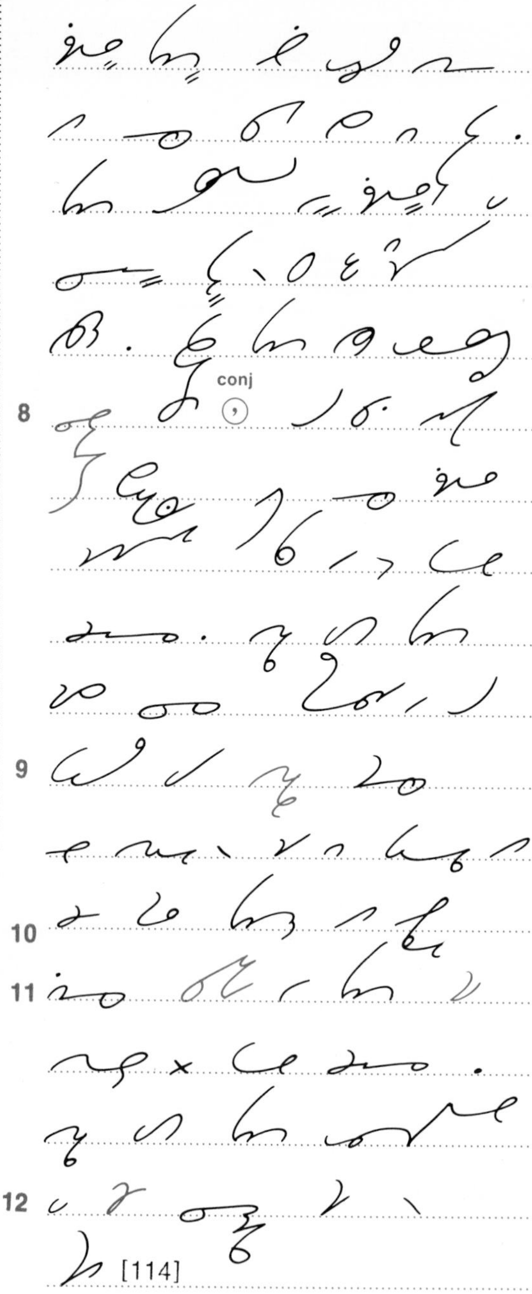

4

5

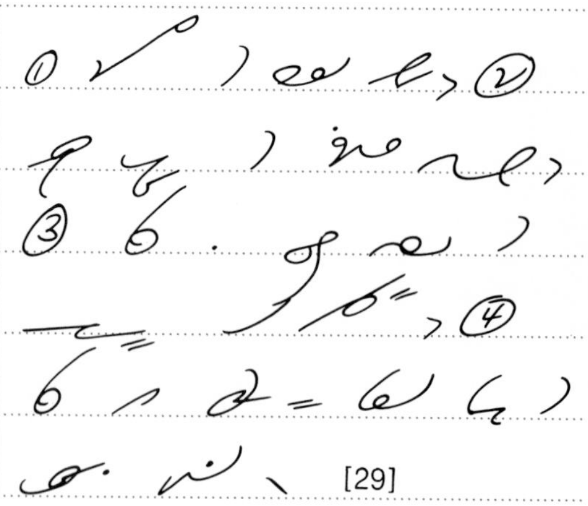

Communication Checkup

whether ■ weather

whether — Meaning "if."

Complete the report whether you feel like it or not.
I do not know whether John or Sue will make the presentation.

weather — Atmospheric conditions such as rain or sunshine.

Today the weather is cloudy.
I will listen to the weather report at 6 p.m.

Building Transcription Skill

Transcription Warmup

10
19
30
40

Transcription Speed Building

11
20
32
42
50
61
70
81

2
Ms. Sara Wade
1221 State Street
Erie, PA 16511

3
Jane Simmon
Publishing Company
1440 Millroad
Los Angeles, CA 90011

1 ma•jor
2 ad•vis•er
3 com•mit•tee
4 here
5 per•son•al
6 en•roll
7 great

1

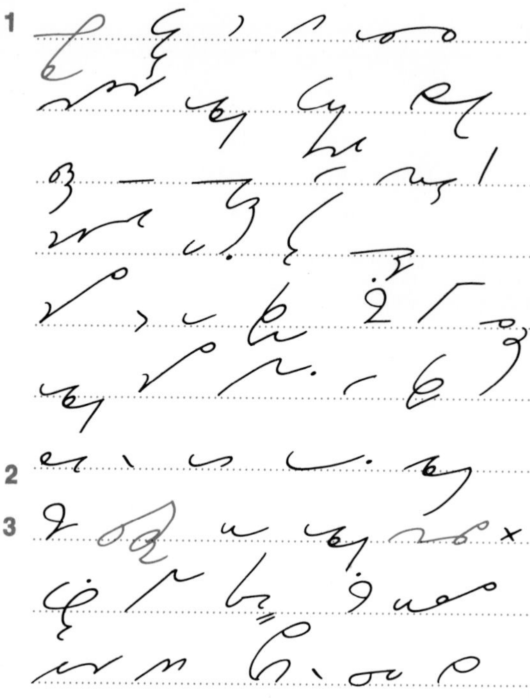

2

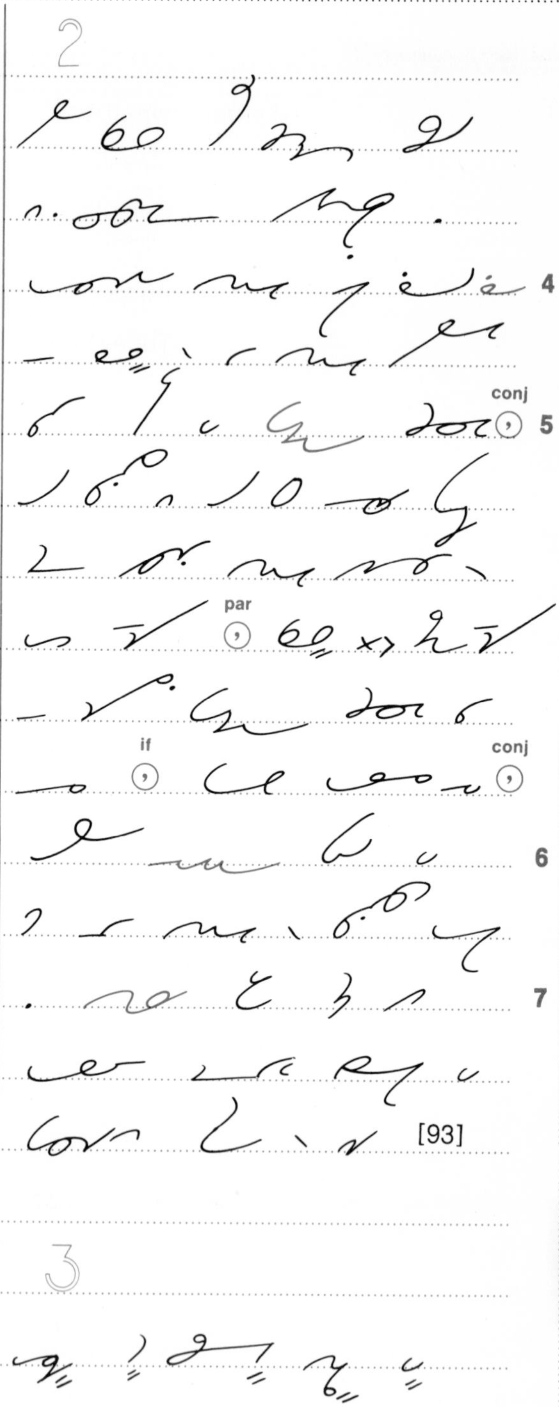

Transcription Quiz

Transcribe the following letter, adding the appropriate punctuation to your transcript.

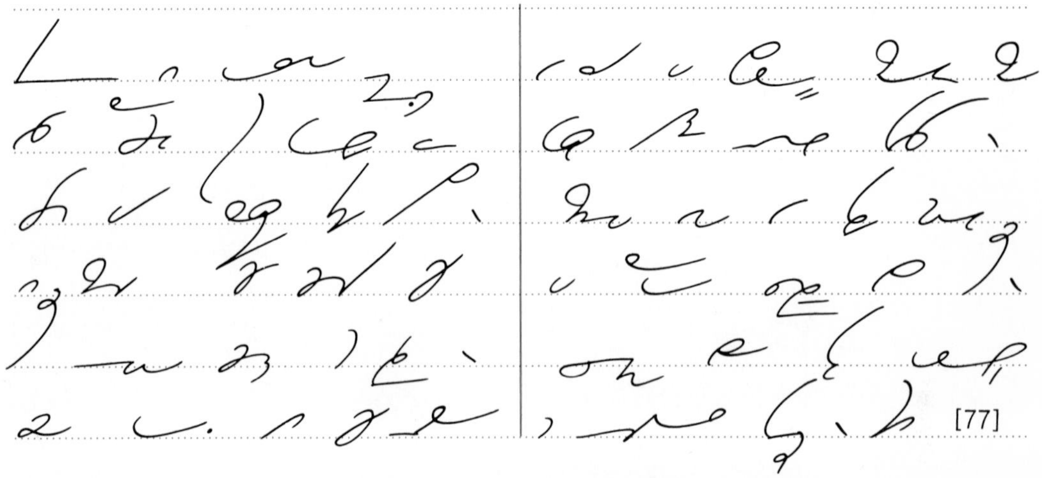

[77]

Mailable Letter Production

1
Midwestern National Bank
20 Michigan Avenue
Chicago, IL 60611

1 **Chi·ca·go**
2 **in·di·vid·u·als**
3 **some·time**

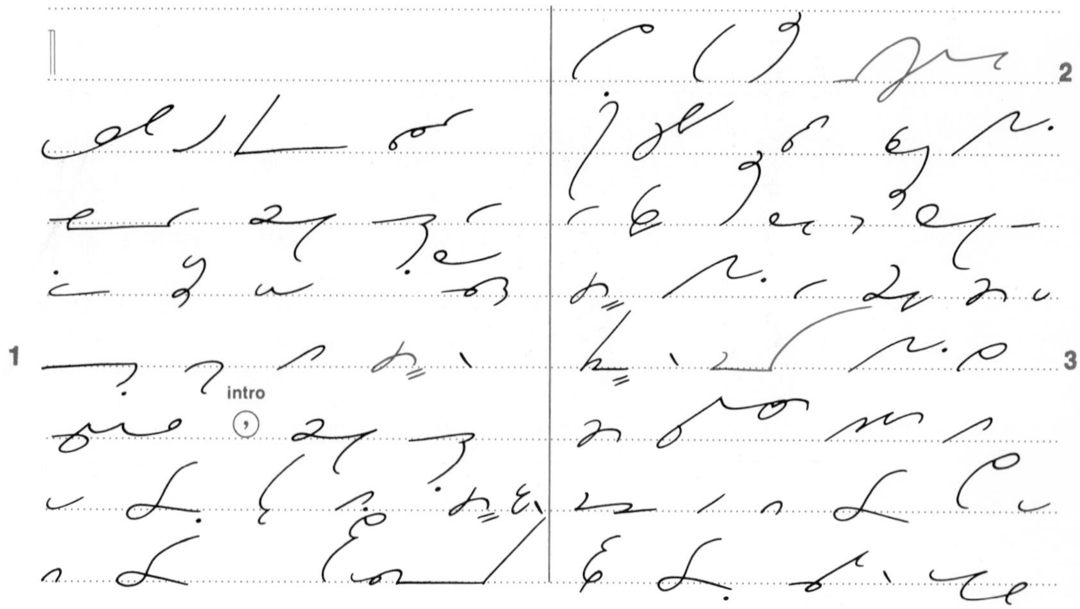

Transcription Quiz

Transcribe the following letter, adding the appropriate punctuation to your transcript.

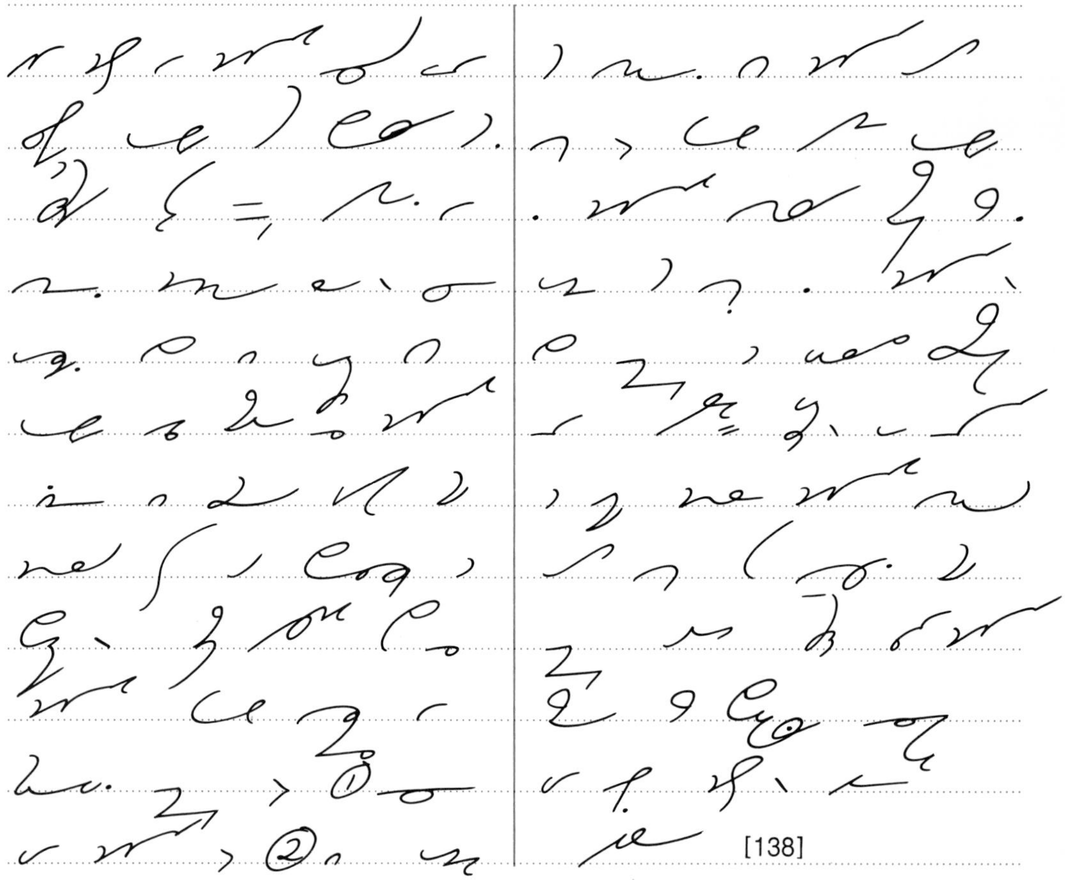

Mailable Letter Production

1
Dr. Julian Hess
Central Business
College
1719 Main Street
Bismarck, ND 58501

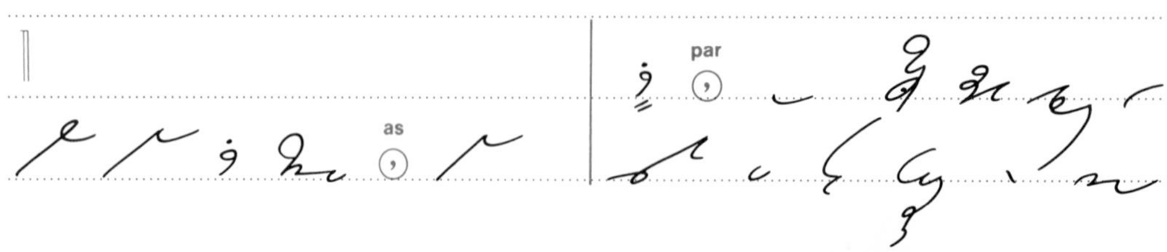

2
Mrs. Claire Phillips
Phillips Real Estate
4027 Beloit Road
Milwaukee, WI 53211

3
Mr. Dean James
612 Sherman Avenue
San Francisco, CA
94111

4 write
5 some time
6 wheth·er
7 an·nu·al

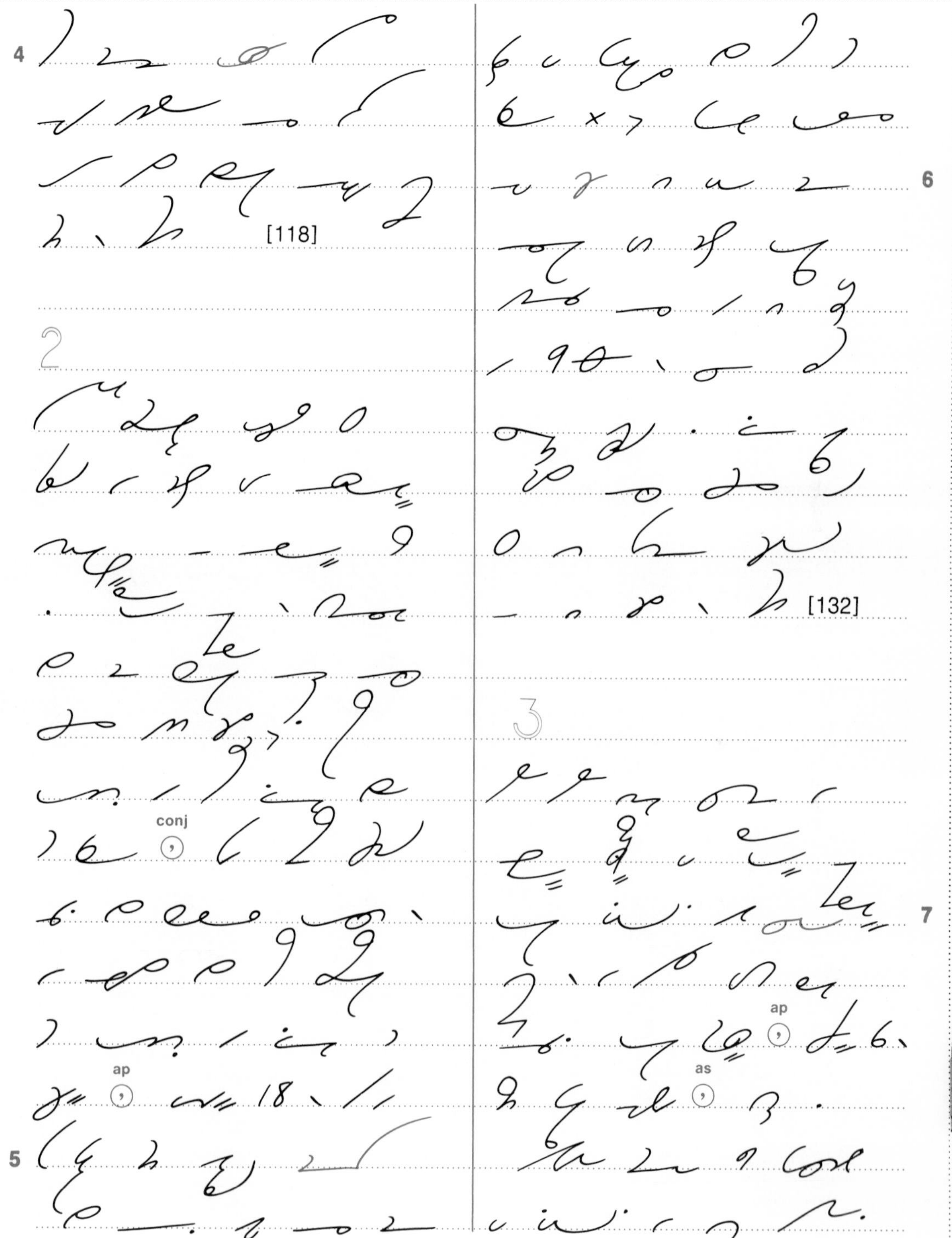

Building Transcription Skill

Transcription Warmup

10
20
30
40

Transcription Speed Building

10
23
30
40
48
56
66
75
81

[118]

4

To Do List For The Boss

8 bro·chure
9 ses·sions
10 ban·quet

8

9

10

if

[36]

Most libraries store documents—even whole newspapers—on microforms. A secretary may take notes from the documents projected on a reader.

43

Building Professional Skills

Shorthand for the Professional ■ Confidentiality

The root word of the word *secretary* is *secret.* The suffix *ary* means "one who." Literally then, a secretary is one who keeps secrets. A more practical definition is that a secretary is the executive's closest and most trusted employee. By working so closely with an executive, a secretary naturally learns a lot of information that must be kept confidential. This is one more aspect of office work in which shorthand proves to be valuable.

If the executive has done the proper job of hiring a secretary, there will be no other person on the staff who can be trusted more than the secretary. It is not surprising then, that when an executive wants to dictate a document about which the strictest confidentiality needs to be mainained, the executive will dictate to the private secretary who takes shorthand rather than having a voice recording transcribed by some anonymous person in a stenopool or word processing center.

Communication Checkup

spelling family ■ -ize -ise -yze

Words ending in -ize

recognize realize utilize
organize familiarize apologize

Words ending in -ise

enterprise rise advise
comprise supervise advertise

Words ending in -yze

analyze paralyze

21

Building Professional Skills

Listening for Main Ideas

We must work at the job of listening. There are times when we must do a good job of listening even though the person we are listening to is not doing a good job of communicating. Perhaps the speaker goes off on tangents or presents so much detail as to be boring. Perhaps the speaker is disorganized and hard to follow. Under these circumstances the good listener keeps the point of the message in mind and tries to overlook the extra detail or the poor organization.

When listening to a class lecture, the good listener identifies the major points that the speaker makes and uses them for the main headings when taking notes in outline form. By identifying a speaker's main ideas and keeping them in mind, the listener is less likely to be distracted and more likely to do a better job of listening.

Communication Checkup

guessed ■ guest

guessed — Having made a supposition.

Ron guessed at the answers to two of the test questions.
She guessed that the weather would be cold and wore a coat.

guest — A visitor.

Sue was his guest for dinner.
Will you be my guest at the banquet?

11 ar-ti-cle
12 re·ceiv·ing
13 cost
14 any·thing

11

par

12

13

14

if

[118]

When dictating confidential material, an executive prefers to dictate to a secretary rather than to a machine.

Building Transcription Skill

Transcription Warmup

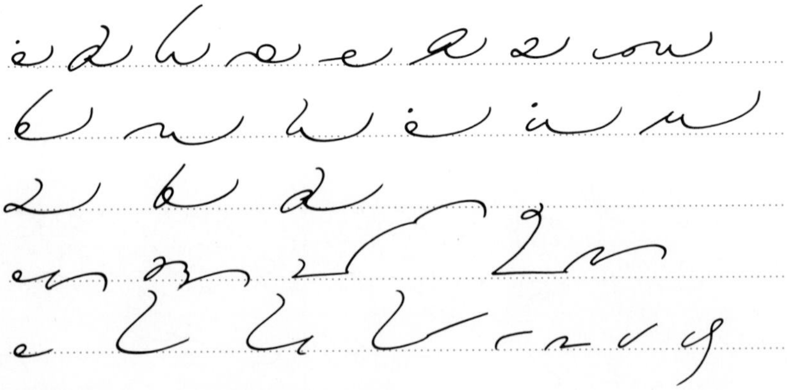

10
20
30
40

Transcription Speed Building

10
18
29
37
49
58
68
75
82

2
Dr. Anna Sharp
1911 14th Street
Lexington, KY 40511

3
Ms. Jean O'Neil, Editor
Today's Office
Magazine
417 Washington Street
Pine Bluff, AR 71600

4 itin·er·ary
5 guest
6 wheth·er
7 here
8 Transcribe: seven
9 ad·vis·er
10 Transcribe: 20

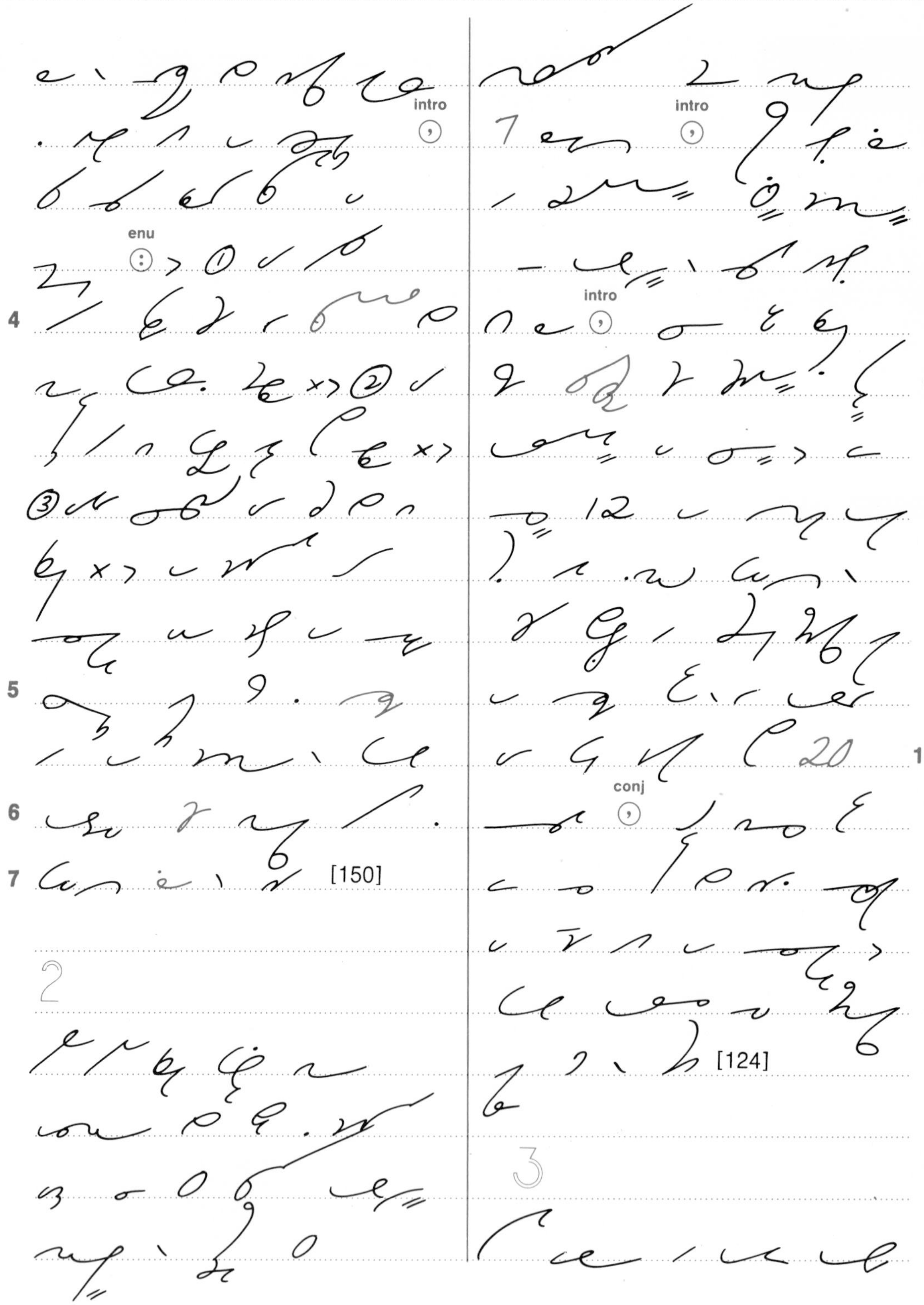

Transcription Quiz

Transcribe the following letter, adding the appropriate punctuation to your transcript.

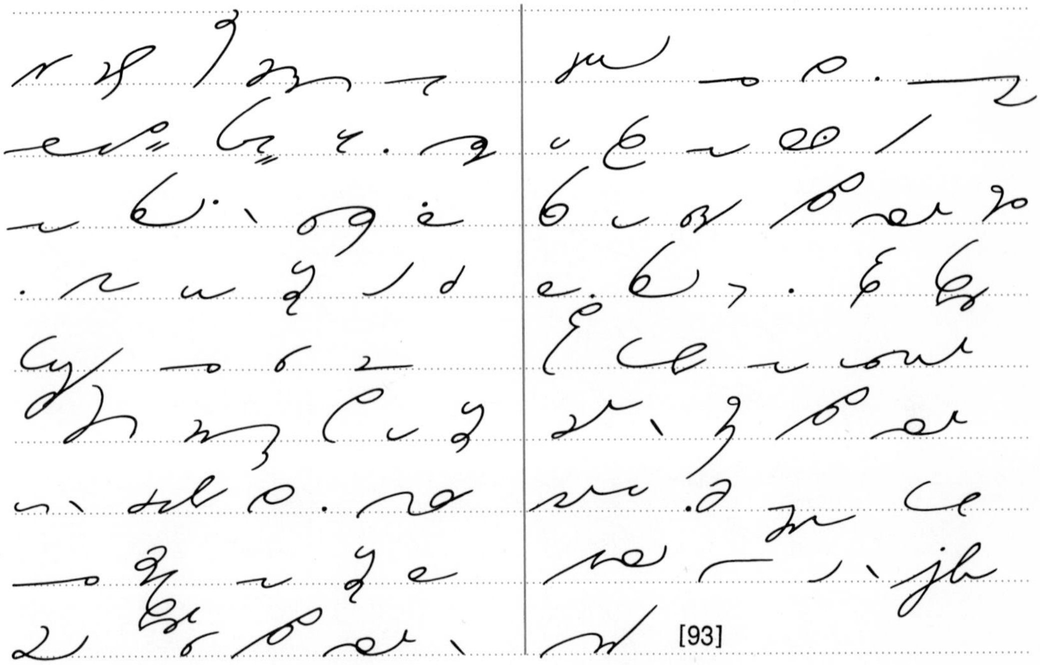

Mailable Letter Production

1
Mrs. Mary Temple
201 Franklin Street
Gary, IN 46411

1 open·ing

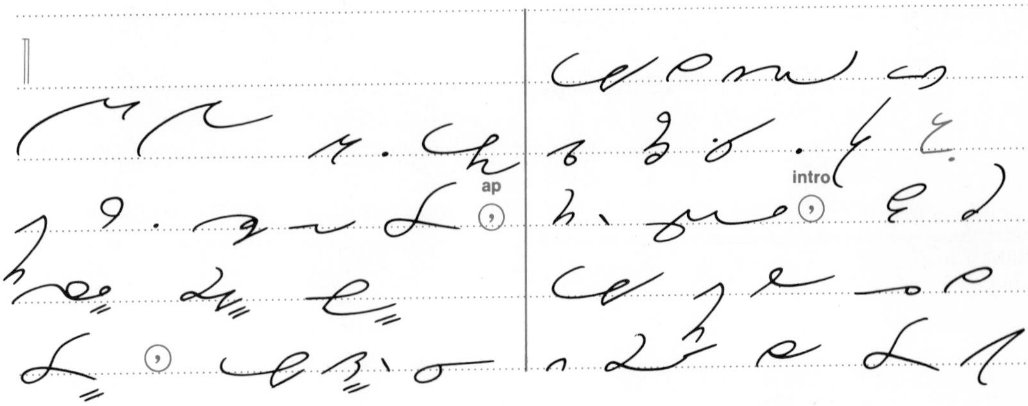

1

Transcription Quiz

Transcribe the following letter, adding the appropriate punctuation to your transcript.

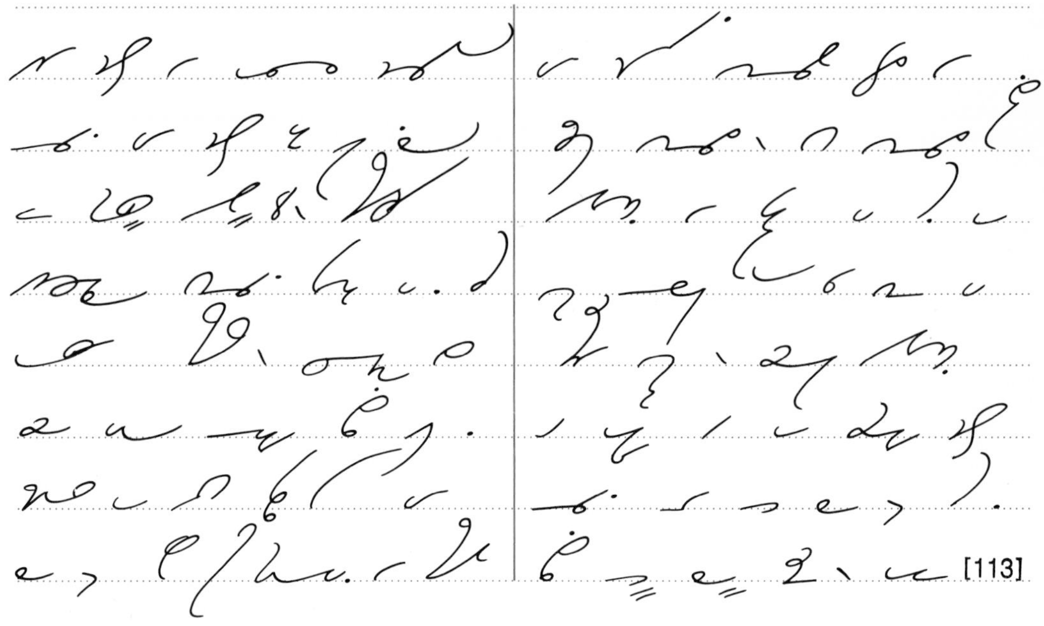

[113]

Mailable Letter Production

1
Mr. Nelson Mitchell
867 Laurel Avenue
Hollywood, CA 91150

1 re·views
2 lec·ture
3 cam·pus

2
Mr. Edward Flint
Dearborn State Bank
313 Detroit Avenue
Dearborn, MI 48100

2 va·can·cy
3 write
4 may be
5 some·time
6 in·quire
7 mort·gage
8 neigh·bor·hood
9 ad·di·tion·al
10 of·fer

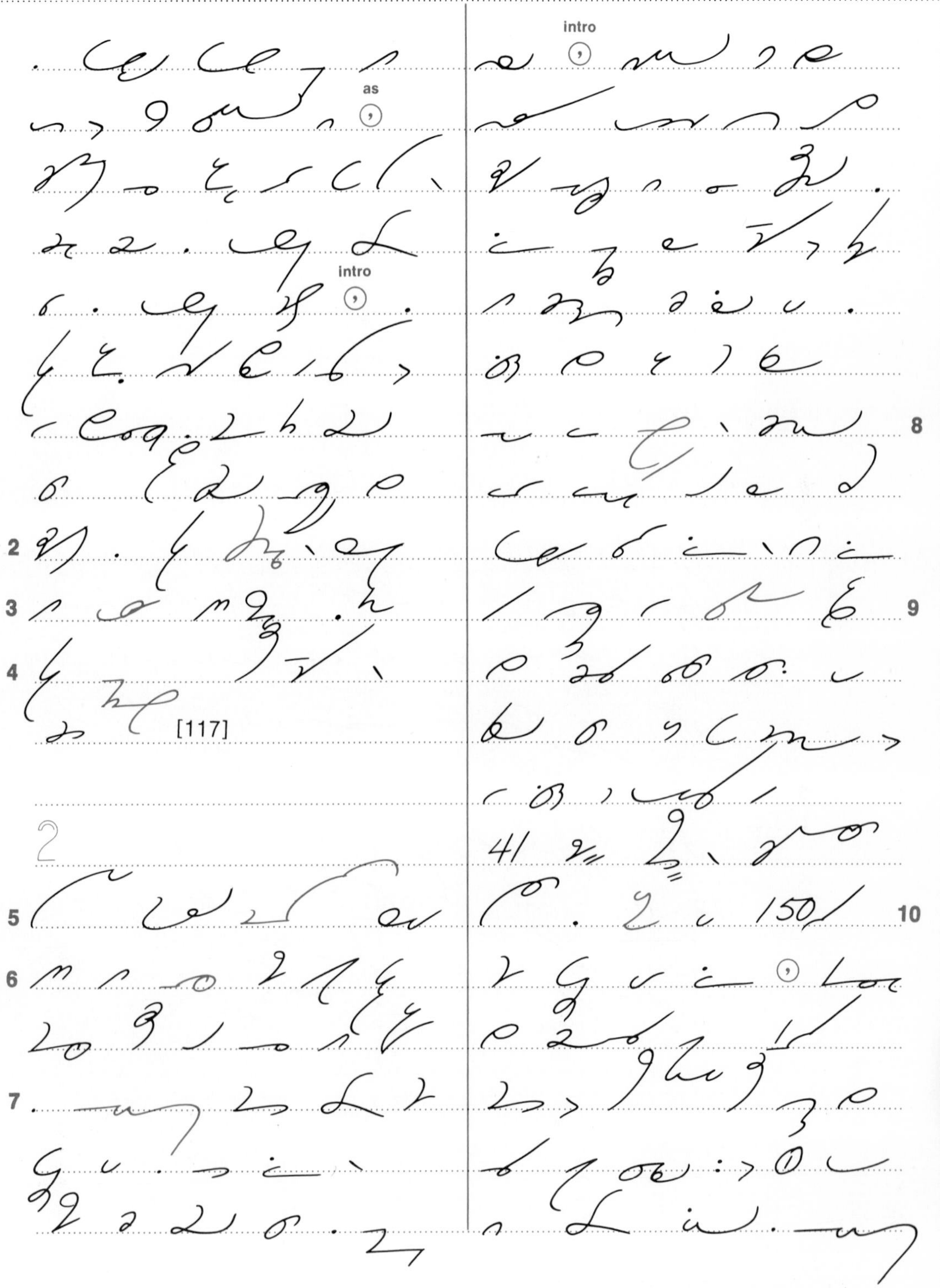

Building Transcription Skill

Transcription Warmup

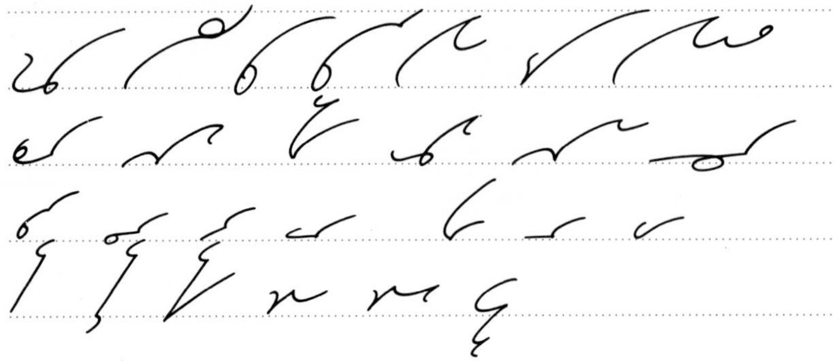

10
20
32
42

Transcription Speed Building

10
20
30
40
52
61
71
81

3
First National Bank
of Iowa
1221 Folsum Street
Iowa City, IA 52240

11 write
12 ca•reer
13 of•fered
14 val•ued
15 guessed

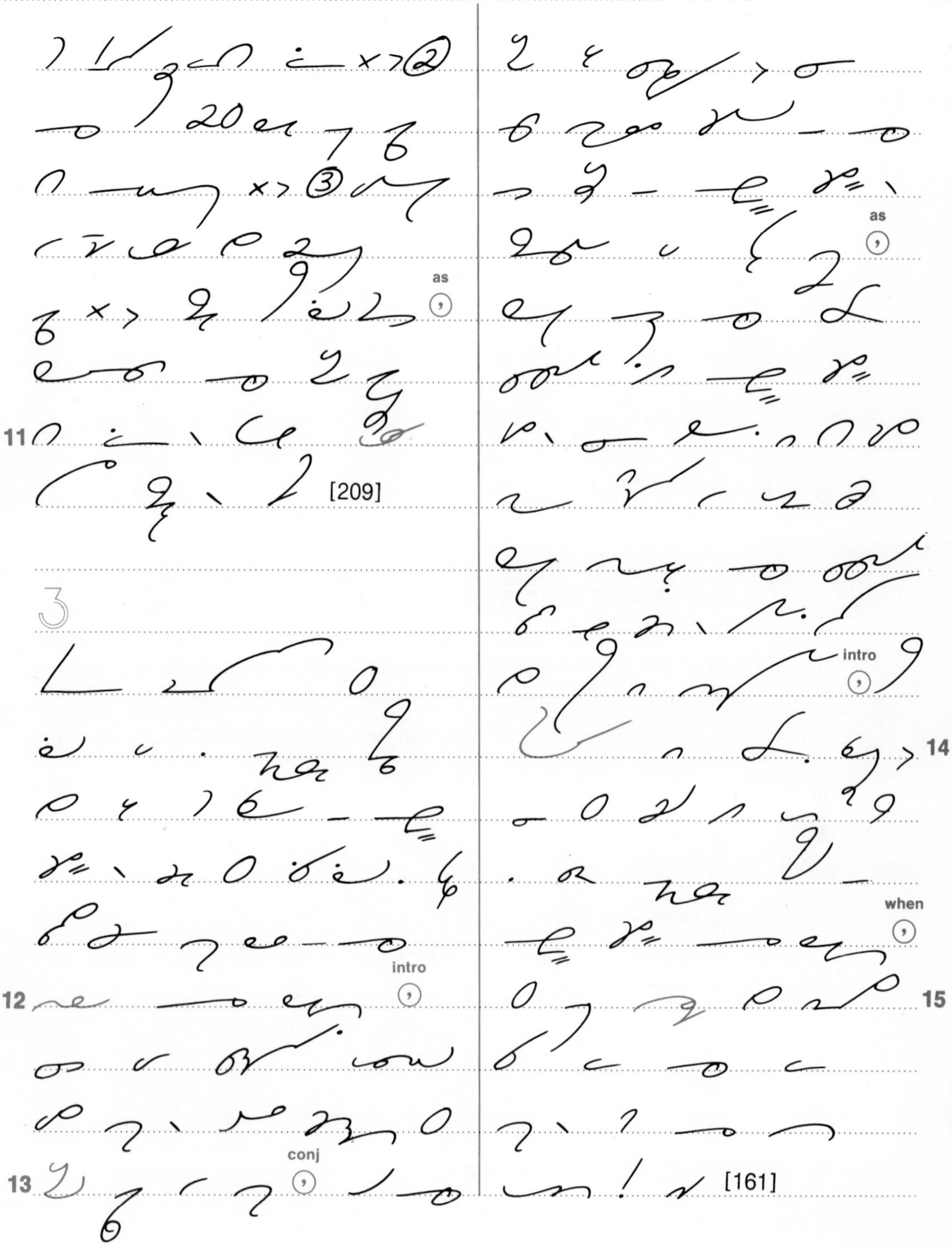

42

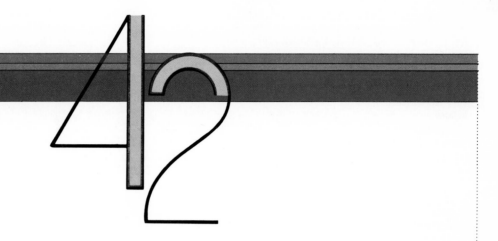

Building Professional Skills

Punctuation Checkup

, geographic expressions

Commas are used to separate geographic expressions from each other. For example, a comma is used between the name of a street and the name of a city, and between the name of a city and the name of a state.

> Send the package to **2406 East Hamilton Avenue, Detroit, Michigan**.
> She is a resident of **Miles City, Montana**.

Communication Checkup

all most ■ almost

all most Meaning an extreme degree for everyone in a group.

> You are all most welcome to attend the meeting.
> We are all most happy to be here today.

almost Meaning not quite.

> We are almost ready for the class to begin.
> The lake is almost frozen.

22

Building Professional Skills

Punctuation Checkup

, when

Introductory clauses beginning with the word *when* are followed by a comma.

When Mark arrives, the meeting will begin.
When the weather clears up, we will go camping.
When the coat has been found, we will let you know.

Communication Checkup

residents ■ residence

residents — The people who live in a building.

Some of our residents are elderly.
All the residents of the neighborhood are invited to the meeting.

residence — The building in which people live.

Please give me the adress of your residence.
We repair both commercial buildings and residences.

4
Instructions From The Boss

7 dem·on·stra·tion

A customer service representative, sometimes called a personal banker, spends a great deal of time on the telephone gathering information from or for account holders. Shorthand aids in this process, insuring accuracy.

Building Transcription Skill

Transcription Warmup

10
20
30
40

Transcription Speed Building

10
20
30
40
52
58
69
80

2
Mr. Jerry Birk
1027 Pine Place
Casper, WY 82601

3
Ms. Shelley Hill
5550 Olson Drive
Columbia, SC 29200

2 for•ward
3 in•creas•ing
4 of•fer
5 re•ferred
6 helped

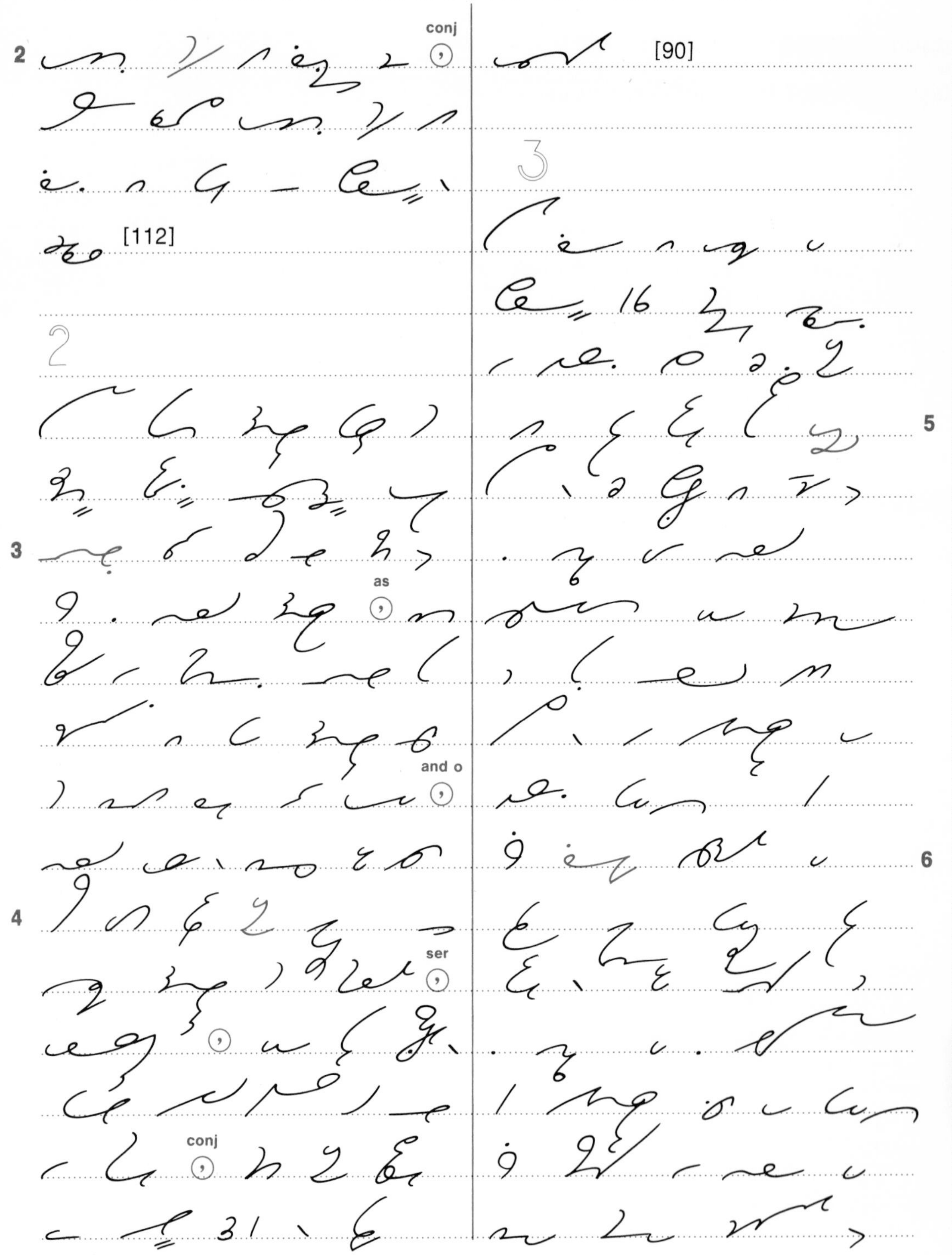

Transcription Quiz

Transcribe the following letter, adding the appropriate punctuation to your transcript.

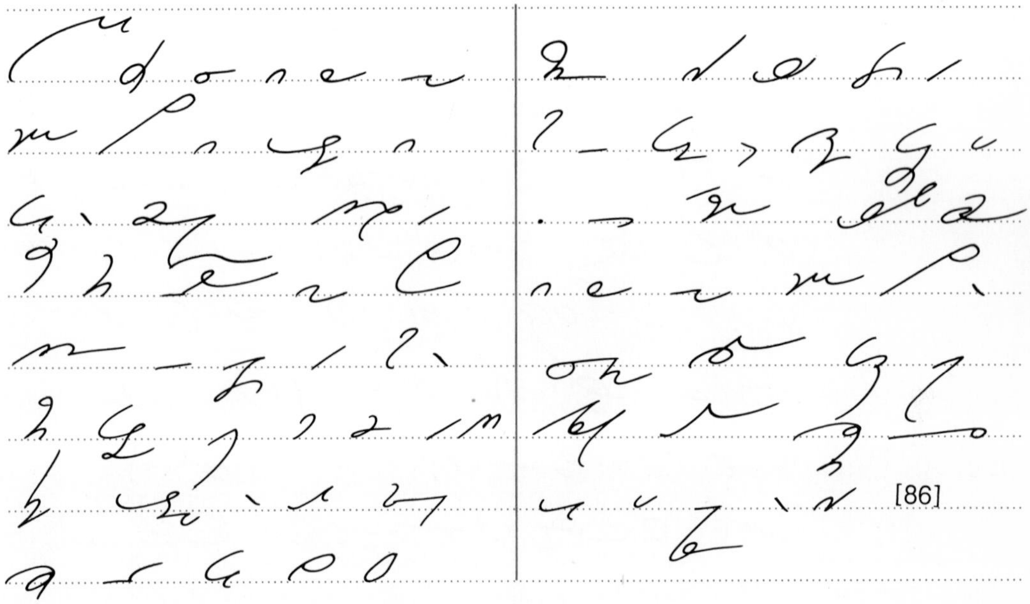

Mailable Letter Production

1
Mr. Barry Davis
2905 Windsor Drive
Manchester, NH 03100

1 Tech•ni•cal
2 re•al•izes

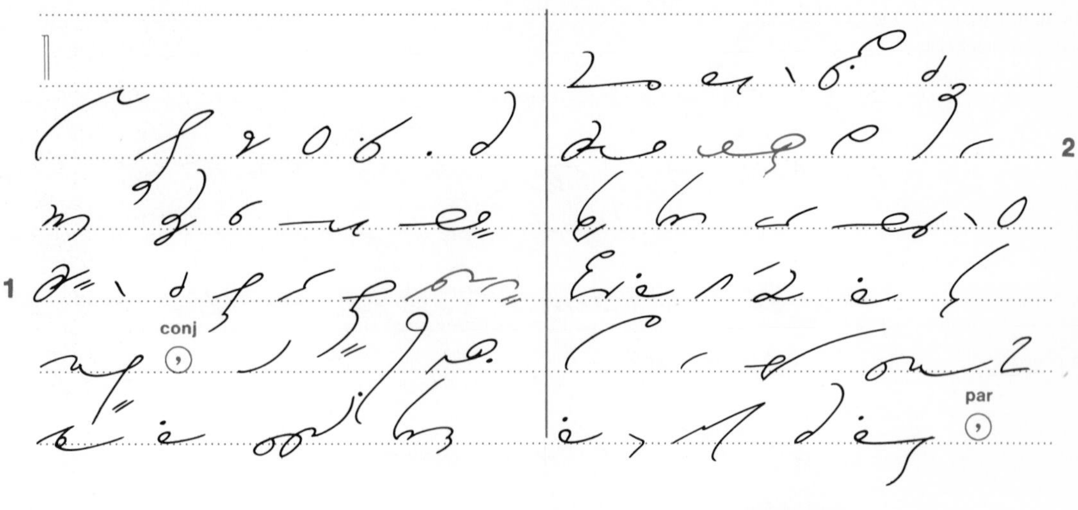

Transcription Quiz

Transcribe the following letter, adding the appropriate punctuation to your transcript.

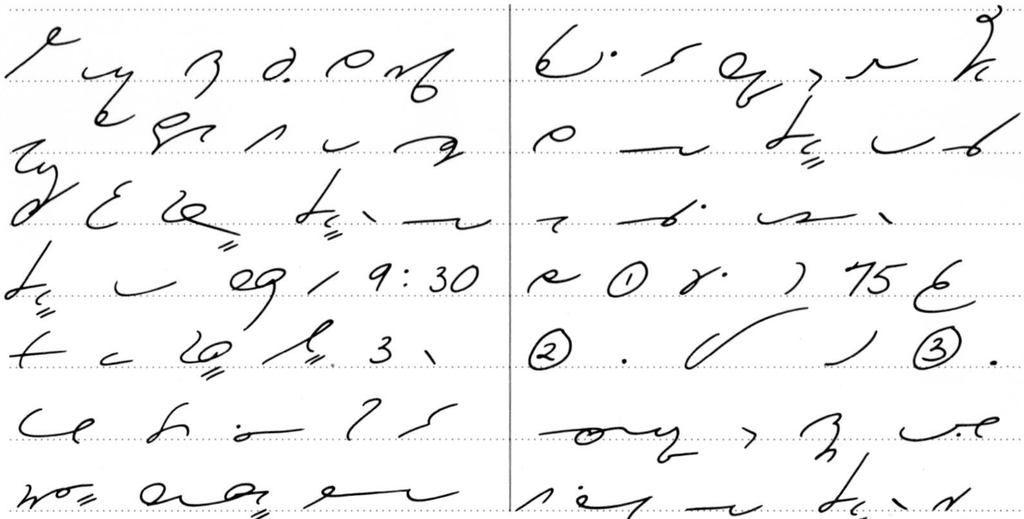

[88]

Mailable Letter Production

1
Dr. Doris Carter
4130 Preston Road
Trenton, NJ 08611

1 en·gage·ment

1

2
Mr. Mark Blackstone
Seattle Transportation
Company
1446 Deerfield Road
Seattle, WA 98199

3 re•ceive
4 piece
5 res•i•dence
6 edi•tion
7 some•time

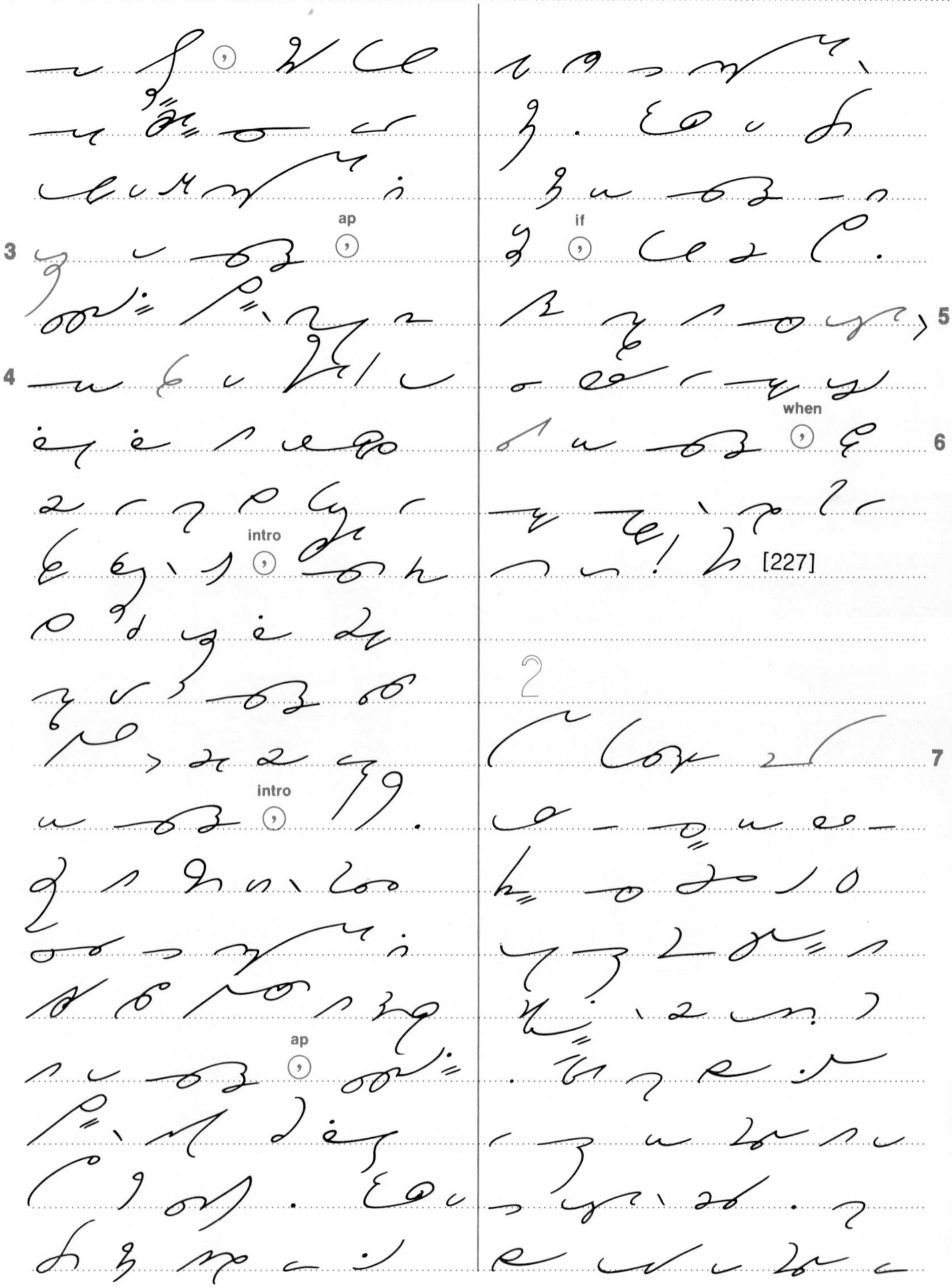

Building Transcription Skill

Transcription Warmup

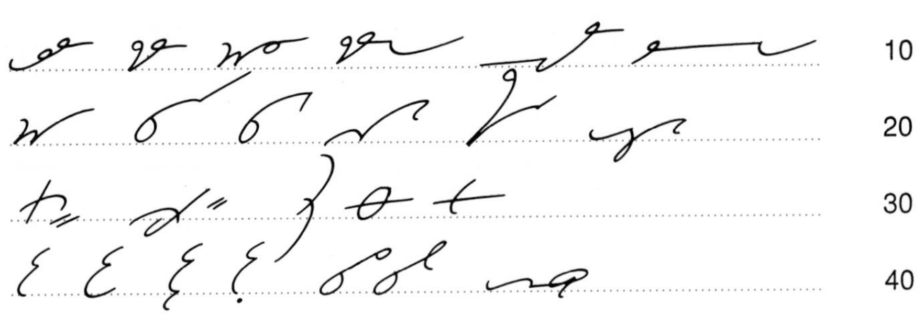

Transcription Speed Building

3
Ms. Jean Billings
4630 City View Drive
Tulsa, OK 74100

8 in·ven·to·ry
9 ev·ery day
10 in·ter·est·ed
11 elec·tron·ic
12 any time

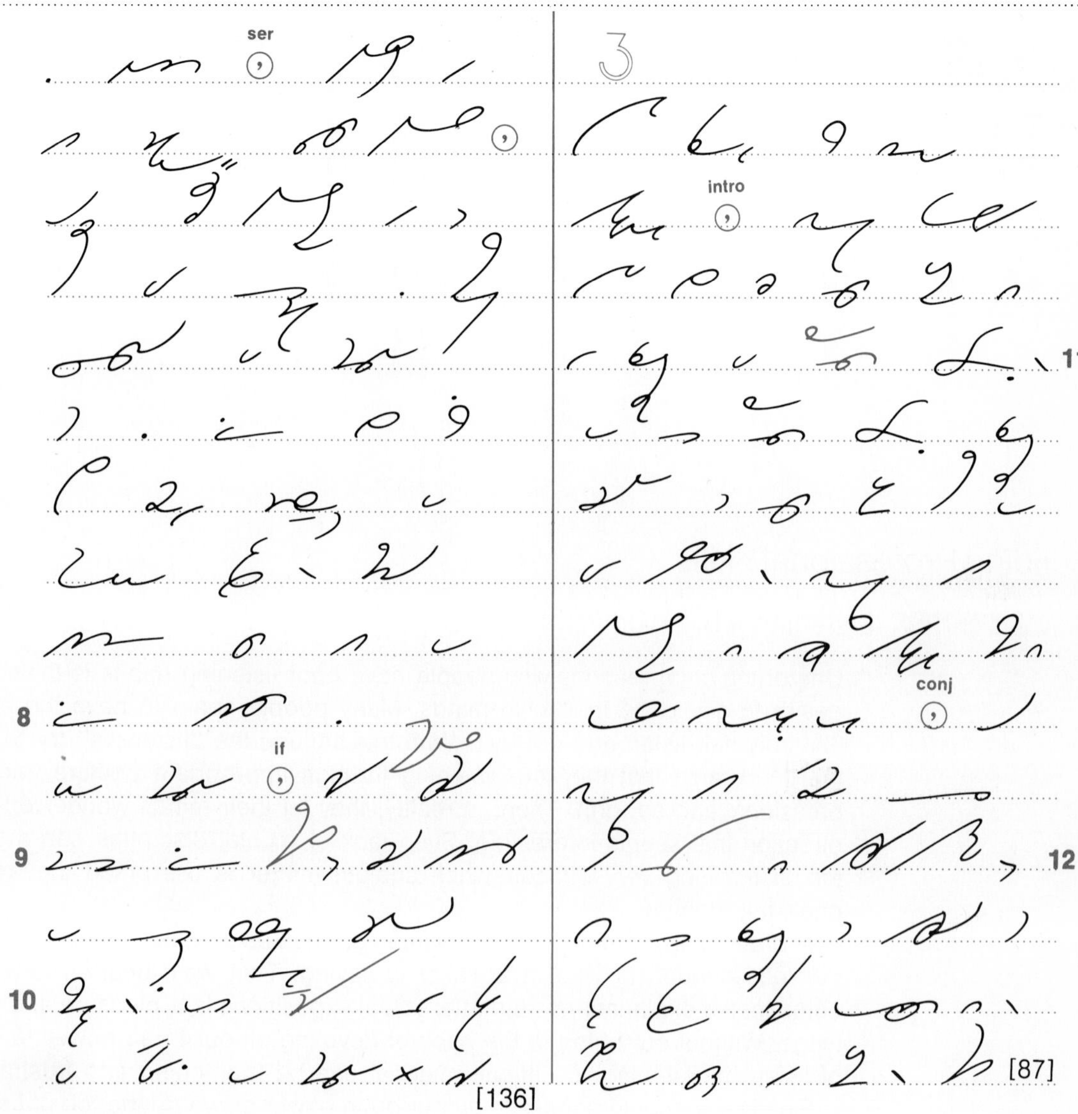

41

Building Professional Skills

Listening ■ Brain power

One of the chief reasons why people have poor listening habits is their lack of desire to discipline their own minds. Many people seem to have the attitude, "I'll only half-listen and get by." With this attitude the "listeners" try to create the impression that they are listening through appropriate posture, facial expressions, and so forth. Then, in reality, they let their minds wander off in any direction that seems interesting. Such lack of mental discipline can make the job of listening very difficult when subject matter is presented that requires one's full attention.

In order to do an effective job of listening, we need to make a habit of directing our full attention to what a speaker is saying. That way, hearing new ideas, complicated explanations, and intellectual expositions is a pleasure and a challenge. Without our being in the habit of devoting all our brain power to the job of listening, listening to difficult material can be frightening and frustrating.

Finally, we should capitalize on our brain power as we do the job of listening, because it represents one of the key traits of a person who excels in human relations.

Communication Checkup

affect ■ effect

affect — To change; to influence.

The plans for the word processing center will not affect my job.

effect — (noun) Result; outcome.
(verb) To bring about.

What will be the effect of that decision?
How will you effect your plans?

23

Building Professional Skills

Shorthand ■ Intelligent Note-Taking

One of the most valuable uses for shorthand is the taking of "intelligent" notes. The person who knows shorthand and has good listening habits has a tremendous advantage over other people in terms of personal efficiency. To the student, shorthand means that all the key points of a lecture can be recorded in class notes for later study. To the secretary, shorthand means that all the elements of a list of instructions can be retained the first time the executive gives those instructions, thus avoiding mistakes and embarrassment later. To the executive, shorthand means that once a business meeting has been concluded, details of agreements will be remembered and commitments met.

Whether you are taking notes as a student, a secretary, or an executive, shorthand enables you to record all the pertinent information—and *only* the pertinent information. Shorthand is the only recording device that allows for editing of the proceedings at the point of recording. It is tied to no more sophisticated equipment than a pen and a piece of paper.

Communication Checkup

some time ■ sometime

some time An amount of time.

Please spend some time in my office today.
I received your check some time ago.

sometime An indefinite time.

Please telephone me sometime.
Sometimes he has been late for work.

5
Instructions For Karen

9 re•ceiv•er

conj

par

[213]

5

[24]

9

When leaving on a business trip, a manager may dictate last-minute instructions that are to be carried out in his absence.

Building Transcription Skill

Transcription Warmup

10
20
30
41

Transcription Speed Building

10
20
30
40
51
59
69
78
82

3
Ace Oil Company
1406 Platt Avenue
Union, PA 15300

4
To: Mary Petroe
From: Frank Adams
Subject: Electronic Mail

6 in·ter·rup·tion
7 doc·u·ments
8 min·i·mal

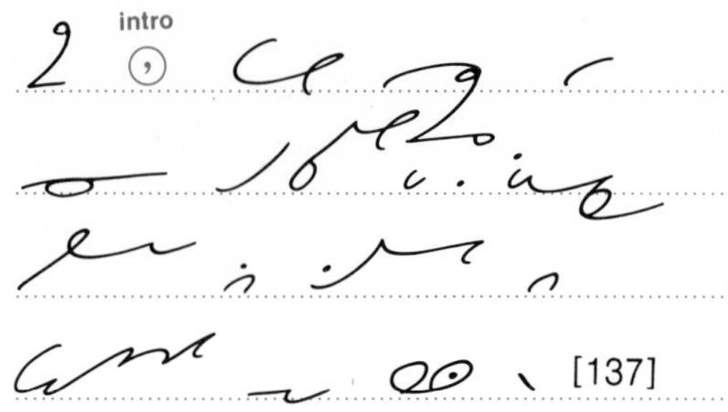

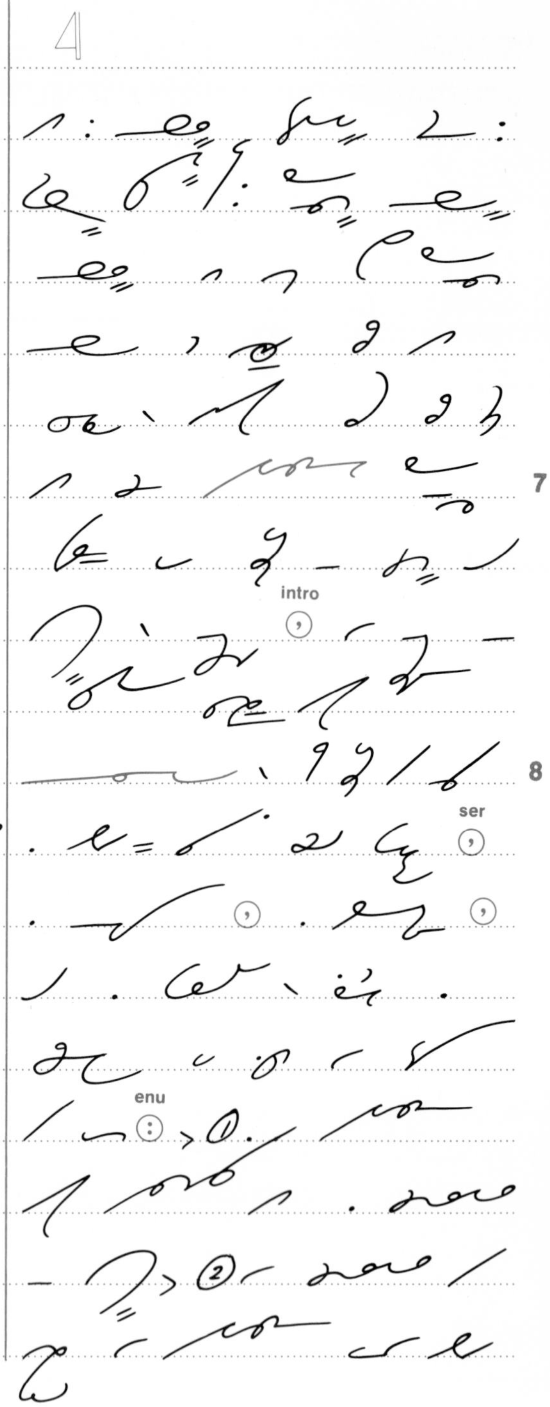

Transcription Quiz

Transcribe the following letter, adding the appropriate punctuation to your transcript.

[118]

Mailable Letter Production

1
Mrs. Susan Miles
Overland Publishing Company
2214 Laurel Avenue
New York, NY 10020

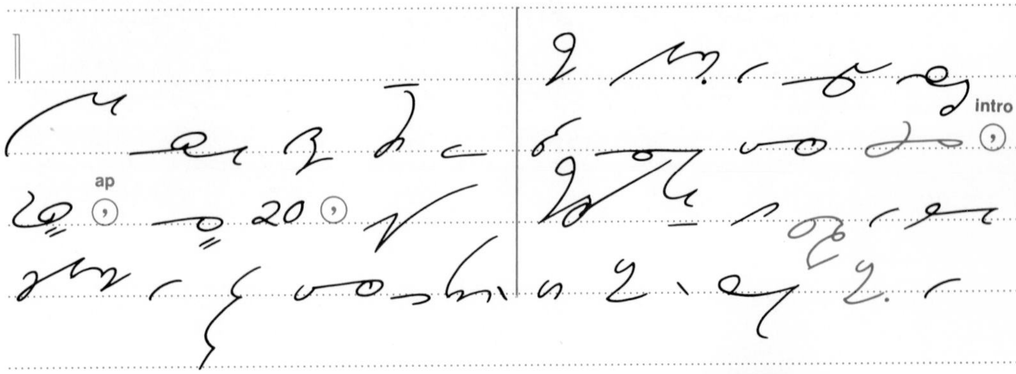

1
2
3

1 fam·i·ly
2 ac·cept
3 of·fer·ing

2
Variety Office Product
555 Bayview Drive
Worcester, MA 01600

1 two
2 ac·quired
3 as·so·ci·ates
4 wheth·er
5 week

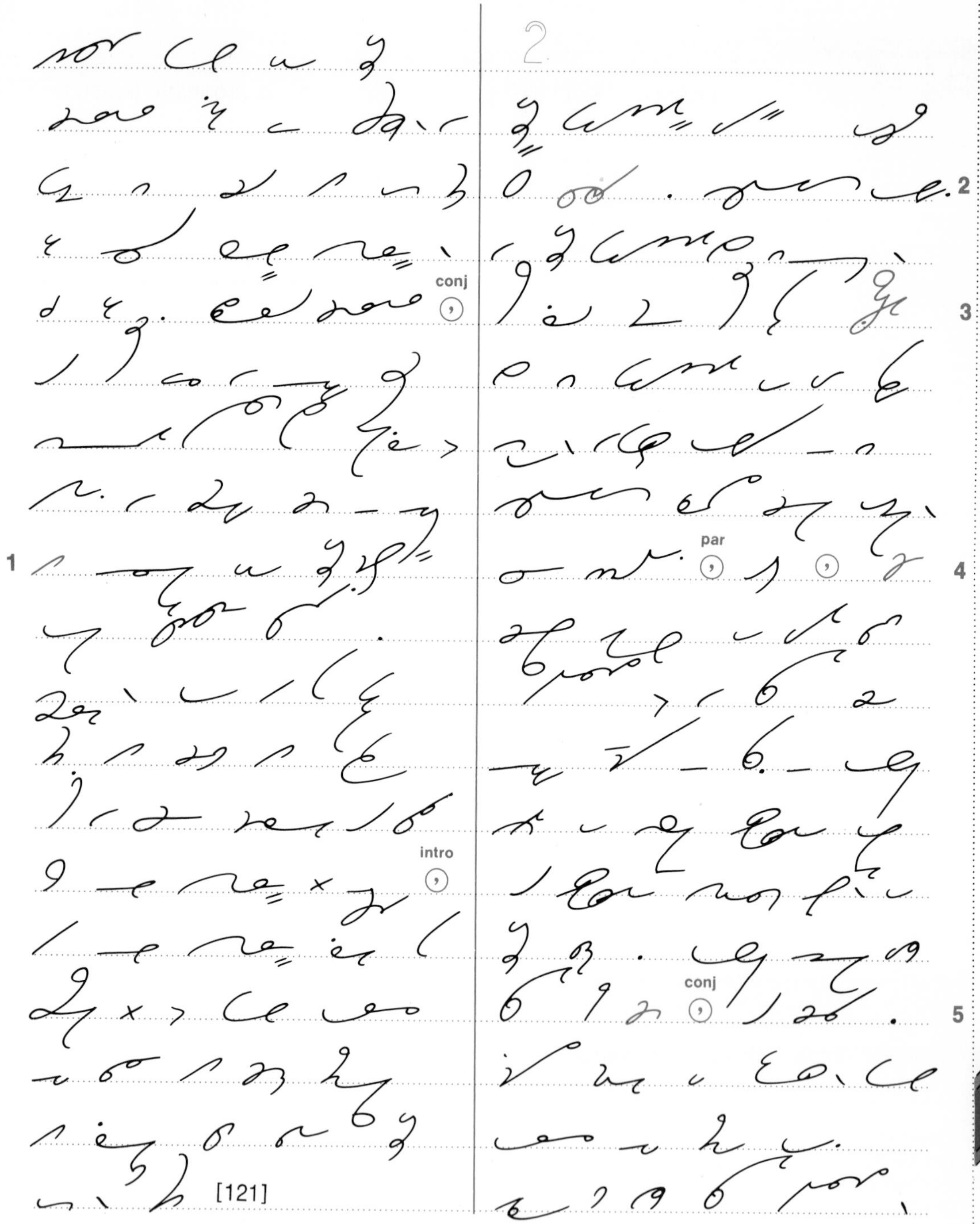

2
Boston Publishing Company
2744 Birch Street
Boston, MA 02100

4 al·low
5 suf·fi·cient
6 re·ceived
7 cop·ies
8 er·ror
9 pur·sue

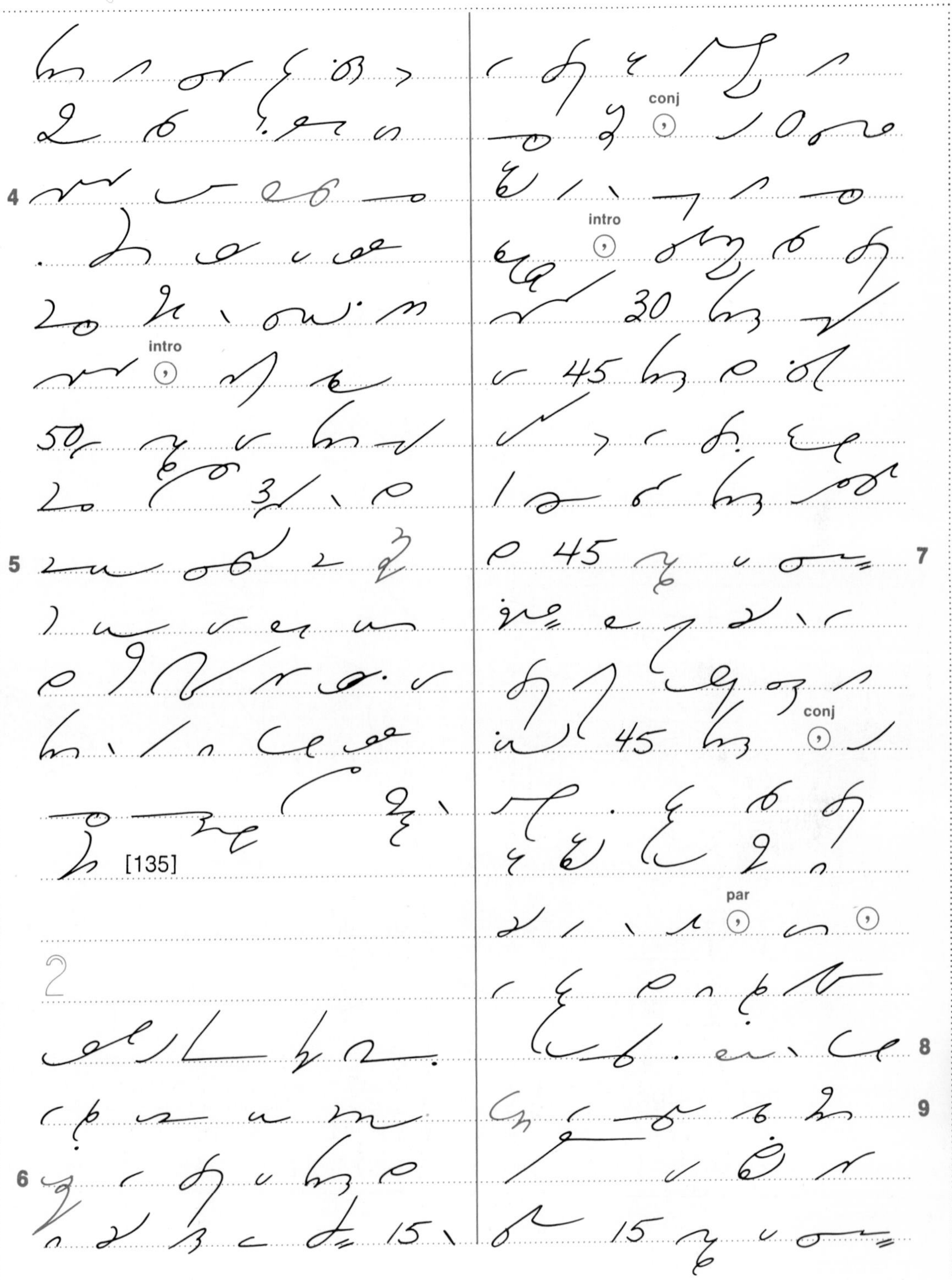

Transcription Quiz

Transcribe the following letter, adding the appropriate punctuation to your transcript.

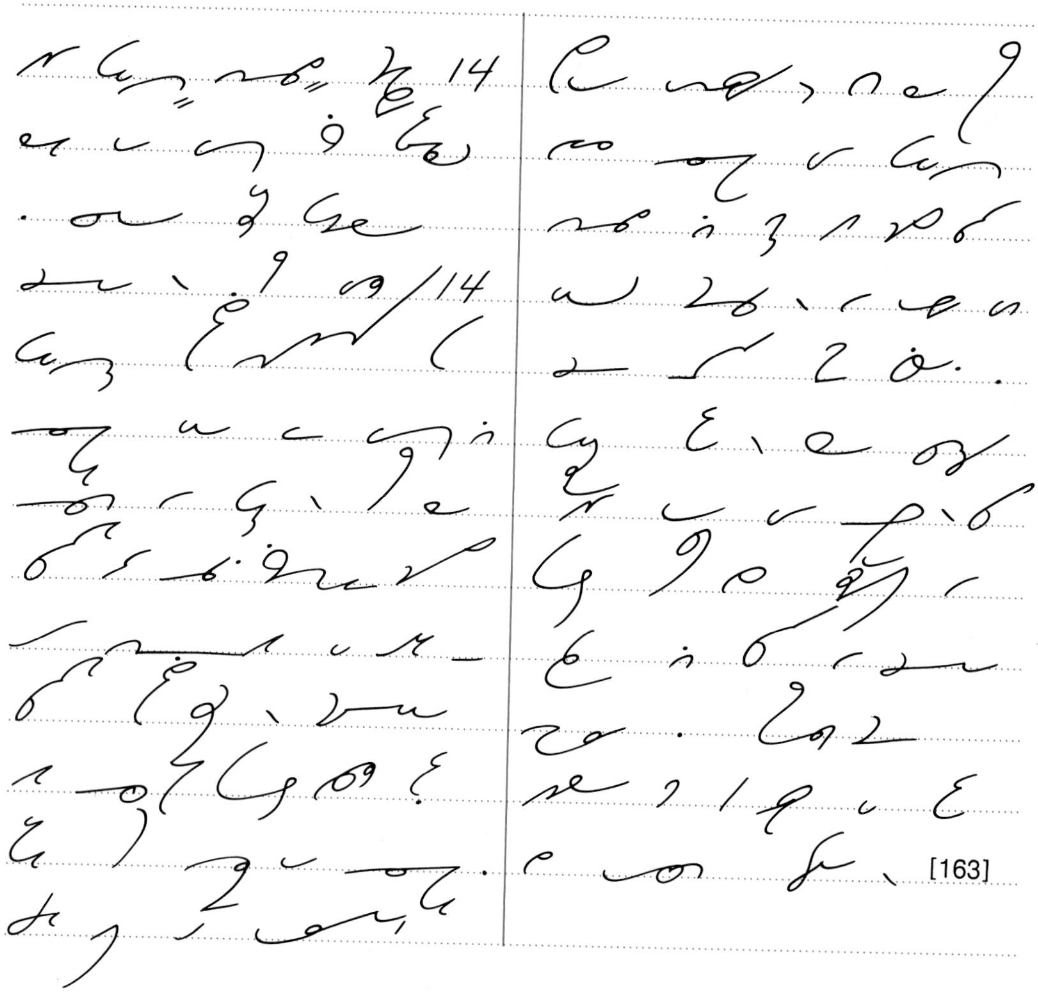

[163]

Mailable Letter Production

1
Mr. James Hart
Office Temporary
Services
8058 Jupiter Street
Hartford, CT 06420

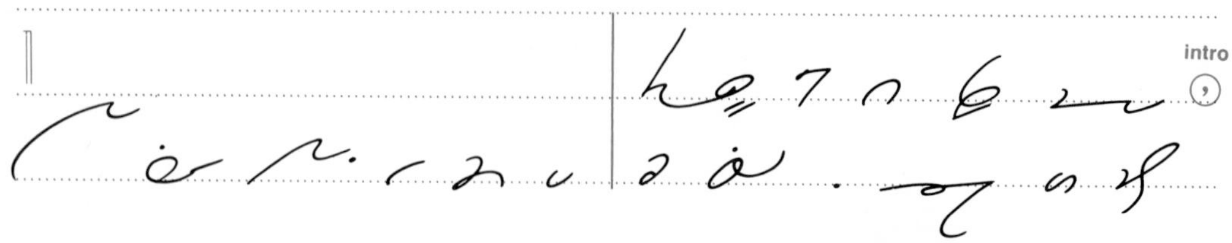

3
Mrs. Marsha James
1507 Wilson Drive
Lincoln, NE 68511

10 some time
11 al·ready
12 some·time
13 res·i·dents
14 ef·fec·tive
15 their
16 Transcribe:
30 percent

In a business meeting, shorthand enables an executive to record only the pertinent information, editing out unnecessary facts, and concentrate on the proceeding.

Building Transcription Skill

Transcription Warmup

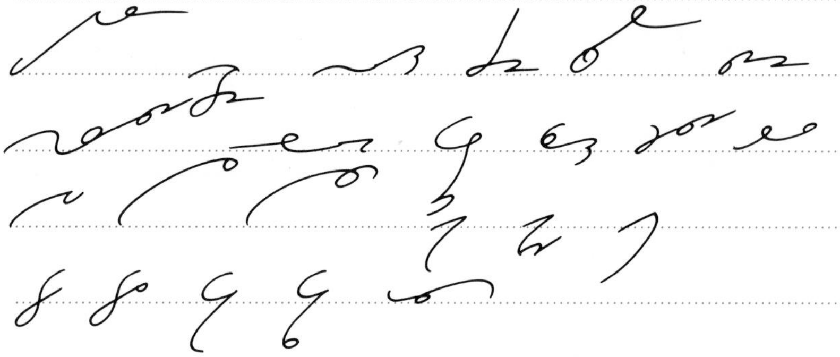

10 20 30 40

Transcription Speed Building

8 19 27 34 42 49 61 74 82

24

Building Professional Skills

Punctuation Checkup

, introductory

A comma is used to separate an introductory phrase from the main part of a sentence. Many introductory phrases begin with the words *if, as,* and *when.* Any number of words or phrases can, of course, be used in an introductory way. Here are some examples:

While I understand the statement, I do not agree with it.
Although it was early, he closed the office.
Before you sign the contract, discuss it with your lawyer.
Furthermore, the report was incomplete.
On the contrary, you are responsible.
For your convenience, I am enclosing an envelope.

Communication Checkup

week ■ weak

week — A period of time consisting of seven days.

The weather has been cold for several weeks.
Stop in to see me sometime next week.

weak — Lacking strength.

The bridge is too weak to be considered safe.
He is still weak as a result of his illness.

40

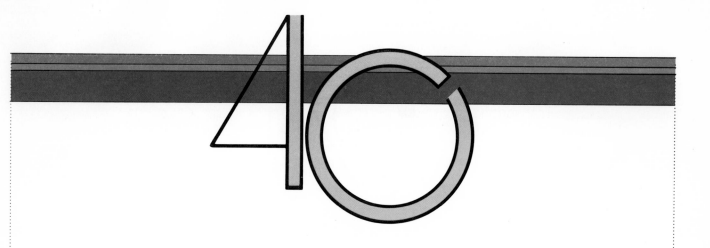

Building Professional Skills

Shorthand for the Professional ■ Recording Instructions

One of the most valuable uses for shorthand skill is the recording of instructions on the job. This skill is equally useful for people at all levels of the organization, whether a file clerk recording instructions from the records manager or the president of the company recording instructions from the board of directors. By recording our supervisor's instructions in shorthand, we can ensure that the instructions are accurate. Shorthand enables us to take the instructions without having to ask the speaker to slow down or to repeat major points. The use of shorthand also means that the instructions are much more likely to be complete, thus avoiding the embarrassment of our having to go back to our supervisor to ask for the instructions a second time. Finally, recording instructions in shorthand is mark of professionalism. The supervisor who sees us recording instructions in shorthand knows that we are well prepared for the job, conscientious, and competent.

Communication Checkup

accede ■ exceed

accede — To agree to or go along with.

The lawmaker will accede to the will of the majority.
He accedes to our opinion.

exceed — To go beyond certain limits.

His decision exceeded his authority.
Do not exceed the speed limit while driving.

Building Transcription Skill

Transcription Warmup

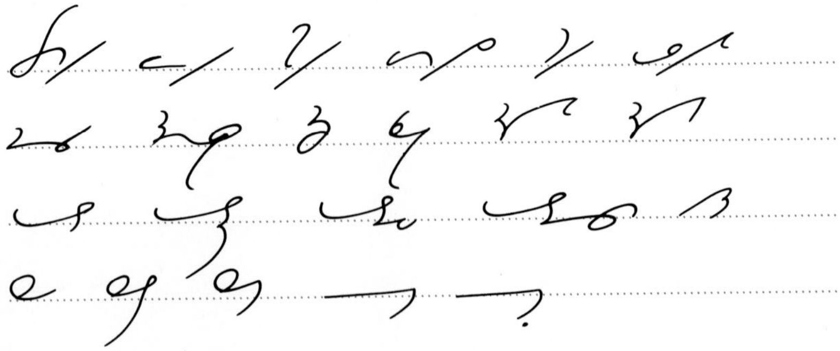

10
20
31
41

Transcription Speed Building

10
20
30
40
49
59
70
80
82

10 doc·u·ment
11 wheth·er
12 ac·cept·able
13 hear·ing

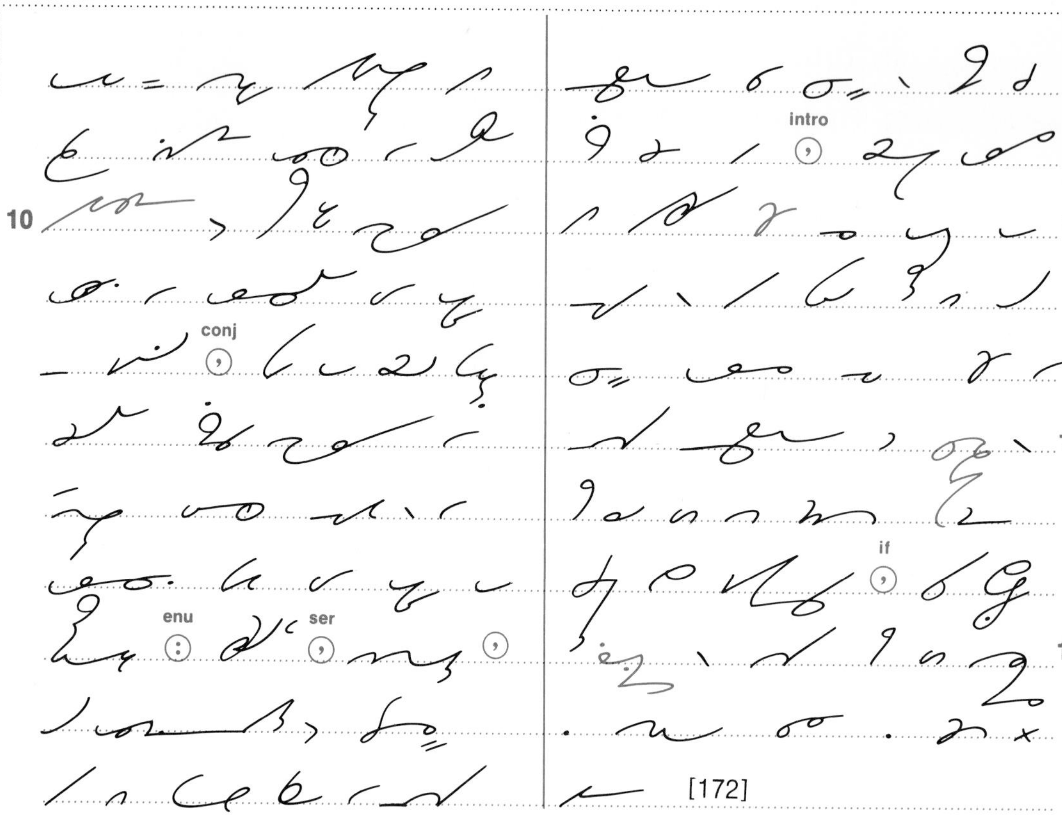

Secretaries often input data from shorthand notes into mirocomputers.

Transcription Quiz

Transcribe the following letter, adding the appropriate punctuation to your transcript.

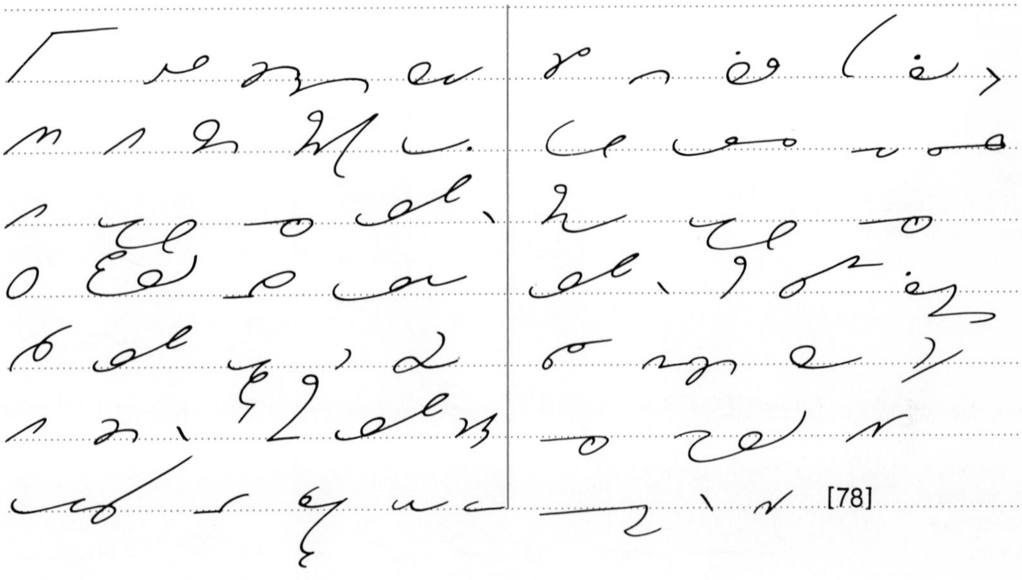

Mailable Letter Production

1
Mr. Thomas Cole
1433 East Madison
Avenue
Pueblo, CO 81011

1 fa·cil·i·ties
2 eas·i·ly

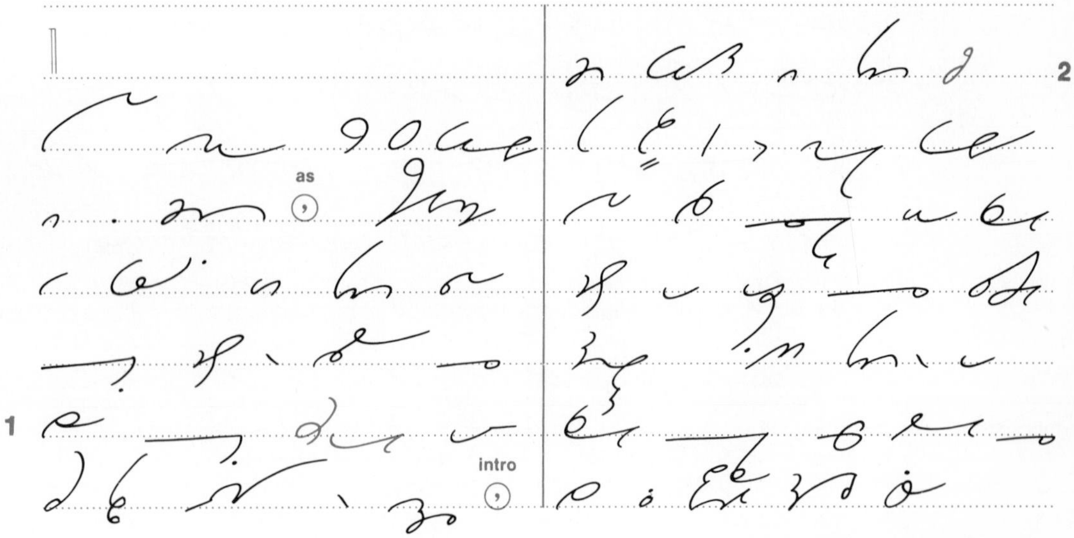

2
Mr. John Melrose,
Convention Chairman
421 Smith Hall
Southern State College
Bowling Green, KY
42101

3
Mrs. Margaret
Woodford
1131 Barron Street
Providence, RI 02911

4 lun•cheon
5 re•al•ly
6 over•head
7 au•di•ence
8 ex•cit•ing
9 sum•ma•ry

2

Mr. John Morris
Michigan Paper
Company
710 Maple Street
Flint, MI 48512

3 than
4 edi·tion
5 suf·fered
6 burst
7 ream
8 sealed
9 some

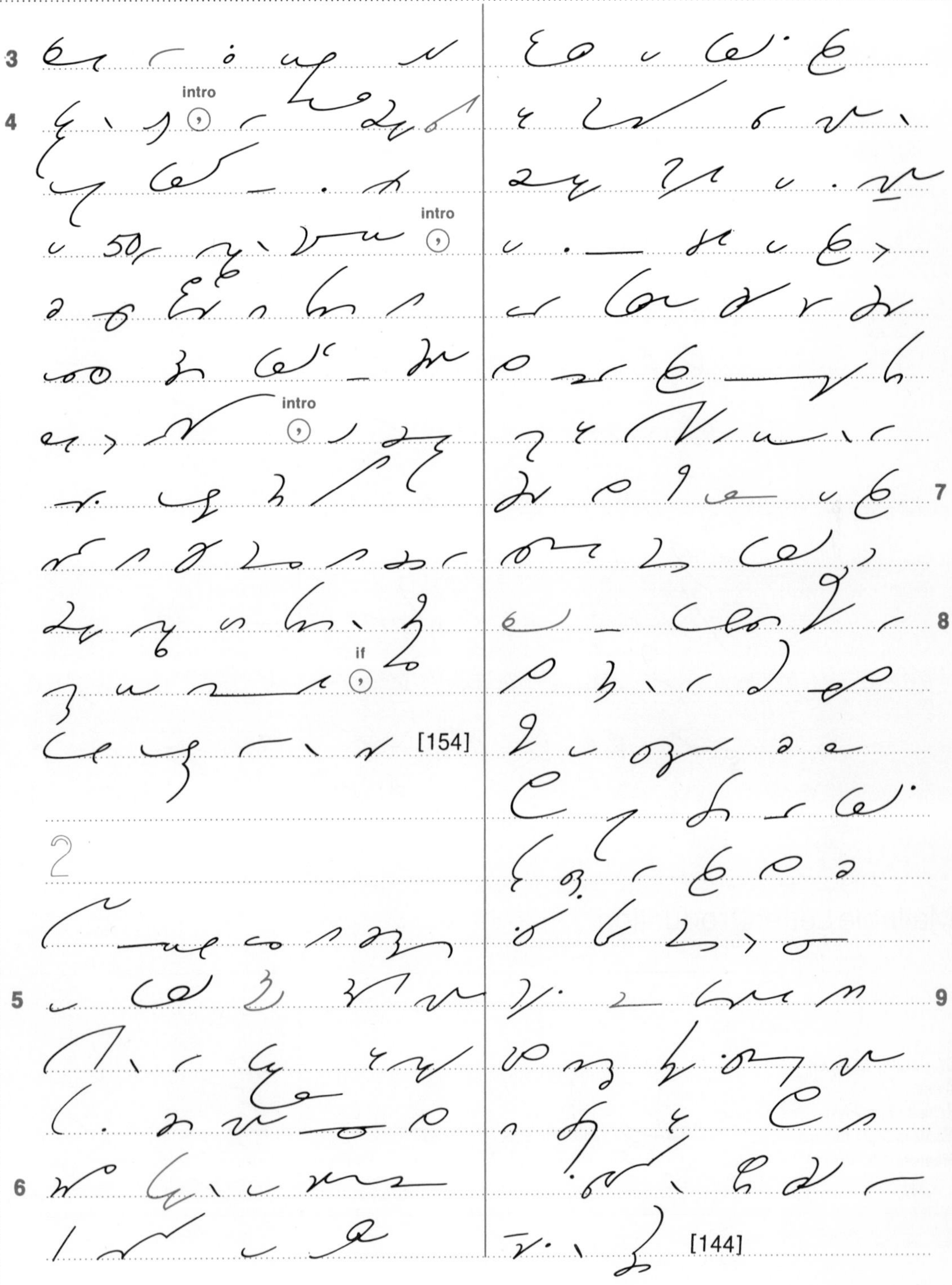

Transcription Quiz

Transcribe the following letter, adding the appropriate punctuation to your transcript.

[127]

Mailable Letter Production

1
Dr. Dorothy Eastman, Dean
School of Business
Madison State College
Madison, WI 53711

1 Sec•re•tary's
2 bro•chure
3 ses•sions

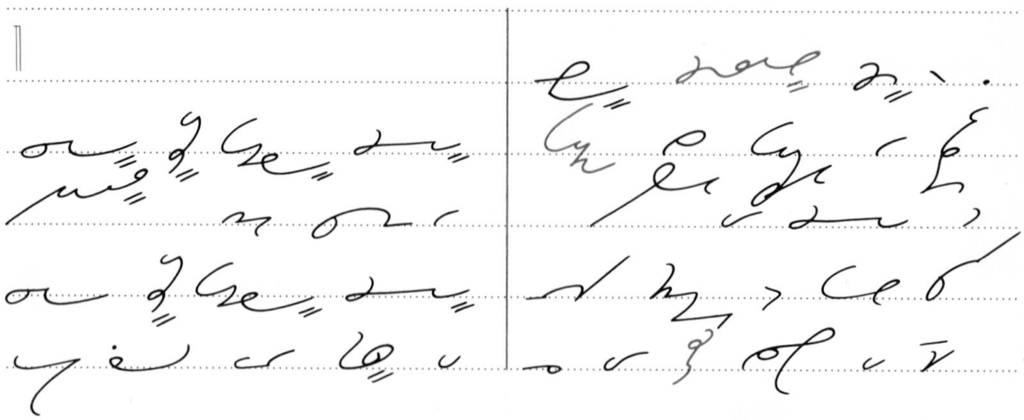

1
2
3

3

Mr. Joseph Green
Erie Publishing
Company
1409 Canal Street
Cumberland, MD
21502

10 for·ward
11 their
12 thor·ough
13 cus·tom·ers'

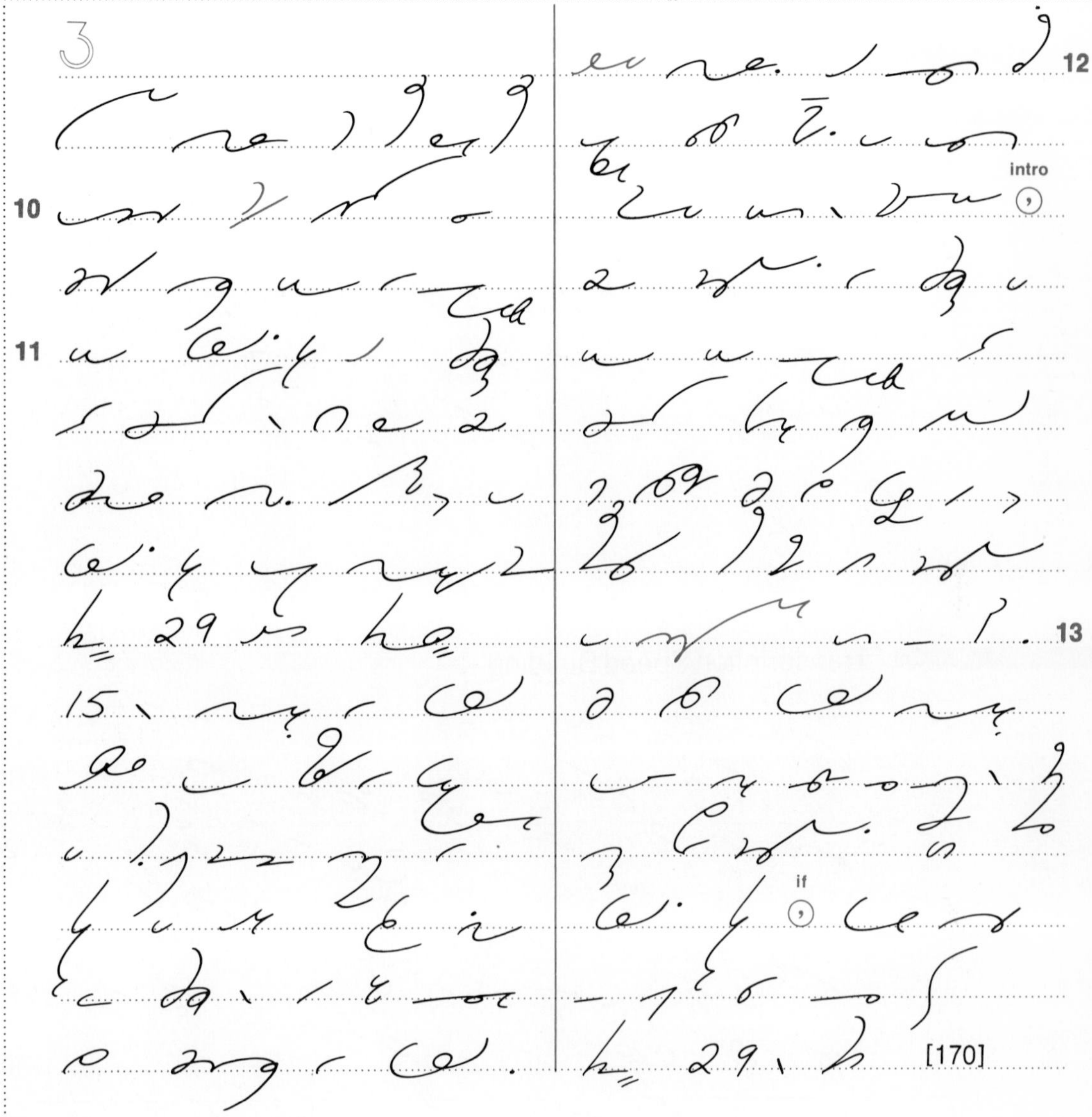

Building Transcription Skill

Transcription Warmup

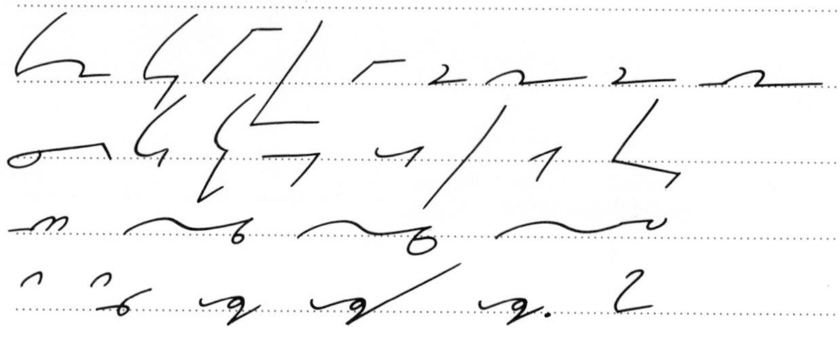

10
20
30
41

Transcription Speed Building

12
24
30
41
49
62
72
82

25

Building Professional Skills

Punctuation Checkup

, dates

Commas are used to separate from each other the various components of a description of a day and time. If more than one component is used, the last is also followed by a comma.

Her birth date is March 17, 1949.
Please see me on Monday, April 2, at 5 p.m.
The contract was signed on Friday, March 7, 1963.

Communication Checkup

numbers ■ basic rule

The basic rule for number expression is to spell the numbers one through ten and to use numerals for numbers larger than ten. One of several exceptions to this basic rule is that the first word of a sentence is always spelled, even if it is a number larger than ten.

Jean gave me ten dollars for the tickets.
I began studying shorthand when I was 17
Eleven days remain until vacation.

39

Building Professional Skills

Punctuation Checkup

: enumeration

When a series or list of such things as people, items, or events is introduced in a sentence, a colon follows that introduction. The items in the series may follow each other sequentially in the sentence, separated by commas, or the series may be displayed as an enumerated list with each item being typed on a separate line in vertical format.

All of the students studied the following: history, geography, and English.

All personnel files should contain the following:

1. Grade reports.
2. A copy of the degree plan.
3. Letters of recommendations.

Communication Checkup

prefix mis-

In English the prefix *mis-* indicates that something is wrong or an error.

mislead	To give the wrong information.
misfortune	A distressing occurrence; ill luck.
misappropriate	To make the wrong use of something.

Building Transcription Skill

Transcription Warmup

10
20
32
42

Transcription Speed Building

10
21
30
43
51
61
70
78
85

3
Mrs. Olive Norton
1558 MacArthur
Avenue
Springfield, IL 62711

12 El·e·men·ta·ry
13 hear·ing
14 com·mit·tee
15 in·for·ma·tion·al
16 agen·da

[161]

3

12

par

13

ap

12

14

intro

15

10

16

10

[142]

An executive who needs a document transcribed immediately often gives on-the-spot dictation.

Transcription Quiz

Transcribe the following letter, adding the appropriate punctuation to your transcript.

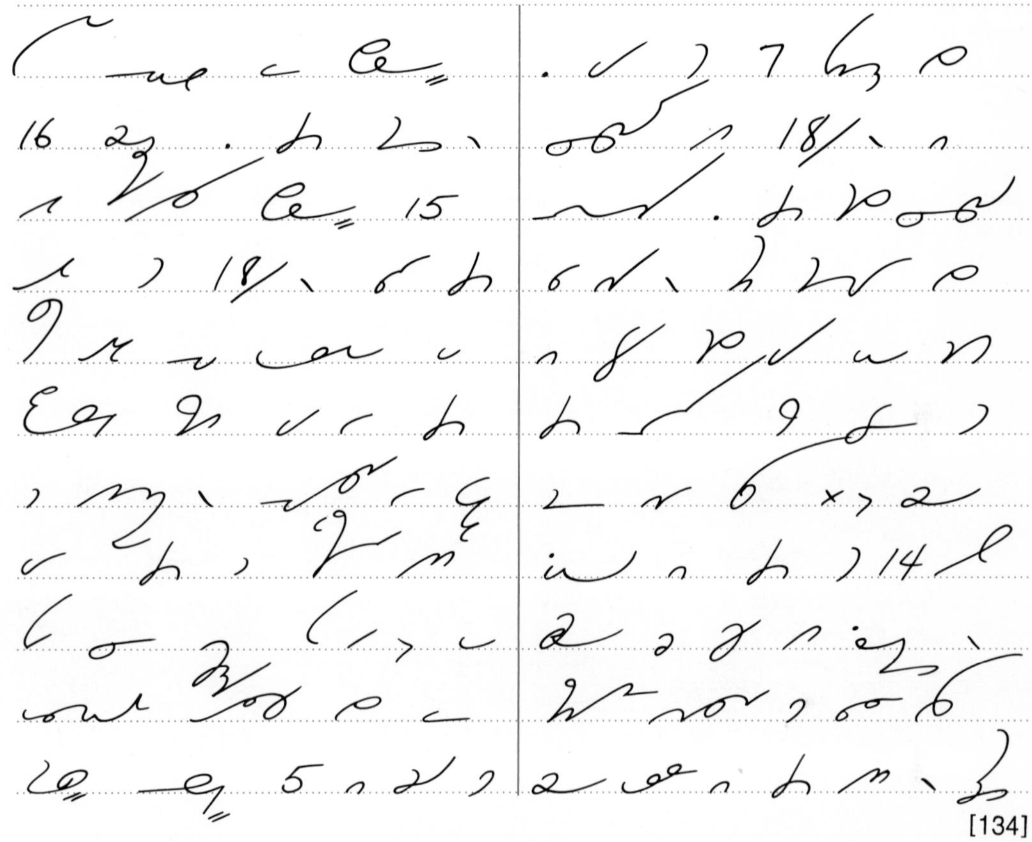

[134]

Mailable Letter Production

1
Ms. Elaine Alan
Windsor Corporation
28 Kirk Drive
Rockford, IL 61100

1 **at·tend**

2
Ms. Kelly Carter
Midwestern Real
Estate Association
430 Water Street
Dover, DE 19901

5 su·perb
6 fur·ther
7 re·al·ize
8 right
9 valu·able
10 sea·sons
11 wheth·er

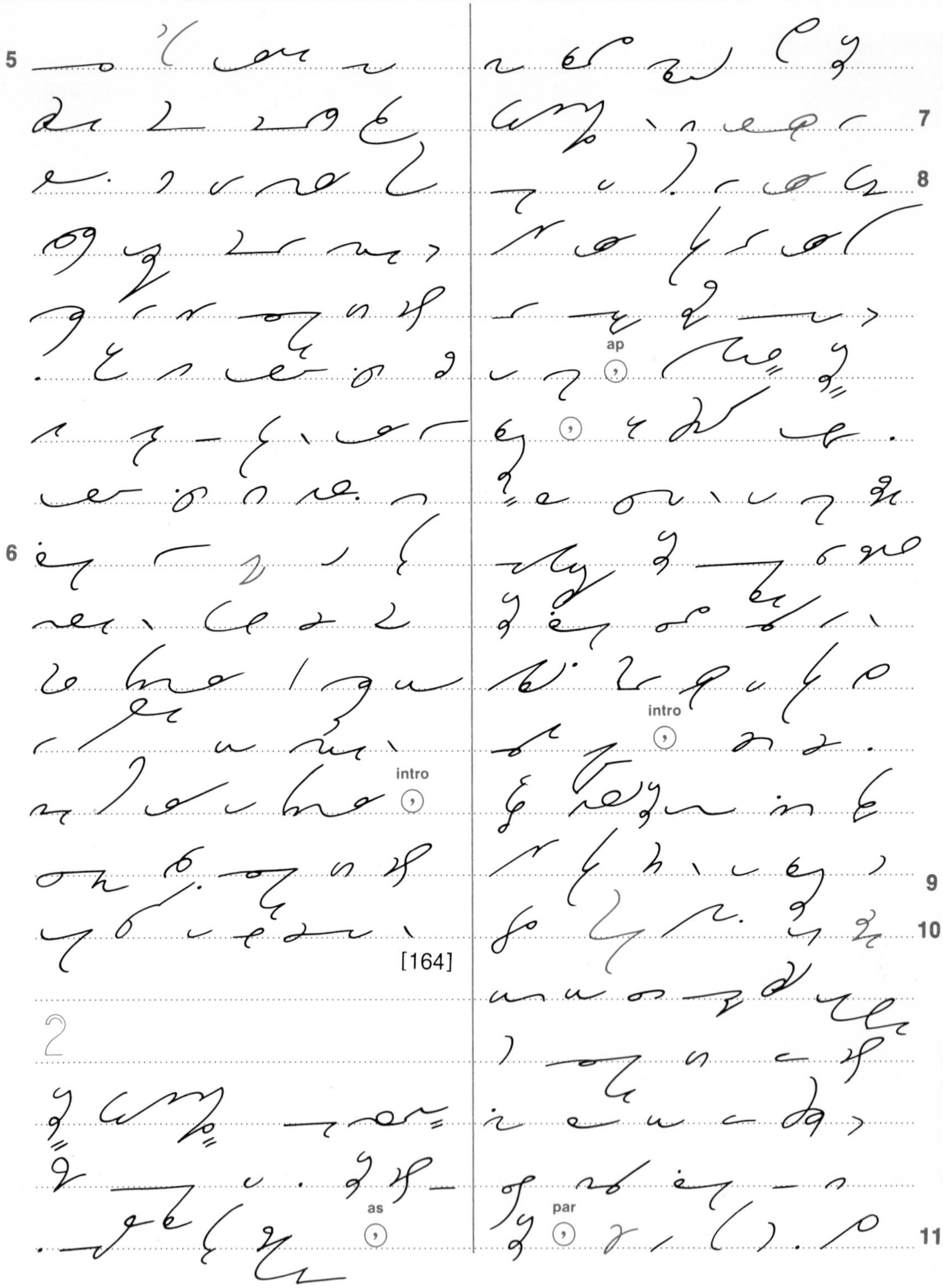

2
Ms. Toni Decker
2524 Shore Road
Atlantic City, NJ 08411

2 su·perb
3 com·mit·tee
4 shipped
5 quite
6 ap·pear·ance

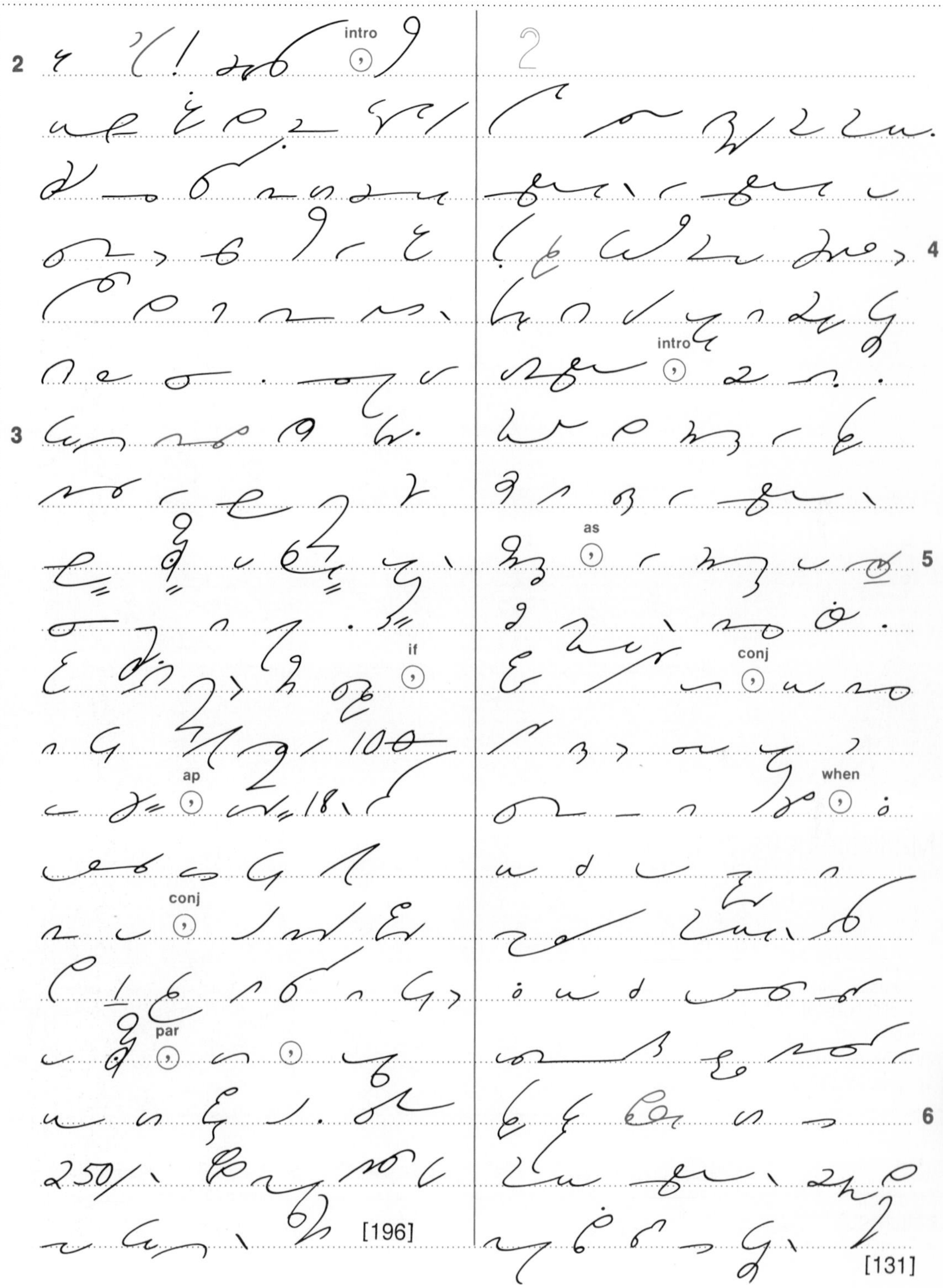

Transcription Quiz

Transcribe the following letter, adding the appropriate punctuation to your transcript.

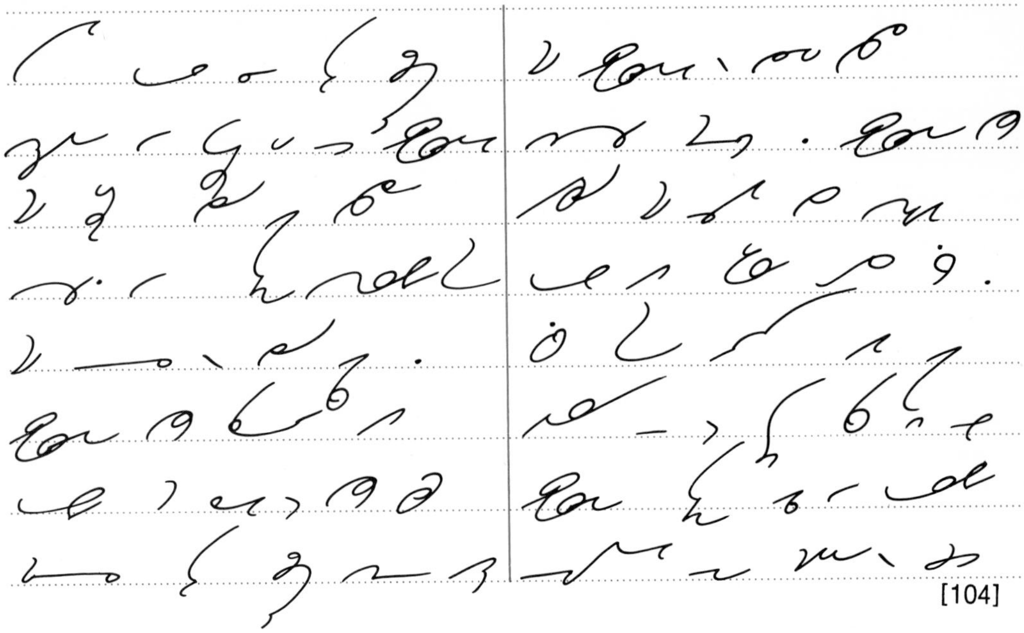

[104]

Mailable Letter Production

1
Ms. Marsha Wong
Central Investment
Corporation
2915 Jupiter Avenue
Spokane, WA 99200

1 abil·i·ty
2 ef·fec·tive
3 Transcribe: seven
4 Transcribe: 7,000

1
2
3

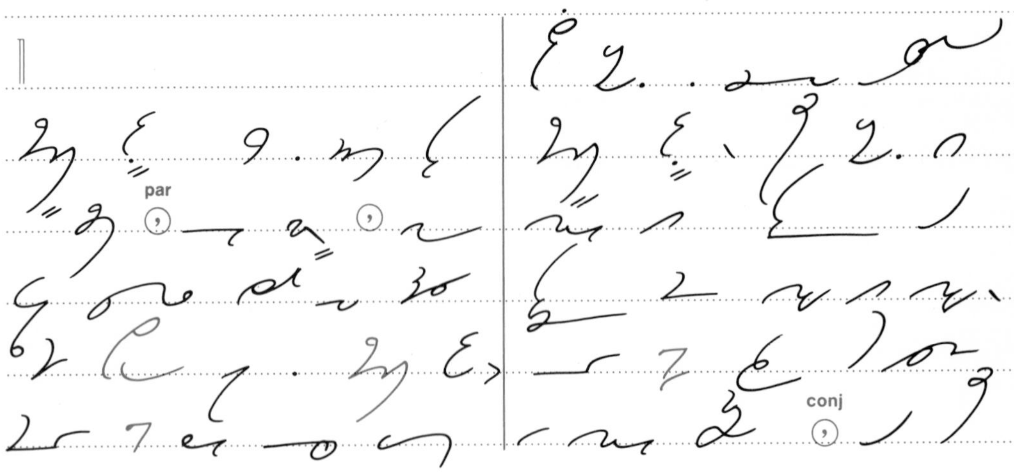

4

3
Ms. Jean Dayton
Dayton Insurance Agency
513 State Street
Greenville, SC 29600

4
To: Pat Jordon, President
From: Stephanie Smith, Sales Manager
Subject: Request For New Word Processor

7 bor·row·ing
8 pieces
9 ver·i·fy

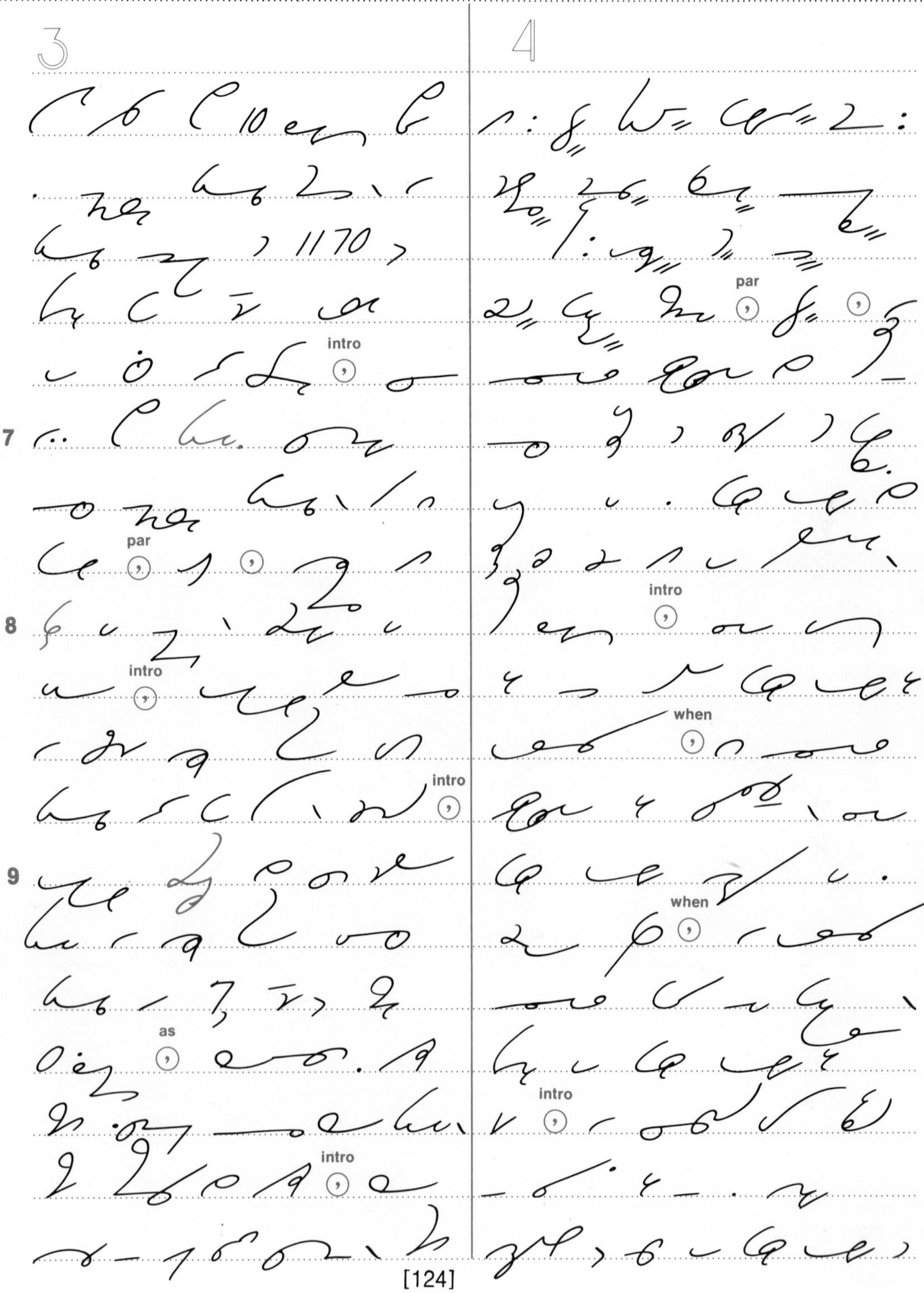

[124]

Building Transcription Skill

Transcription Warmup

10
20
30
40

Transcription Speed Building

10
20
29
40
50
59
66
80

10 ed·i·to·ri·al
11 pro·duc·tiv·i·ty
12 es·ti·mate

Secretaries are often asked to do research in order to assist their managers in the development of major reports; shorthand makes this job easier and more efficient.

NORTHGATE SECURITY SYSTEMS
648 Lockwood Avenue, Windsor, CT 06095

March 25, 19XX

Ms. Maria Sanchez
Madison Real Estate Company
3210 Oak Street
Hartford, CT 06106

REFERENCE FOR MS. LINDA MICHAELS

It is a pleasure for me to serve as a job reference for Ms. Linda Michaels. In fact, this should be one of the easiest business letters that I have ever had to write.

Ms. Michaels came to work for us a little over three years ago. In her first job with us she worked as an operator in our word processing center. She proved to be an excellent proofreader and did the highest quality work. Because of her shorthand skill, many people began to dictate to her the corrections they desired to have made in their rough draft typed material. Also because of her shorthand skill, Linda was identified for promotion to the position of private secretary.

As the secretary to one of our vice presidents, Linda proved to be very dependable and productive. Because of her mastery of the English language, Linda was given the job of writing much of the routine correspondence formerly handled by the executive.

Ms. Michaels decided to resign her position with us because we are a rather small company and simply do not have any further job opportunities for her. We believe, however, that she will make a valuable contribution to any business that is lucky enough to hire her.

Stanley J. Urbanek

STANLEY J. URBANEK, PERSONNEL ADMINISTRATOR

ABJ

26

Building Professional Skills

Shorthand ■ Research Notes

A common assignment that most students face is to write a research paper based upon resources available in the library. Business people—executives and secretaries—are also called upon to prepare reports that involve extensive research. Anyone who has written such a paper knows the long hours of painstaking work that can be involved in making longhand notes from research data. While photocopies can be made, this can be a costly process if a great number of pages must be copied, and photocopy machines cannot edit. They copy an entire page, even though the researcher may desire to quote only a sentence or two.

The person who knows shorthand has a real advantage when it comes to taking research notes. Data can be quickly scanned, with major points noted in shorthand. Crucial data and quotations that support those major points are also easily noted in shorthand. Since shorthand can be written at a speed several times that of longhand, it can easily cut research time in half. Virtually everyone can appreciate that kind of contribution toward more effective time management.

Communication Checkup

Fractions Alone

In letters and memos, fractions that occur by themselves should be represented by words. The two elements of a fraction are separated by a hyphen.

We sent a notice to two-thirds of the members.

Fractions in Reports

In technical reports, fractions are expressed with figures. A diagonal is used to separate the two elements of the fraction.

The micrometer revealed an error of 3/32 inch.

38

Building Professional Skills

Letter Styles ■ Simplified

The simplified letter style shown on page 186 was created in order to make business letters more conversational and to reduce the cost of producing them. The basic feature of the simplified letter is the omission of both the salutation and the complimentary closing. The reason for these omissions is that these two letter parts are purely traditional and have little, if anything, to do with the way people normally communicate with each other face-to-face.

In place of the salutation the simplified letter customarily includes a subject line. The word *subject* is omitted and the subject line itself is typed in all capital letters. This typing style makes for the fastest keyboarding, and the routine inclusion of a subject line in a letter aids in the sorting of incoming mail according to work priorities.

Communication Checkup

prefix in-

In English, the prefix *in-* means *not.*

informal	Not formal.
incomplete	Not complete.
inadequate	Not adequate.

Mixed Numbers

When whole numbers and fractions occur together, the mixed numbers are expressed in figures.

The attendance was 2½ times greater than expected.

Fractions at the Beginning of a Sentence

As with all numbers at the beginning of a sentence, fractions at the beginning of a sentence are spelled as words.

One-half of the class was absent today.

Building Transcription Skill

Transcription Warmup

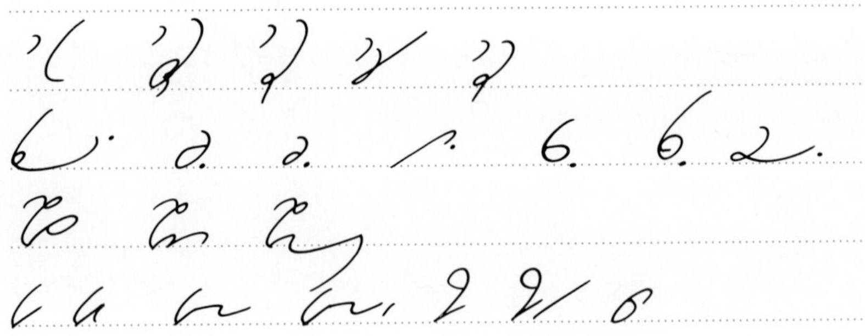

10
20
31
41

Transcription Speed Building

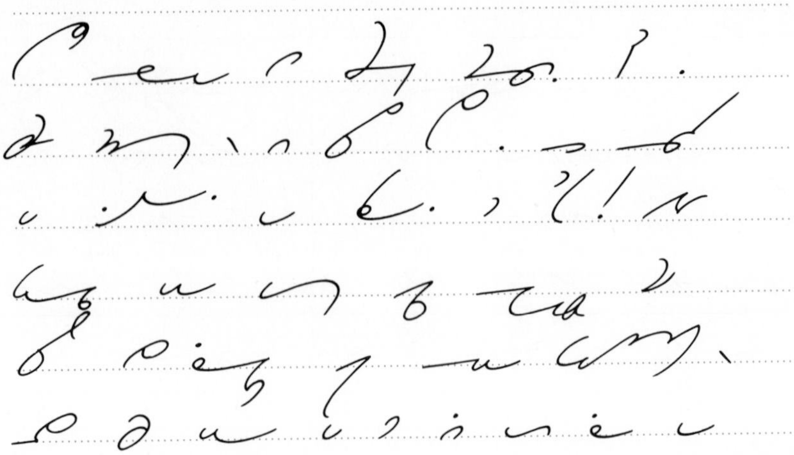

11
20
30
40
49
57

3

Mrs. Ann West
Central City Bank
706 Madison Avenue
New York, NY 10020

14 com·mu·ter
15 course
16 au·dio
17 too
18 of·fered
19 ac·cept
20 cop·ies

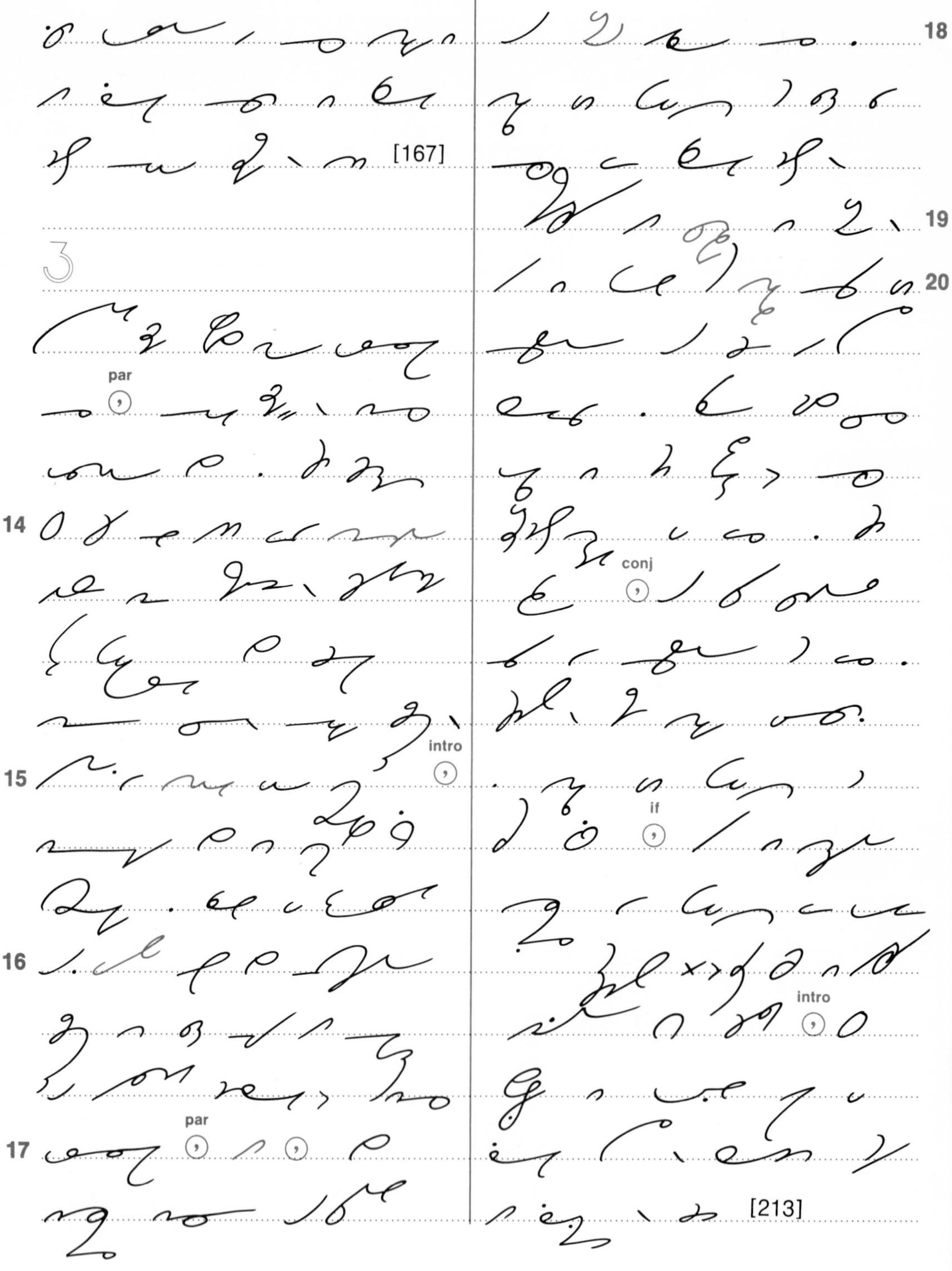

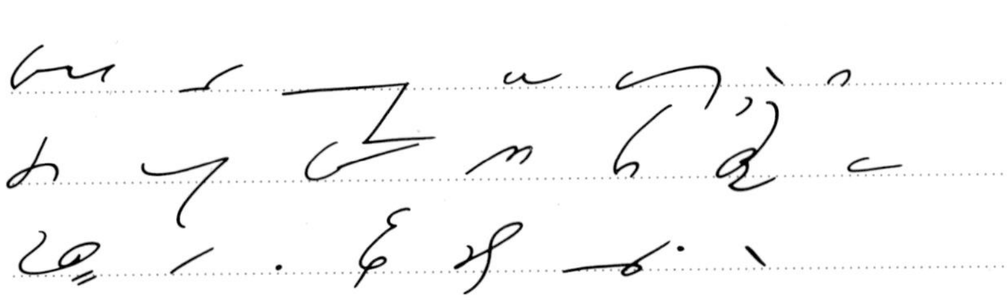

68

79

85

Transcription Quiz

Transcribe the following letter, adding the appropriate punctuation to your transcript.

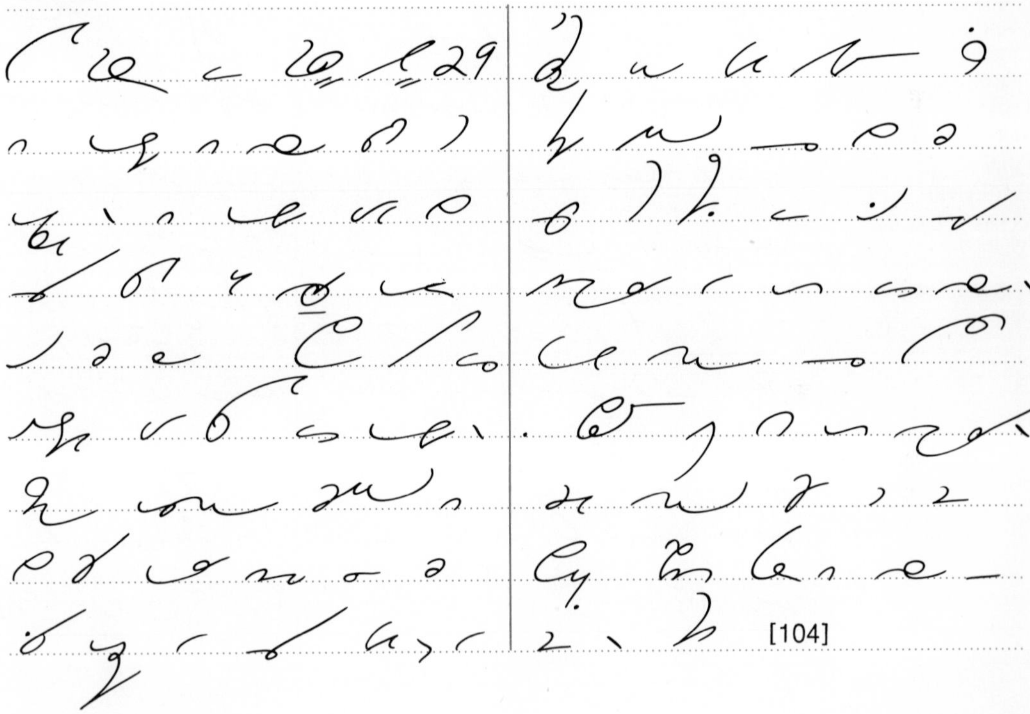

[104]

Mailable Letter Production

1
Ms. Sharon Bruce
1004 Third Avenue
Long Beach, CA 90811

1 write

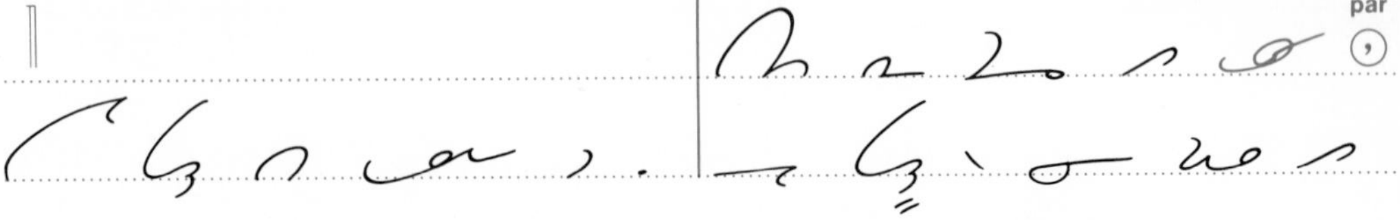

par 1

2

Mr. Thomas Duffy
United Manufacturing Enterprises
202 Howard Avenue
Salt Lake City, UT
84100

3 va·ri·ety
4 cit·ies
5 of·fer·ing
6 ben·e·fit
7 com·pa·nies
8 re·duc·ing
9 cost
10 ex·ists
11 their
12 ef·fi·cient
13 Transcribe: 25

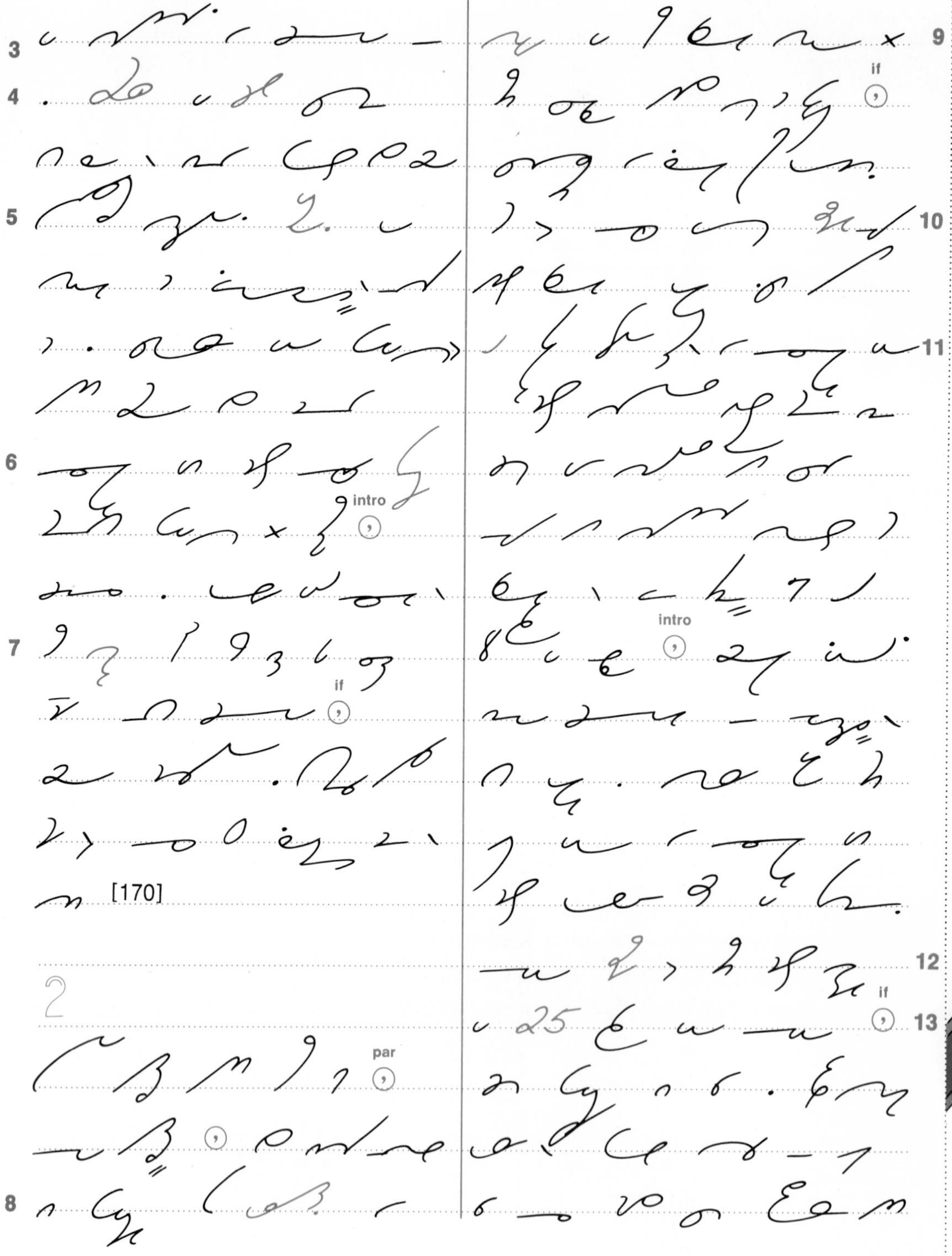

2
Mr. Ralph Macy
915 Platte Avenue
Denver, CO 80211

2 pre·mi·um
3 lose
4 may·be
5 in·stall·ment
6 hear
7 cov·er·age
8 Transcribe:
   2½
9 re·place·ment
10 cost

2

3

4

if

5

6

[125]

2

ser

as

7

8

9

if

10

if

[127]

Transcription Quiz

Transcribe the following letter, adding the appropriate punctuation to your transcript.

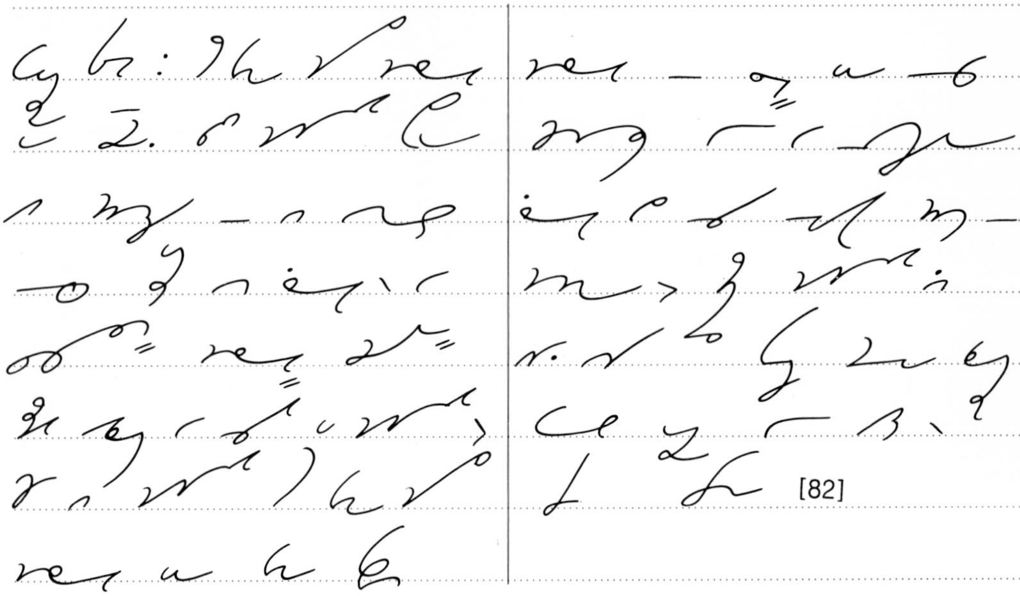

Mailable Letter Production

1
Mr. Arnold Kline
Anderson
Manufacturing
Company
2422 Corona Street
Honolulu, HI 96800

1 se·ries
2 sem·i·nars

1
2

3
Mrs. Diane Gunderson
1217 St. Claire Avenue
Billings, MT 59100

4
Notes From
The Library

11 their
12 won·der·ing
13 pa·per·work
14 than
15 one-half
16 fire·proof

3

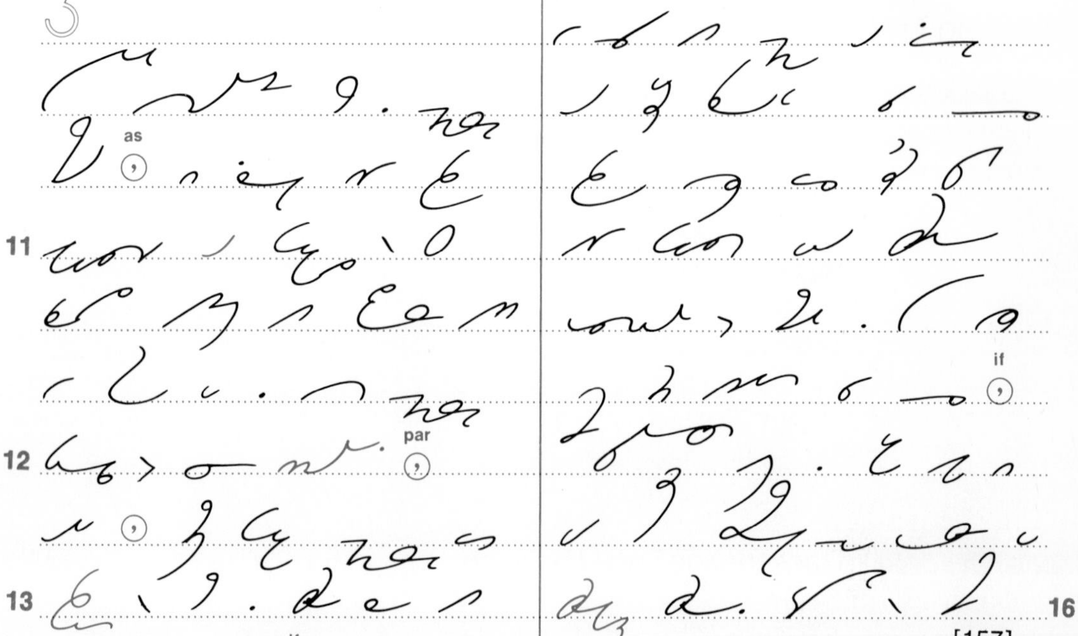

[157]

4

[38]

Transcription Warmup

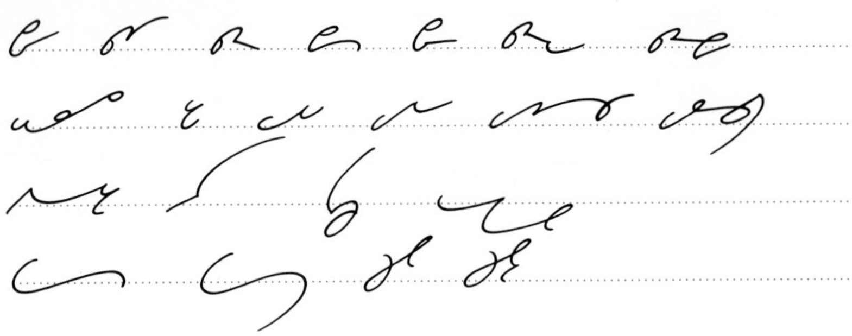

9
19
29
39

Transcription Speed Building

10
19
27
37
44
53
62
70
80

27

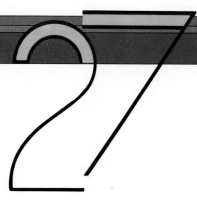

Building Professional Skills

Punctuation Checkup

, numbers

Commas are used to separate thousands in numbers. That is, a comma is used every three digits to the left of the decimal point. Commas are not used to the right of the decimal point. In numbers having only four digits, the comma may be omitted.

5000
49,000
1,200,000

Communication Checkup

titles of complete works

The title of a complete publication such as a book, a magazine, a newspaper, or a brochure is typed with the first letter of every major word capitalized and with the entire title underlined.

Please send me a copy of your new book, Accounting Today.
I read the entire sports section of The Morning Times.
The booklet, Home Repairs Made Easy, was helpful.

37

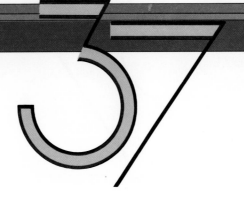

Building Professional Skills

Listening ■ Planning a Response

One of the problems in being a good listener is that the human mind can do more than one thing at a time. We can listen to someone speak, and yet we can also be thinking of other things, too. In order to keep our minds on the subject that the speaker is talking about, we can effectively apply this excess intelligence to the job of listening.

Instead of letting our minds wander while listening to someone, we can use intelligence to anticipate the logical conclusion to which the speaker's line of reasoning is leading. We can be planning our wording and recalling supportive evidence for how we are to either support or dispute what the speaker has said. Good listeners do not monopolize a conversation. They give the other person equal time. But when it is their turn to speak, good listeners have planned ahead so that their remarks are articulate, logical, and to the point.

Communication Checkup

prefix inter-

The prefix *inter-* means between or among.

interpret	To bring about understanding between two people.
interruption	A division in an event.
interfere	To come between.

Building Transcription Skill

Transcription Warmup

10
20
30
40

Transcription Speed Building

10
20
32
40
50
61
74
83

6 anx·ious
7 ac·cept
8 any time

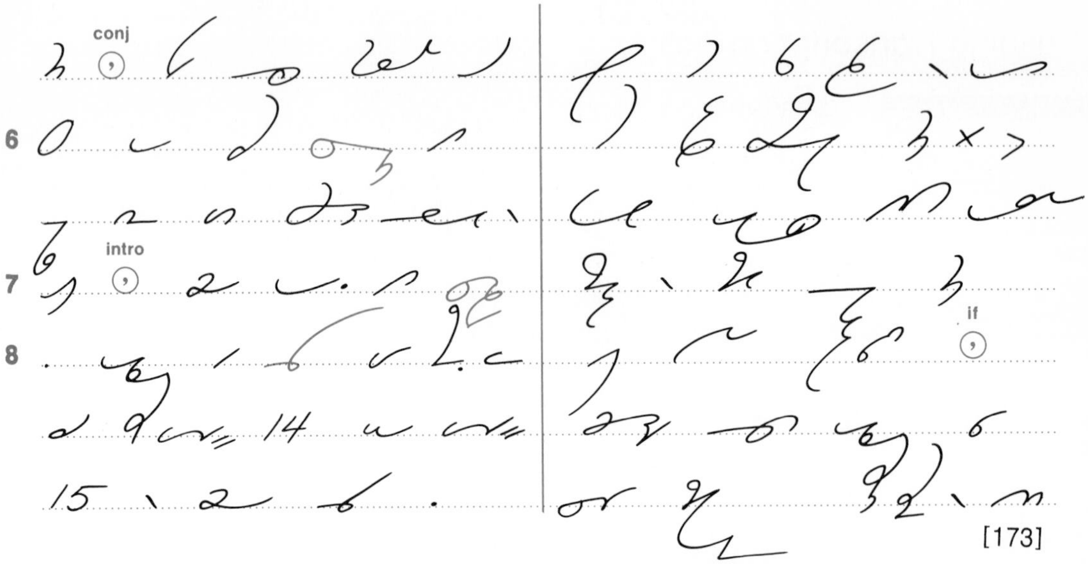

[173]

An executive may leave a meeting in order to dictate information that must be transcribed and brought back into the meeting.

Transcription Quiz

Transcribe the following letter, adding the appropriate punctuation to your transcript.

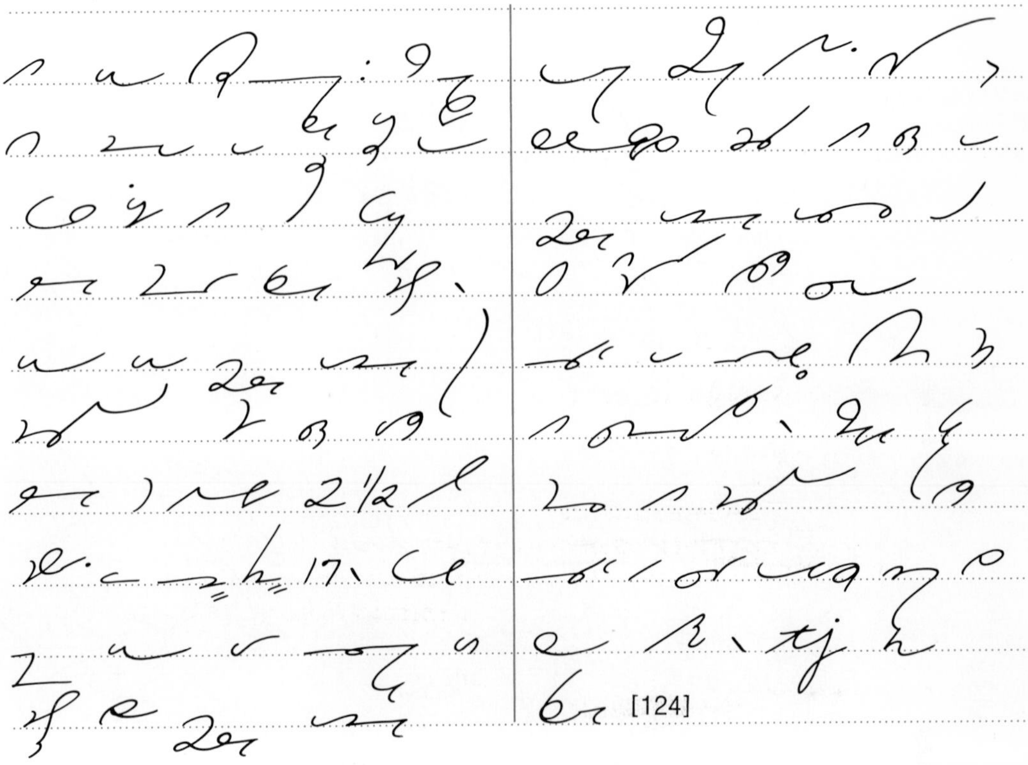

Mailable Letter Production

1
Mr. Roger Parsons
712 Mason Avenue
Des Moines, IA 50311

1 brief
2 Transcribe: seven

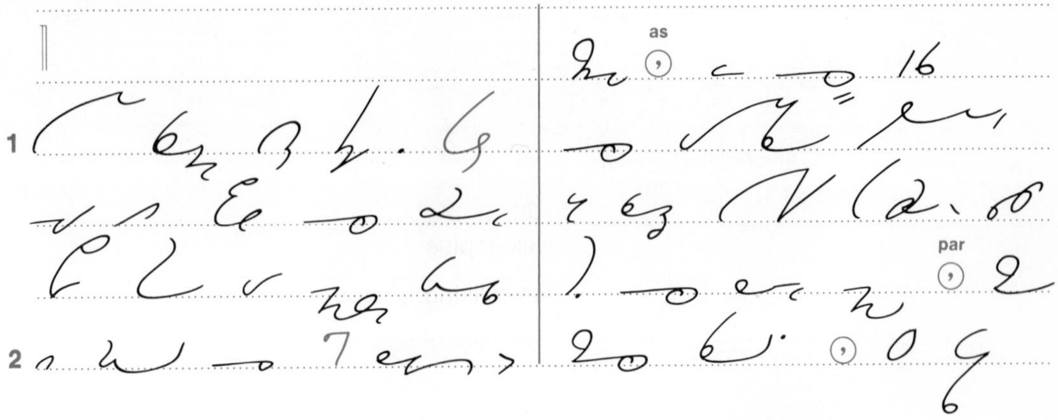

2
Mountain View Hotel
112 Webster Avenue
Nashville, TN 37211

3
Lake View Restaurant
1532 Shore Drive
Burlington, VT 05401

2 night's
3 some·time
4 cost
5 rep·u·ta·tion

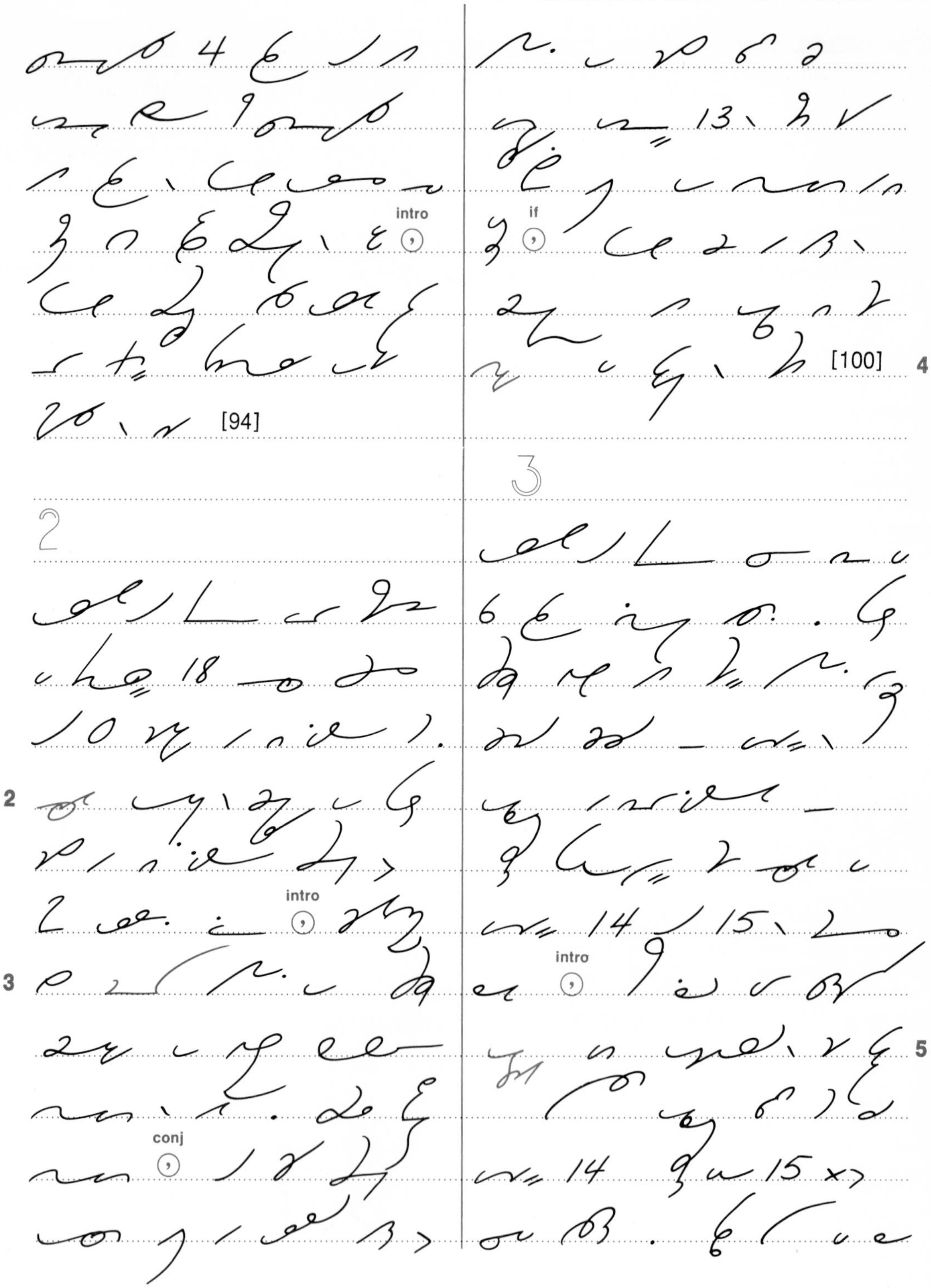

2
Mrs. E. D. Bailey
116 East Tyler Avenue
Cleveland, OH 44111

3
Mr. Ralph Drew
25 Pine Ridge Court
Oxford, MI 48051

3 cov•er•age
4 ev•ery•one
5 some
6 re•al•ize
7 its
8 re•built

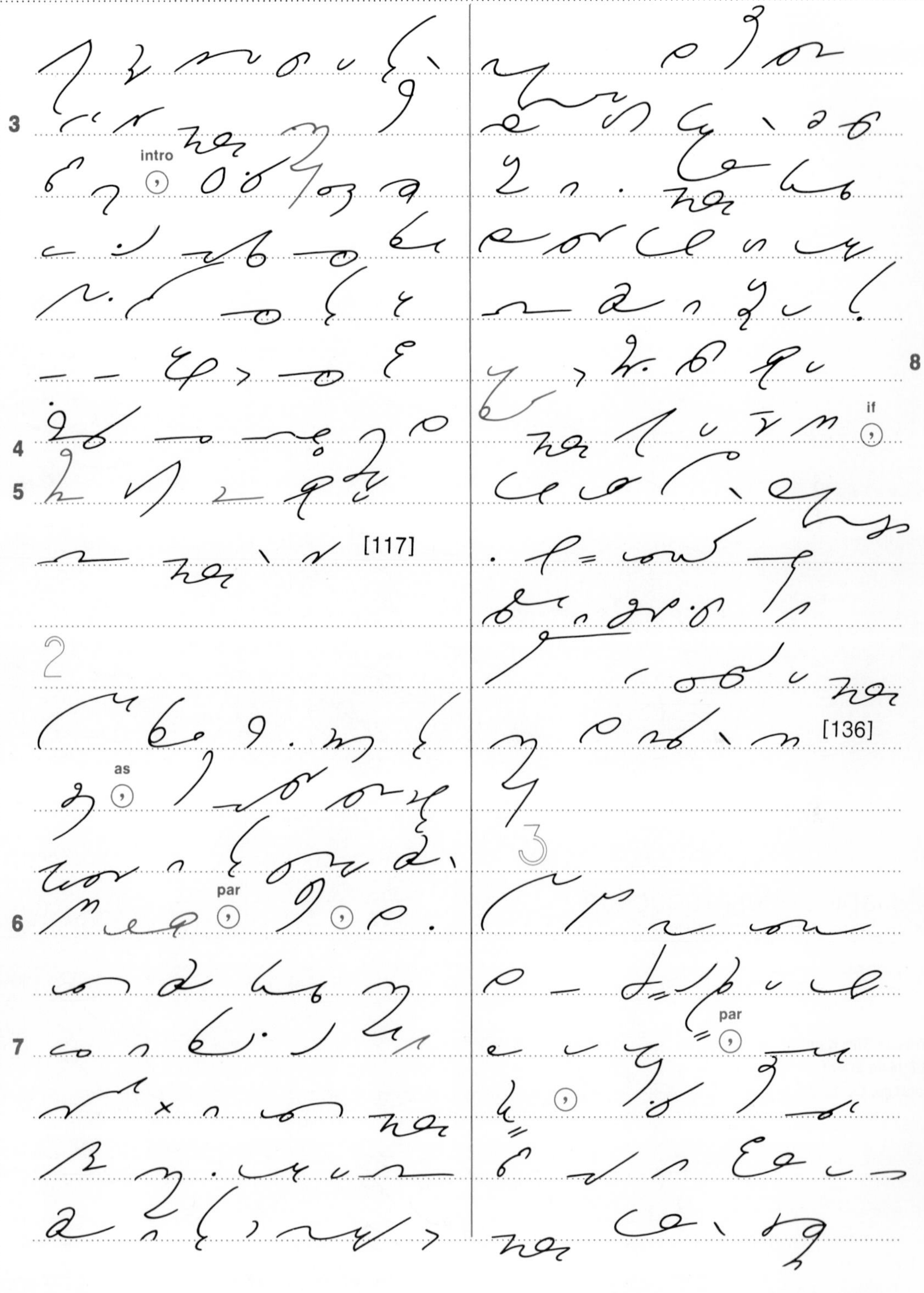

Transcription Quiz

Transcribe the following letter, adding the appropriate punctuation to your transcript.

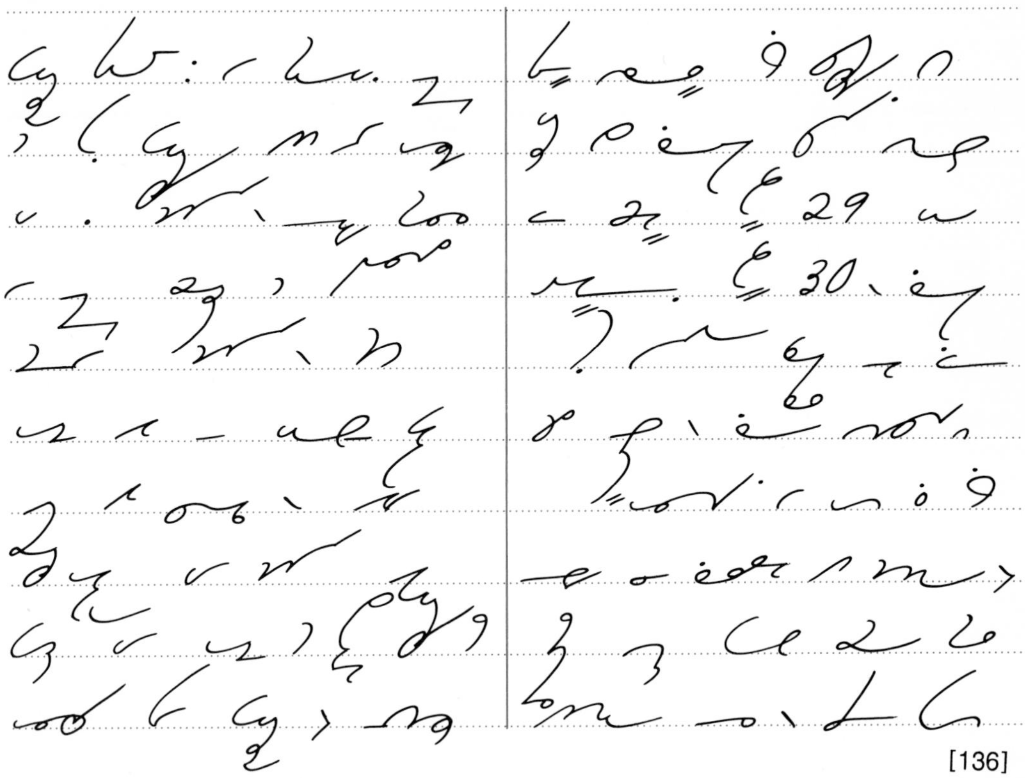

[136]

Mailable Letter Production

1
Western Star Hotel
458 Main Street
Durango, CO 81301

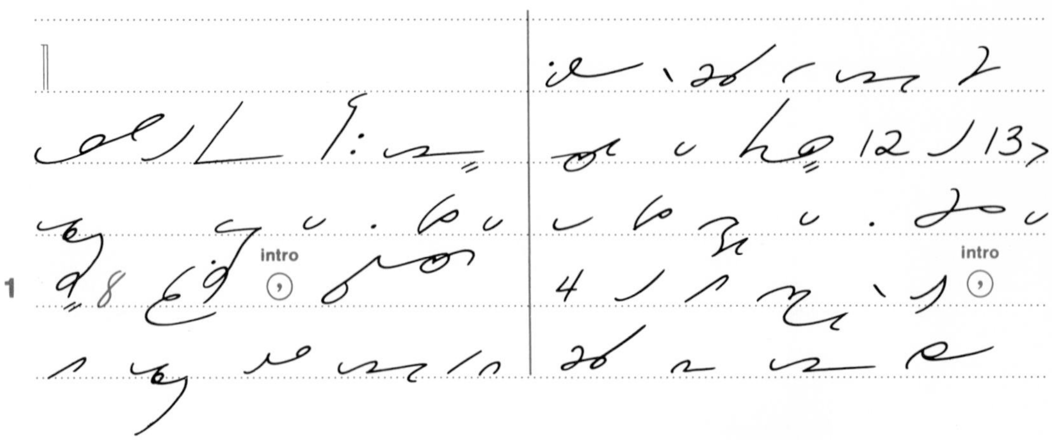

1 Transcribe:
eight

4
Mr. Edward Crane
2005 Fountain Street
Youngstown, OH
44511

9 costs
10 ben·e·fits
11 touch
12 ea·ger
13 ad·di·tion
14 Transcribe: $48
15 an·nu·al

Building Transcription Skill

Transcription Warmup

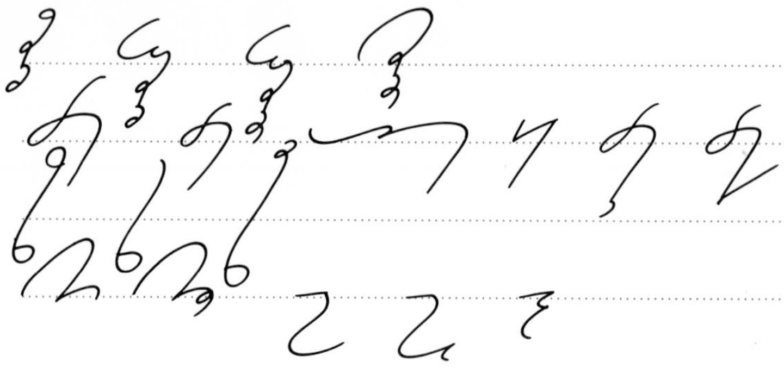

10
20
30
41

Transcription Speed Building

11
24
34
43
53
62
68
78
81

28

Building Professional Skills

Listening ■ Judge the Message

Oftentimes we are called upon to decide whether we agree with what a speaker is saying. The speaker may be a political candidate, a lecturer in a meeting, a teacher in a class, or a friend with whom we are having a conversation. In any case, when we make a decision about agreeing or disagreeing, we must make sure that we are really reacting to the message and not something else.

It is easy for people to mistakenly think that they oppose an idea when what they really dislike is the speaker's attitude, appearance, communication ability, or personality. In order to do an intelligent job of listening, we must judge the content of what is being said and not judge the way in which it is being said. Judging the content of a message, instead of judging the speaker, is not only good listening, it is good human relations. It is one more way in which to develop a better personality within ourselves, and to master the communication skill of listening.

Communication Checkup

adjacent numbers

When two numbers occur next to each other in a sentence, it is best for the sake of clarity to express one in figures and the other as a spelled word. Usually we spell the first number of the pair and represent the second number in figures. If the first number, however, would make a very long spelled word, we can express it in figures and spell the second word. When two numbers occur together in a sentence, it is usually because the second number is part of a hyphenated expression.

My class consists of seven 5-year-old boys and girls.
I am grading three 2-page reports.
However, we printed 7,000 two-page leaflets.

36

Building Professional Skills

Shorthand for the Professional ■ The Immediate Deadline

The concept of "turnaround time" is becoming more and more important as people are increasingly concerned with office productivity. Simply put, turnaround time is the number of minutes or hours that elapse from the time an executive finishes dictating a letter until that letter is ready for the executive's signature.

The executive who knows how to dictate and the secretary who is a good transcriber form an unbeatable team in the quest for rapid turnaround time. An executive with a private secretary knows exactly what the secretary's work priorities are. The executive with a private secretary also knows from experience what level of productivity to expect when the secretary is under pressure. No stenopool or word processing center is likely to beat the turnaround time of a private secretary who has just been told, "Take this letter in shorthand, and give me a typewritten transcript now!"

Communication Checkup

prefix dis-

In English *dis-* tells us that words have a negative meaning. Sometimes *dis-* means opposition to something; at other times the prefix means the lack of something. Here are a few examples:

dislike	The opposite of liking.
displeasure	The opposite of being pleased.
disregard	The lack of paying attention.
disparity	The lack of being equal.

Building Transcription Skill

Transcription Warmup

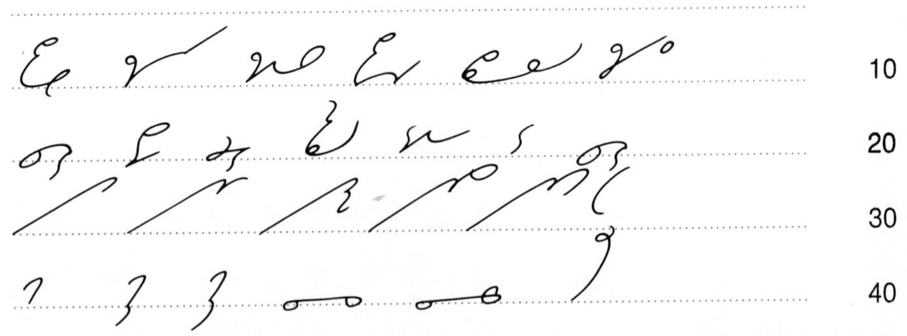

Transcription Speed Building

4
To: James Clark
From: Lorraine Melrose
Subject: Let's Upgrade Our Word Processing Printer

12 strength
13 ev·er·in·creas·ing

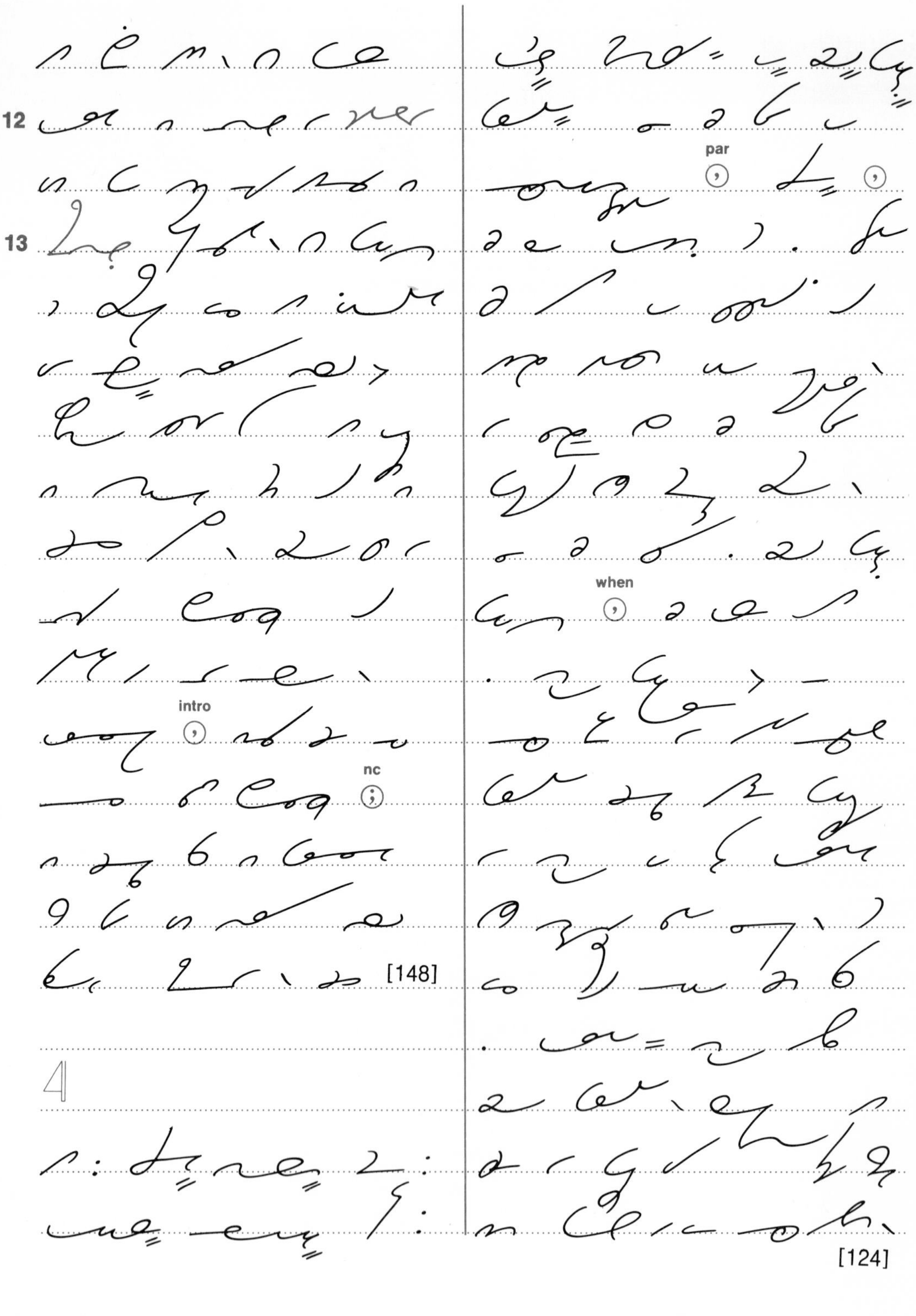

Transcription Quiz

Transcribe the following letter, adding the appropriate punctuation to your transcript.

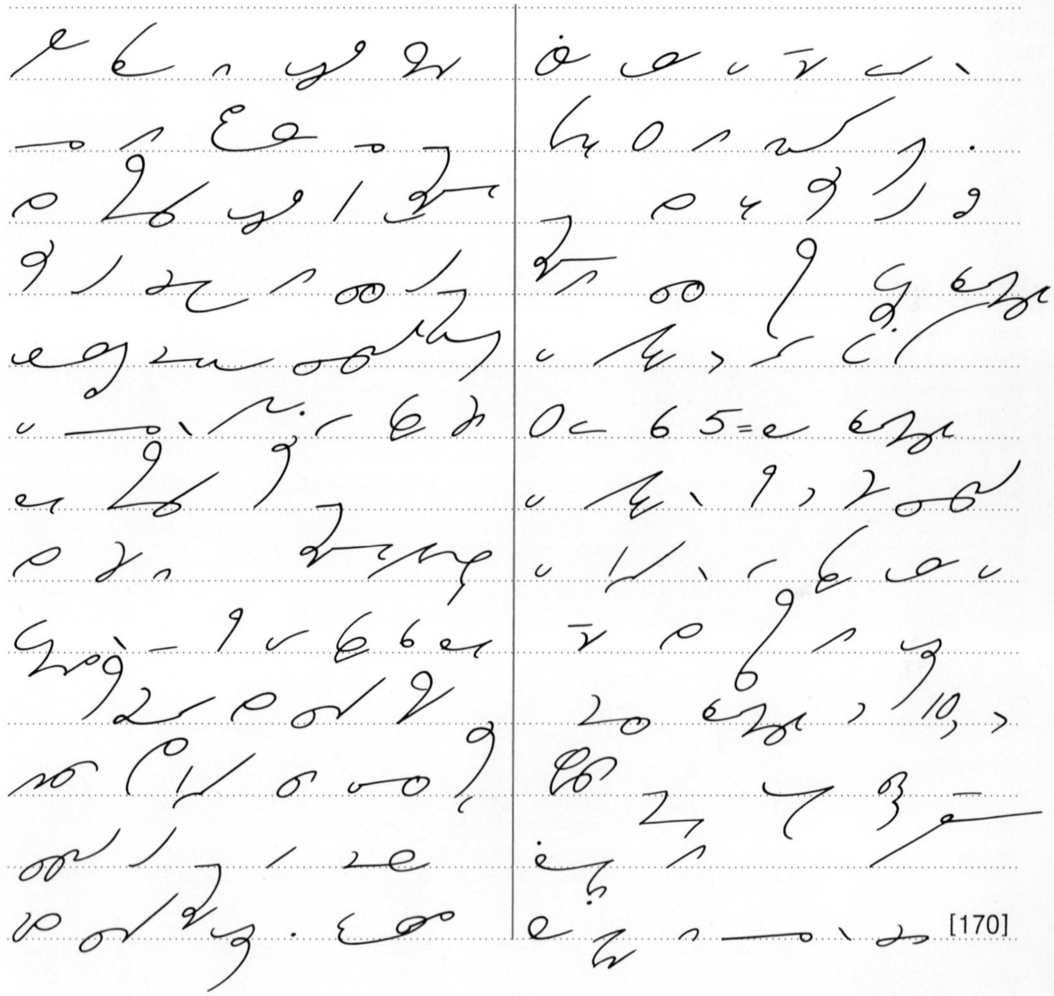

2
Ms. Cindy Nelson
Western Life
Insurance Company
3004 Lee Street
Salem, OR 97311

3
Mr. Lee Harrison
809 Blake Street
Arlington, VA 22211

4 vis·i·tor
5 two-draw·er
6 three
7 nec·es·sary
8 re·al·ly
9 valu·able
10 as·sets
11 cri·sis

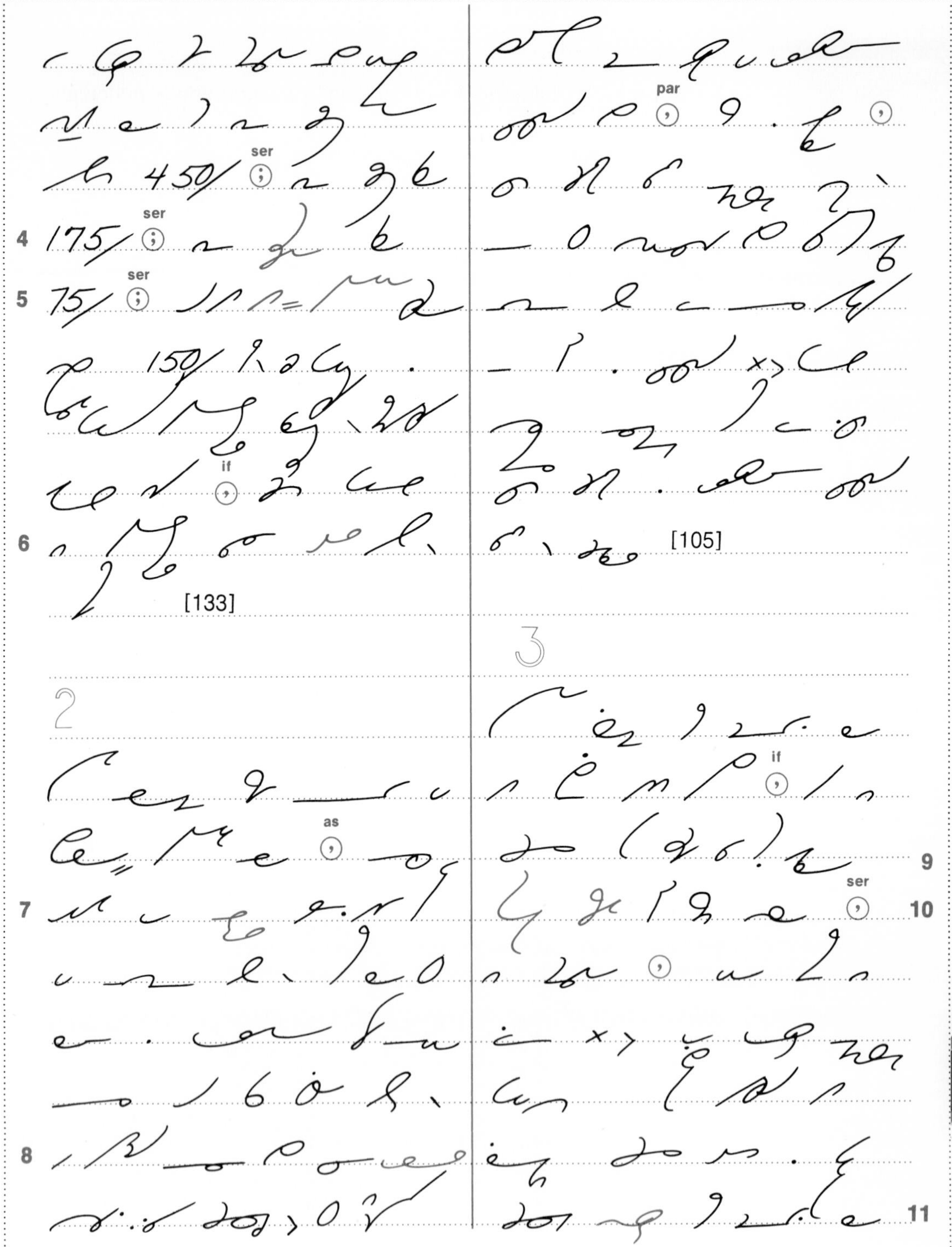

Mailable Letter Production

1
Mrs. Mary Davis
Kansas Property
Insurance Company
1605 Hamilton Avenue
Kansas City, KS 66100

2
Ms. Judy Frank
423 Mead Street
Fargo, ND 58100

1 great
2 ga•rage
3 it•self

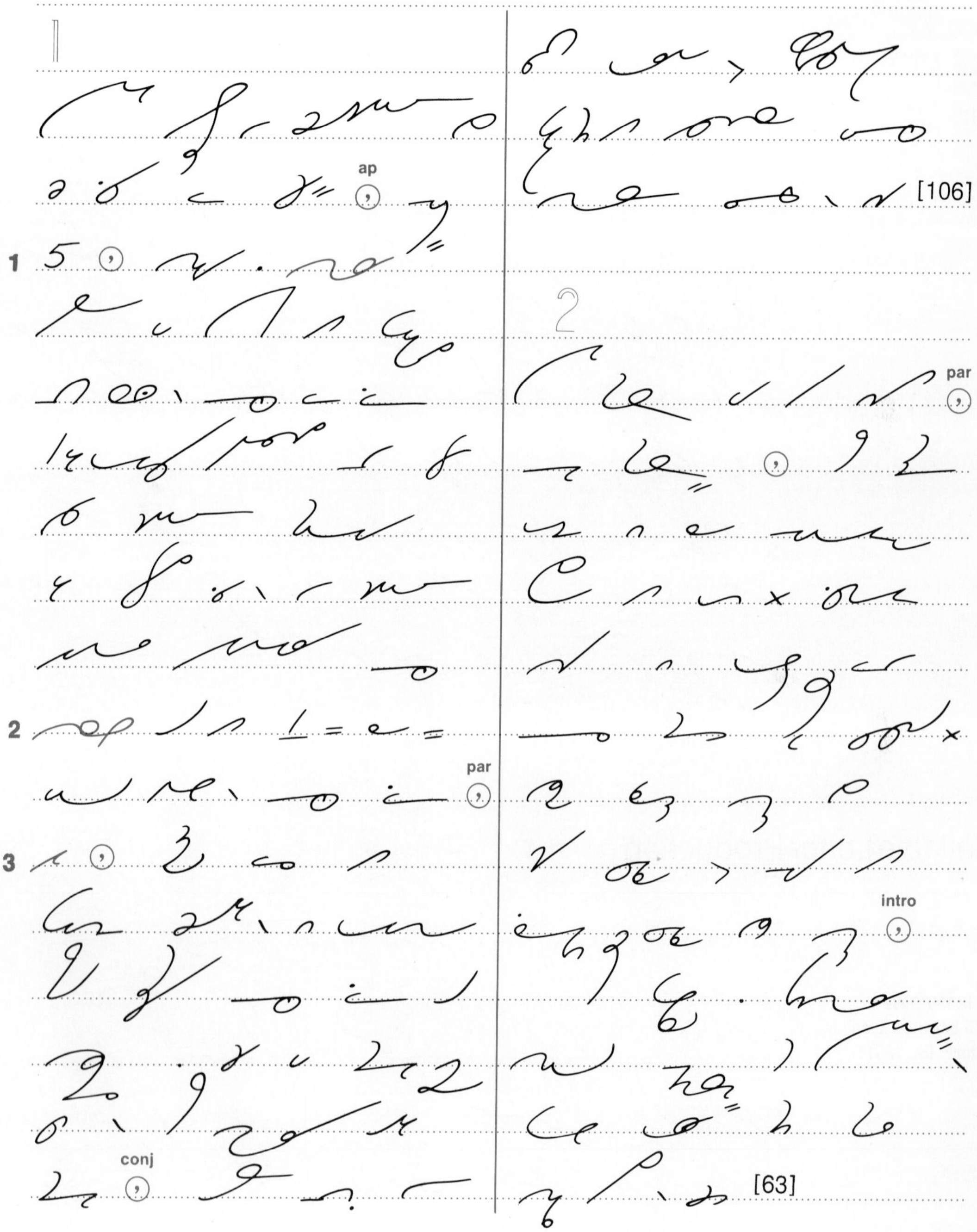

Transcription Quiz

Transcribe the following letter, adding the appropriate punctuation to your transcript.

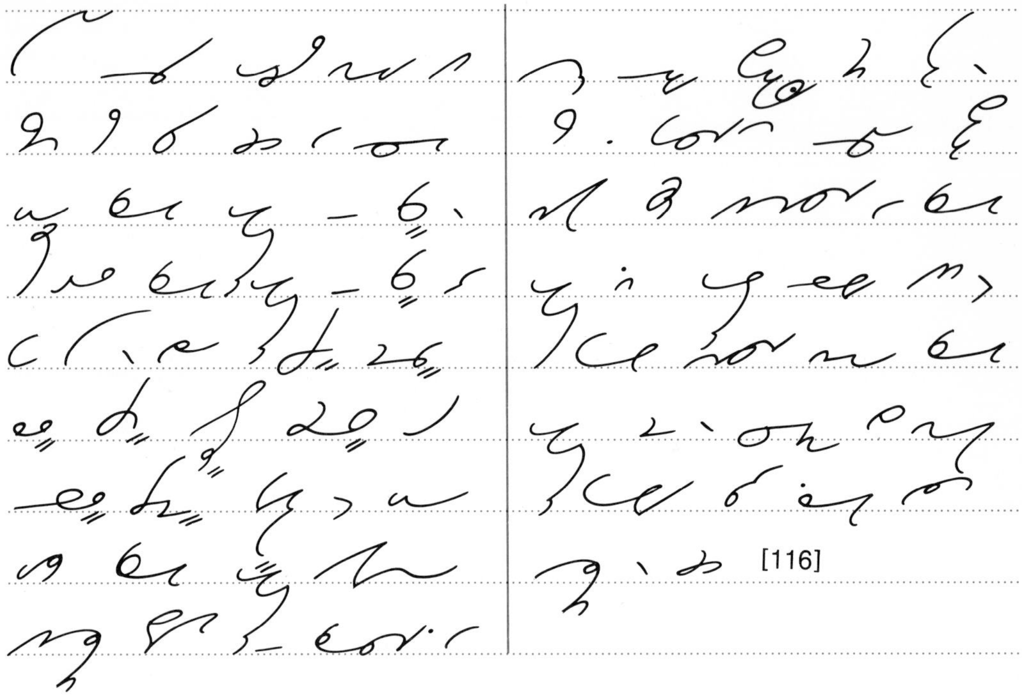

[116]

Mailable Letter Production

1
Mr. Lester Novak
2615 Seymour Road
Norman, OK 73011

1 some time
2 length
3 ris·ing

1

2

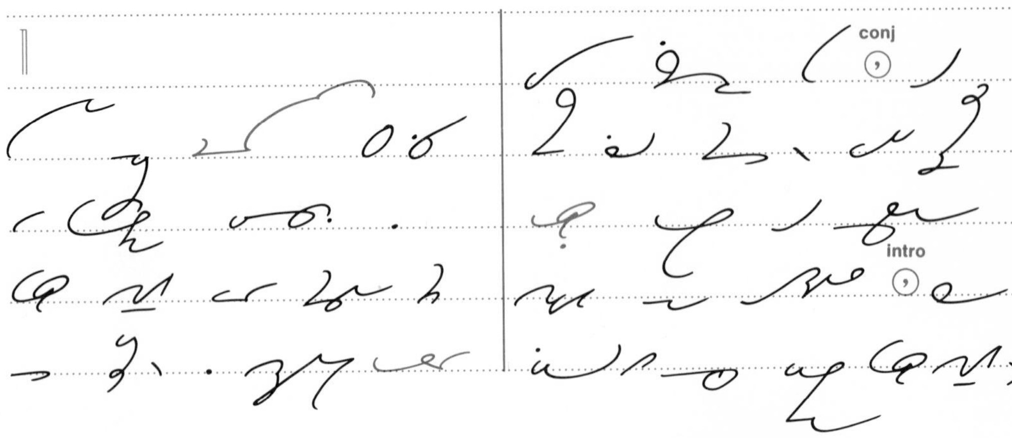

3

3
Mrs. Edna Pace
307 Dodge Street
Louisville, KY 40211

4
Mr. Rico Sanchez
1431 Russell Road
Wilmington, DE 19811

4 **know**
5 **Transcribe:**
  $120
6 **ei•ther**
7 **re•ceive**
8 **ef•fect**

Building Transcription Skill

Transcription Warmup

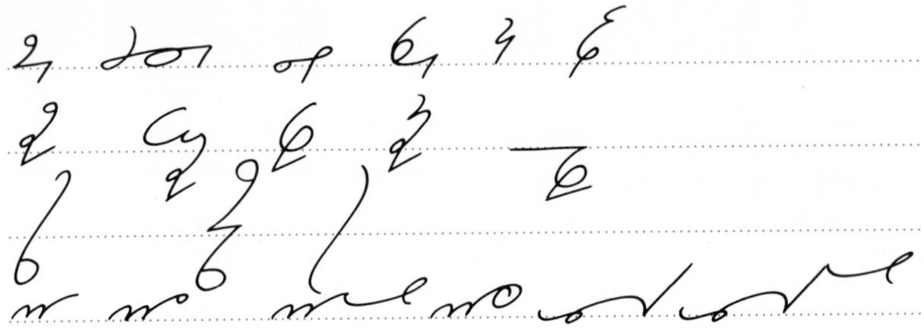

10
20
30
40

Transcription Speed Building

10
20
29
35
45
54
65
73
82

29

Building Professional Skills

Punctuation Checkup

, compound sentence

Sometimes two simple sentences are joined together. This is usually done when two sentences are very short and are closely related. Usually the sentences are joined by a conjunction such as *and, for,* or *but.* This type of sentence is called a compound sentence, and the conjunction is preceded by a comma.

Today is stormy, and I want to stay home.
He expected to do well on the test, but he failed to answer many questions.
I really enjoy travel, for I find the change of pace relaxing.

Communication Checkup

dates

In business communications it is common practice for the month to precede the date. In expressing dates in this common way, it is not appropriate to use *th, st,* or *d.*

On July 4, 1984, we had a celebration.
Your letter arrived on April 24.

If, for some reason, the date precedes the month, then it is appropriate to use *th, st,* or *d.*

On the 17th of March the Senate will vote.

35

Building Professional Skills

Punctuation Checkup

; series

When one or more items within a series contains a comma, the items in the series are separated from each other by semicolons.

The officers are Vincent Rossi, President; Kim Lau, Vice-President; and Mary Baker, Secretary.
The exams will be given on Monday, November 1; Monday, November 8; and Wednesday, November 17.

Communication Checkup

assistance ■ assistants

assistance Help or aid.

Thanks for your assistance with the newsletter.
The assistance with our new members was quite valuable.

assistants People who help.

I need two assistants who can operate cash registers.
Several of the assistants made valuable suggestions.

Building Transcription Skill

Transcription Warmup

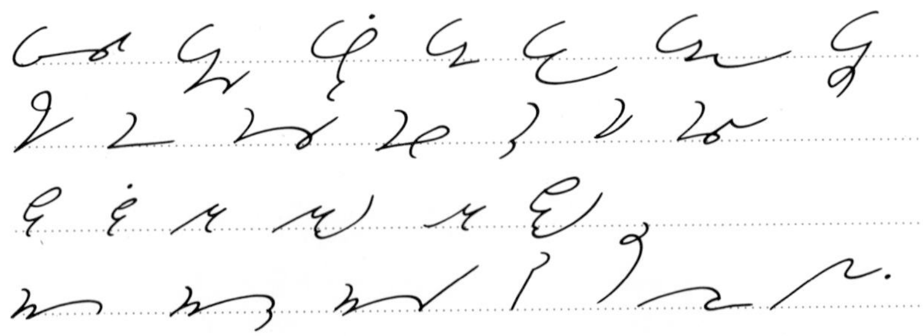

11
21
32
42

Transcription Speed Building

10
21
31
40
48
59
69
79
80

4
Ms. Lynda Higgins
623 Walnut Street
Charlotte, NC 28211

11 ar·ti·cle
12 we're
13 ac·com·mo·date

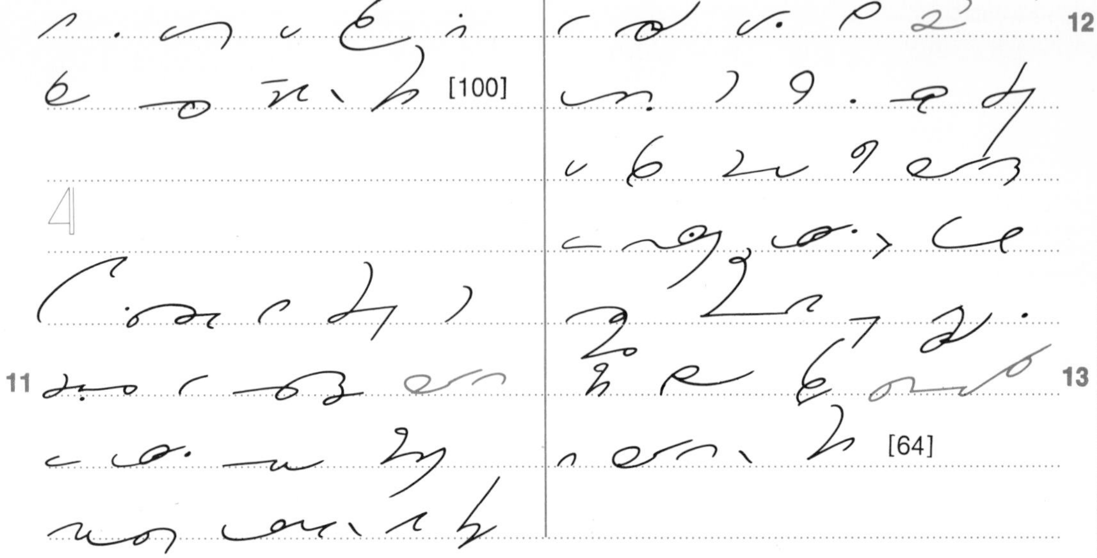

Word processors use magnetic media to store transcribed documents. The stored documents serve as file copies and can be played back, if necessary, for verification, revision, or additional hard copies.

Transcription Quiz

Transcribe the following letter, adding the appropriate punctuation to your transcript.

[123]

Mailable Letter Production

1
Southwest Insurance Corporation
113 Carson Street
Santa Fe, NM 87501

1 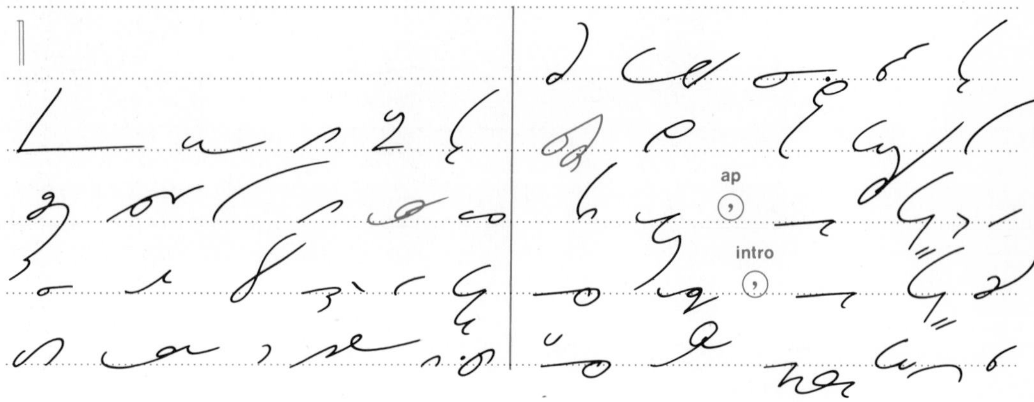

2

1 write
2 ad·vice

2
Mr. John Troy
417 Washington Street
Aberdeen, SD 57401

3
Ms. Barbara Lynn
Executive Director
National Hiking Club
405 Madison Street
Cleveland, OH 44111

6 **one**
7 **two**
8 **wheth·er**
9 **fre·quent**
10 **Hik·ing**

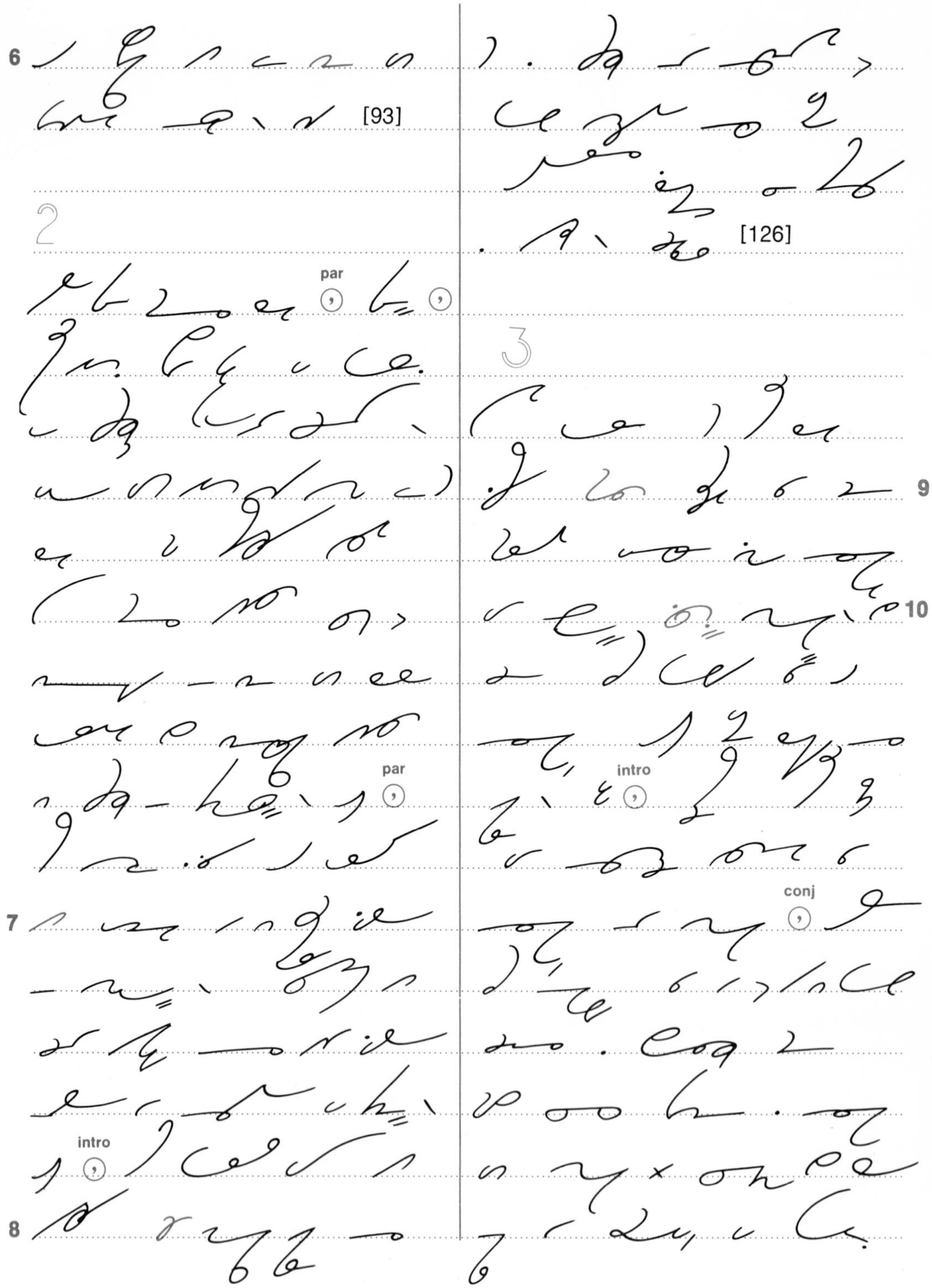

2
Mr. Glen Gordon
2905 Ellis Street
Duluth, MN 55811

3
Dawson Insurance
Agency
1620 Adams Avenue
Boston, MA 02100

3 sum•ma•rize
4 there
5 stor•age

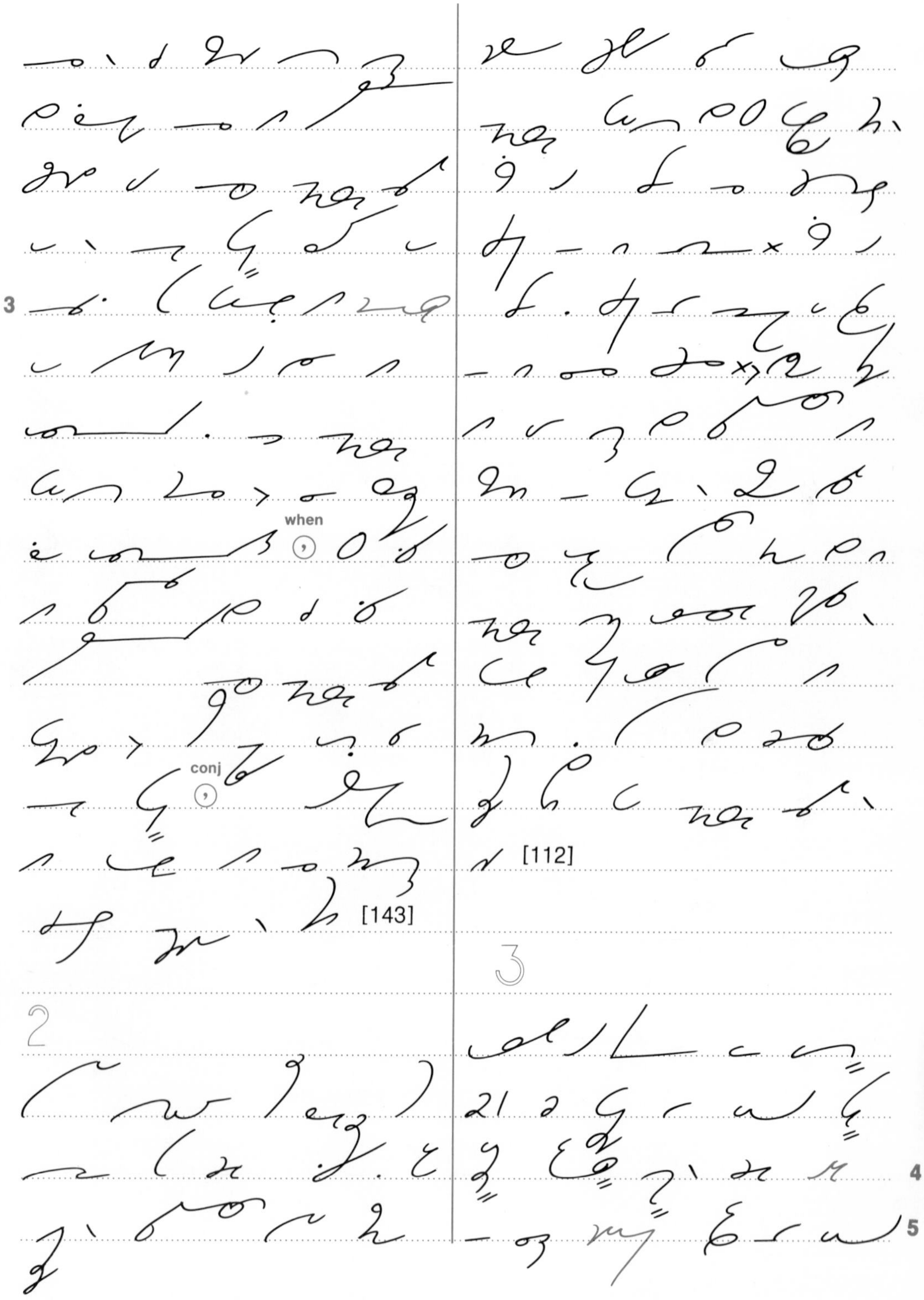

Transcription Quiz

Transcribe the following letter, adding the appropriate punctuation to your transcript.

Mailable Letter Production

1
Mr. Lyle Fulton
225 Summit Avenue
Manchester, MO 63011

1 avail·able
2 va·ri·ety
3 know·ing
4 typ·i·cal
5 sin·cere·ly

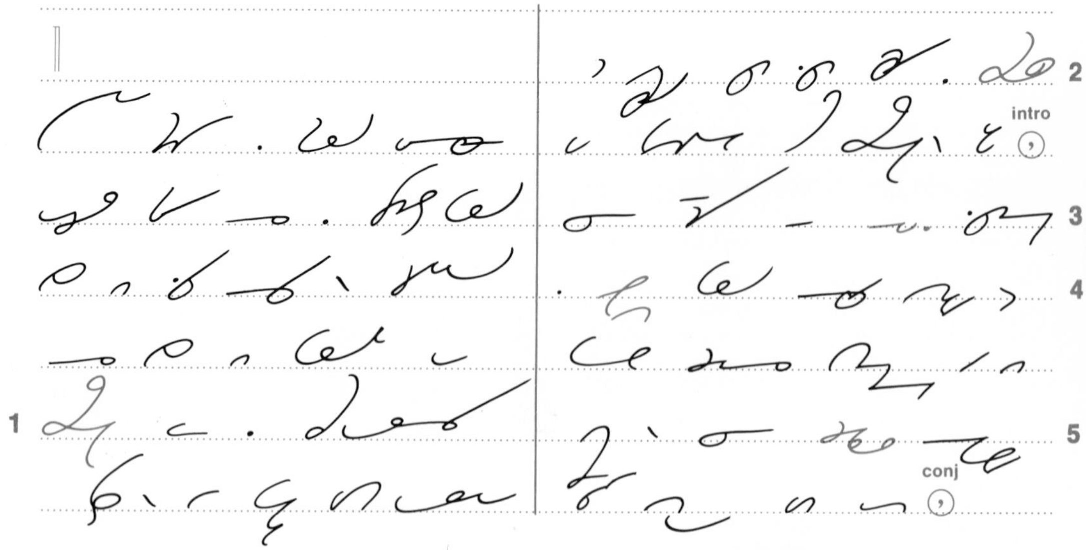

6 **Transcribe:**
17th
7 **low·est**
8 **af·ford**

[146]

After completing research for a business report, the secretary may prepare the first draft in shorthand.

Building Transcription Skill

Transcription Warmup

10
20
31
42

Transcription Speed Building

12
23
30
39
47
54
63
71
81

30

Building Professional Skills

Shorthand ■ Capturing Thoughts and Writing Rough Drafts

Anyone who has ever completed a writing assignment knows that writing can be a difficult job. Much thought is required in order to formulate clear sentences and paragraphs in the writer's mind. All too often, those thoughts are fleeting. A person may spend several minutes trying to compose a smooth sentence mentally, only to have the thoughts disappear during the slow, laborious process of writing them down in longhand. You *could* compose a rough draft by dictating to a tape recorder, but tape-recorded thoughts are very difficult to review when you are trying to compose one sentence after another with grammatical precision, a certain progression of ideas, and a smooth style.

Shorthand, then, is the perfect medium for capturing fleeting thoughts—those bursts of genius that we may never be able to recreate verbatim again. While capturing our thoughts, the shorthand rough draft also provides the paper copy that we need for continual review in those instances when elements of grammar, logic, and style are critical.

Communication Checkup

comparisons

In describing the difference between two people or objects comparative language is used. Examples of comparative terms are *bigger, taller, smaller,* and so forth.

Jim is taller than Ed.
The lake is wider than the river.

When making comparisons among three or more objects or people, superlatives are used. Examples of superlatives are *biggest, tallest, brightest,* and so forth.

Mario is the tallest boy in the class.
Today is the hottest day of the year.

34

Building Professional Skills

Punctuation Checkup

, series

Items within a sentence that are listed in the form of a series are separated from each other by commas. The last two items in a series are usually connected by the word *and*; the placement of a comma before the word *and* is optional.

The folder contained letters, memos, and forms.
Meetings will be held in Chicago, Boston, Los Angeles, and Seattle.

Communication Checkup

their ■ there ■ they're

their — Indicating possession.

I eagerly read their report.
Their business forms were difficult to understand.

there — An instance or a place.

There is not enough light at my desk.
Please stack the paper over there.

they're — Plural possessive.

They're not ready for the meeting.
Do you know where they're going?

Building Transcription Skill

Transcription Warmup

10
20
30
41

Transcription Speed Building

10
18
26
36
47
57
70
80

3

Ms. Nancy Grant
509 Ripley Avenue
Atlanta, GA 30300

10 al·ready
11 ac·knowl·edge
12 lun·cheon
13 ac·knowl·edg·ment

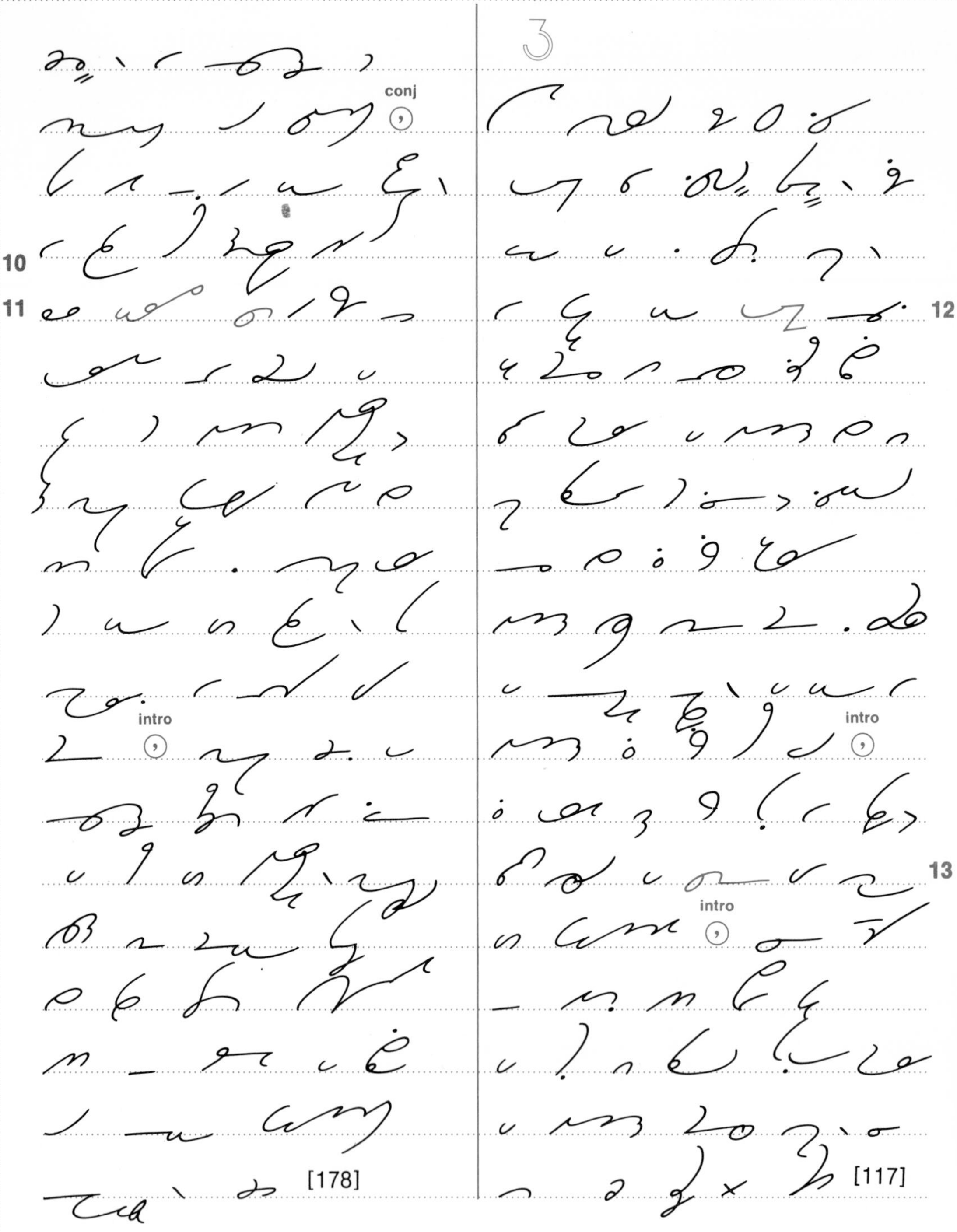

Transcription Quiz

Transcribe the following letter, adding the appropriate punctuation to your transcript.

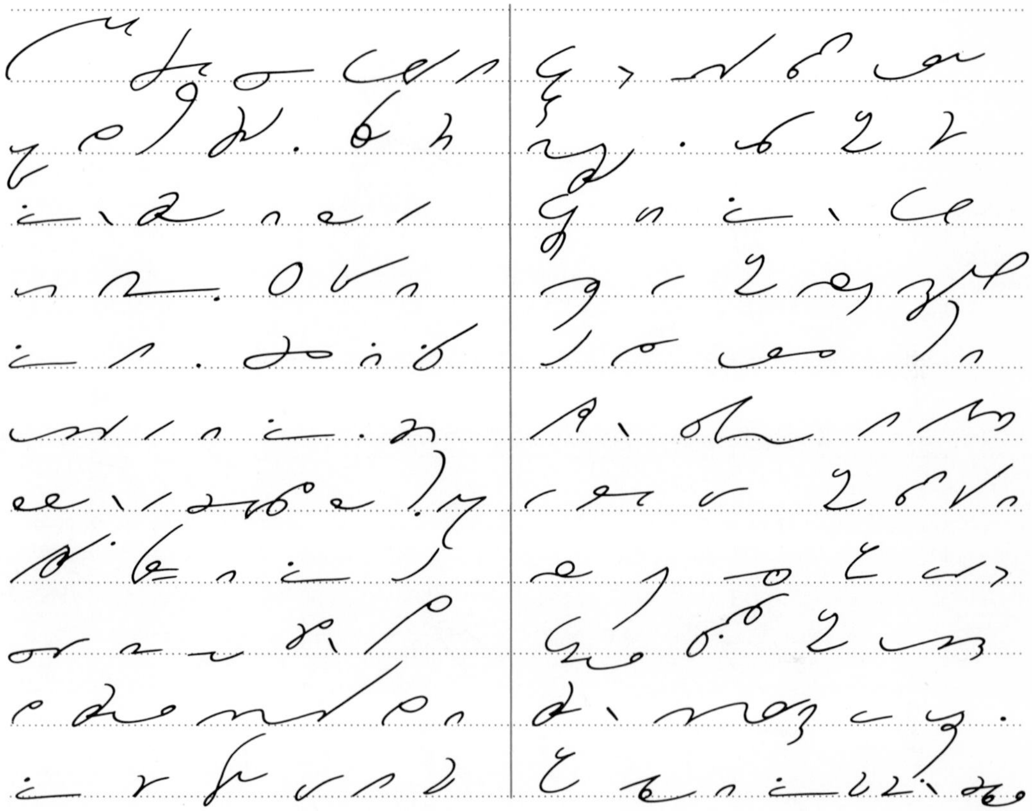

[141]

Mailable Letter Production

1
Mr. Ralph Henning
The Seven Seas
Restaurant
417 Congress Street
Chicago, IL 60611

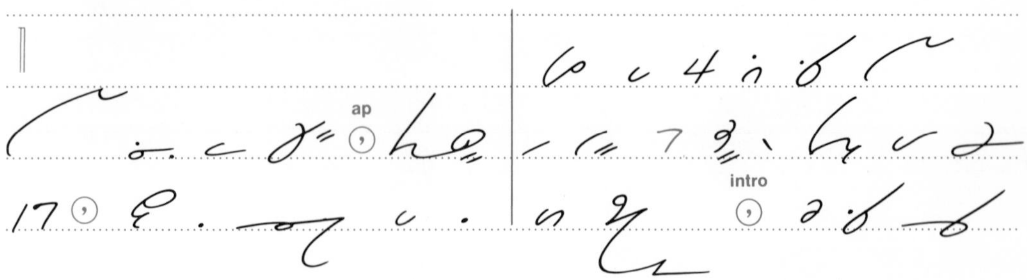

1

1 Transcribe:
Seven

2

Mr. Howard Jones
4610 University Avenue
El Paso, TX 79911

1 haul·ing
2 sites
3 ve·hi·cle
4 al·lows
5 arise
6 ef·fec·tive·ly
7 ap·plied
8 their
9 be·gin·ning

2

Mr. Edward Riley
American Tire Center
1221 Pacific Avenue
Ashland, OR 97520

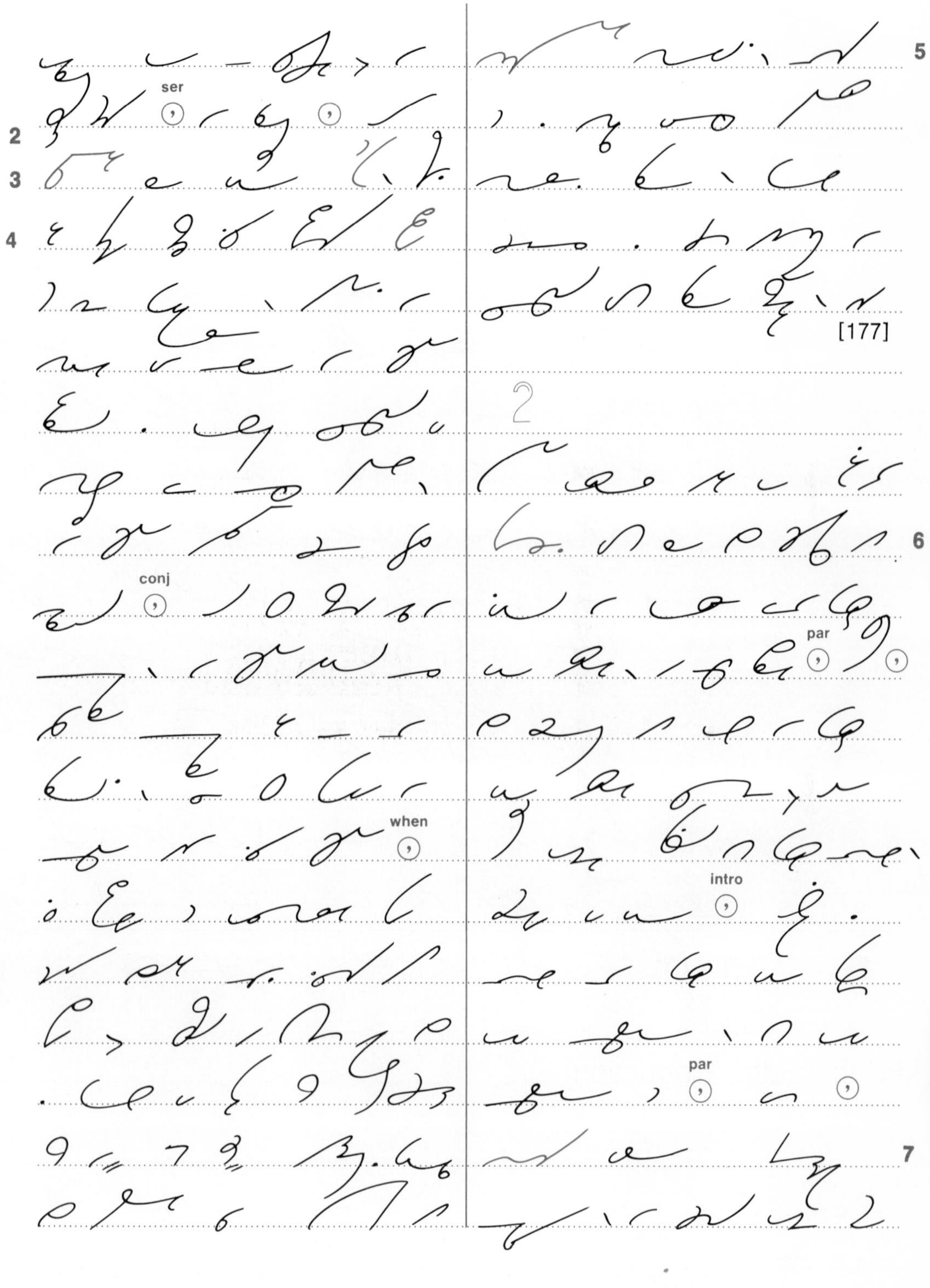

2 at·mo·sphere
3 su·perb
4 ex·cept
5 cus·tom·ers'
6 be·gin·ning
7 crude

Transcription Quiz

Transcribe the following letter, adding the appropriate punctuation to your transcript.

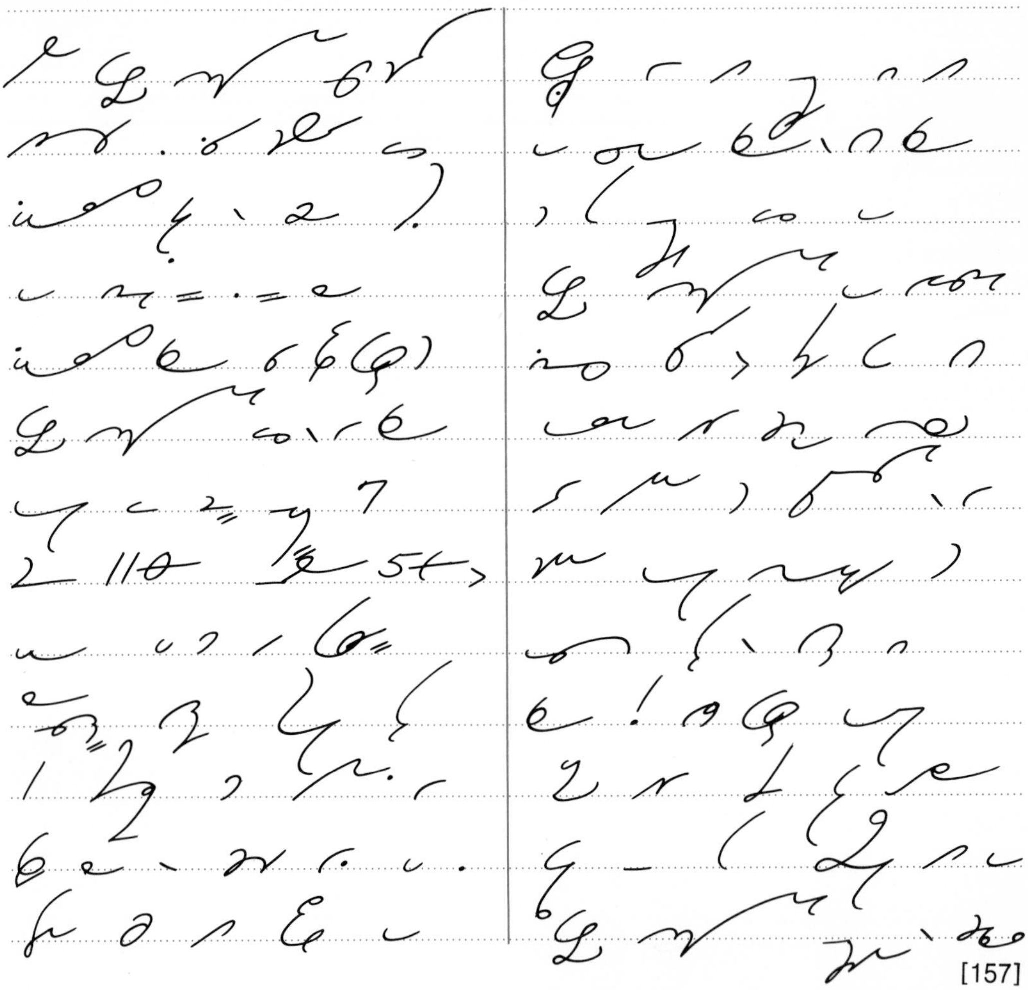

[157]

Mailable Letter Production

1
Mr. Bruce Walters
241 Henry Avenue
Wheeling, WV 26003

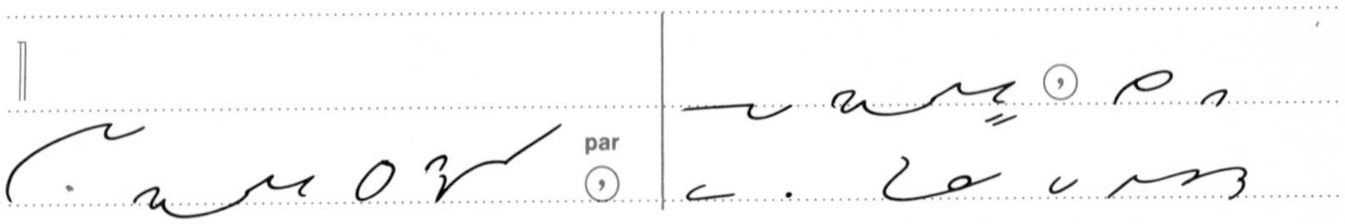

3
Ms. Mary Forest
709 Main Street
Reno, NV 89511

4
Ms. Mary Green
604 State Street
Mobile, AL 36600

8 of•fer
9 sin•cere•ly
10 ac•ces•so•ries
11 owe

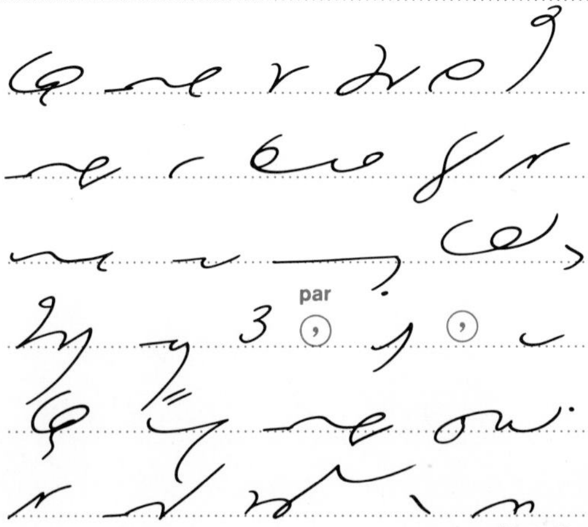

[118]

[111]

3

4

[73]

Building Transcription Skill

Transcription Warmup

Transcription Speed Building

31

Building Professional Skills

Listening ■ Keep Your Mind on the Subject

The human mind is an interesting place. Through our imagination we can be in any place and do anything we please. This ability does help to make life interesting, but it can also be counterproductive. If we use our imagination merely as an escape from reality, we have done ourselves a disservice. It is so easy for our minds to wander that we must really work at the job of listening.

In order to do an effective job of communication, it is critical that we keep our mind on the subject when someone else is speaking. We can do this by keeping an open mind, by trying to identify the main points the speaker is making, and by applying our critical thinking to the main points of the speaker's message rather than concentrating on distractions.

Communication Checkup

choose ■ chose

choose — To make a choice in the present or the future.

I choose to abstain from voting today.
I will choose my successor in a few months.

chose — A choice made in the past.

We chose our replacements early last week.
She was chosen for the award in 1982.

OFFICE PRO TEMPS

1890 West Edgewater Avenue, Chicago, IL 60660

February 14, 19XX

Miss Judy Taylor
616 Navarre Place
Detroit, MI 48214

Dear Judy:

Thank you for sending me a copy of your research study. The
findings of your study about the use of shorthand in the modern business office are most interesting to me. As I am sure
you realize, your study agrees with several other studies
that have been done recently. Basically, all of these studies
have found that the best way for a secretary to be hired and
to be promoted is for that secretary to know shorthand.

As you know, our company is one of the largest temporary office help agencies in the nation. We find jobs for hundreds
of secretaries in cities all across the nation each year.
For those secretaries who wish to improve their skills, we
offer classes in shorthand, typewriting, and word processing.
Also, we publish a magazine for secretaries.

I would like to have you write an article for our magazine
based upon the findings of your study. I know that our
readers would be as interested in your study as I am. May
I expect an article from you soon?

Sincerely,

Helen Goldman

Mrs. Helen Goldman
Manager

HG:FL

Building Transcription Skill

Transcription Warmup

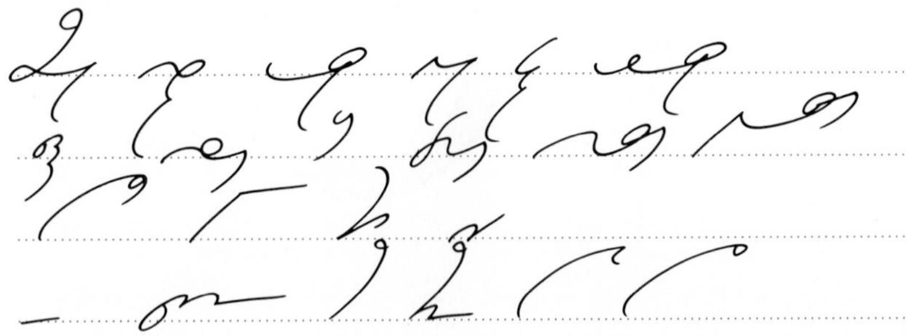

Transcription Speed Building

33

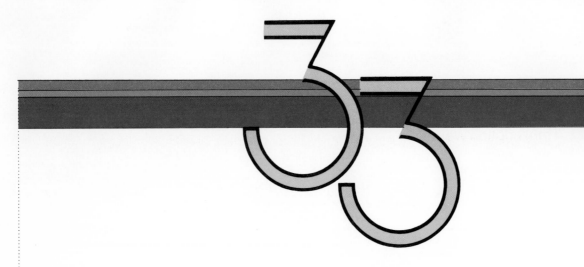

Building Professional Skills

Letter Styles ■ Block

A block style letter is one in which every line begins at the left margin. Since no tabs are used, a block style letter requires less production time than the modified block style as shown on page 160.

Communication Checkup

subject and verb

Subjects and verbs must agree in number. That is, a singular verb must be used with a singular subject, while a plural verb must be used with a plural subject.

Our representatives are glad to help you.
Our plumber is not available today.
Your bill for April is enclosed.
Your letters are ready for mailing.

Including phrases such as *in addition to, as well as,* or *along with* does not affect the number of the verb.

Our sales representative, as well as our manager, is looking forward to serving you.
Your canceled checks, along with your bank statements, are mailed each month.

Transcription Quiz

Transcribe the following letter, adding the appropriate punctuation to your transcript.

[161]

Mailable Letter Production

1
Mr. Barry Smith
520 Hayden Street
Boise, ID 83700

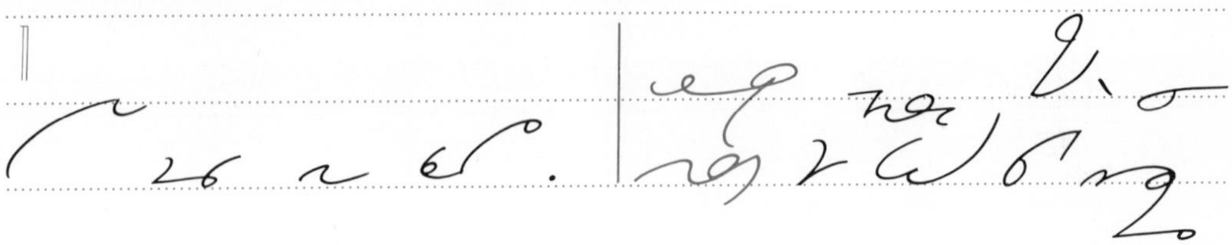

1
2

1 re·li·able
2 grate·ful

3
Mr. Dale Heinz
605 Cedar Street
Lexington, KY 40511

11 your
12 some time
13 per·son·al

[158]

3

11

12

13

[136]

2
Raleigh Tires
919 Carolina Avenue
Raleigh, NC 27611

3 tree's
4 ar·rived
5 two
6 paid
7 its
8 suf·fered
9 ca·pa·ble
10 as·sur·ance
11 Transcribe: 20,000
12 wear
13 ex·ces·sive

2
Miss Helen Lopez
2833 Lyndon Square
Las Vegas, NV 89100

3 Christ•mas
4 their
5 month's
6 va•cant
7 con•sists
8 acres
9 some time
10 fair

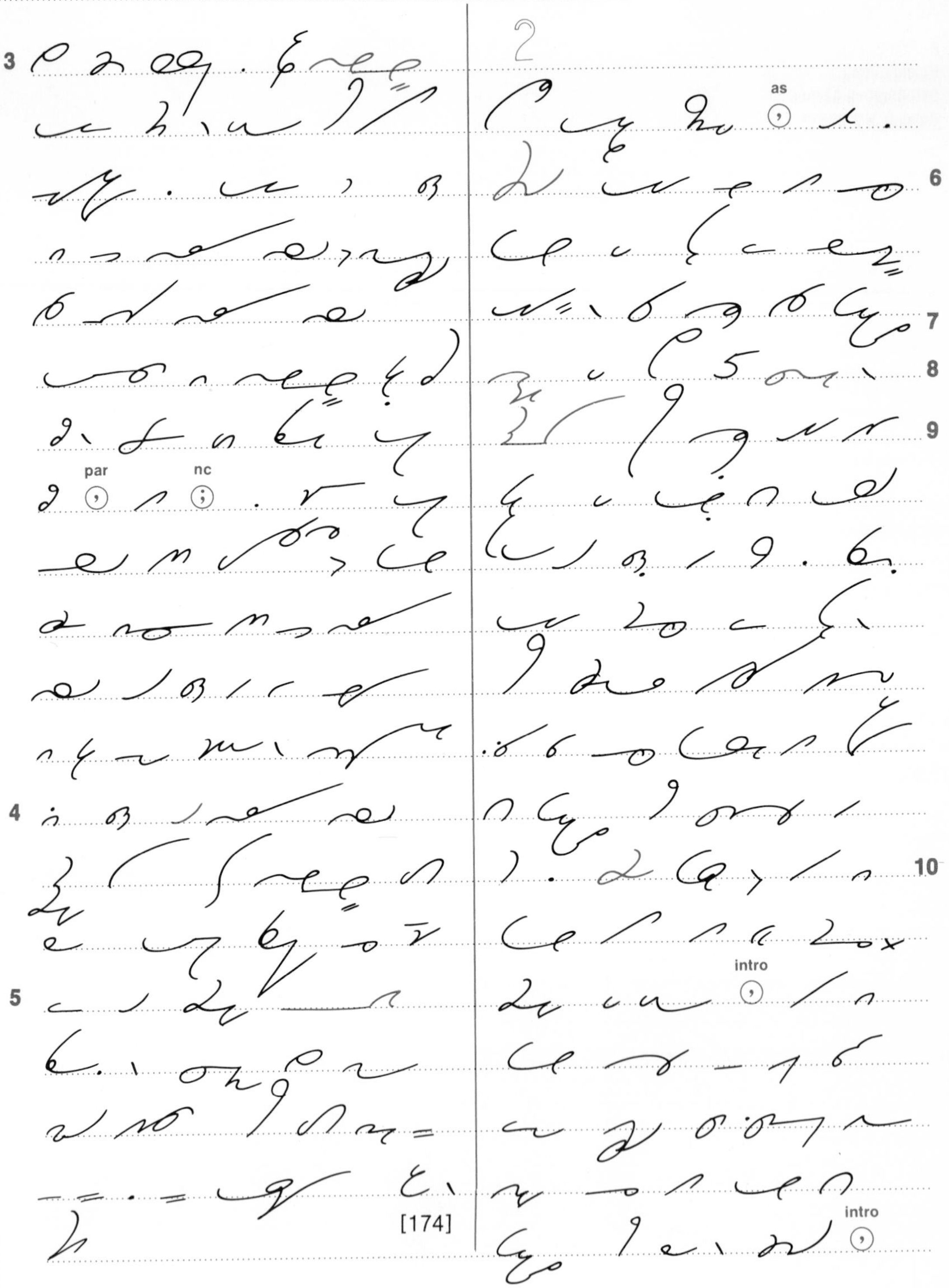

3
Dr. James Klein
1819 Lynn Drive
Houston, TX 77011

14 some·day
15 chair·per·son
16 com·mit·tee
17 speak·er
18 wel·come

Transcription Quiz

Transcribe the following letter, adding the appropriate punctuation to your transcript.

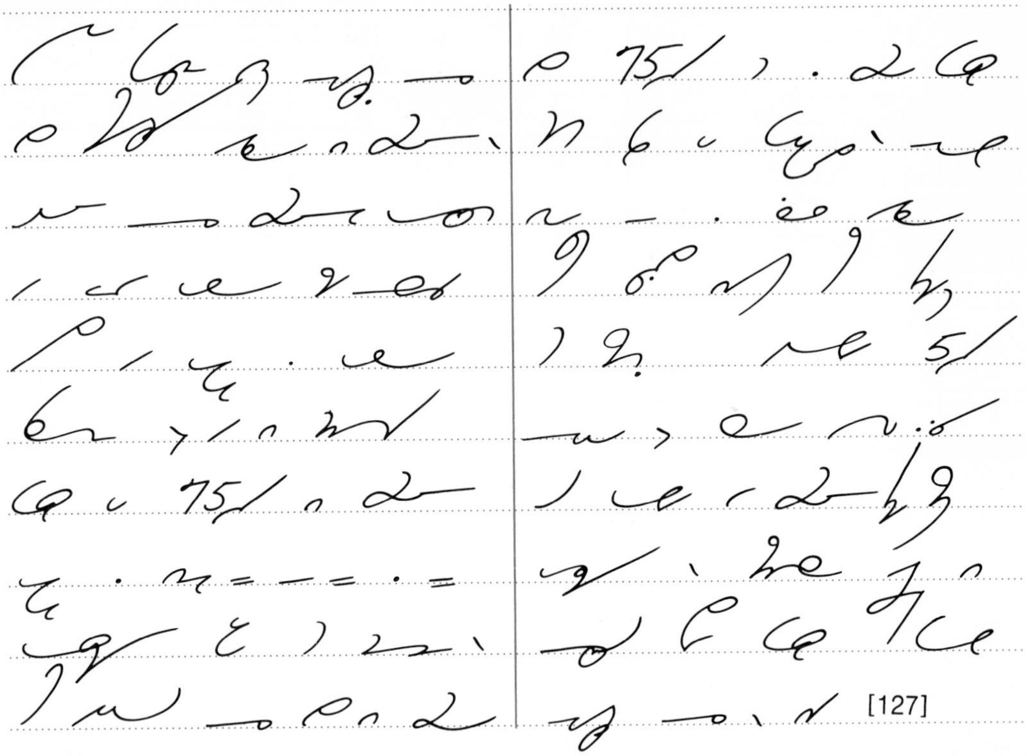

Mailable Letter Production

1
Mr. Raymond Tyler
1910 Water Street
Omaha, NE 68100

1 sea•son
2 hol•i•days

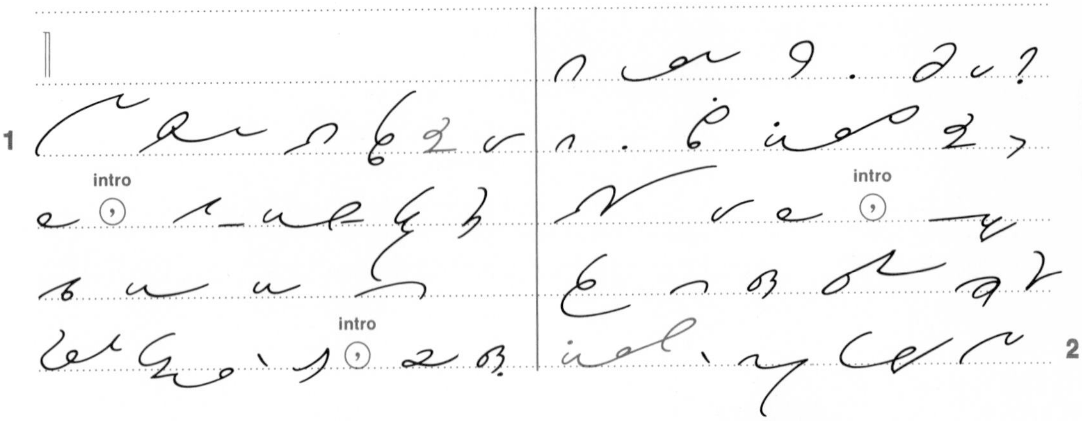

32

Building Professional Skills

Punctuation Checkup

; compound sentence

Sometimes two independent clauses are joined together to form a compound sentence. Usually a comma and a conjunction such as *and* are used to join the two clauses. If it is the writer's wish to join the two independent clauses without a comma and a conjunction, then a semicolon is used in their place.

Today the weather is rainy; it makes me feel depressed.
Some of the students will attend the meeting in the morning; some will attend in the afternoon.
The program sounds interesting; I wish to attend.

Communication Checkup

compound modifier

Sometimes in modifying (describing) a noun, two or more words will be joined together to express a single meaning.

We can offer you a once-in-a-lifetime opportunity.
He plans to buy a state-of-the-art stereo.
We attended a run-of-the-mill presentation.

Building Transcription Skill

Transcription Warmup

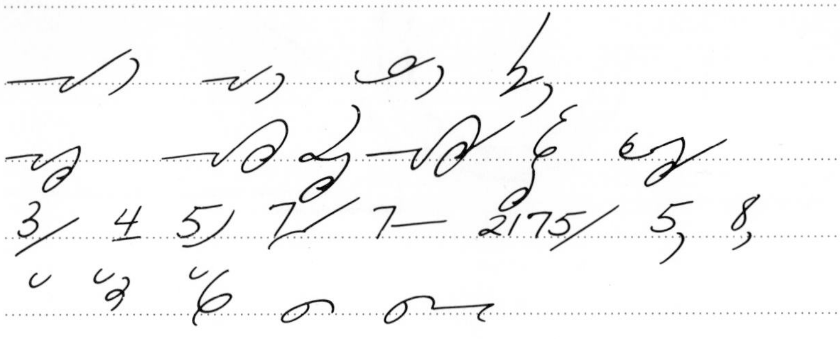

10
20
32
42

Transcription Speed Building

13
20
28
40
49
59
69
80